Shakespeare's
MACBETH

THE **MANGA EDITION**

Shakespeare's
MACBETH

THE MANGA EDITION

Adam Sexton • Eve Grandt • Candice Chow

WILEY

Wiley Publishing, Inc.

Published by Wiley Publishing, Inc., Hoboken, New Jersey

For general information on our other products and services or to obtain technical support please contact our Customer Care Department within the U.S. at (800) 762-2974, outside the U.S. at (317) 572-3993 or fax (317) 572-4002.

Wiley also publishes its books in a variety of electronic formats. Some content that appears in print may not be available in electronic books. For more information about Wiley products, please visit our web site at www.wiley.com.

Library of Congress Number: 2007940643

ISBN: 978-0-470-09759-5

Printed in the United States of America

10 9 8 7 6 5 4 3

Book design by Elizabeth Brooks
Book production by Wiley Publishing, Inc. Composition Services

CONTENTS

Suiting the Action to the Word:
Shakespeare and Manga ... 1

Act I ... 5

Act II ... 35

Act III ... 81

Act IV ... 117

Act V ... 155

Adam Sexton is the author of *Master Class in Fiction Writing* and the editor of the anthologies *Love Stories, Rap on Rap,* and *Desperately Seeking Madonna.* He has written on art and entertainment for *The New York Times* and *The Village Voice,* and he teaches fiction writing and literature at New York University and critical reading and writing at Parsons School of Design. A graduate of Columbia University and the University of Pennsylvania, he lives in Brooklyn with his wife and son.

Eve Grandt works in an animal shelter by day and draws comics by night. She lives in New York City with her roommate, two cats, and two rabbits. This is her first published work, and you can e-mail her about it or anything else at eve@inuwashi.net. To see more of her comics and illustrations please visit www.bloodandtheartofbaking.com.

Candice Chow has always had an interest in anime and manga. She started pursuing animation and eventually graduated with a degree from the School of Visual Arts. After college, Candice found herself heading toward the field of comics and manga. Besides her love for Japanese animations and manga, Candice's other hobbies include video games, piano, and shopping.

Suiting the Action to the Word: Shakespeare and Manga

by Adam Sexton

Suit the action to the word, the word to the action...
— *Hamlet* (Act III, Scene 2)

Four hundred years after the writing of William Shakespeare's plays, it is clear that they are timeless. This is due in part to their infinite adaptability. The plays have been translated into dozens of languages and performed all over the world. Famously creative stage productions have included a version of *Julius Caesar* set in fascist Europe during the 1930s and a so-called "voodoo *Macbeth*." Nor have gender and age proved barriers to casting Shakespeare's characters. The role of Hamlet is occasionally played by a woman—an appropriate reversal, considering that boys acted all the female roles in Shakespeare's day—while the teenaged Romeo and Juliet have been portrayed by couples in their forties and fifties.

It is common knowledge that the plays of Shakespeare transfer especially well to the movie screen. Such has been the case since Thomas Edison made one of the first sound films ever using a scene from *As You Like It*. Recent cinema standouts include *William Shakespeare's Romeo + Juliet*, directed by Baz Luhrmann, and Michael Almereyda's *Hamlet*. Both take place in the present day or near future: Leonardo DiCaprio's Romeo wears a Hawaiian shirt—and Julia Stiles' Ophelia wears a wire, so Claudius and Polonius can eavesdrop on her conversation with Hamlet. Otherwise, these adaptations remain surprisingly faithful to Shakespeare's texts. And both hit the audience as hard as conventional stage productions in which the actors are outfitted with doublets and hose, crossed swords, and what Hamlet calls "a bare bodkin"—his unsheathed dagger (replaced in Almereyda's movie by a gun).

Shakespeare's plays have been set to music as well, in operas and ballets by composers such as Verdi, Tchaikovsky, and Prokofiev. The early comedy *Two Gentlemen of Verona* was adapted for Broadway by the composer of *Hair*, and it won the Tony award for Best Musical the same year that *Grease* was nominated. In the words of theater critic Jan Kott, Shakespeare is indeed "our contemporary."

In short, though some consider the plays of William Shakespeare to be sacrosanct, they have been cut, expanded (it was common in the Victorian era to add songs and even happy endings to the tragedies), and adapted to multiple media, emerging none the worse for wear. Although we cannot be sure of this, it seems likely that the writer, who was a popular artist and a savvy businessman as well as an incomparable poet, would approve.

The graphic novels known as *manga* (Japanese for "whimsical pictures") are a natural medium for Shakespeare's work. Like his tragedies, comedies, histories, and romances, which are thrillingly dynamic if properly staged, manga are of course visual. In fact, a manga is potentially *more* visual than a stage production of one of the plays of Shakespeare. Unbound by the physical realities of the theater, the graphic novel can depict any situation, no matter how fantastical or violent, that its creators are able to pencil, ink, and shade.

Take *Romeo and Juliet*'s famous Queen Mab speech. Even the most creative stage director cannot faithfully present the minuscule fairy described by Mercutio. Manga artists can. The same is true of the drowning of Ophelia in *Hamlet*. It is precisely because these vignettes are unstageable that Shakespeare has his characters describe Queen Mab and the death of Ophelia in such great detail—they must help us imagine them. In its unlimited ability to dramatize, the graphic novel more closely resembles a contemporary film with a colossal special-effects budget than anything produced onstage in the Elizabethan era or since.

At the same time, manga are potentially no less verbal than Shakespeare's spectacularly wordy plays, with this crucial difference: in a production of one of the plays onstage or onscreen, we can hear the words but can't see them. Though Shakespeare is never easy, reading helps. And that is precisely what manga adaptations of the plays allow. Perusing a Shakespeare manga, the reader can linger over speeches, rereading them in part or altogether. Especially in the long and intricate soliloquies typical of Shakespearean tragedy, this allows for an appreciation of the playwright's craft that is difficult if not impossible as those soliloquies move past us during a performance.

Overall, turning the pages of a manga version of one of Shakespeare's plays is something like reading the text of that play while attending a performance, but at one's own pace. Manga is not merely a new medium for the plays of William Shakespeare, but one that is distinctly different from anything to have come before.

A note on authenticity: In order to fit our adaptations into books of less than 200 pages, the writers and editors of *The Manga Editions* have cut words, lines, speeches, even entire scenes from Shakespeare's plays, a practice almost universal among stage and film directors. We have never paraphrased the playwright's language, however, nor have we summarized action. Everything you read in *The Manga Editions* was written by William Shakespeare himself. Finally, footnotes don't interrupt the characters' speeches here, any more than they would in a production of one of Shakespeare's plays onstage or on film.

In contrast to American comics, manga appeal to girls and women as much as they do to boys and men. And although the cast of

Macbeth includes only a handful of female characters, they loom large in this bloody story of royal succession in medieval Scotland. The opening lines of the play ("When should we three meet again?/In thunder, lightning, or in rain?") are spoken by the First Witch, in a scene where no men appear. Arguably, the single most sympathetic figure in the play is a woman: Lady Macduff. And then there's Lady Macbeth, one of the best-known female characters in all of literature. Her "Out, damned spot" scene has transcended *Macbeth* altogether and grown familiar to many who have neither read this tragedy nor seen a production of it, while her name has become a universal (if sexist) synonym for distaff ambition.

Indeed, the women of *Macbeth* are probably the most powerful characters in the play, as they drive the action from start to finish. Without the Weird Sisters and his wife, Macbeth himself would not pursue, and then defend, the crown—another way of saying that, in the absence of its female characters, *Macbeth* would not exist at all.

The other aspect of *Macbeth* that makes it particularly manga-worthy is the tragedy's surfeit of the magical and violent. Onstage, the scene that takes place in the witches' cave, with its child apparitions and parade of Banquo's descendants, can easily fail to convince. Not here. The same goes for *Macbeth*'s many murders; when one character chops off another's head, in a manga it is very much that head on a sword in the following scene, and not a facsimile devised by the props department. A manga provides the literalness—the "gore" that Macbeth himself refers to, in describing the scene of King Duncan's murder—that Shakespeare's *Macbeth* cries out for. By no means do we miss out on the play's poetry, however. Manga makes room for both.

Act I

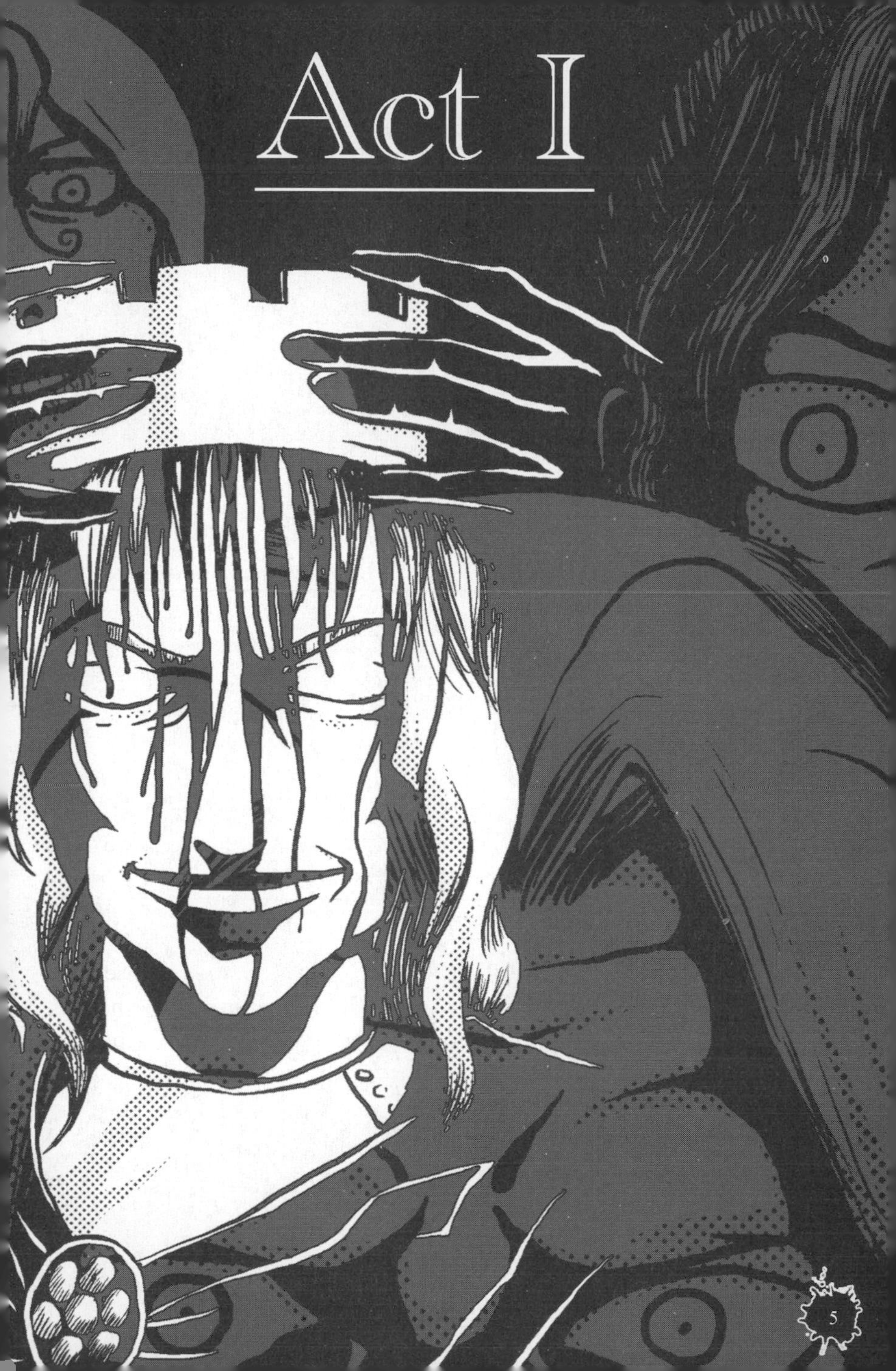

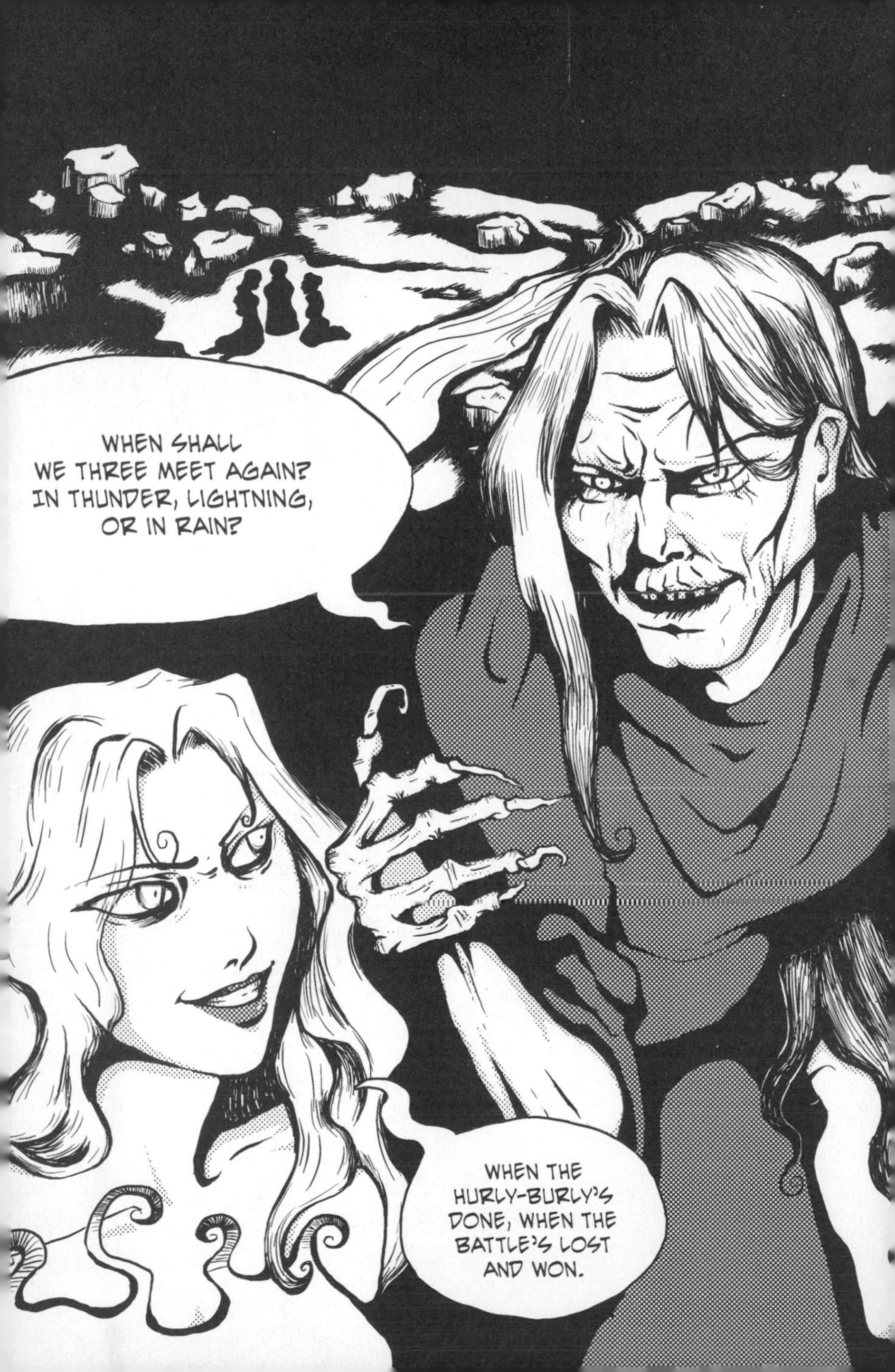
WHEN SHALL WE THREE MEET AGAIN? IN THUNDER, LIGHTNING, OR IN RAIN?
WHEN THE HURLY-BURLY'S DONE, WHEN THE BATTLE'S LOST AND WON.

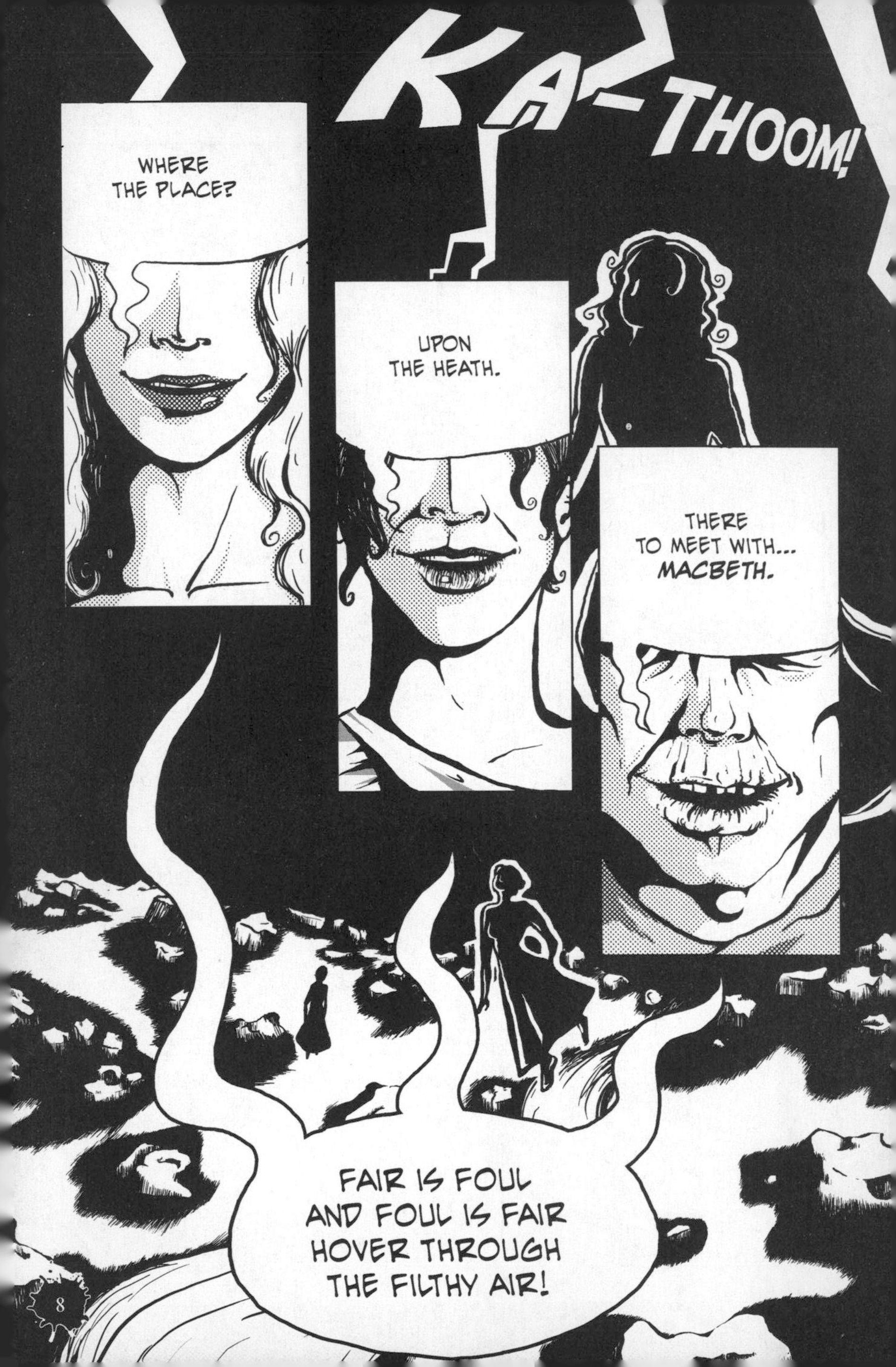
KA-THOOM!
WHERE THE PLACE?
UPON THE HEATH.
THERE TO MEET WITH... MACBETH.
FAIR IS FOUL AND FOUL IS FAIR HOVER THROUGH THE FILTHY AIR!

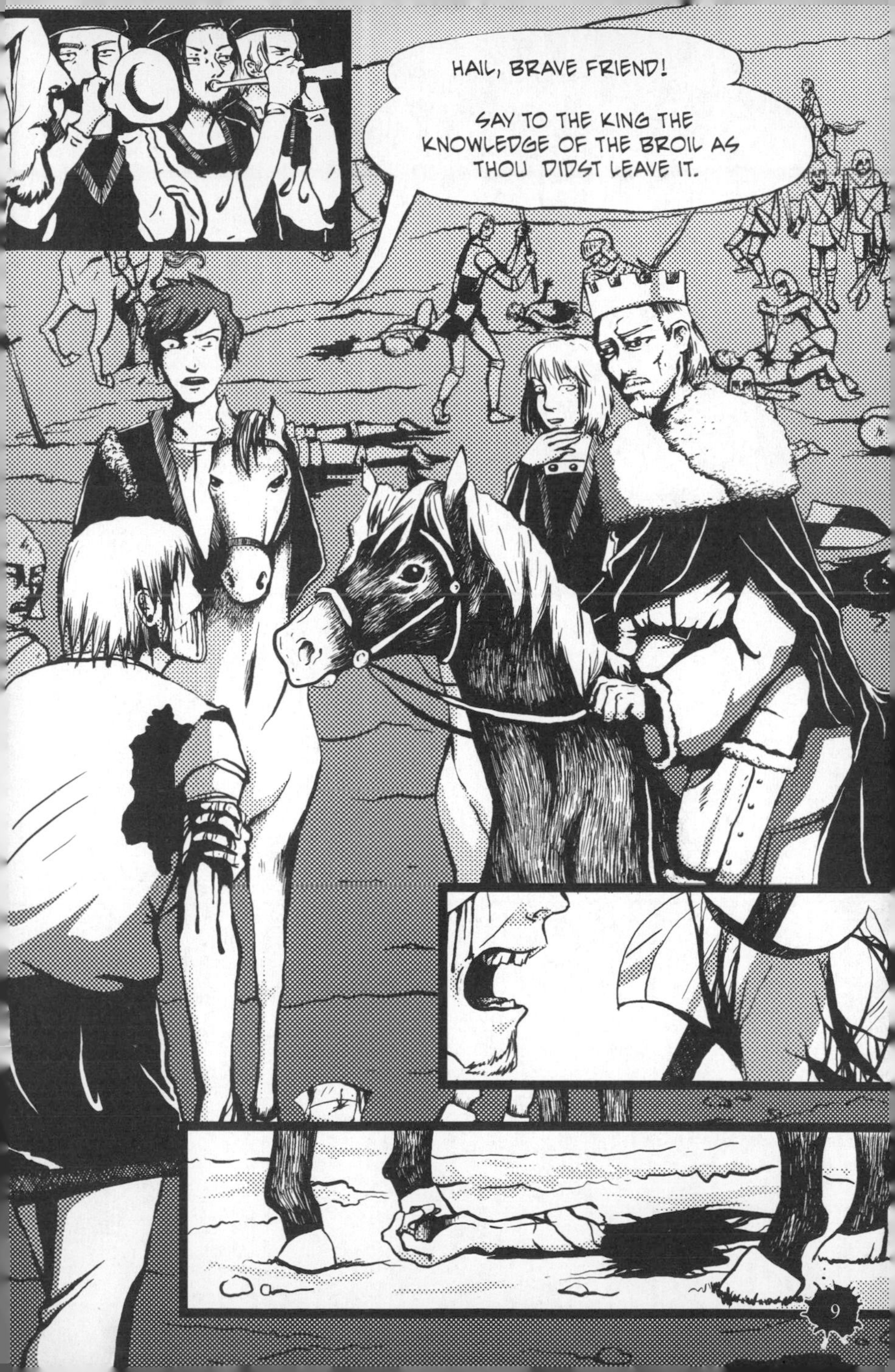
HAIL, BRAVE FRIEND!
SAY TO THE KING THE KNOWLEDGE OF THE BROIL AS THOU DIDST LEAVE IT.

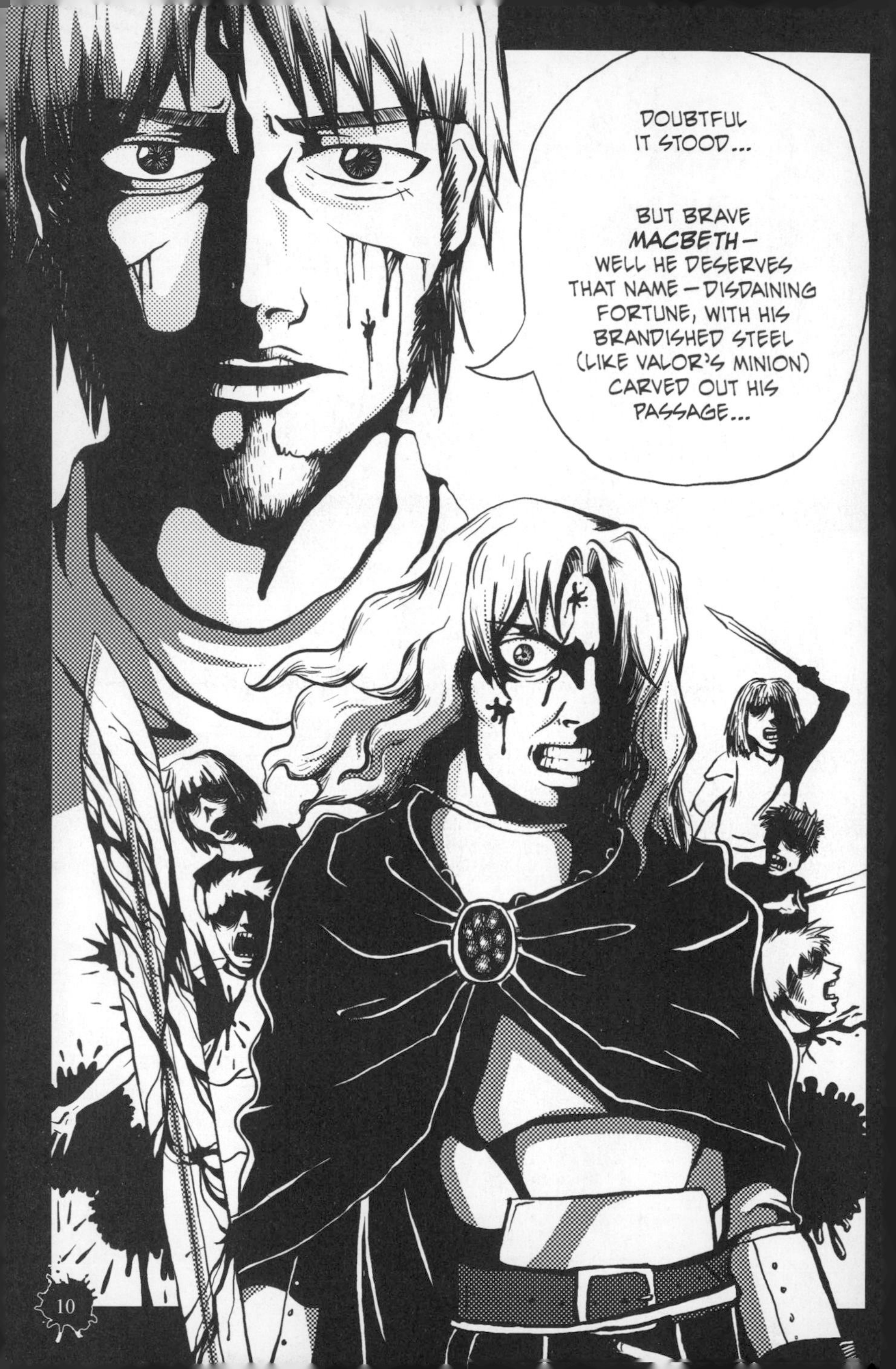
DOUBTFUL IT STOOD...
BUT BRAVE **MACBETH**— WELL HE DESERVES THAT NAME—DISDAINING FORTUNE, WITH HIS BRANDISHED STEEL (LIKE VALOR'S MINION) CARVED OUT HIS PASSAGE...

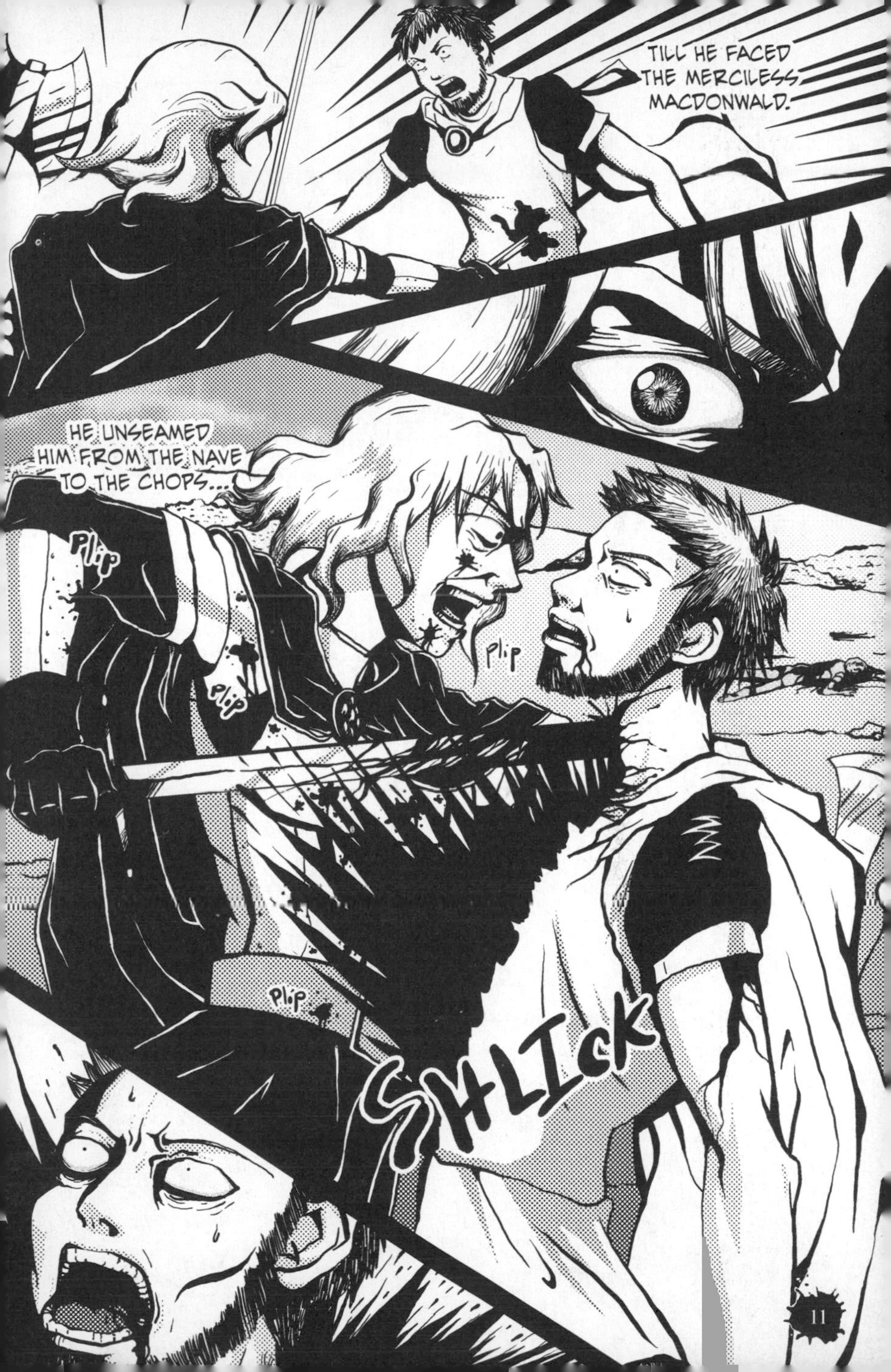
TILL HE FACED THE MERCILESS MACDONWALD.
HE UNSEAMED HIM FROM THE NAVE TO THE CHOPS...
Plip
plip
Plip
Plip
SHLICK

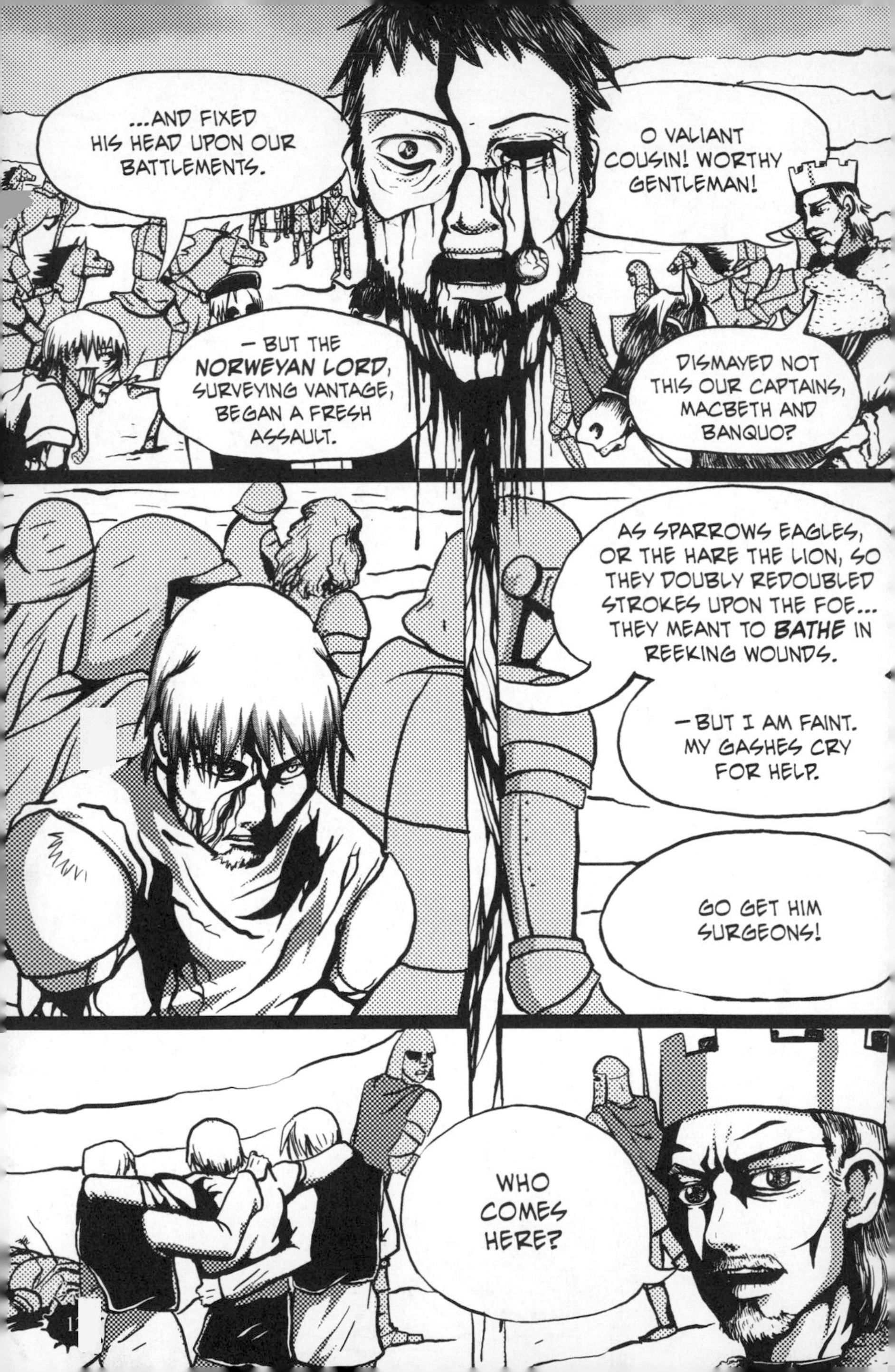
...AND FIXED HIS HEAD UPON OUR BATTLEMENTS.
O VALIANT COUSIN! WORTHY GENTLEMAN!
— BUT THE **NORWEYAN LORD**, SURVEYING VANTAGE, BEGAN A FRESH ASSAULT.
DISMAYED NOT THIS OUR CAPTAINS, MACBETH AND BANQUO?
AS SPARROWS EAGLES, OR THE HARE THE LION, SO THEY DOUBLY REDOUBLED STROKES UPON THE FOE... THEY MEANT TO **BATHE** IN REEKING WOUNDS.
—BUT I AM FAINT. MY GASHES CRY FOR HELP.
GO GET HIM SURGEONS!
WHO COMES HERE?

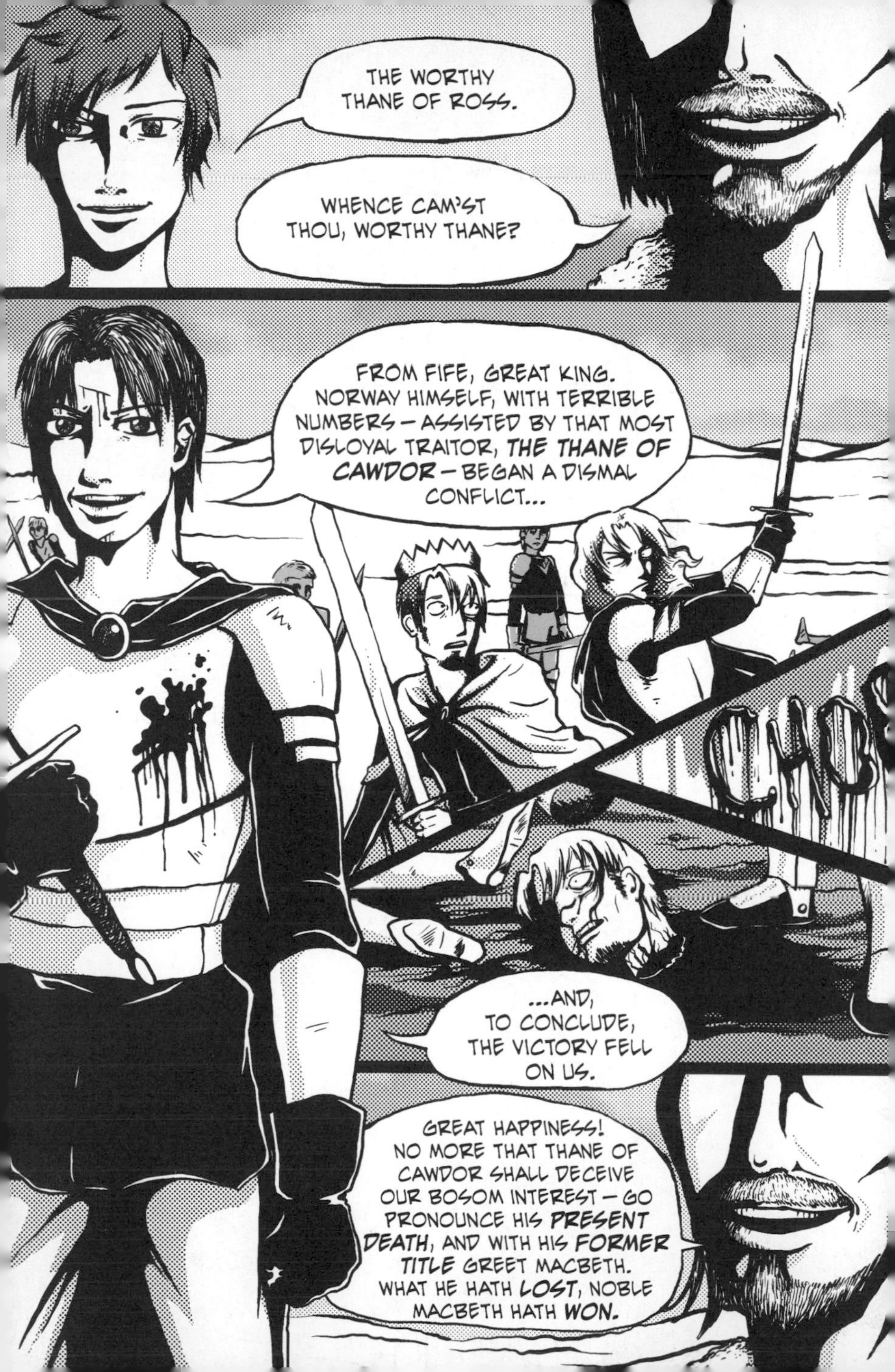
THE WORTHY THANE OF ROSS.
WHENCE CAM'ST THOU, WORTHY THANE?
FROM FIFE, GREAT KING. NORWAY HIMSELF, WITH TERRIBLE NUMBERS—ASSISTED BY THAT MOST DISLOYAL TRAITOR, **THE THANE OF CAWDOR**—BEGAN A DISMAL CONFLICT...
...AND, TO CONCLUDE, THE VICTORY FELL ON US.
GREAT HAPPINESS! NO MORE THAT THANE OF CAWDOR SHALL DECEIVE OUR BOSOM INTEREST—GO PRONOUNCE HIS **PRESENT DEATH**, AND WITH HIS **FORMER TITLE** GREET MACBETH. WHAT HE HATH **LOST**, NOBLE MACBETH HATH **WON.**

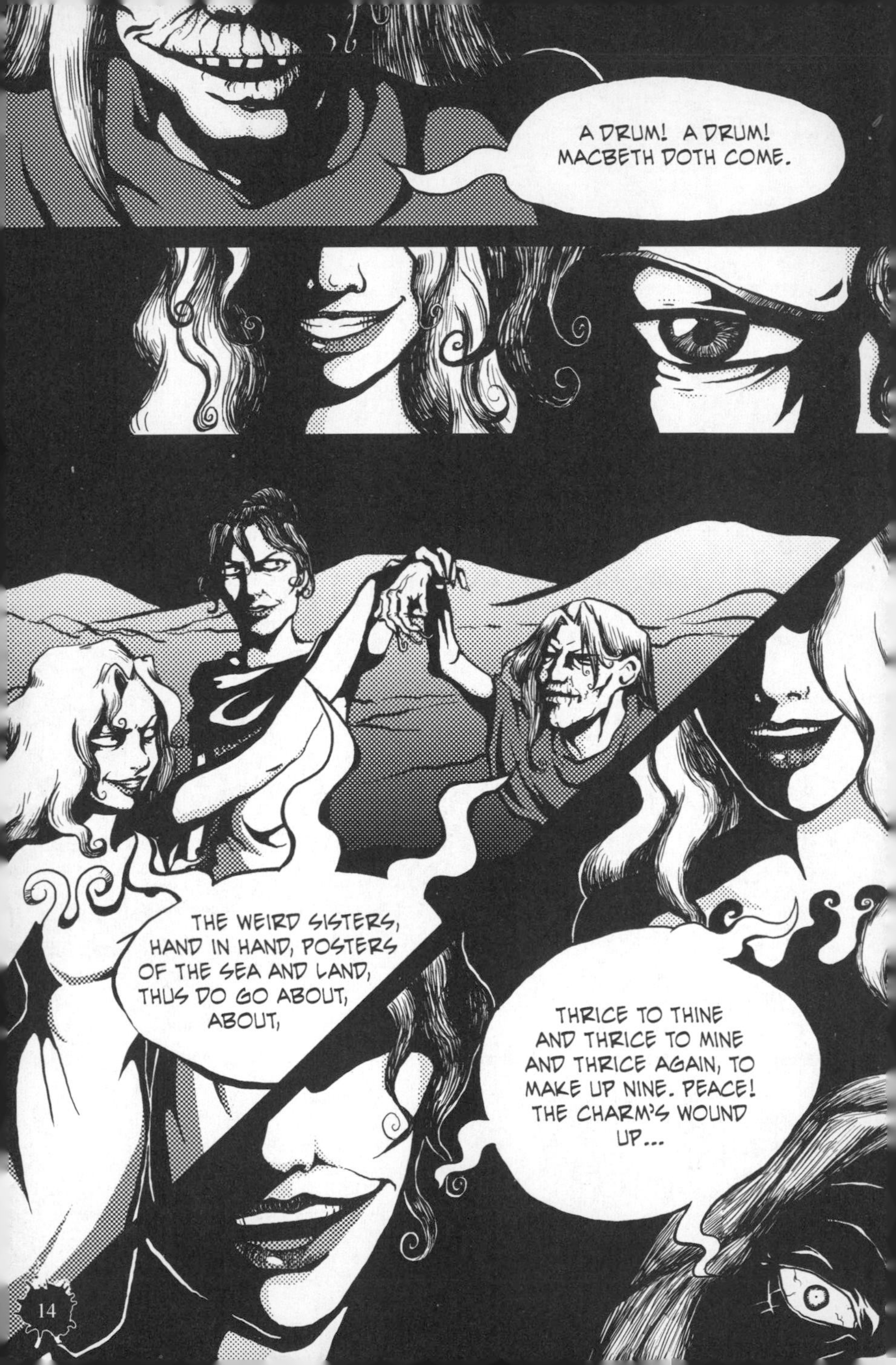
A DRUM! A DRUM! MACBETH DOTH COME.
THE WEIRD SISTERS, HAND IN HAND, POSTERS OF THE SEA AND LAND, THUS DO GO ABOUT, ABOUT,
THRICE TO THINE AND THRICE TO MINE AND THRICE AGAIN, TO MAKE UP NINE. PEACE! THE CHARM'S WOUND UP...

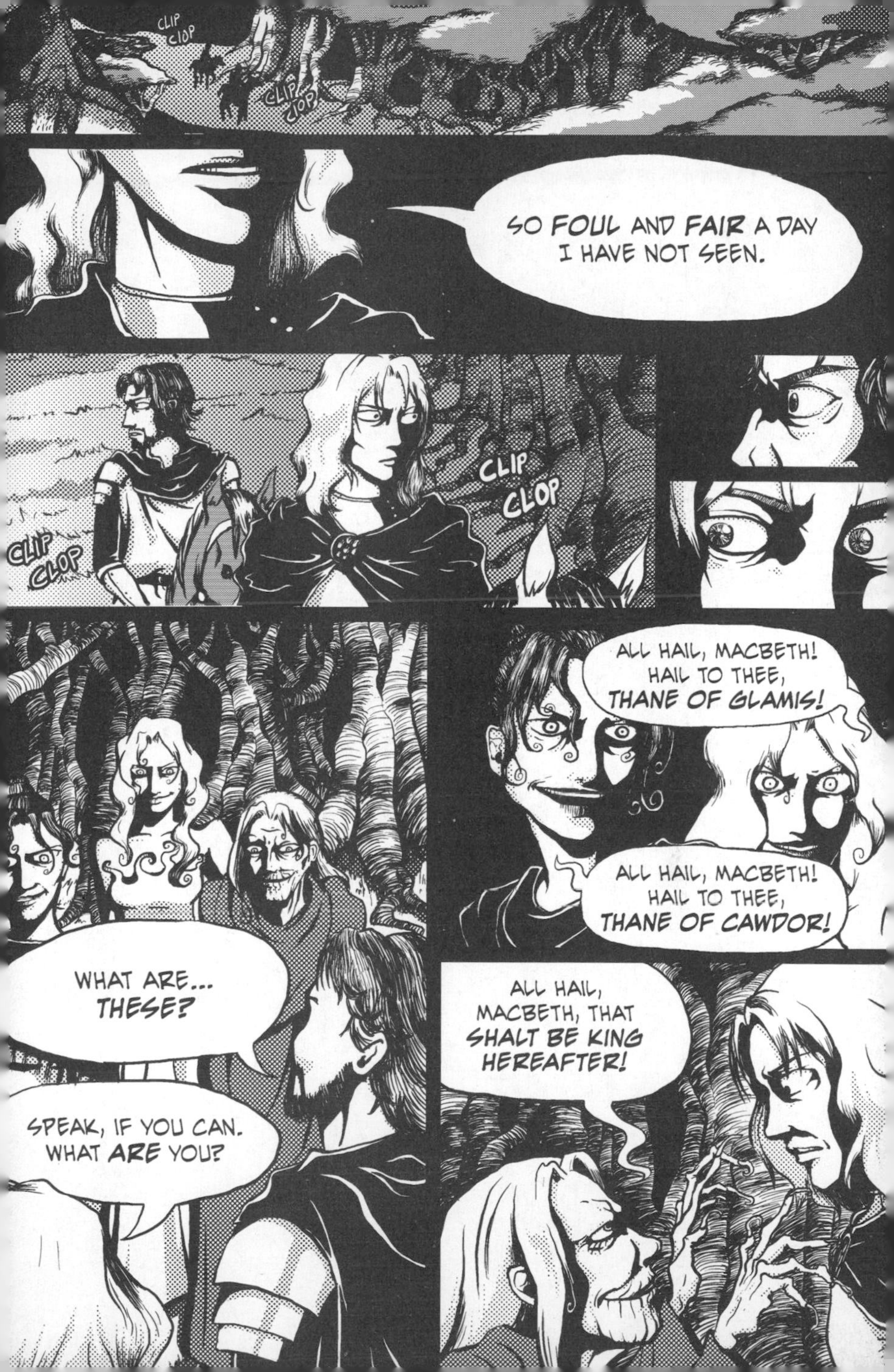
CLIP CLOP
CLIP CLOP
SO FOUL AND FAIR A DAY I HAVE NOT SEEN.
CLIP CLOP
CLIP CLOP
WHAT ARE... THESE?
SPEAK, IF YOU CAN. WHAT ARE YOU?
ALL HAIL, MACBETH! HAIL TO THEE, THANE OF GLAMIS!
ALL HAIL, MACBETH! HAIL TO THEE, THANE OF CAWDOR!
ALL HAIL, MACBETH, THAT SHALT BE KING HEREAFTER!

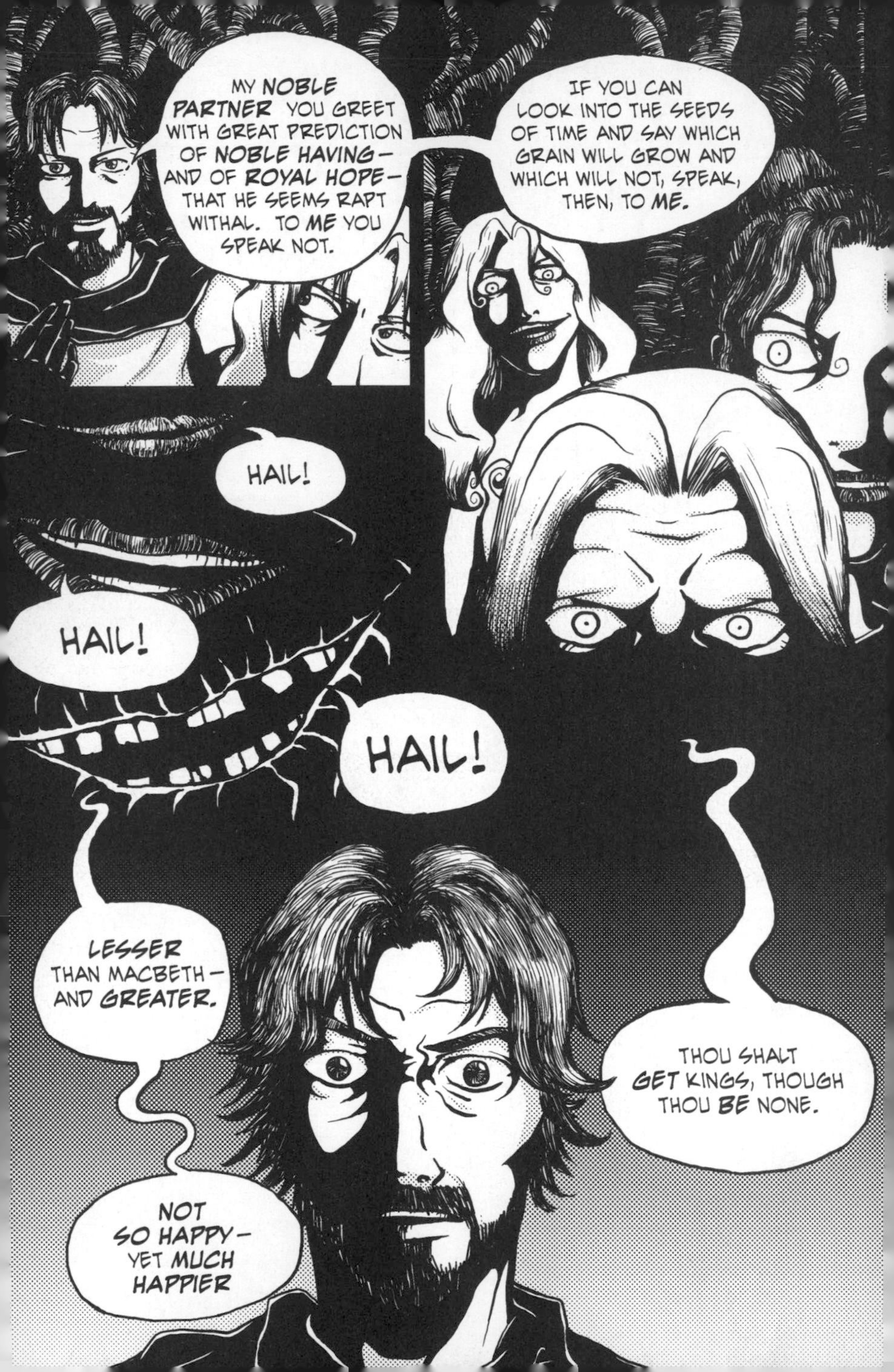
MY NOBLE PARTNER YOU GREET WITH GREAT PREDICTION OF NOBLE HAVING– AND OF ROYAL HOPE– THAT HE SEEMS RAPT WITHAL. TO ME YOU SPEAK NOT.
IF YOU CAN LOOK INTO THE SEEDS OF TIME AND SAY WHICH GRAIN WILL GROW AND WHICH WILL NOT, SPEAK, THEN, TO ME.
HAIL!
HAIL!
HAIL!
LESSER THAN MACBETH– AND GREATER.
NOT SO HAPPY– YET MUCH HAPPIER
THOU SHALT GET KINGS, THOUGH THOU BE NONE.

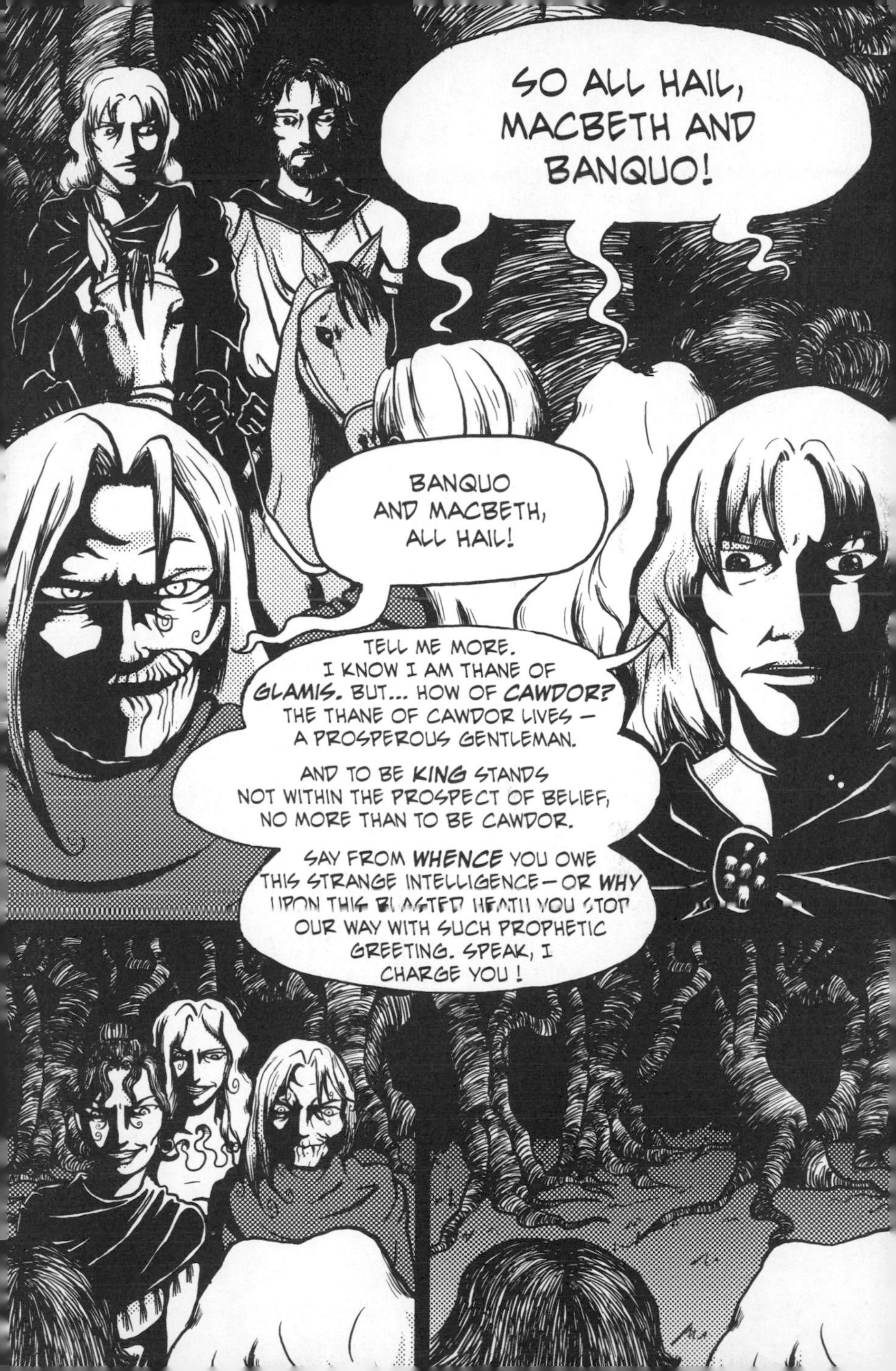
SO ALL HAIL, MACBETH AND BANQUO!
BANQUO AND MACBETH, ALL HAIL!
TELL ME MORE. I KNOW I AM THANE OF GLAMIS. BUT... HOW OF CAWDOR? THE THANE OF CAWDOR LIVES – A PROSPEROUS GENTLEMAN.
AND TO BE KING STANDS NOT WITHIN THE PROSPECT OF BELIEF, NO MORE THAN TO BE CAWDOR.
SAY FROM WHENCE YOU OWE THIS STRANGE INTELLIGENCE–OR WHY UPON THIS BLASTED HEATH YOU STOP OUR WAY WITH SUCH PROPHETIC GREETING. SPEAK, I CHARGE YOU !

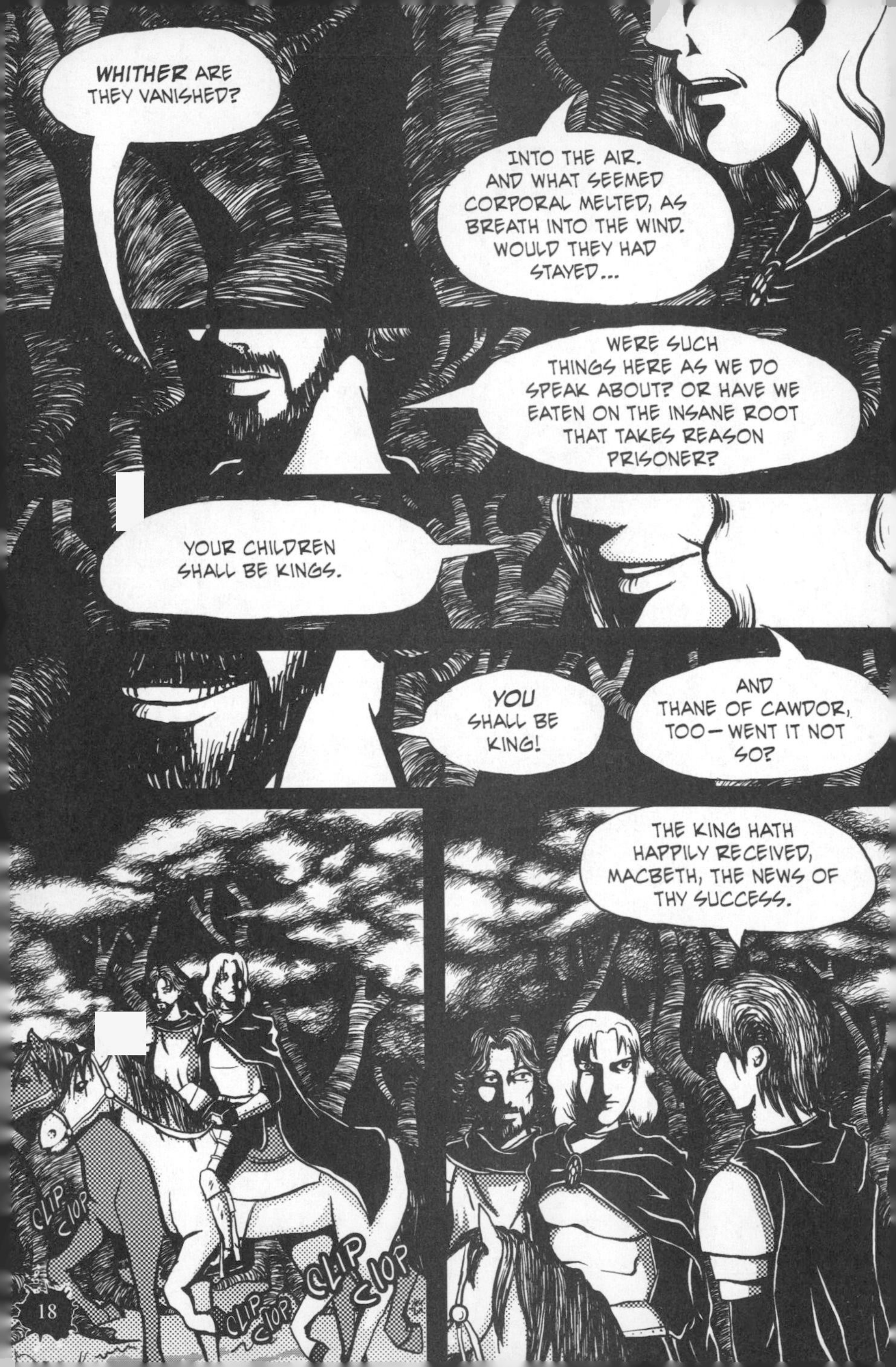
WHITHER ARE THEY VANISHED?
INTO THE AIR. AND WHAT SEEMED CORPORAL MELTED, AS BREATH INTO THE WIND. WOULD THEY HAD STAYED...
WERE SUCH THINGS HERE AS WE DO SPEAK ABOUT? OR HAVE WE EATEN ON THE INSANE ROOT THAT TAKES REASON PRISONER?
YOUR CHILDREN SHALL BE KINGS.
YOU SHALL BE KING!
AND THANE OF CAWDOR, TOO—WENT IT NOT SO?
CLIP CLOP
CLIP CLOP
CLIP CLOP
THE KING HATH HAPPILY RECEIVED, MACBETH, THE NEWS OF THY SUCCESS.

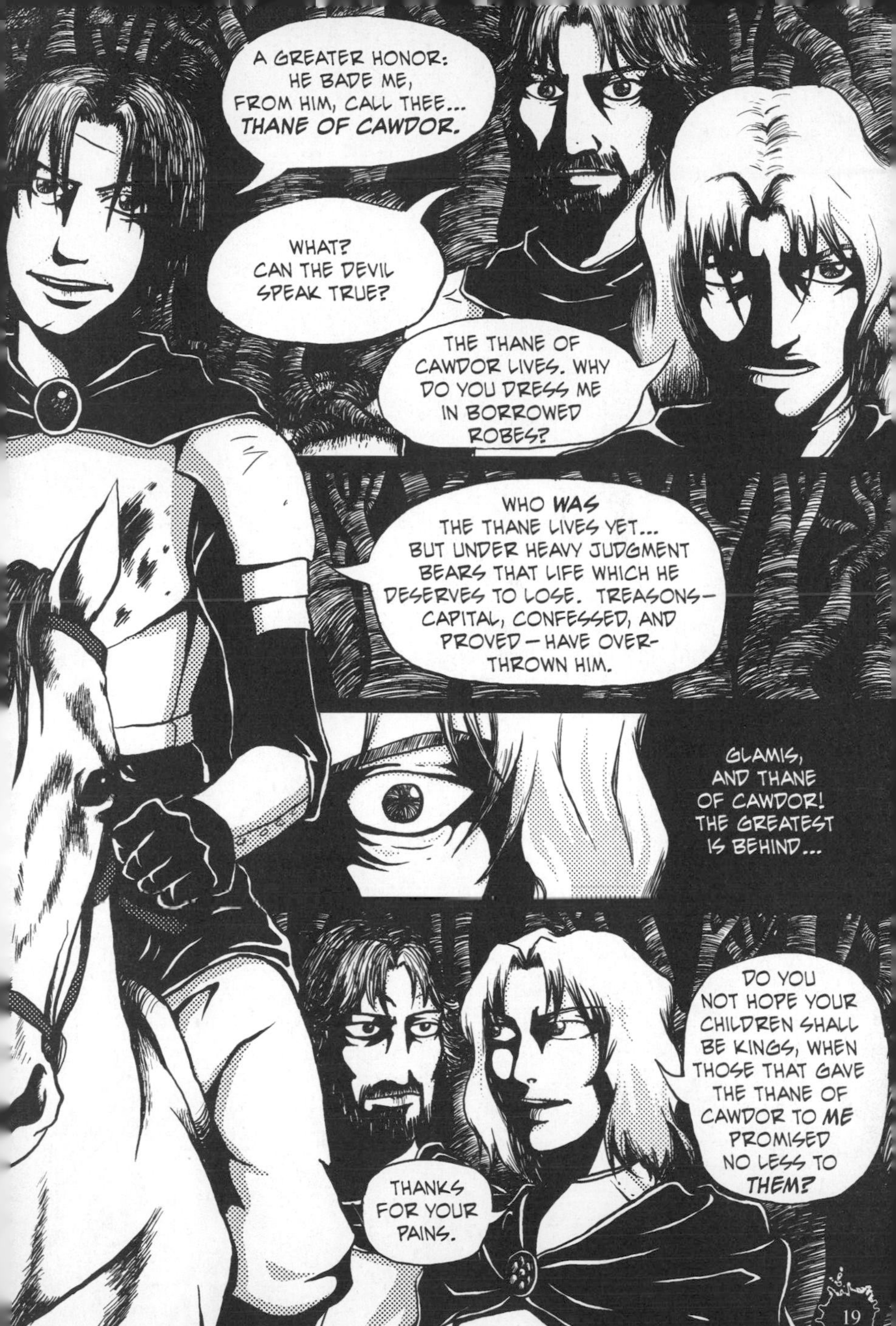
A GREATER HONOR: HE BADE ME, FROM HIM, CALL THEE... THANE OF CAWDOR.
WHAT? CAN THE DEVIL SPEAK TRUE?
THE THANE OF CAWDOR LIVES. WHY DO YOU DRESS ME IN BORROWED ROBES?
WHO WAS THE THANE LIVES YET... BUT UNDER HEAVY JUDGMENT BEARS THAT LIFE WHICH HE DESERVES TO LOSE. TREASONS—CAPITAL, CONFESSED, AND PROVED—HAVE OVERTHROWN HIM.
GLAMIS, AND THANE OF CAWDOR! THE GREATEST IS BEHIND...
THANKS FOR YOUR PAINS.
DO YOU NOT HOPE YOUR CHILDREN SHALL BE KINGS, WHEN THOSE THAT GAVE THE THANE OF CAWDOR TO ME PROMISED NO LESS TO THEM?

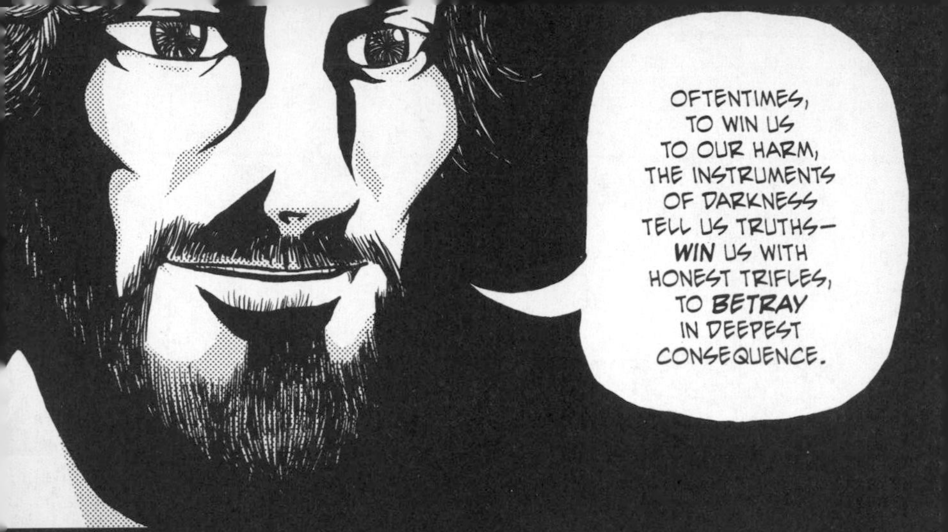
OFTENTIMES, TO WIN US TO OUR HARM, THE INSTRUMENTS OF DARKNESS TELL US TRUTHS— WIN US WITH HONEST TRIFLES, TO BETRAY IN DEEPEST CONSEQUENCE.

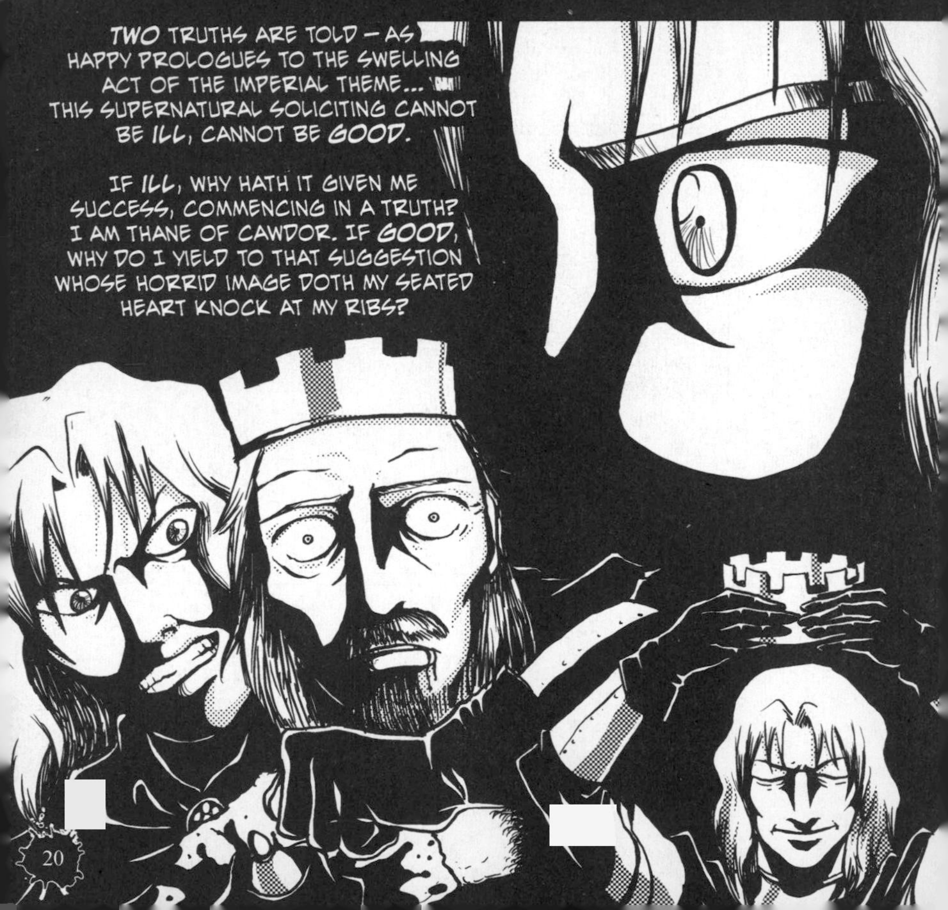
TWO TRUTHS ARE TOLD — AS HAPPY PROLOGUES TO THE SWELLING ACT OF THE IMPERIAL THEME... THIS SUPERNATURAL SOLICITING CANNOT BE ILL, CANNOT BE GOOD.
IF ILL, WHY HATH IT GIVEN ME SUCCESS, COMMENCING IN A TRUTH? I AM THANE OF CAWDOR. IF GOOD, WHY DO I YIELD TO THAT SUGGESTION WHOSE HORRID IMAGE DOTH MY SEATED HEART KNOCK AT MY RIBS?

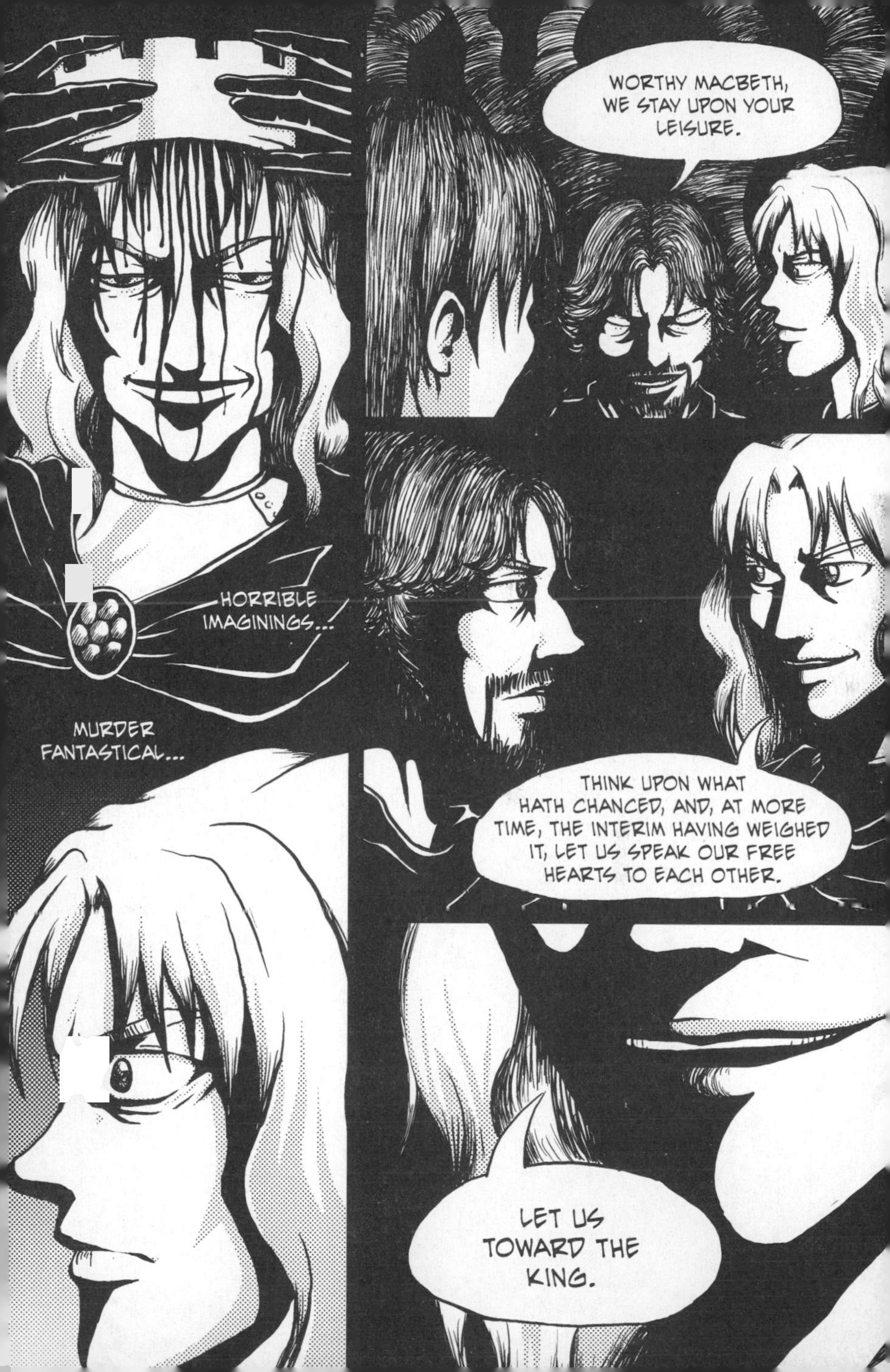
HORRIBLE IMAGININGS...
WORTHY MACBETH, WE STAY UPON YOUR LEISURE.
MURDER FANTASTICAL...
THINK UPON WHAT HATH CHANCED, AND, AT MORE TIME, THE INTERIM HAVING WEIGHED IT, LET US SPEAK OUR FREE HEARTS TO EACH OTHER.
LET US TOWARD THE KING.

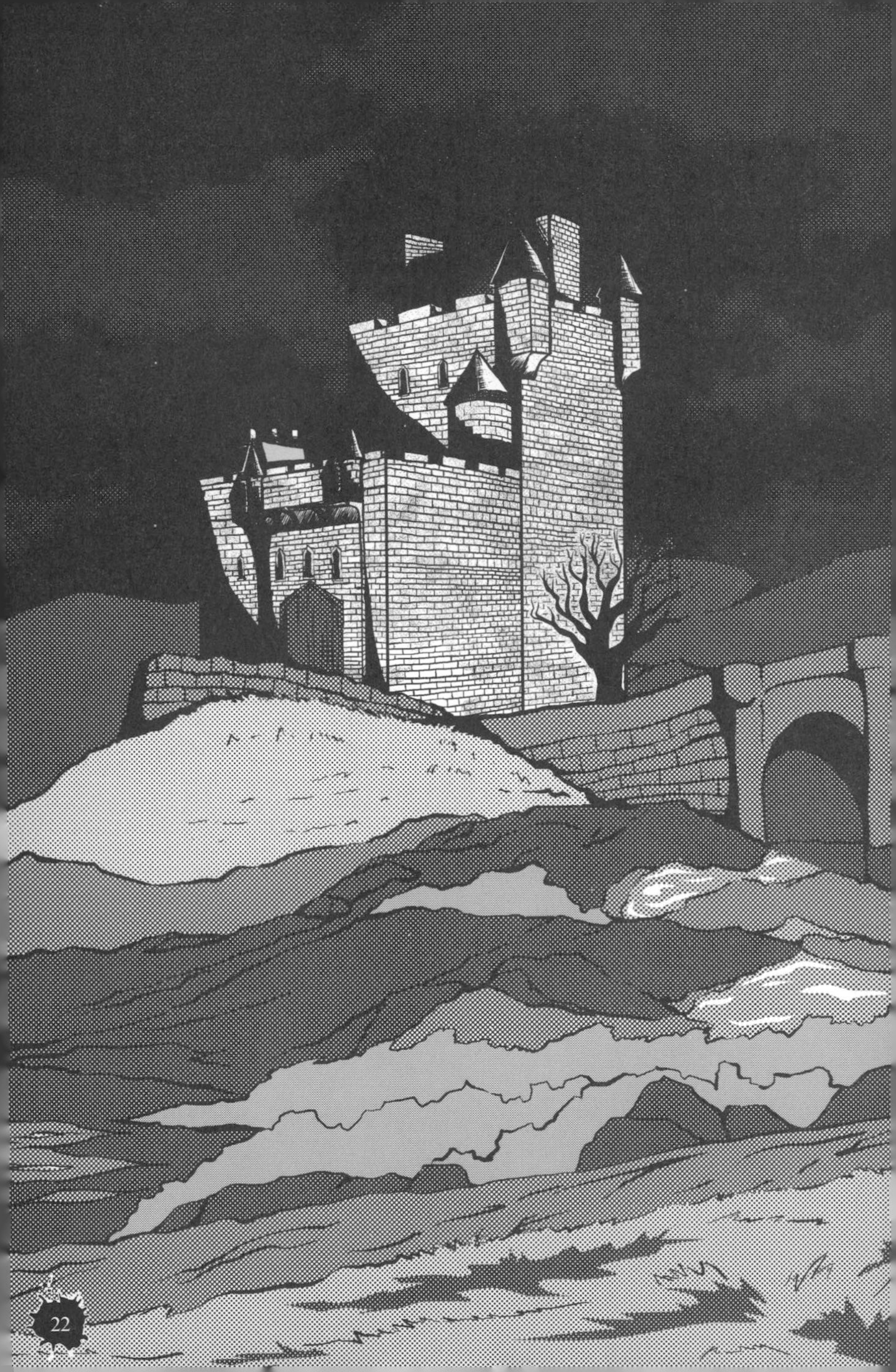

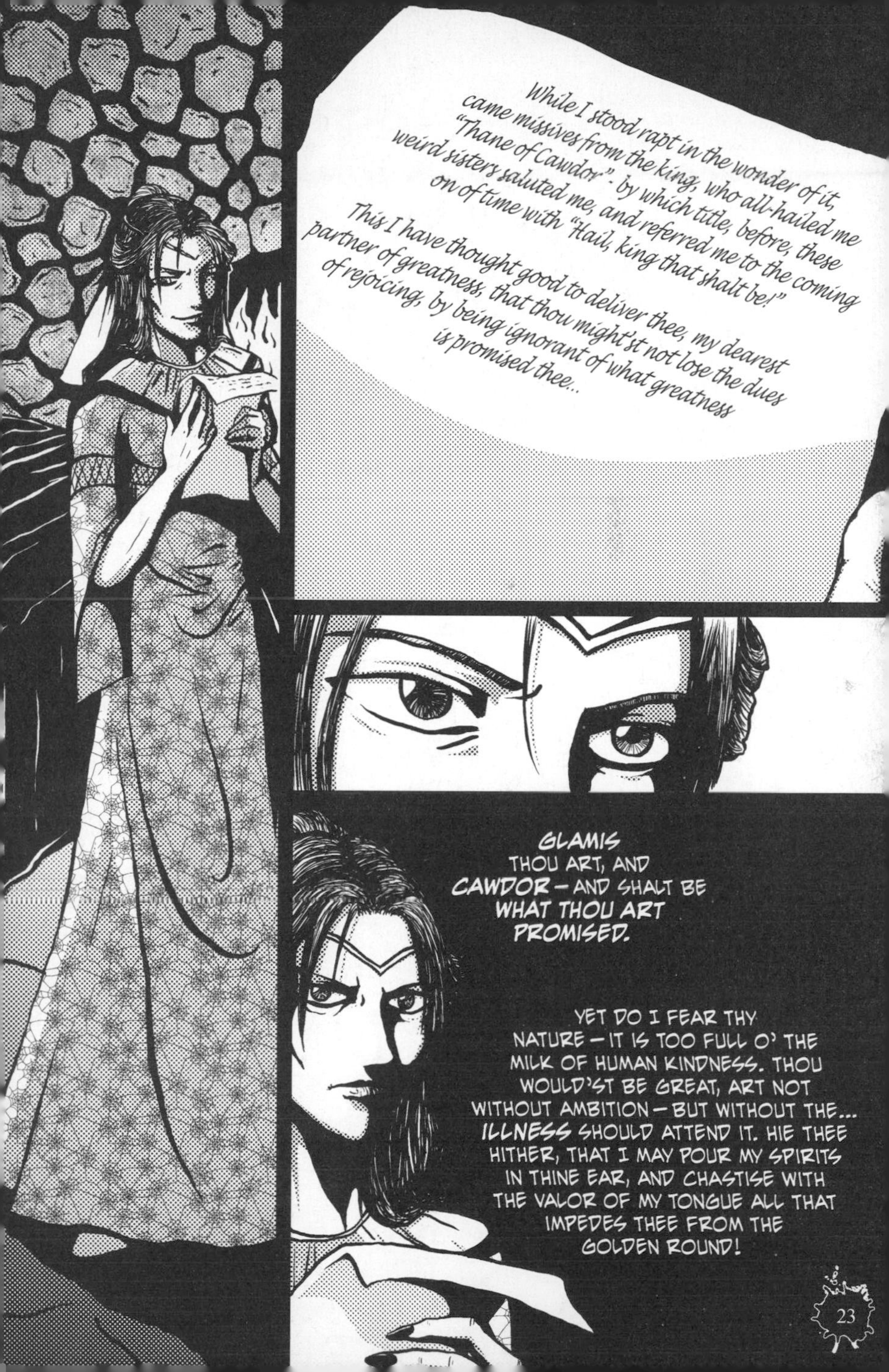
While I stood rapt in the wonder of it, came missives from the king, who all-hailed me "Thane of Cawdor"- by which title, before, these weird sisters saluted me, and referred me to the coming on of time with "Hail, king that shalt be!"
This I have thought good to deliver thee, my dearest partner of greatness, that thou might'st not lose the dues of rejoicing, by being ignorant of what greatness is promised thee...
GLAMIS THOU ART, AND CAWDOR—AND SHALT BE WHAT THOU ART PROMISED.
YET DO I FEAR THY NATURE—IT IS TOO FULL O' THE MILK OF HUMAN KINDNESS. THOU WOULD'ST BE GREAT, ART NOT WITHOUT AMBITION—BUT WITHOUT THE... ILLNESS SHOULD ATTEND IT. HIE THEE HITHER, THAT I MAY POUR MY SPIRITS IN THINE EAR, AND CHASTISE WITH THE VALOR OF MY TONGUE ALL THAT IMPEDES THEE FROM THE GOLDEN ROUND!

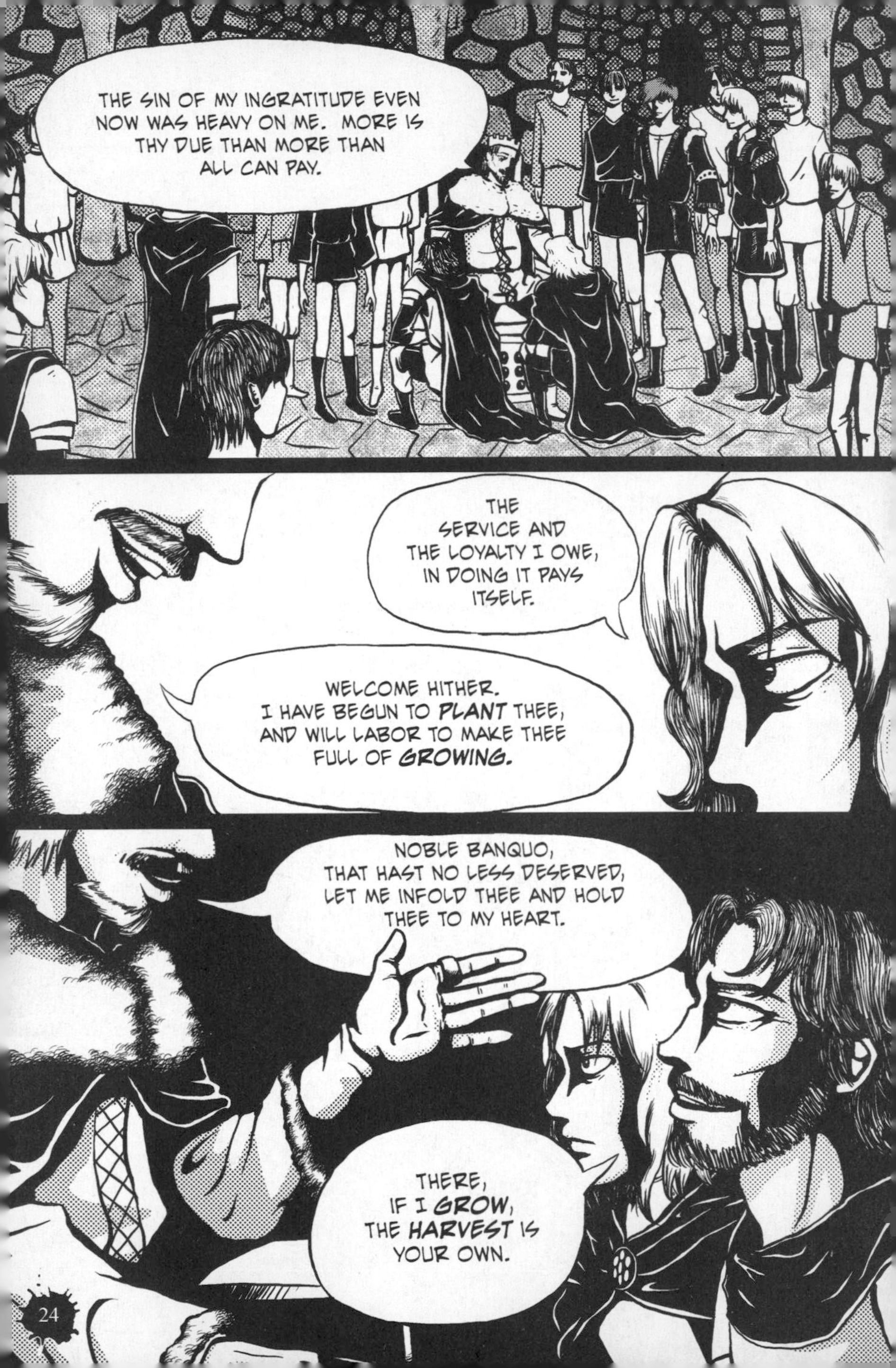
THE SIN OF MY INGRATITUDE EVEN NOW WAS HEAVY ON ME. MORE IS THY DUE THAN MORE THAN ALL CAN PAY.
THE SERVICE AND THE LOYALTY I OWE, IN DOING IT PAYS ITSELF.
WELCOME HITHER. I HAVE BEGUN TO PLANT THEE, AND WILL LABOR TO MAKE THEE FULL OF GROWING.
NOBLE BANQUO, THAT HAST NO LESS DESERVED, LET ME INFOLD THEE AND HOLD THEE TO MY HEART.
THERE, IF I GROW, THE HARVEST IS YOUR OWN.

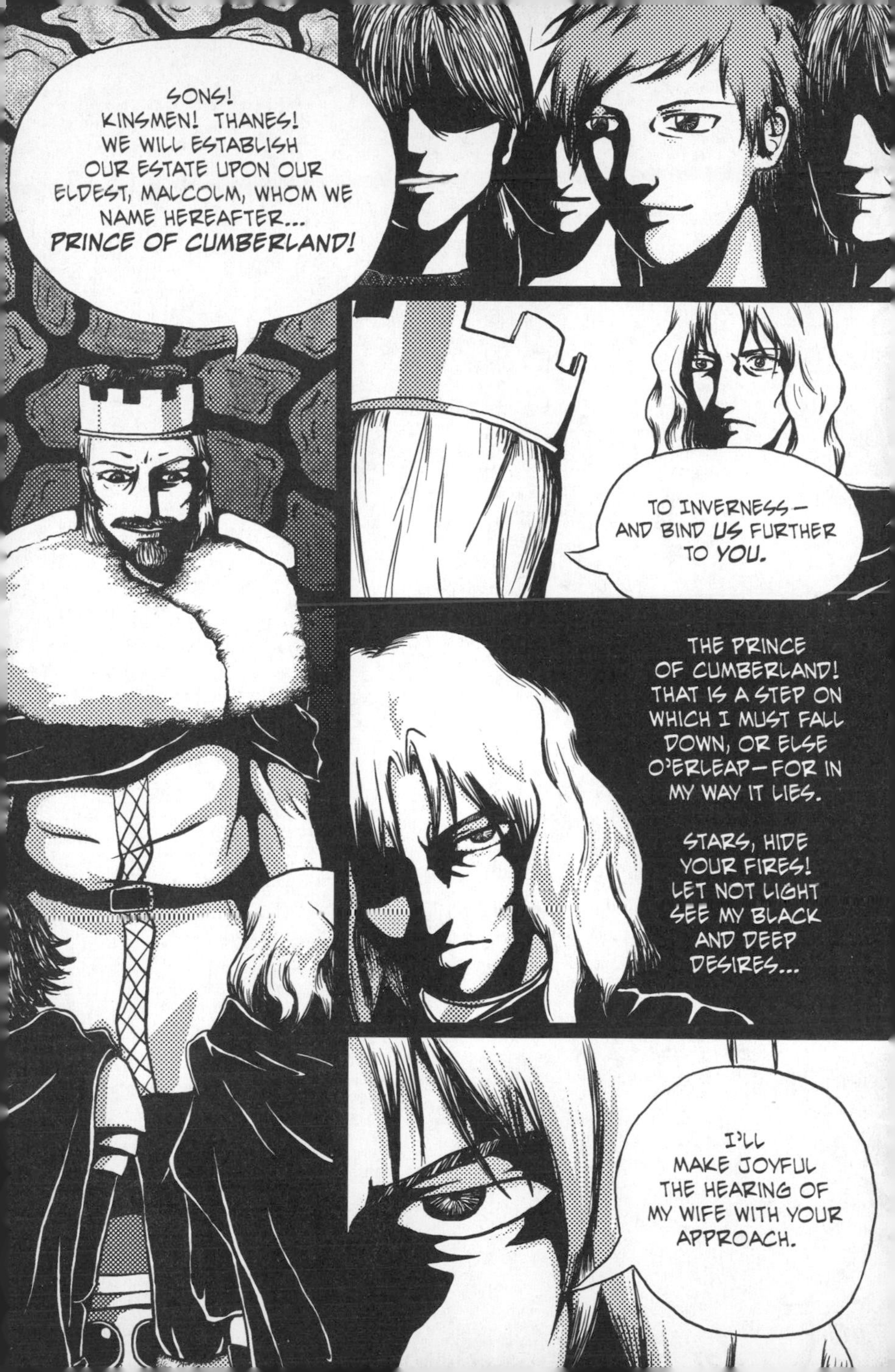
SONS! KINSMEN! THANES! WE WILL ESTABLISH OUR ESTATE UPON OUR ELDEST, MALCOLM, WHOM WE NAME HEREAFTER... PRINCE OF CUMBERLAND!
TO INVERNESS— AND BIND US FURTHER TO YOU.
THE PRINCE OF CUMBERLAND! THAT IS A STEP ON WHICH I MUST FALL DOWN, OR ELSE O'ERLEAP—FOR IN MY WAY IT LIES.
STARS, HIDE YOUR FIRES! LET NOT LIGHT SEE MY BLACK AND DEEP DESIRES...
I'LL MAKE JOYFUL THE HEARING OF MY WIFE WITH YOUR APPROACH.

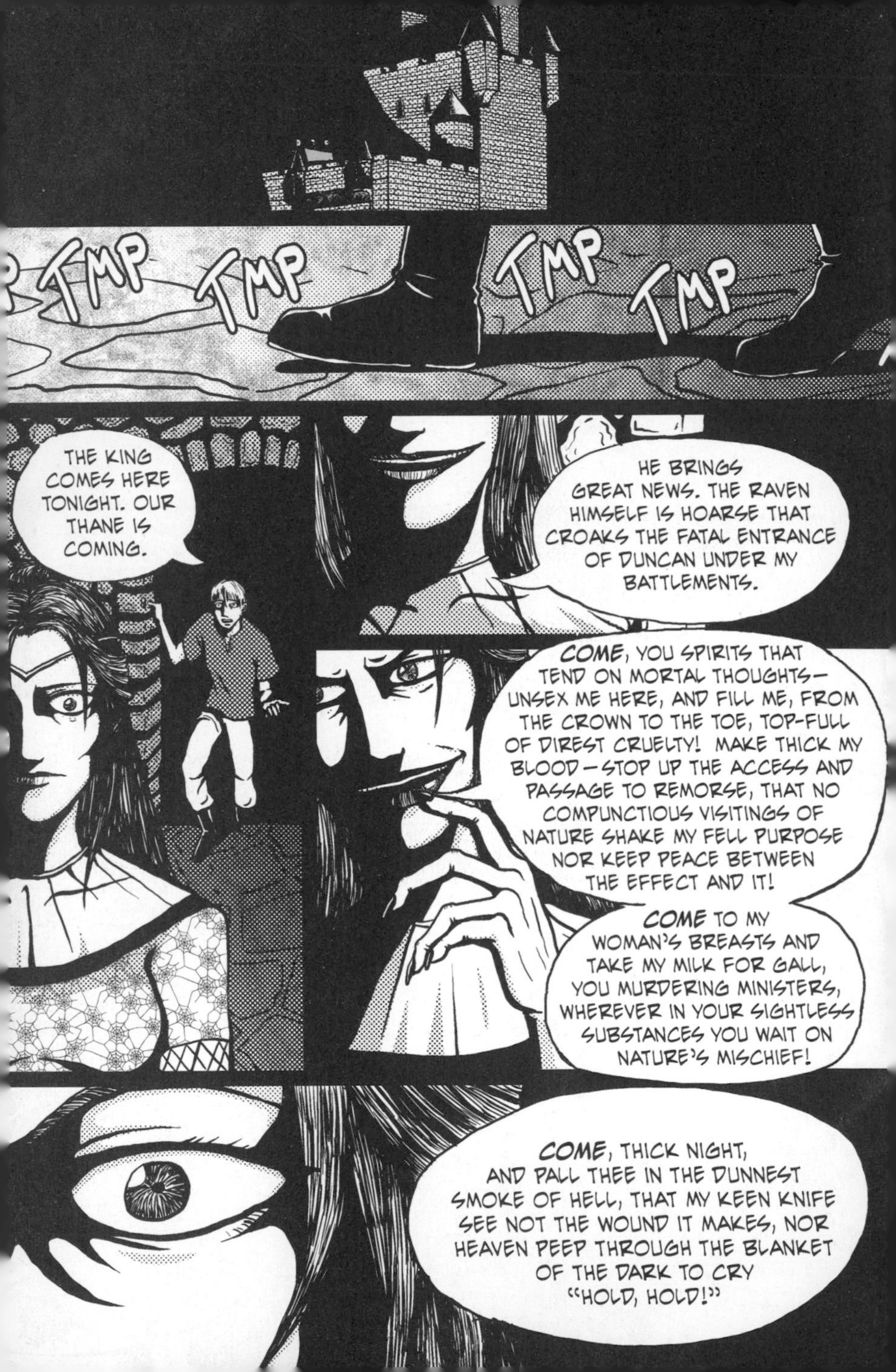
TMP TMP TMP TMP
THE KING COMES HERE TONIGHT. OUR THANE IS COMING.
HE BRINGS GREAT NEWS. THE RAVEN HIMSELF IS HOARSE THAT CROAKS THE FATAL ENTRANCE OF DUNCAN UNDER MY BATTLEMENTS.
COME, YOU SPIRITS THAT TEND ON MORTAL THOUGHTS— UNSEX ME HERE, AND FILL ME, FROM THE CROWN TO THE TOE, TOP-FULL OF DIREST CRUELTY! MAKE THICK MY BLOOD—STOP UP THE ACCESS AND PASSAGE TO REMORSE, THAT NO COMPUNCTIOUS VISITINGS OF NATURE SHAKE MY FELL PURPOSE NOR KEEP PEACE BETWEEN THE EFFECT AND IT!
COME TO MY WOMAN'S BREASTS AND TAKE MY MILK FOR GALL, YOU MURDERING MINISTERS, WHEREVER IN YOUR SIGHTLESS SUBSTANCES YOU WAIT ON NATURE'S MISCHIEF!
COME, THICK NIGHT, AND PALL THEE IN THE DUNNEST SMOKE OF HELL, THAT MY KEEN KNIFE SEE NOT THE WOUND IT MAKES, NOR HEAVEN PEEP THROUGH THE BLANKET OF THE DARK TO CRY "HOLD, HOLD!"

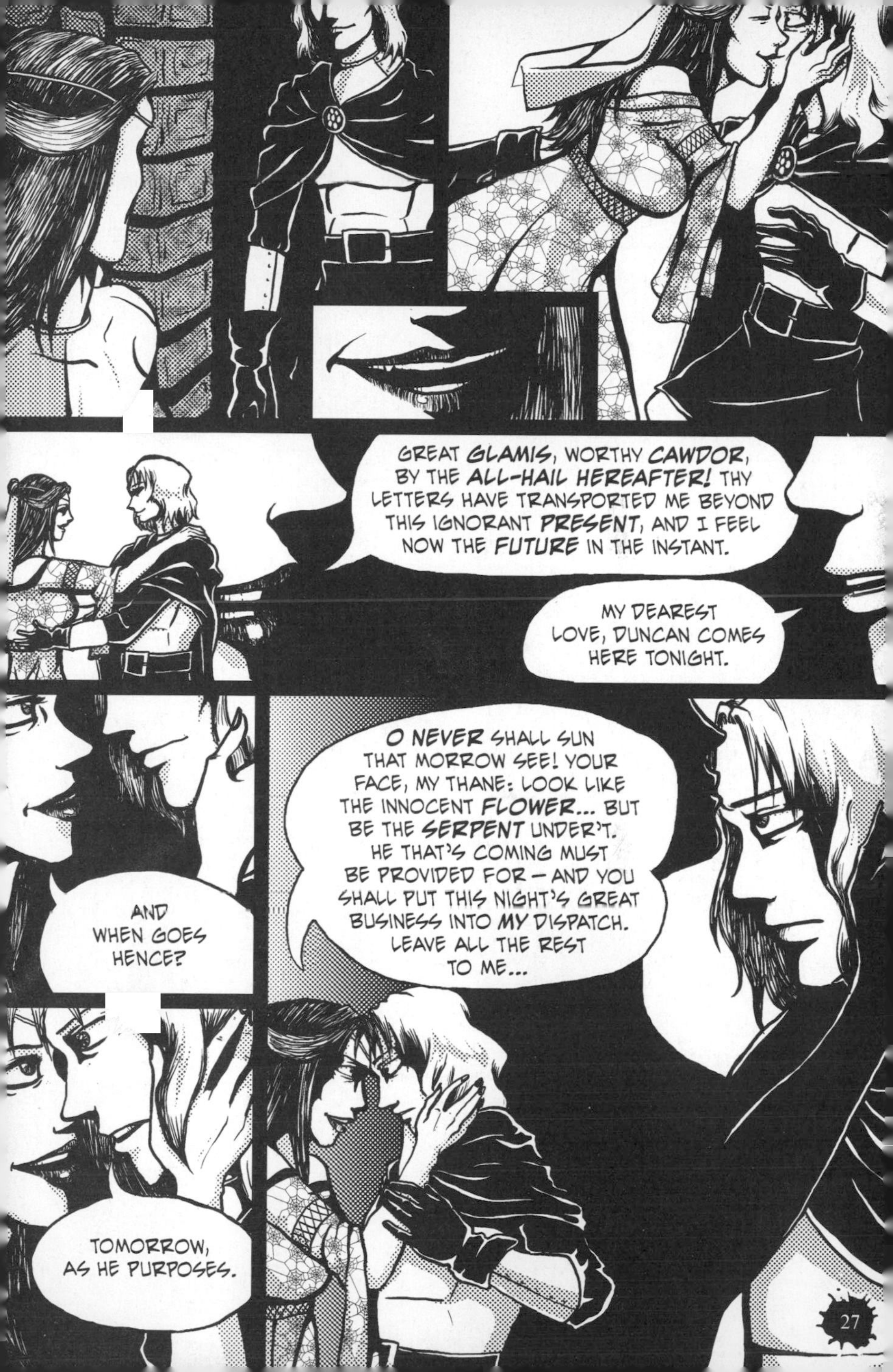
GREAT GLAMIS, WORTHY CAWDOR, BY THE ALL-HAIL HEREAFTER! THY LETTERS HAVE TRANSPORTED ME BEYOND THIS IGNORANT PRESENT, AND I FEEL NOW THE FUTURE IN THE INSTANT.
MY DEAREST LOVE, DUNCAN COMES HERE TONIGHT.
AND WHEN GOES HENCE?
O NEVER SHALL SUN THAT MORROW SEE! YOUR FACE, MY THANE: LOOK LIKE THE INNOCENT FLOWER... BUT BE THE SERPENT UNDER'T. HE THAT'S COMING MUST BE PROVIDED FOR — AND YOU SHALL PUT THIS NIGHT'S GREAT BUSINESS INTO MY DISPATCH. LEAVE ALL THE REST TO ME...
TOMORROW, AS HE PURPOSES.

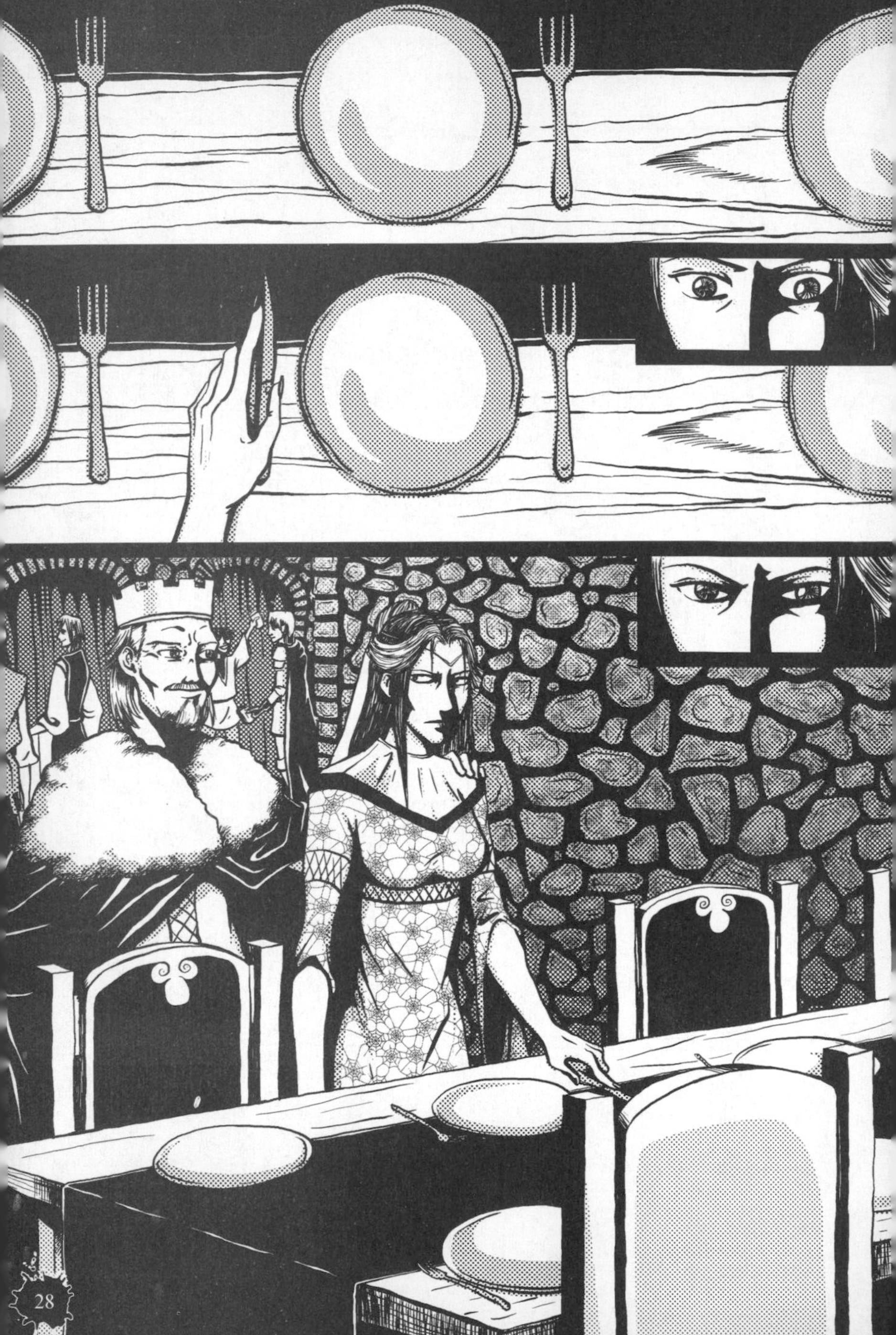

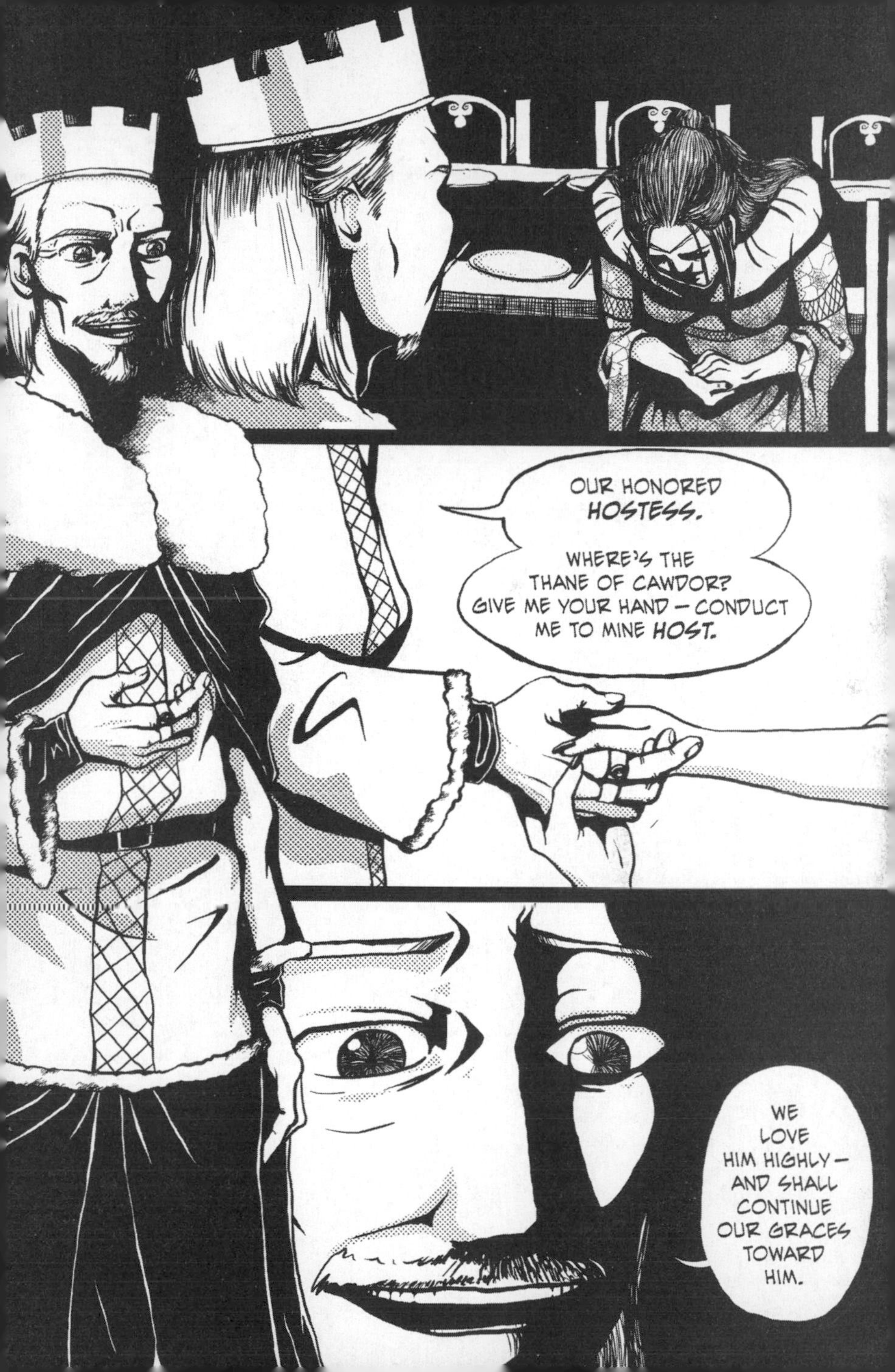
OUR HONORED HOSTESS.
WHERE'S THE THANE OF CAWDOR? GIVE ME YOUR HAND — CONDUCT ME TO MINE HOST.
WE LOVE HIM HIGHLY — AND SHALL CONTINUE OUR GRACES TOWARD HIM.

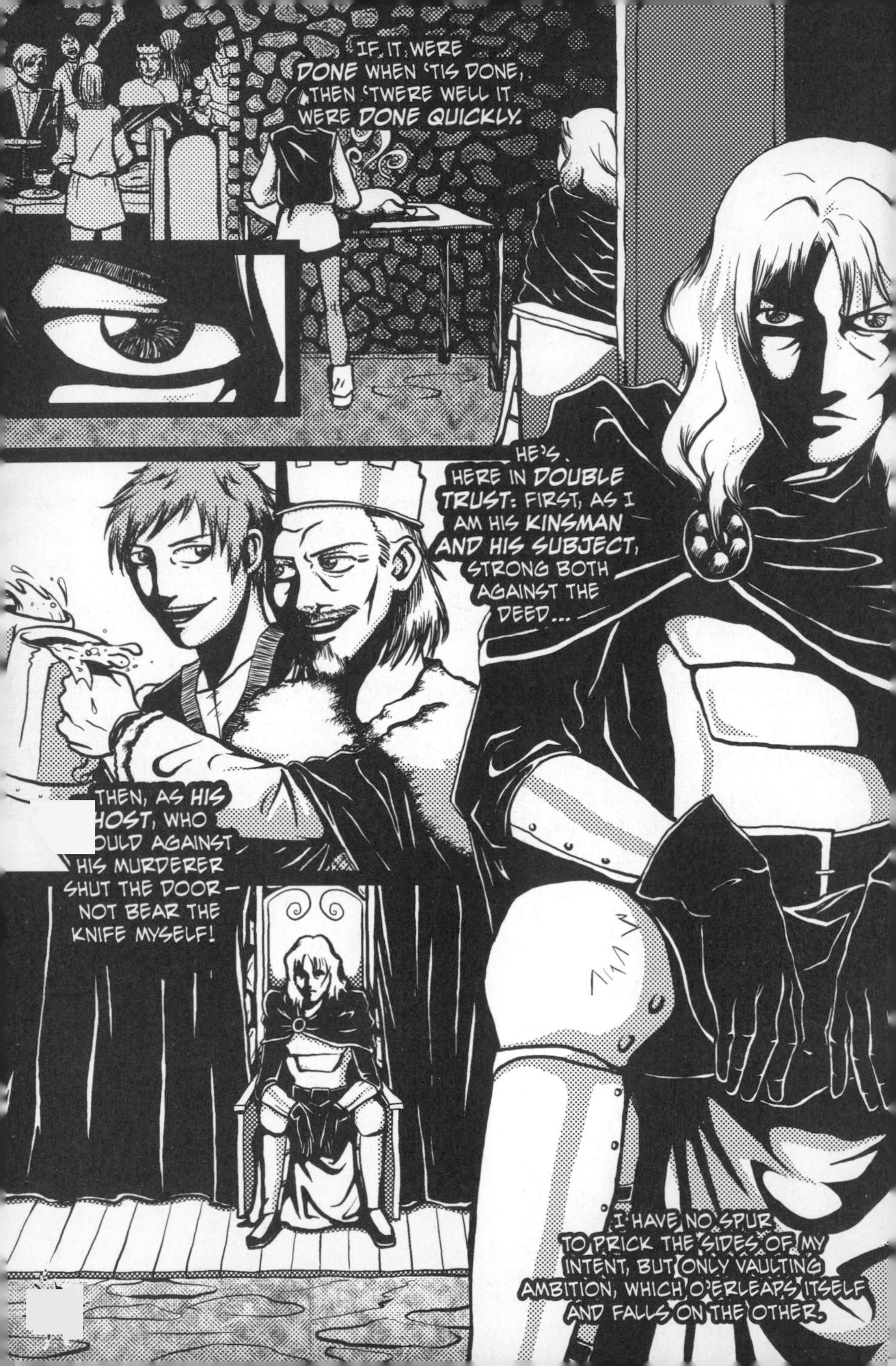
IF IT WERE DONE WHEN 'TIS DONE, THEN 'TWERE WELL IT WERE DONE QUICKLY.
HE'S HERE IN DOUBLE TRUST: FIRST, AS I AM HIS KINSMAN AND HIS SUBJECT, STRONG BOTH AGAINST THE DEED...
THEN, AS HIS HOST, WHO SHOULD AGAINST HIS MURDERER SHUT THE DOOR—NOT BEAR THE KNIFE MYSELF!
I HAVE NO SPUR TO PRICK THE SIDES OF MY INTENT, BUT ONLY VAULTING AMBITION, WHICH O'ERLEAPS ITSELF AND FALLS ON THE OTHER.

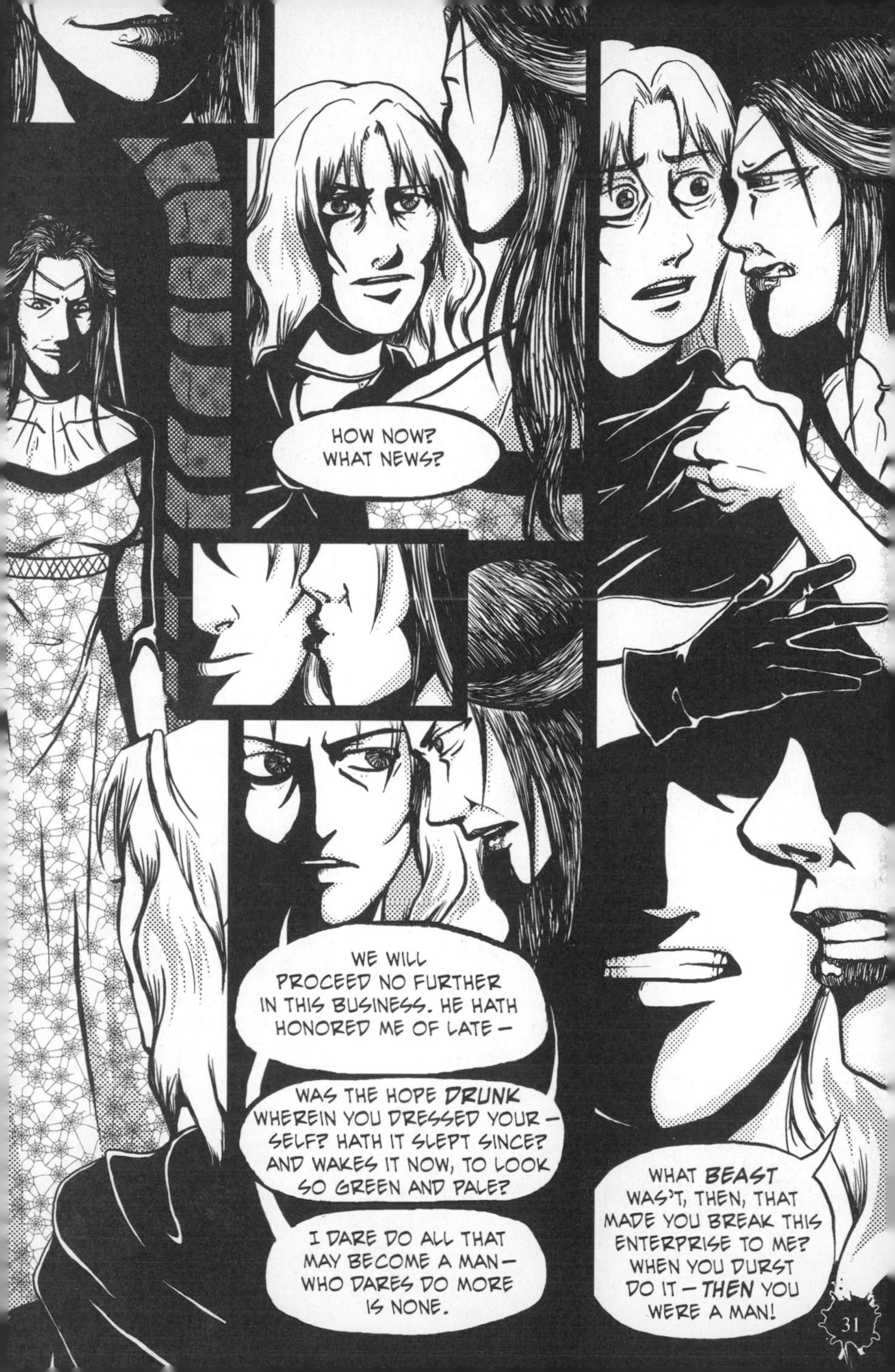
HOW NOW? WHAT NEWS?
WE WILL PROCEED NO FURTHER IN THIS BUSINESS. HE HATH HONORED ME OF LATE—
WAS THE HOPE DRUNK WHEREIN YOU DRESSED YOUR-SELF? HATH IT SLEPT SINCE? AND WAKES IT NOW, TO LOOK SO GREEN AND PALE?
I DARE DO ALL THAT MAY BECOME A MAN—WHO DARES DO MORE IS NONE.
WHAT BEAST WAS'T, THEN, THAT MADE YOU BREAK THIS ENTERPRISE TO ME? WHEN YOU DURST DO IT—THEN YOU WERE A MAN!

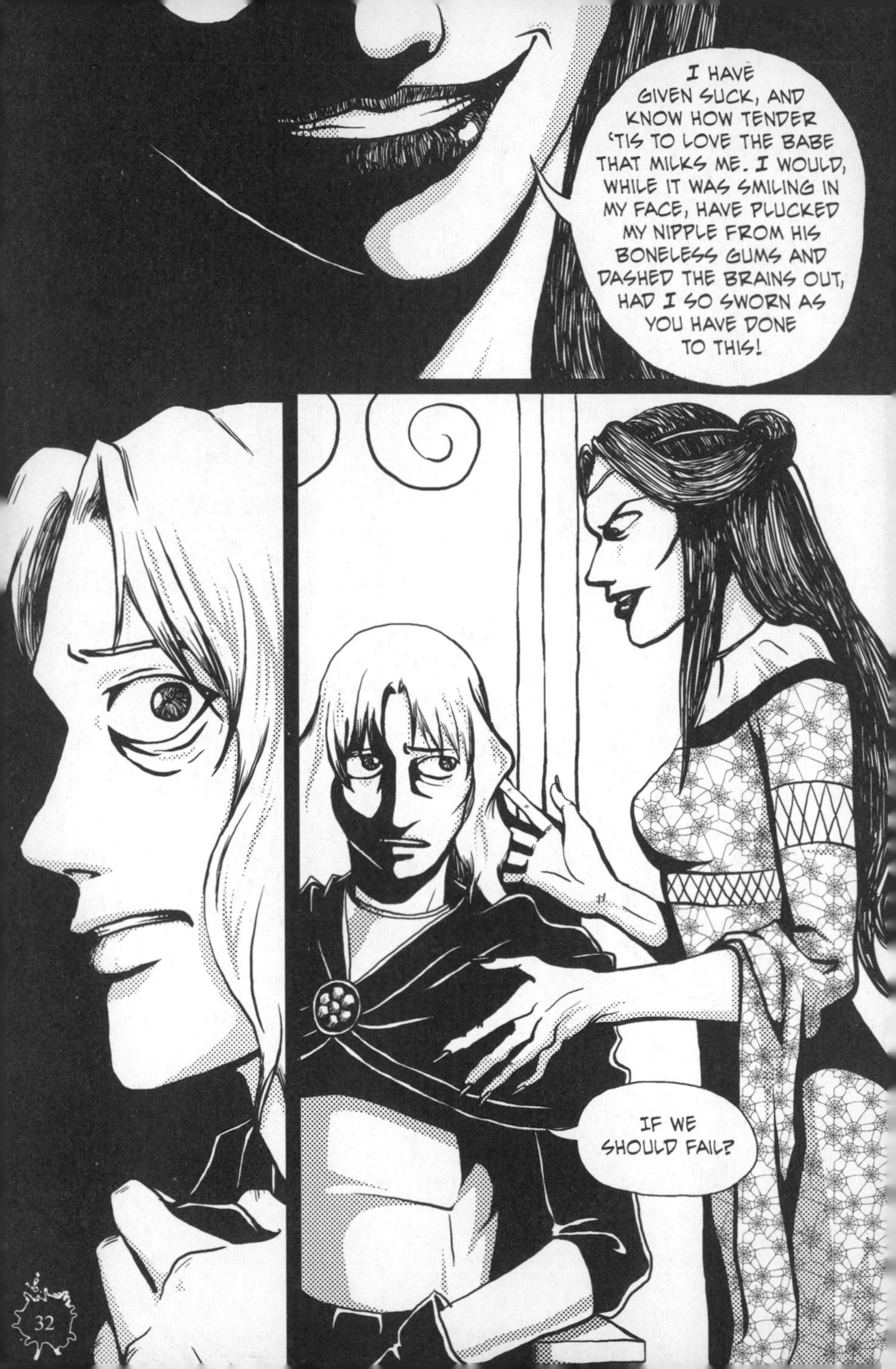
I HAVE GIVEN SUCK, AND KNOW HOW TENDER 'TIS TO LOVE THE BABE THAT MILKS ME. I WOULD, WHILE IT WAS SMILING IN MY FACE, HAVE PLUCKED MY NIPPLE FROM HIS BONELESS GUMS AND DASHED THE BRAINS OUT, HAD I SO SWORN AS YOU HAVE DONE TO THIS!
IF WE SHOULD FAIL?

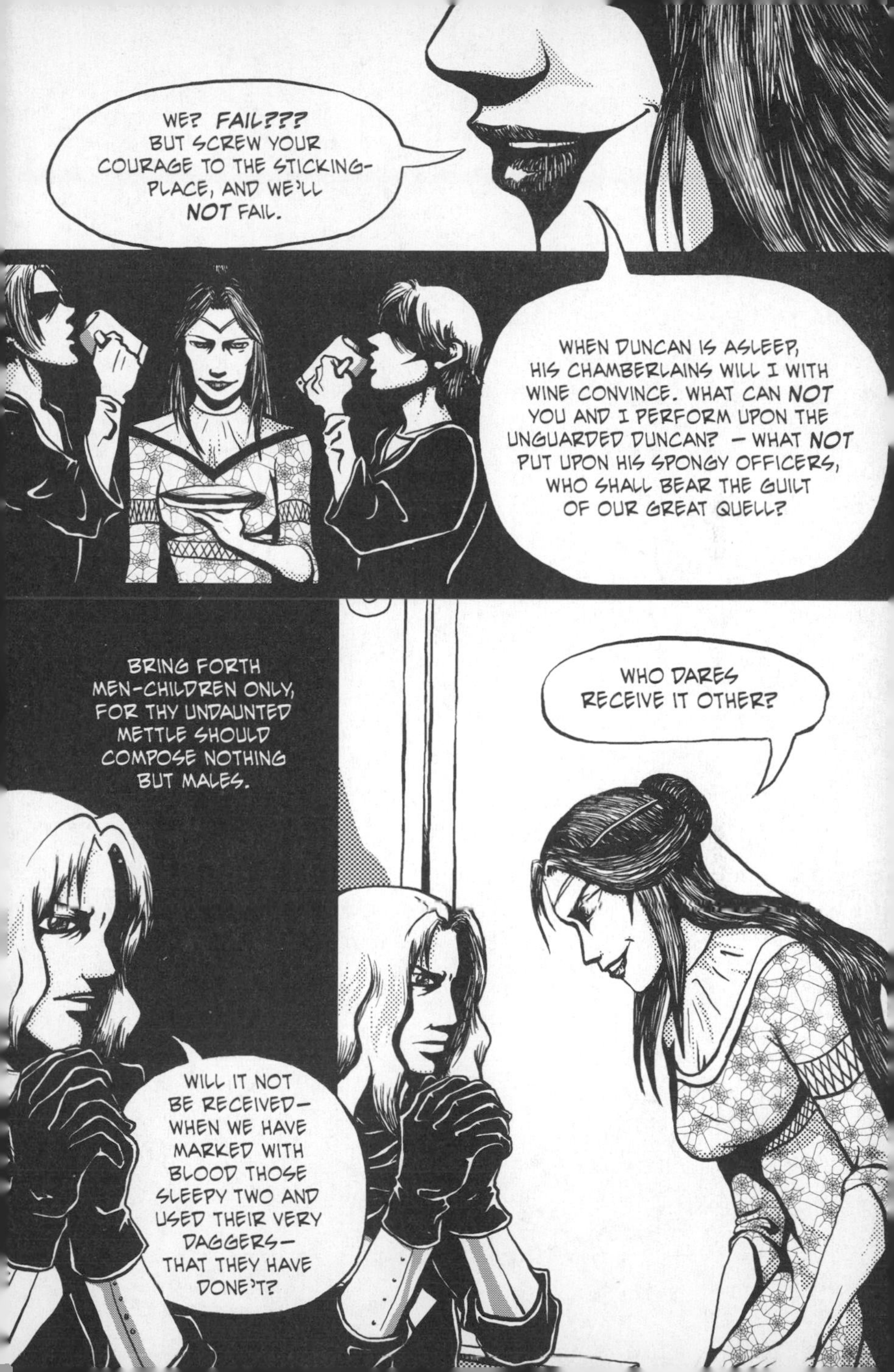
WE? FAIL??? BUT SCREW YOUR COURAGE TO THE STICKING-PLACE, AND WE'LL NOT FAIL.
WHEN DUNCAN IS ASLEEP, HIS CHAMBERLAINS WILL I WITH WINE CONVINCE. WHAT CAN NOT YOU AND I PERFORM UPON THE UNGUARDED DUNCAN? — WHAT NOT PUT UPON HIS SPONGY OFFICERS, WHO SHALL BEAR THE GUILT OF OUR GREAT QUELL?
BRING FORTH MEN-CHILDREN ONLY, FOR THY UNDAUNTED METTLE SHOULD COMPOSE NOTHING BUT MALES.
WILL IT NOT BE RECEIVED— WHEN WE HAVE MARKED WITH BLOOD THOSE SLEEPY TWO AND USED THEIR VERY DAGGERS— THAT THEY HAVE DONE'T?
WHO DARES RECEIVE IT OTHER?

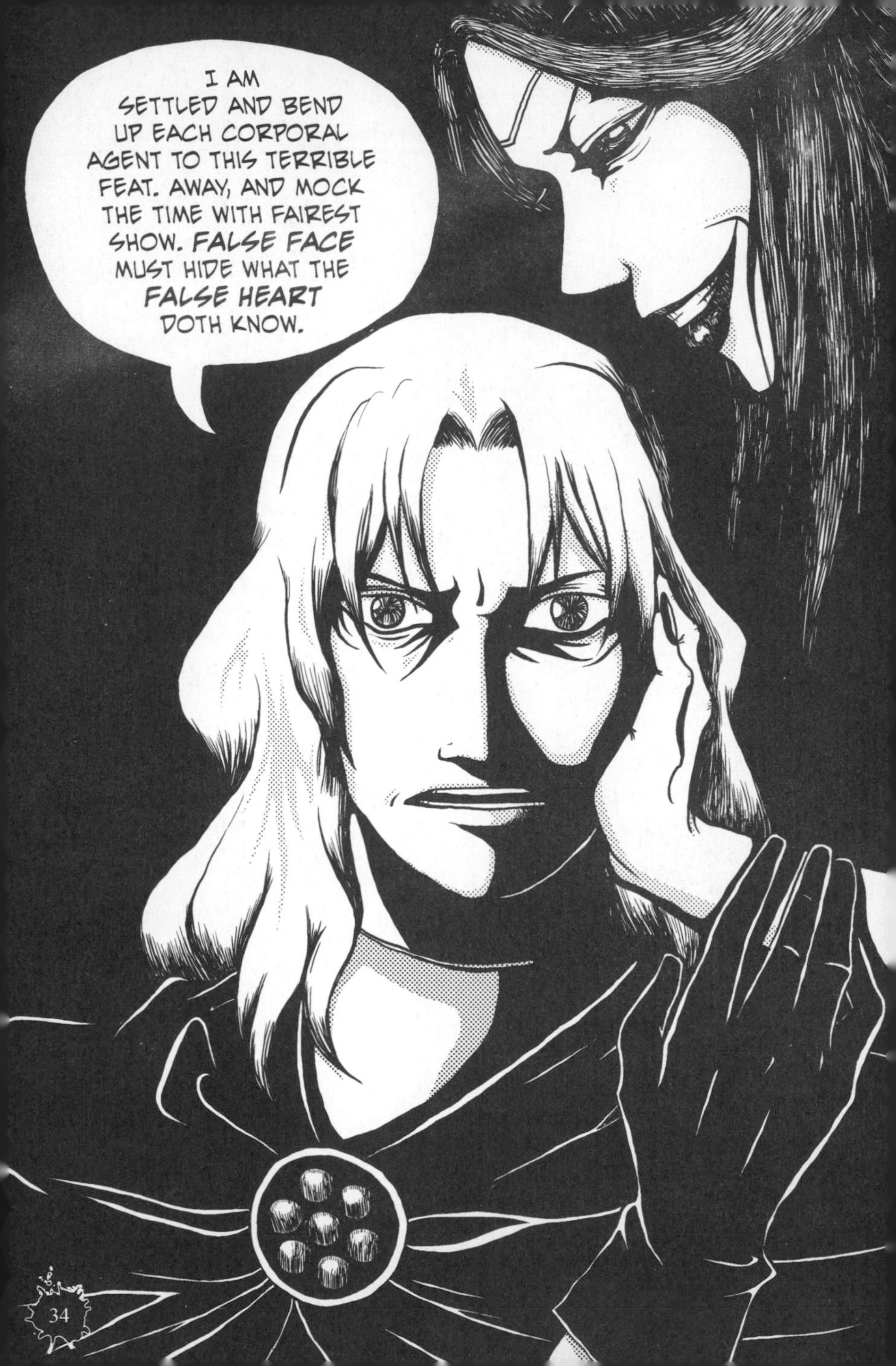
I AM SETTLED AND BEND UP EACH CORPORAL AGENT TO THIS TERRIBLE FEAT. AWAY, AND MOCK THE TIME WITH FAIREST SHOW. FALSE FACE MUST HIDE WHAT THE FALSE HEART DOTH KNOW.

Act II

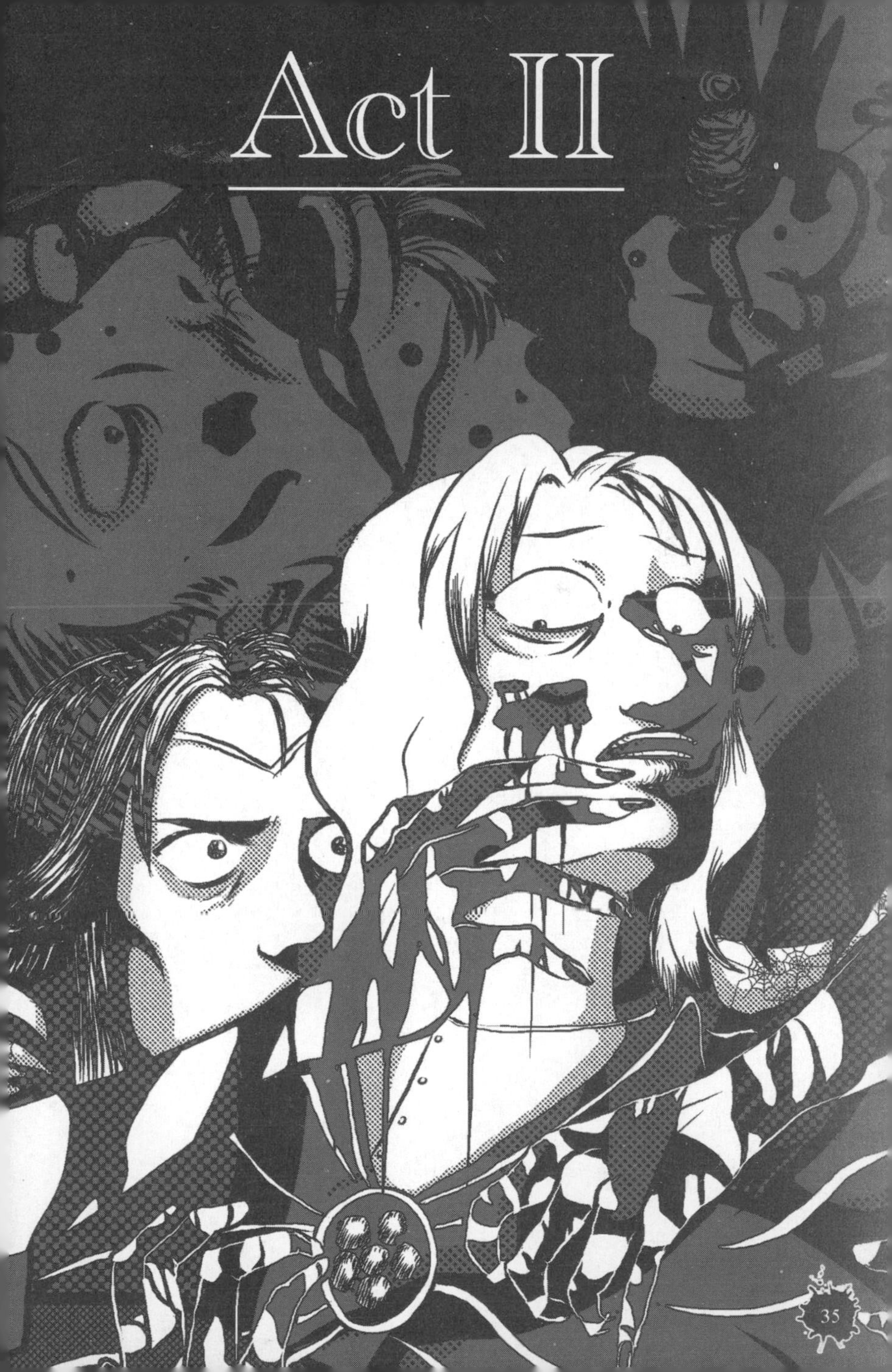

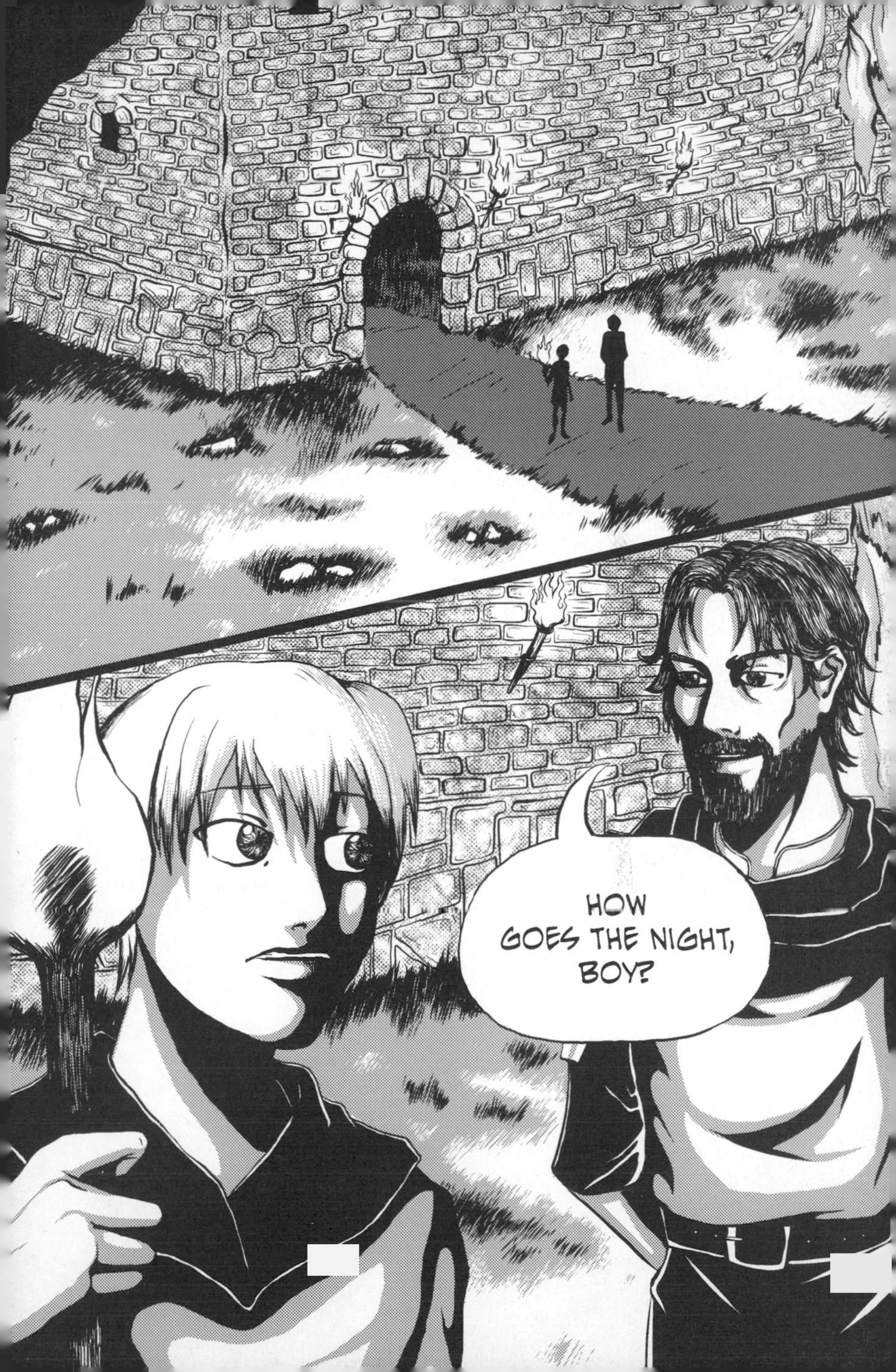
HOW GOES THE NIGHT, BOY?

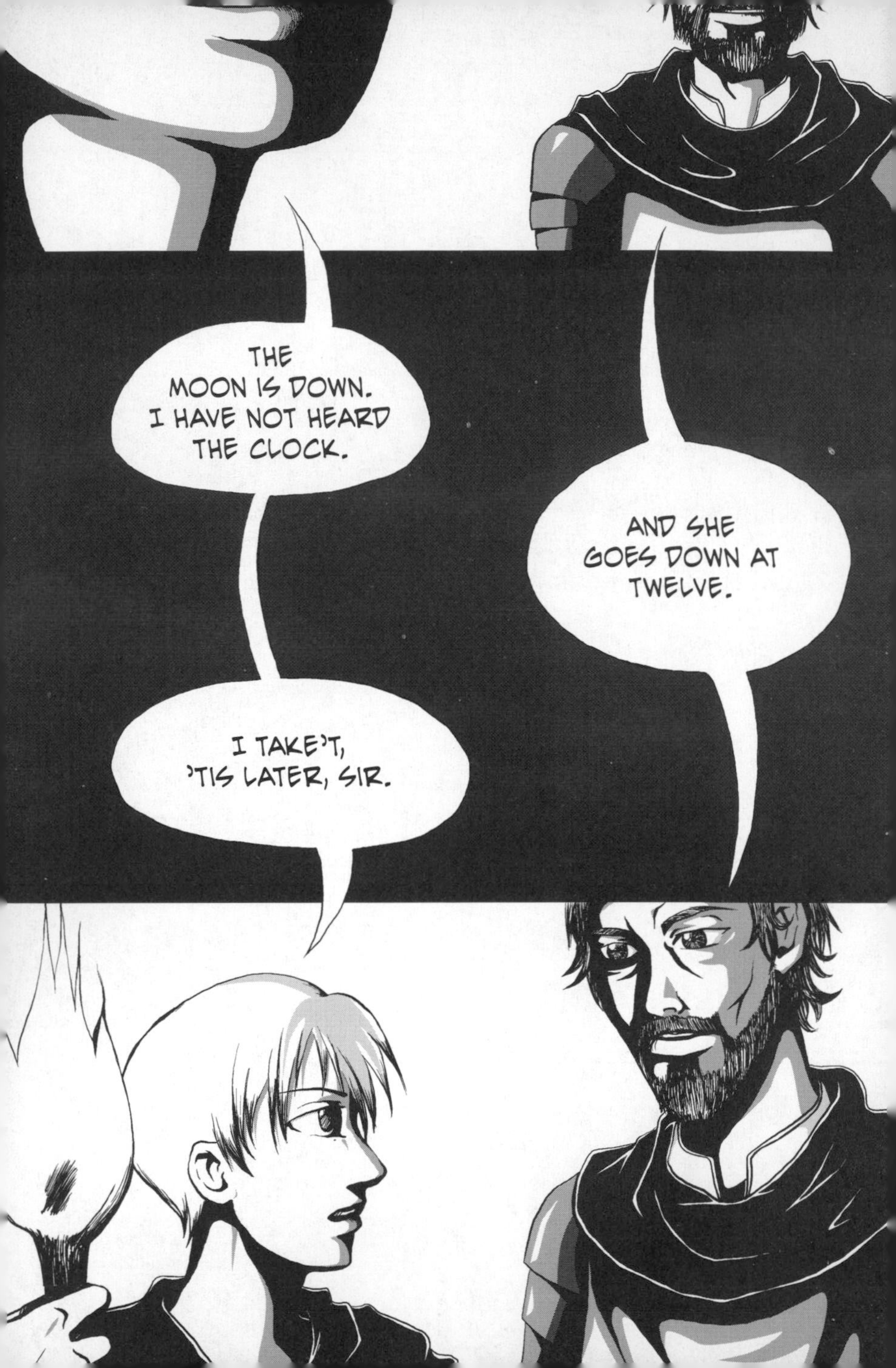
THE MOON IS DOWN. I HAVE NOT HEARD THE CLOCK.
AND SHE GOES DOWN AT TWELVE.
I TAKE'T, 'TIS LATER, SIR.

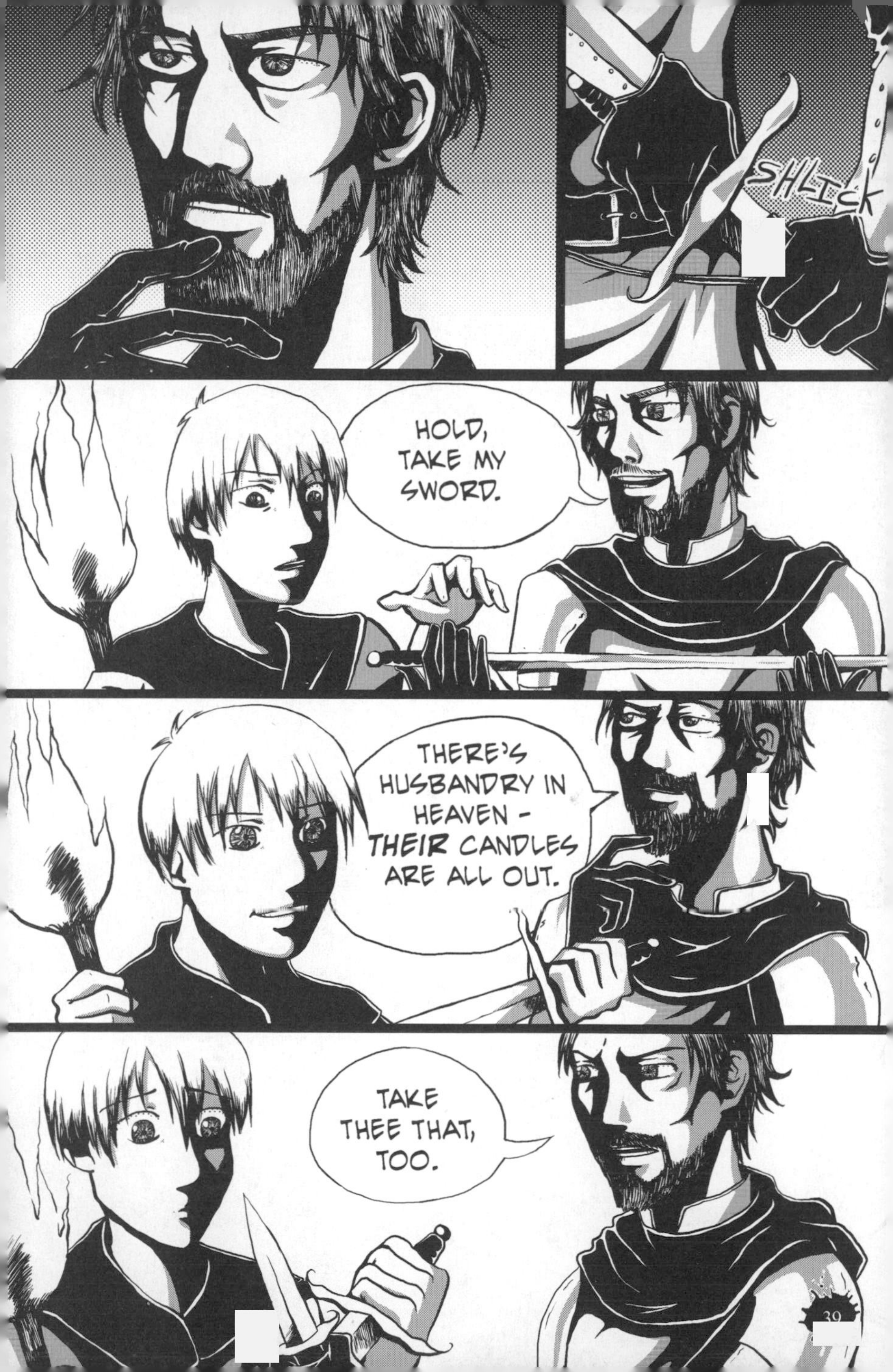
SHLICK
HOLD, TAKE MY SWORD.
THERE'S HUSBANDRY IN HEAVEN - THEIR CANDLES ARE ALL OUT.
TAKE THEE THAT, TOO.

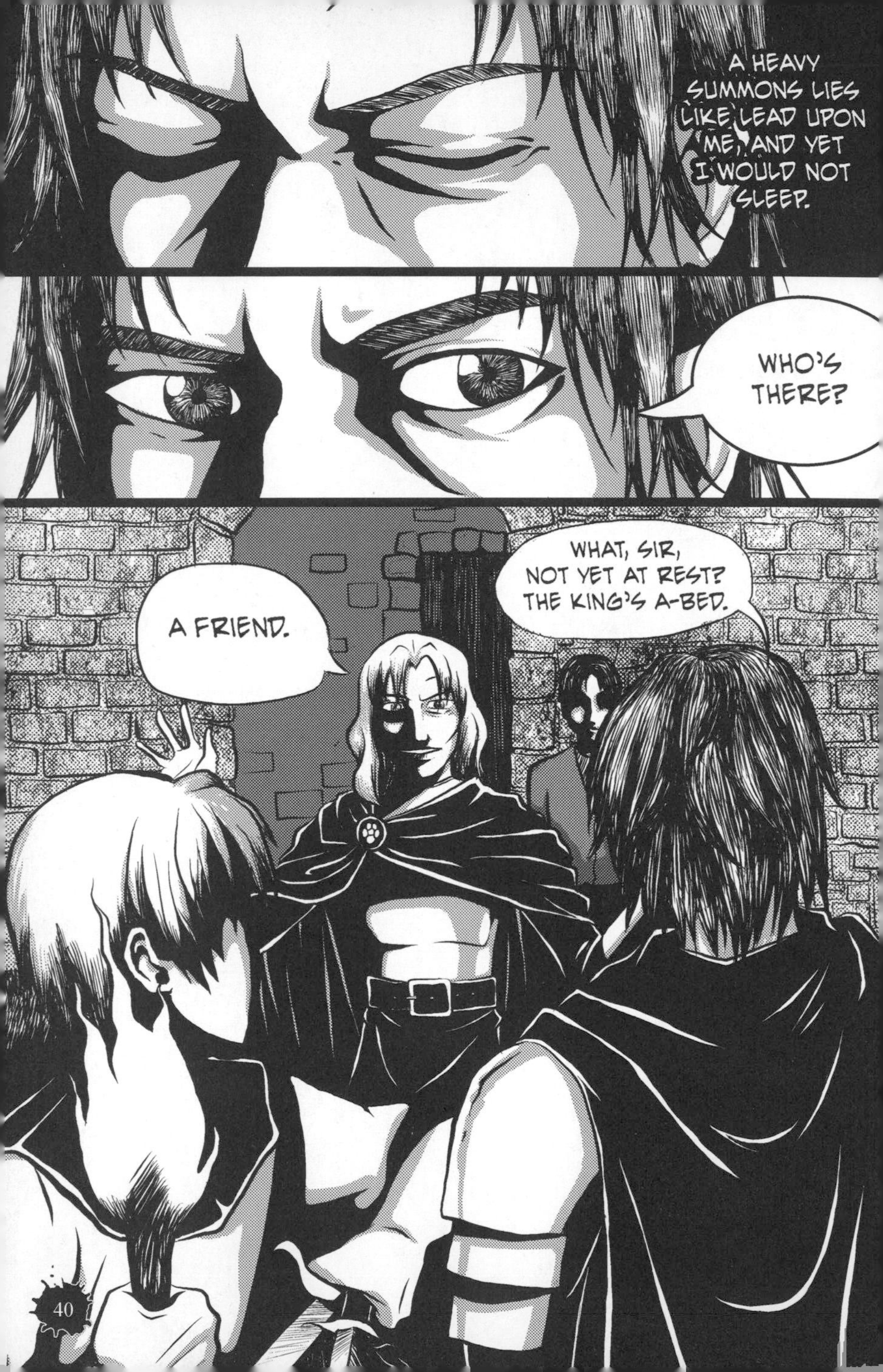
A HEAVY SUMMONS LIES LIKE LEAD UPON ME, AND YET I WOULD NOT SLEEP.
WHO'S THERE?
A FRIEND.
WHAT, SIR, NOT YET AT REST? THE KING'S A-BED.

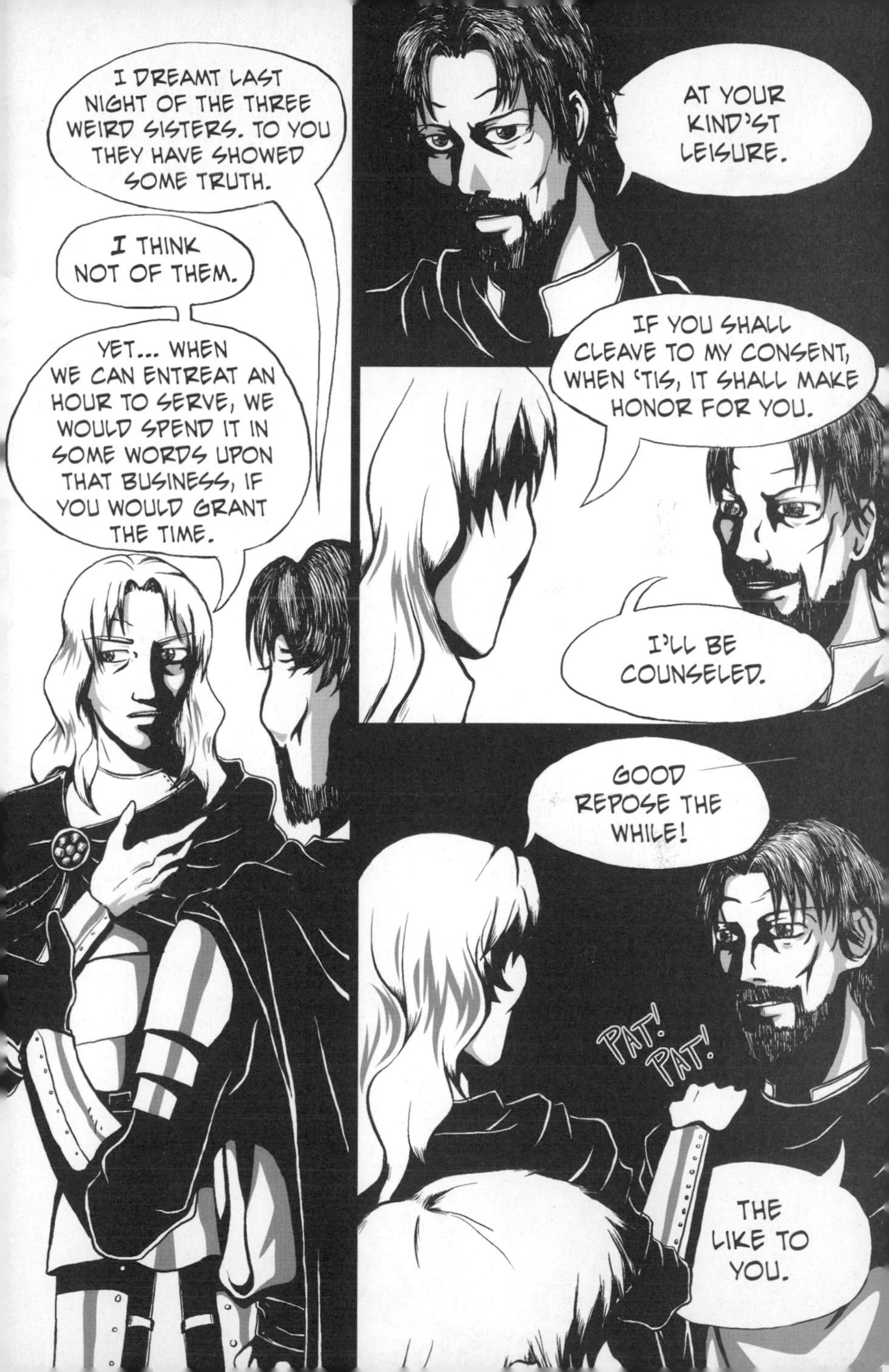
I DREAMT LAST NIGHT OF THE THREE WEIRD SISTERS. TO YOU THEY HAVE SHOWED SOME TRUTH.
I THINK NOT OF THEM.
YET... WHEN WE CAN ENTREAT AN HOUR TO SERVE, WE WOULD SPEND IT IN SOME WORDS UPON THAT BUSINESS, IF YOU WOULD GRANT THE TIME.
AT YOUR KIND'ST LEISURE.
IF YOU SHALL CLEAVE TO MY CONSENT, WHEN 'TIS, IT SHALL MAKE HONOR FOR YOU.
I'LL BE COUNSELED.
GOOD REPOSE THE WHILE!
PAT! PAT!
THE LIKE TO YOU.

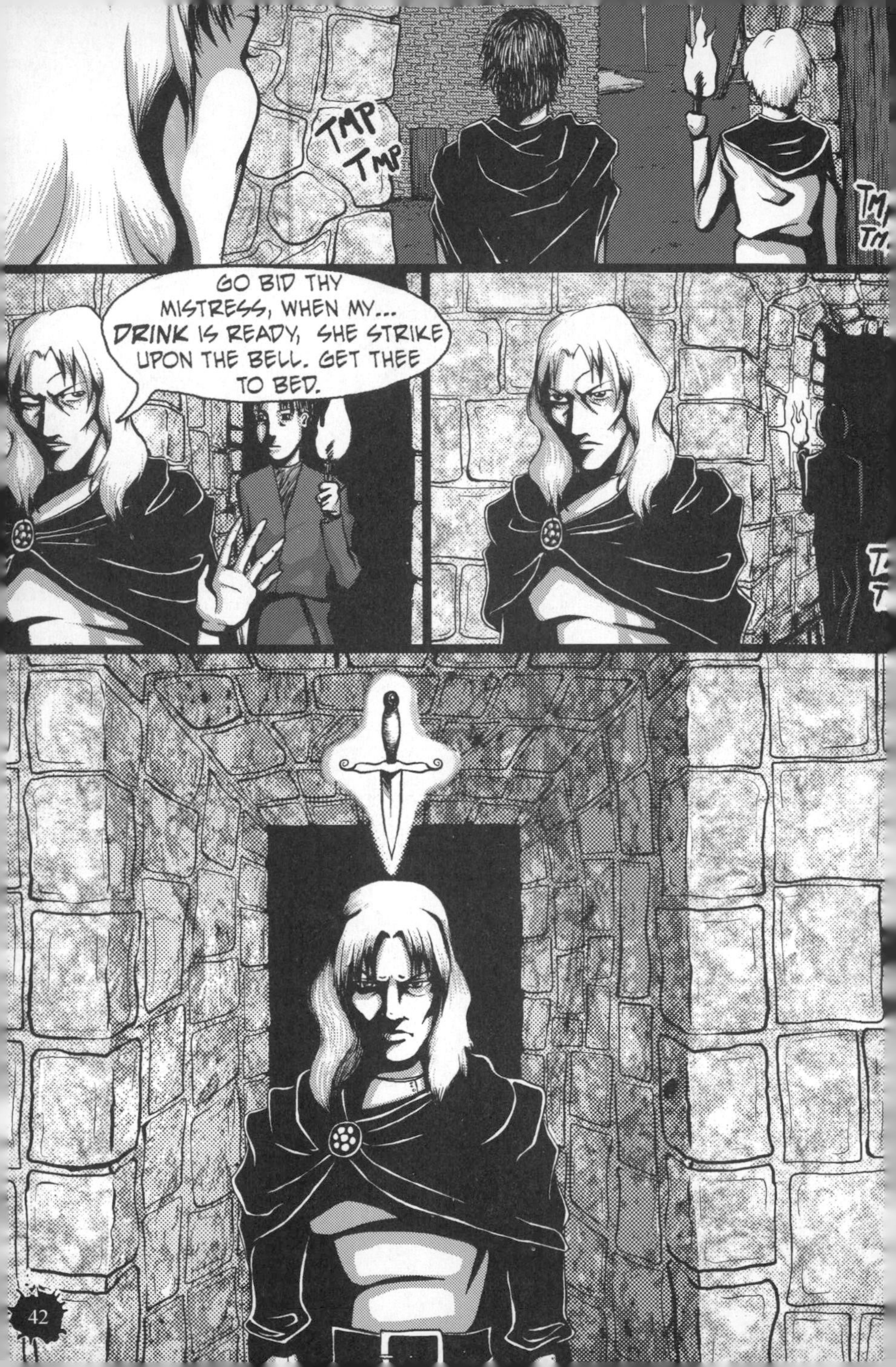
TMP TMP
TMP TMP
GO BID THY MISTRESS, WHEN MY... DRINK IS READY, SHE STRIKE UPON THE BELL. GET THEE TO BED.

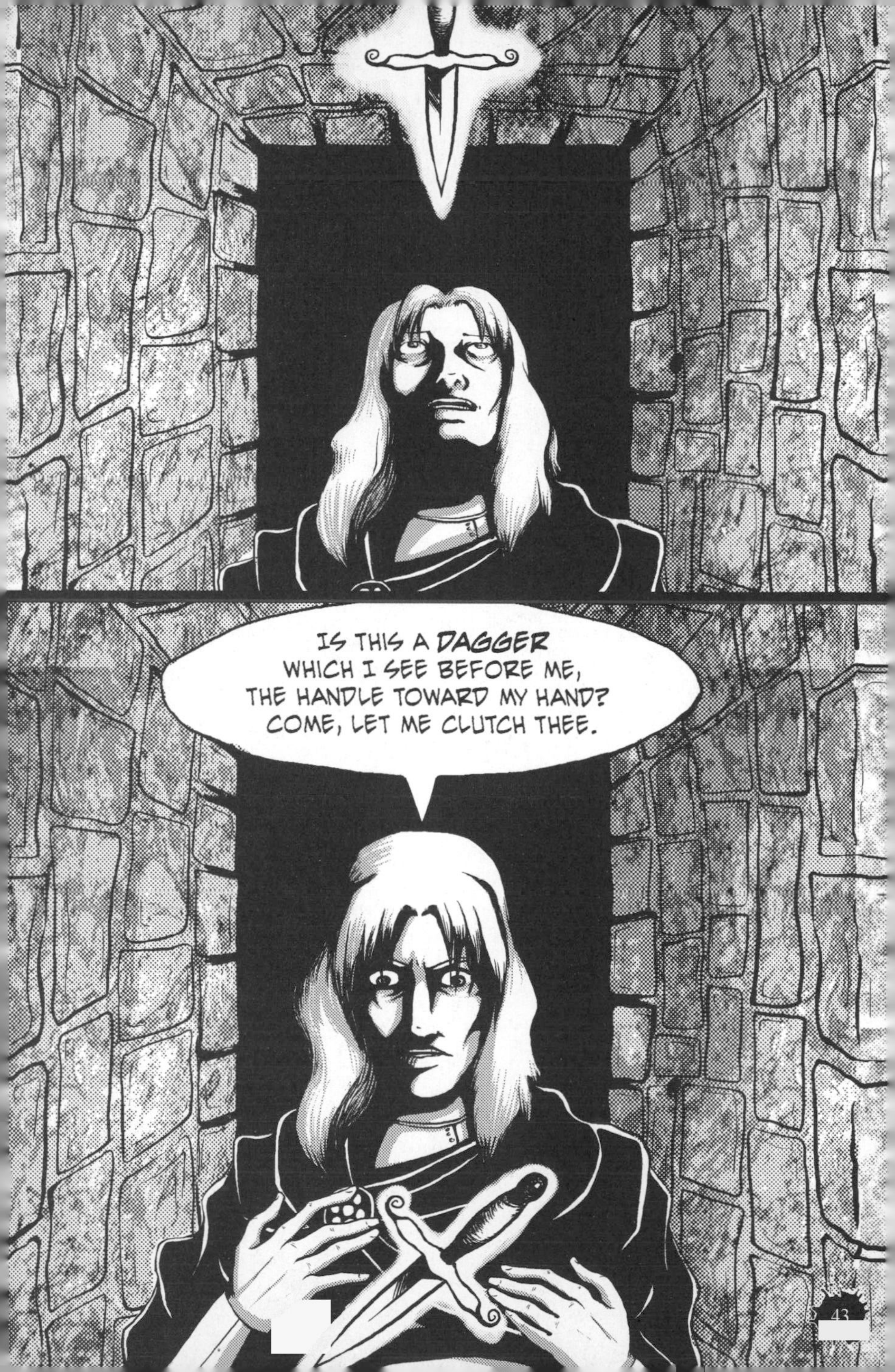
IS THIS A DAGGER WHICH I SEE BEFORE ME, THE HANDLE TOWARD MY HAND? COME, LET ME CLUTCH THEE.

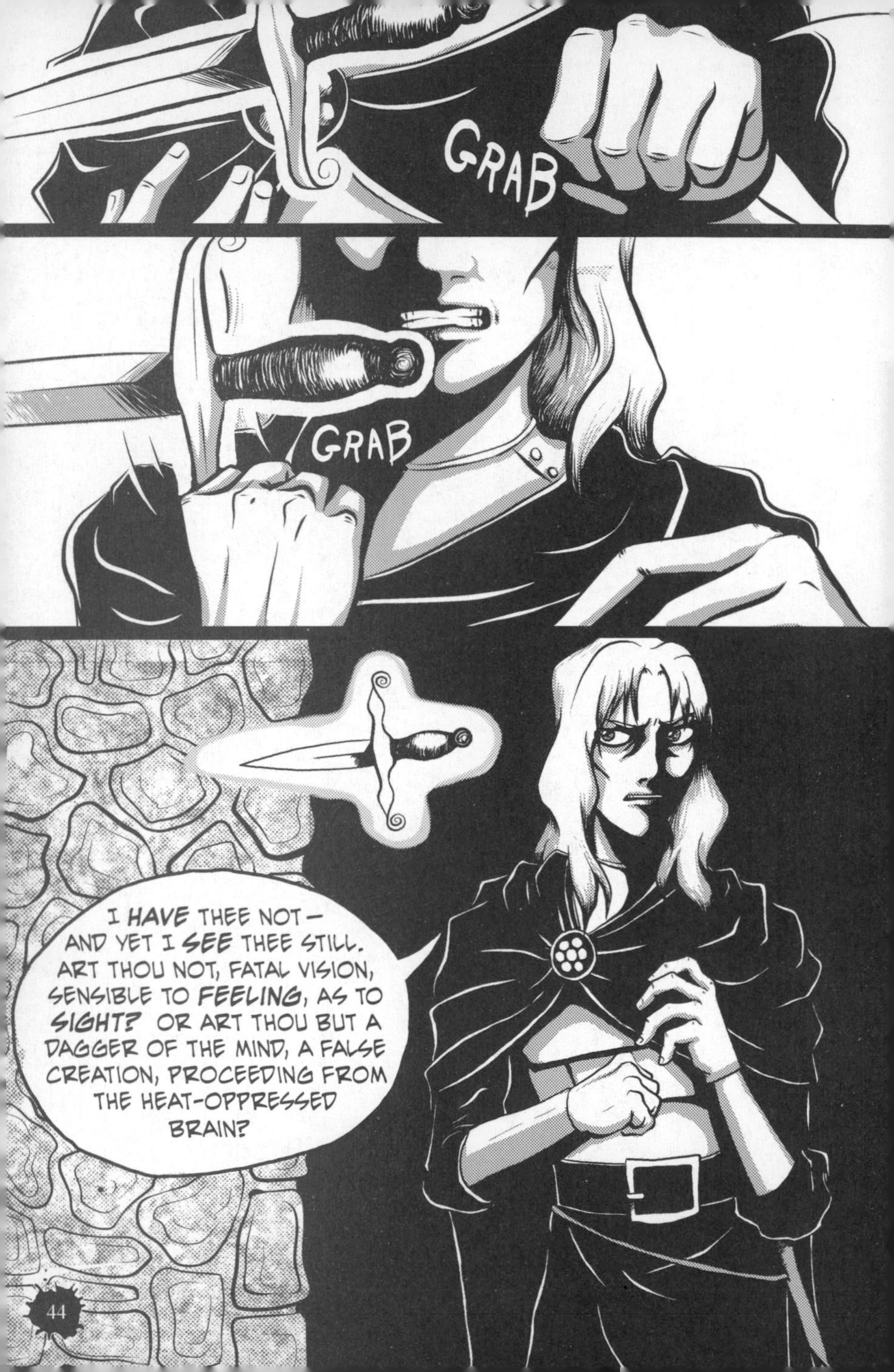
GRAB
GRAB
I HAVE THEE NOT— AND YET I SEE THEE STILL. ART THOU NOT, FATAL VISION, SENSIBLE TO FEELING, AS TO SIGHT? OR ART THOU BUT A DAGGER OF THE MIND, A FALSE CREATION, PROCEEDING FROM THE HEAT-OPPRESSED BRAIN?

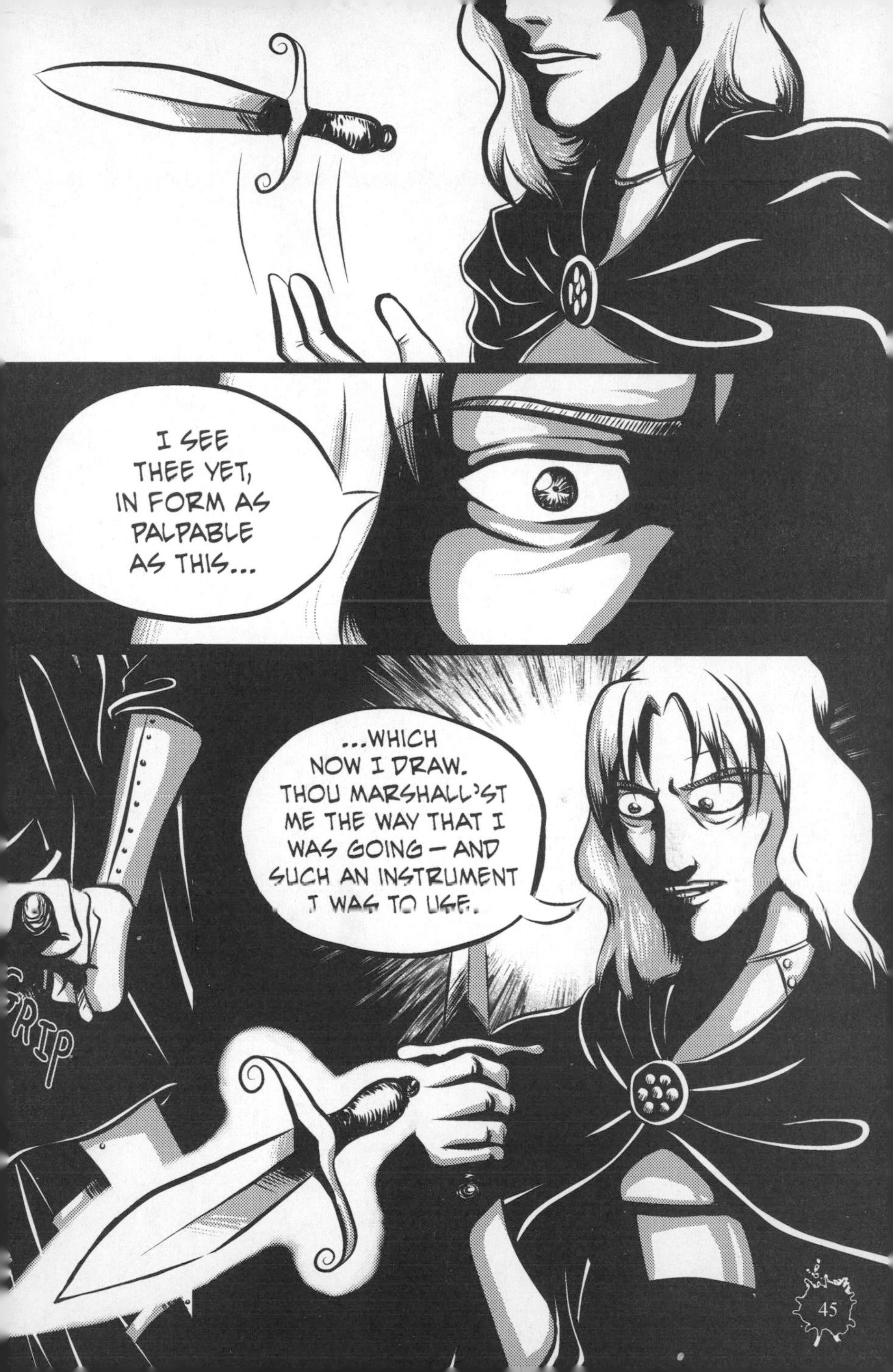
I SEE THEE YET, IN FORM AS PALPABLE AS THIS...
...WHICH NOW I DRAW. THOU MARSHALL'ST ME THE WAY THAT I WAS GOING— AND SUCH AN INSTRUMENT I WAS TO USE.
GRIP

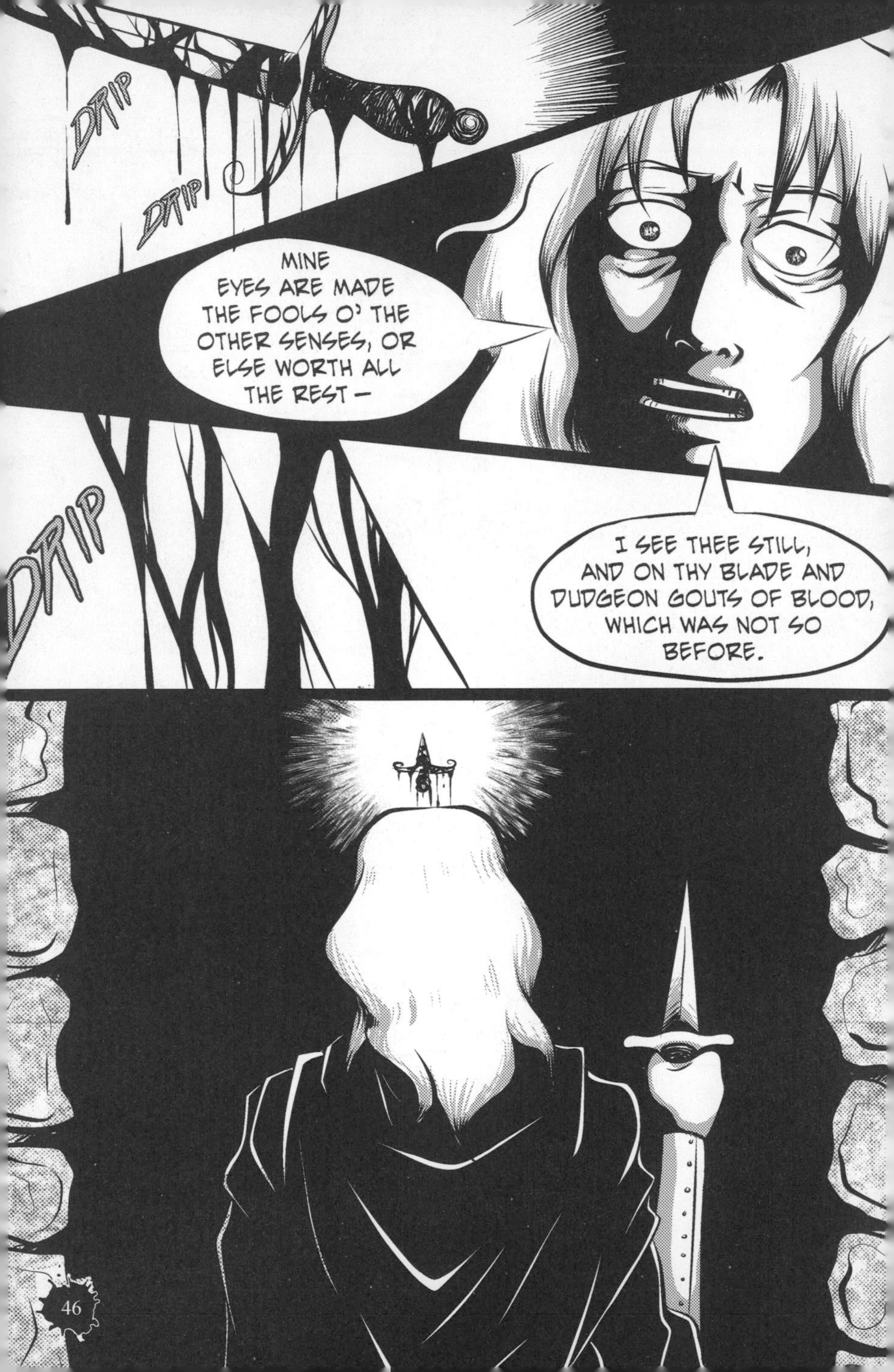
DRIP
DRIP
MINE EYES ARE MADE THE FOOLS O' THE OTHER SENSES, OR ELSE WORTH ALL THE REST —
DRIP
I SEE THEE STILL, AND ON THY BLADE AND DUDGEON GOUTS OF BLOOD, WHICH WAS NOT SO BEFORE.

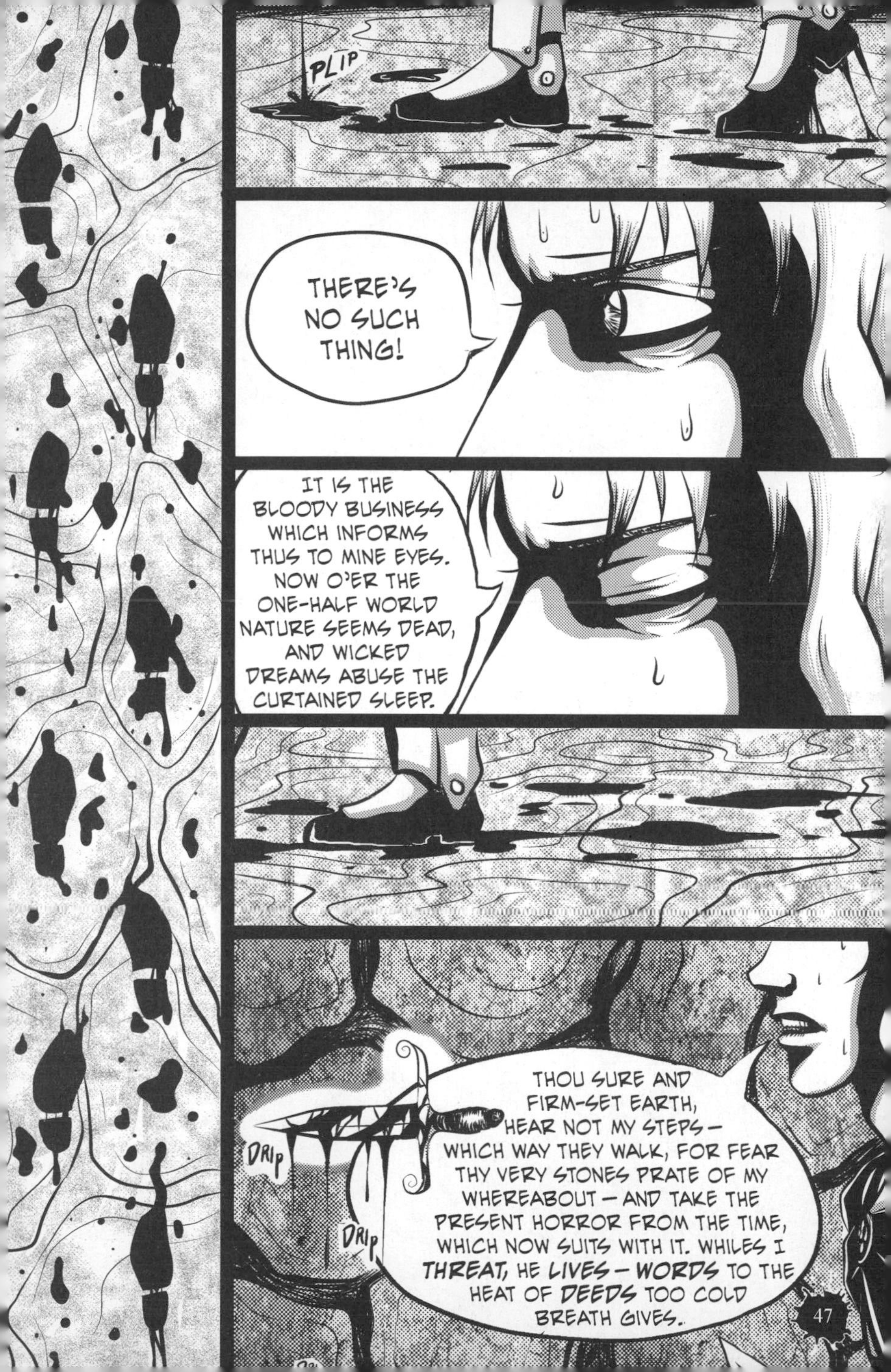
PLIP
THERE'S NO SUCH THING!
IT IS THE BLOODY BUSINESS WHICH INFORMS THUS TO MINE EYES. NOW O'ER THE ONE-HALF WORLD NATURE SEEMS DEAD, AND WICKED DREAMS ABUSE THE CURTAINED SLEEP.
DRIP
DRIP
THOU SURE AND FIRM-SET EARTH, HEAR NOT MY STEPS — WHICH WAY THEY WALK, FOR FEAR THY VERY STONES PRATE OF MY WHEREABOUT — AND TAKE THE PRESENT HORROR FROM THE TIME, WHICH NOW SUITS WITH IT. WHILES I THREAT, HE LIVES — WORDS TO THE HEAT OF DEEDS TOO COLD BREATH GIVES.

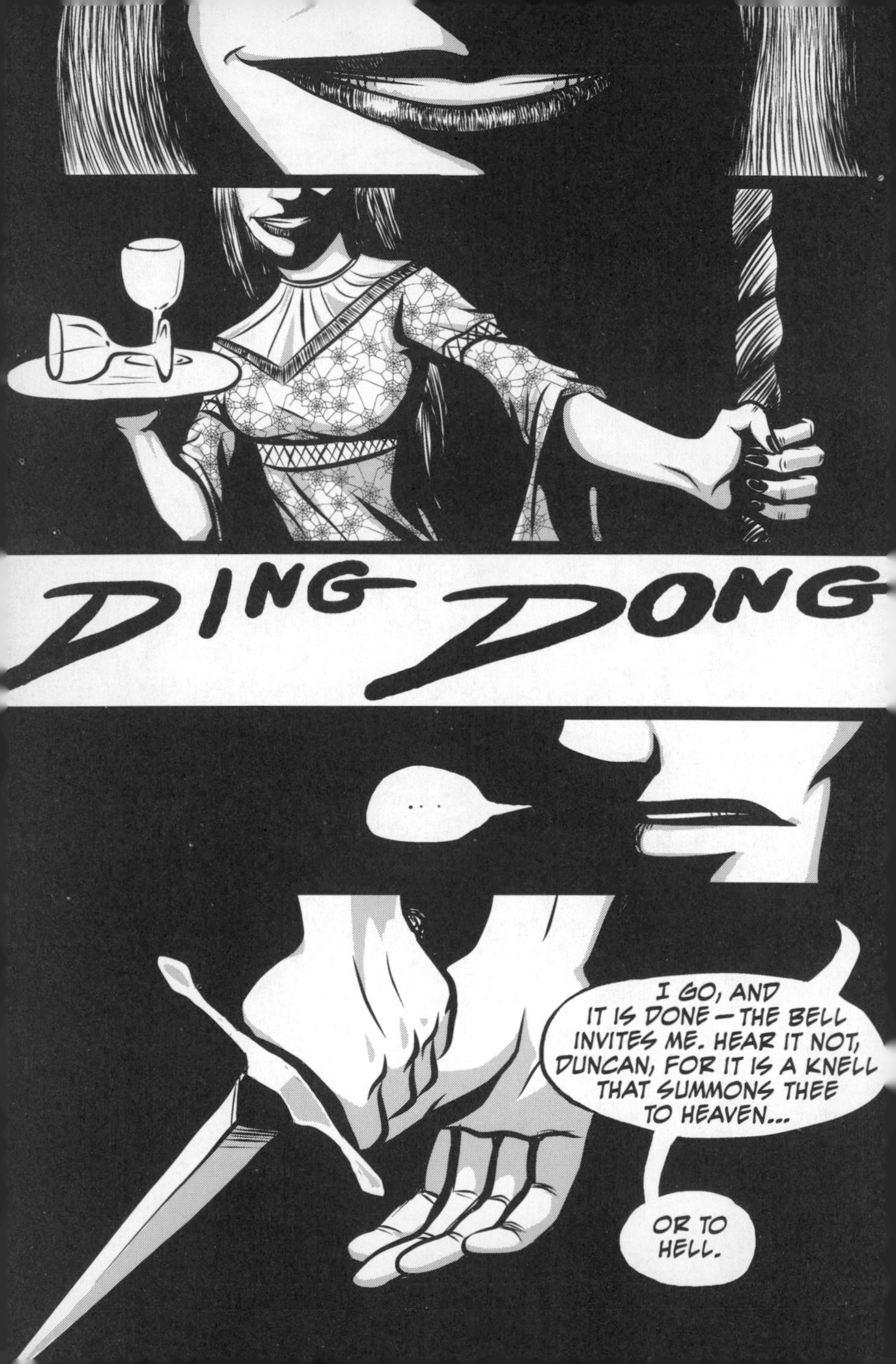
DING DONG
...
I GO, AND IT IS DONE — THE BELL INVITES ME. HEAR IT NOT, DUNCAN, FOR IT IS A KNELL THAT SUMMONS THEE TO HEAVEN...
OR TO HELL.

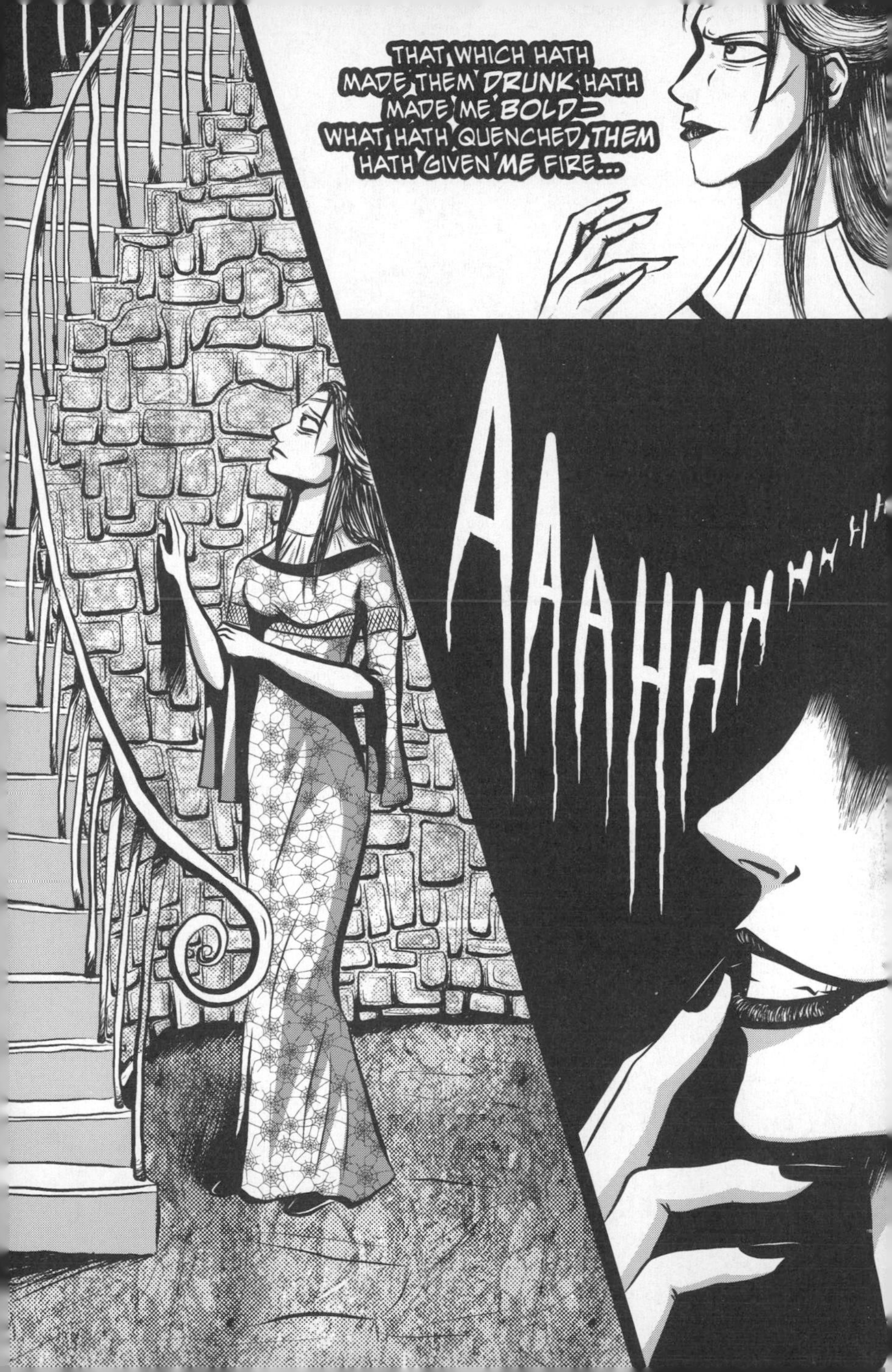
THAT WHICH HATH MADE THEM DRUNK HATH MADE ME BOLD— WHAT HATH QUENCHED THEM HATH GIVEN ME FIRE...
AAAHHHHHHHH

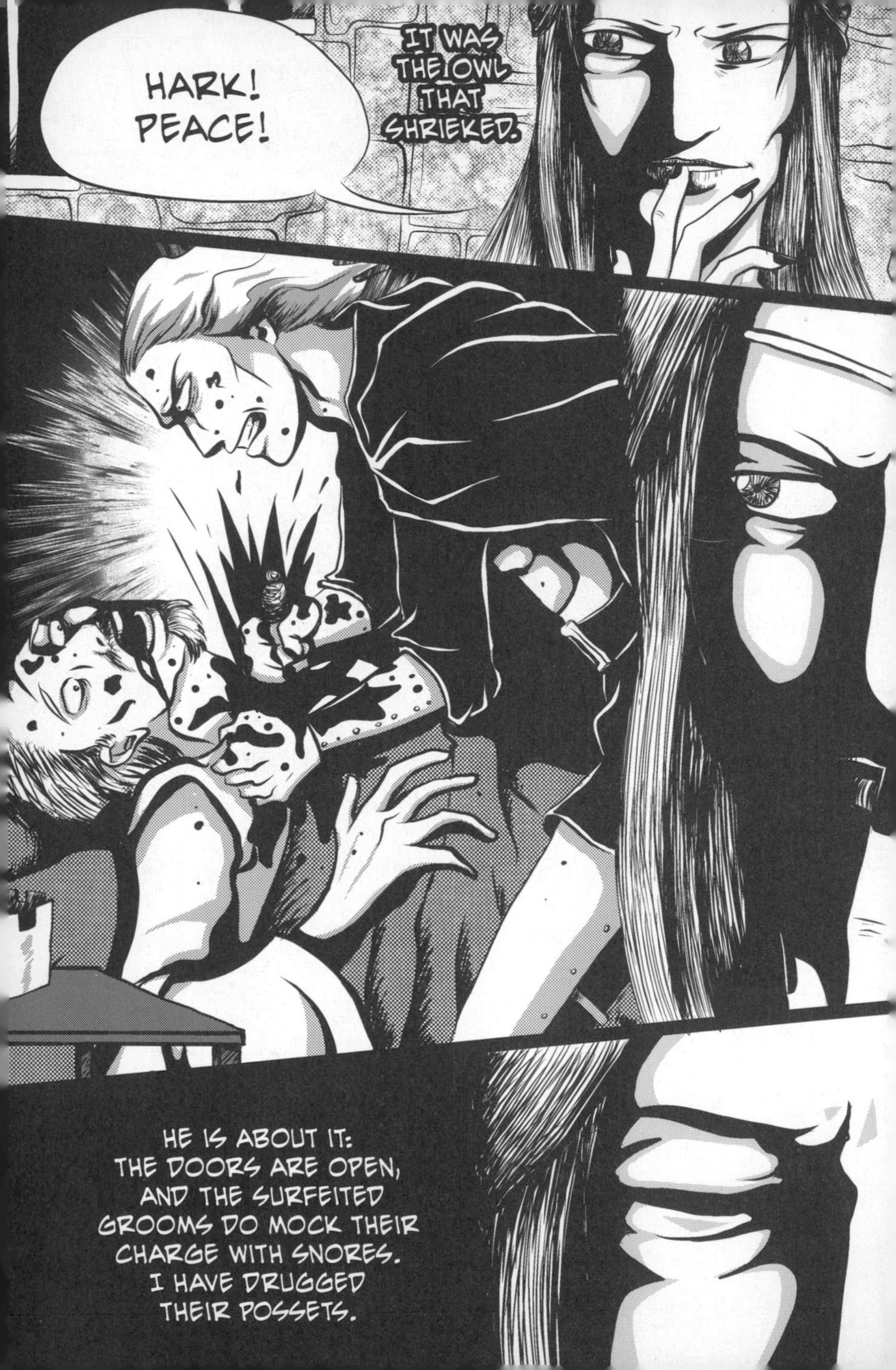
HARK! PEACE!
IT WAS THE OWL THAT SHRIEKED.
HE IS ABOUT IT: THE DOORS ARE OPEN, AND THE SURFEITED GROOMS DO MOCK THEIR CHARGE WITH SNORES. I HAVE DRUGGED THEIR POSSETS.

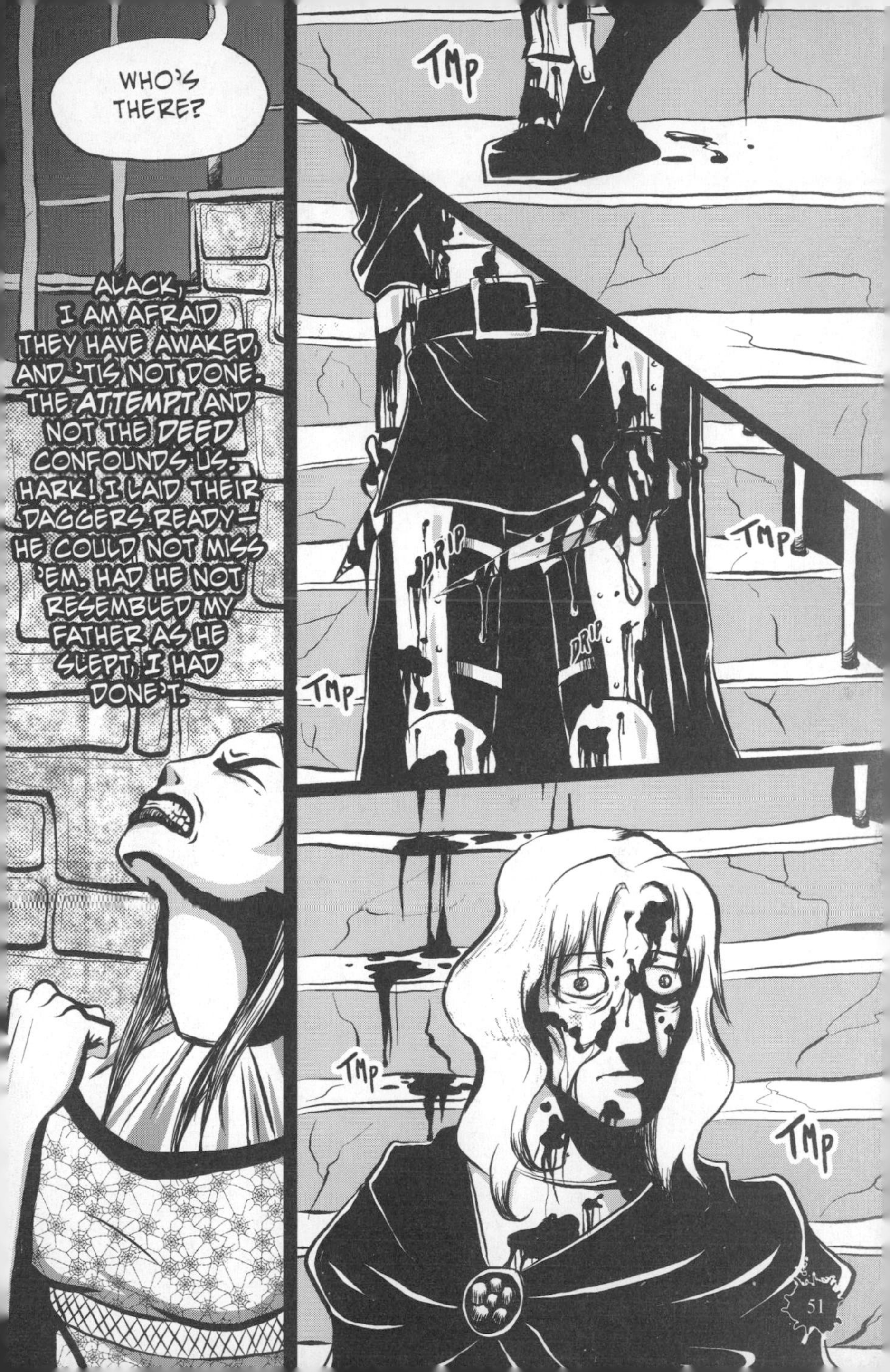
WHO'S THERE?
ALACK, I AM AFRAID THEY HAVE AWAKED, AND 'TIS NOT DONE. THE ATTEMPT AND NOT THE DEED CONFOUNDS US. HARK! I LAID THEIR DAGGERS READY— HE COULD NOT MISS 'EM. HAD HE NOT RESEMBLED MY FATHER AS HE SLEPT, I HAD DONE'T.
TMP
TMP
DRIP
DRIP
TMP
TMP
TMP

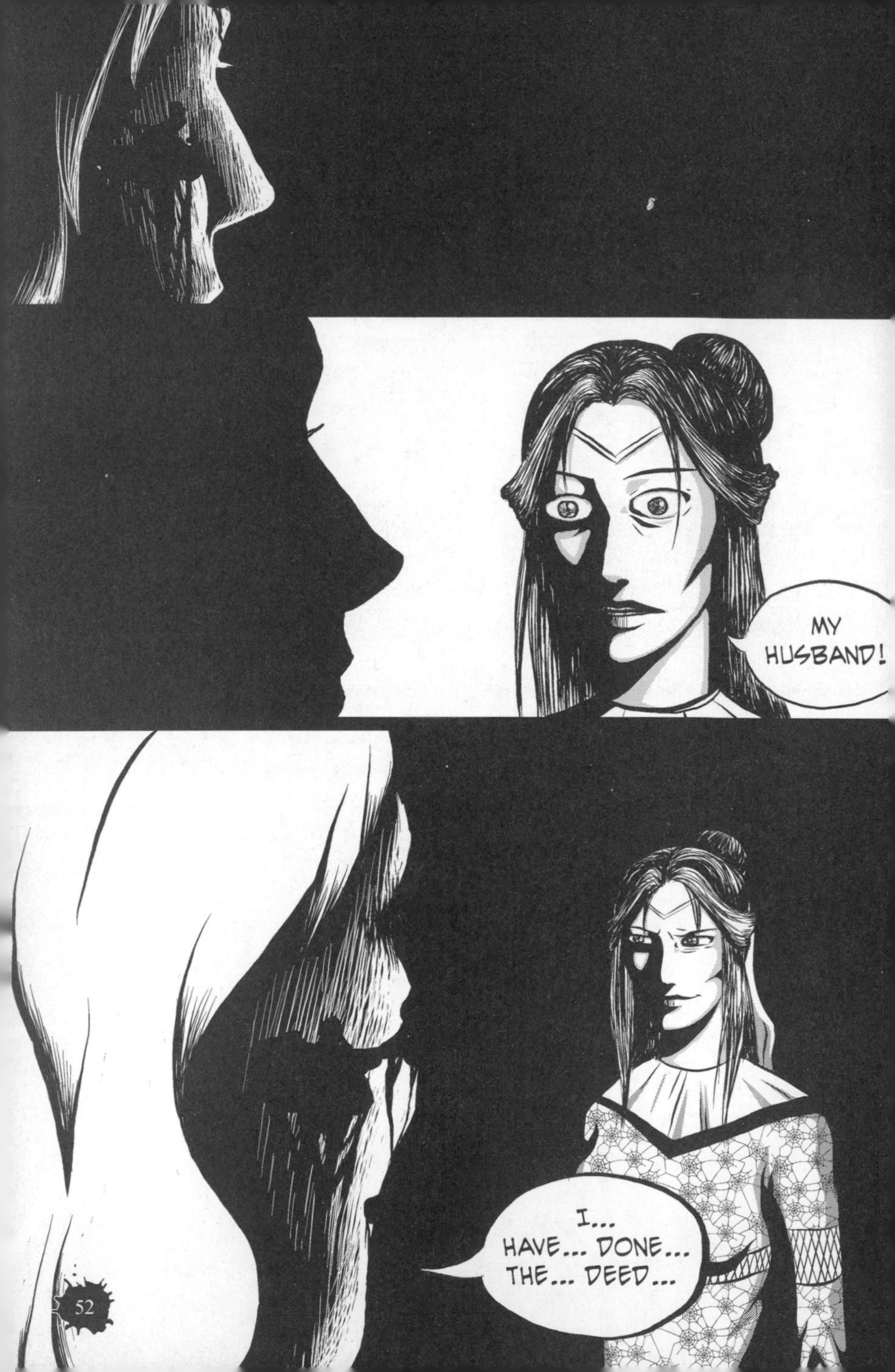
MY HUSBAND!
I... HAVE... DONE... THE... DEED...

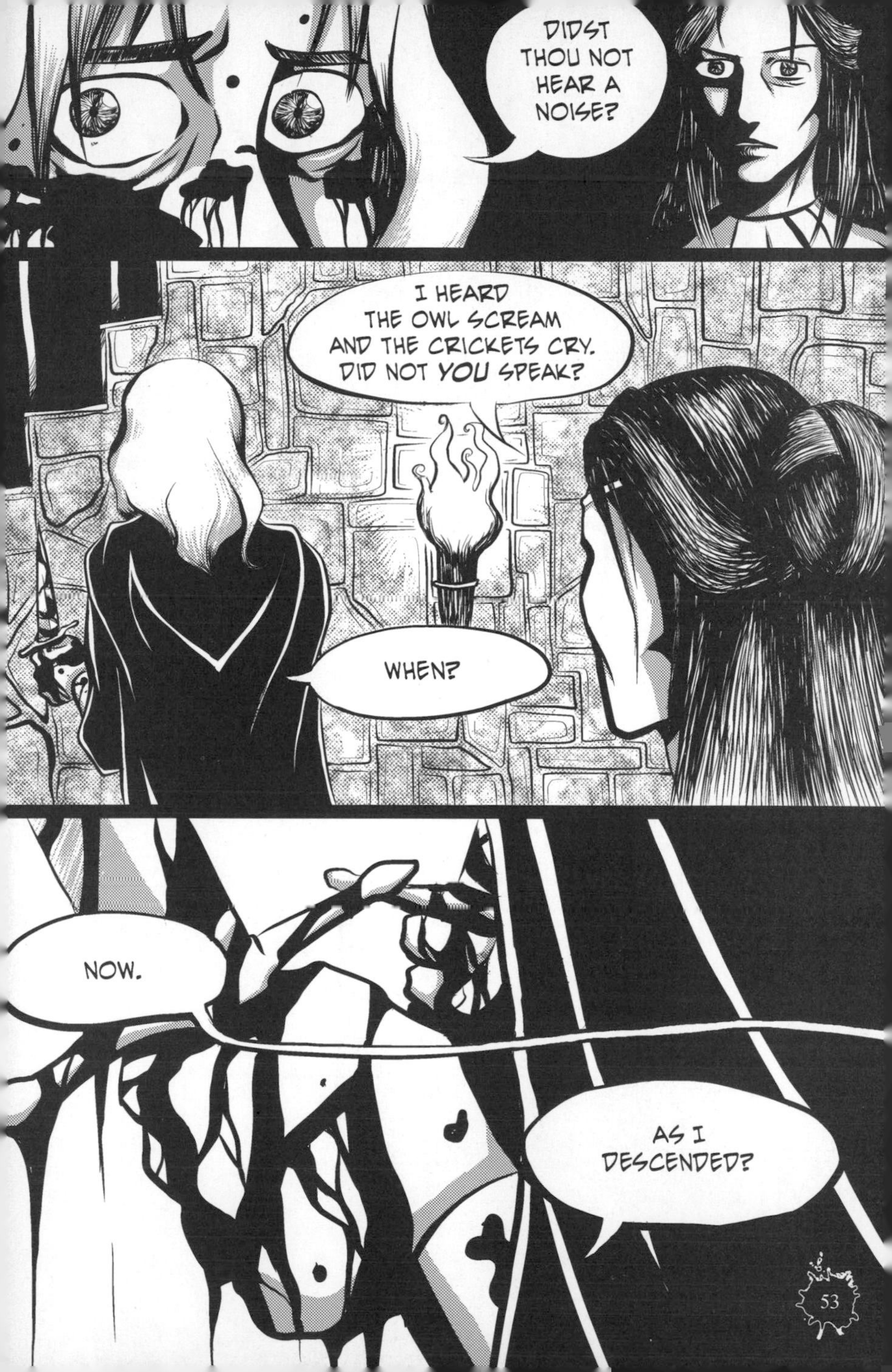
DIDST THOU NOT HEAR A NOISE?
I HEARD THE OWL SCREAM AND THE CRICKETS CRY. DID NOT *YOU* SPEAK?
WHEN?
NOW.
AS I DESCENDED?

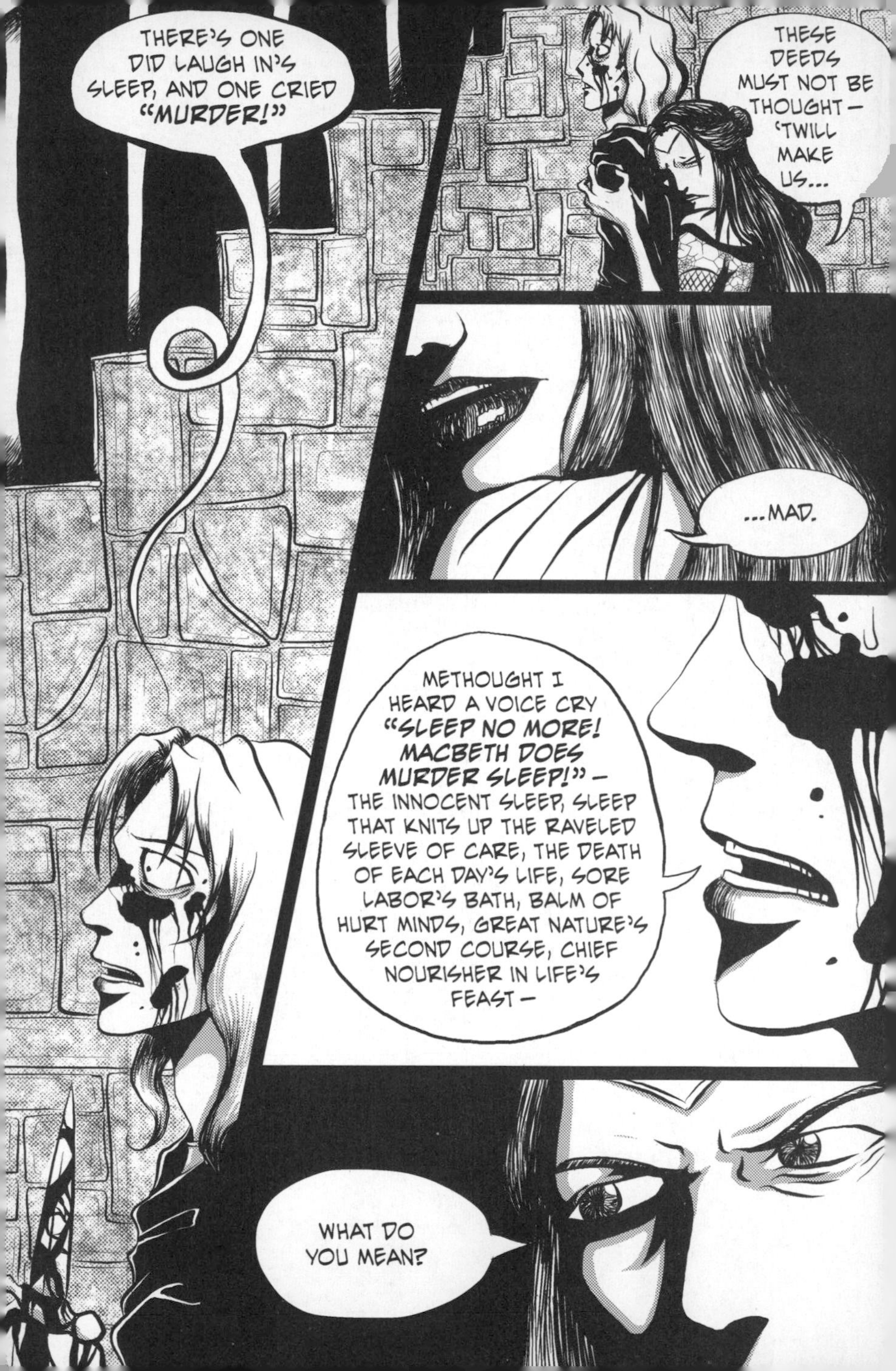
THERE'S ONE DID LAUGH IN'S SLEEP, AND ONE CRIED "MURDER!"
THESE DEEDS MUST NOT BE THOUGHT— 'TWILL MAKE US...
...MAD.
METHOUGHT I HEARD A VOICE CRY "SLEEP NO MORE! MACBETH DOES MURDER SLEEP!"— THE INNOCENT SLEEP, SLEEP THAT KNITS UP THE RAVELED SLEEVE OF CARE, THE DEATH OF EACH DAY'S LIFE, SORE LABOR'S BATH, BALM OF HURT MINDS, GREAT NATURE'S SECOND COURSE, CHIEF NOURISHER IN LIFE'S FEAST—
WHAT DO YOU MEAN?

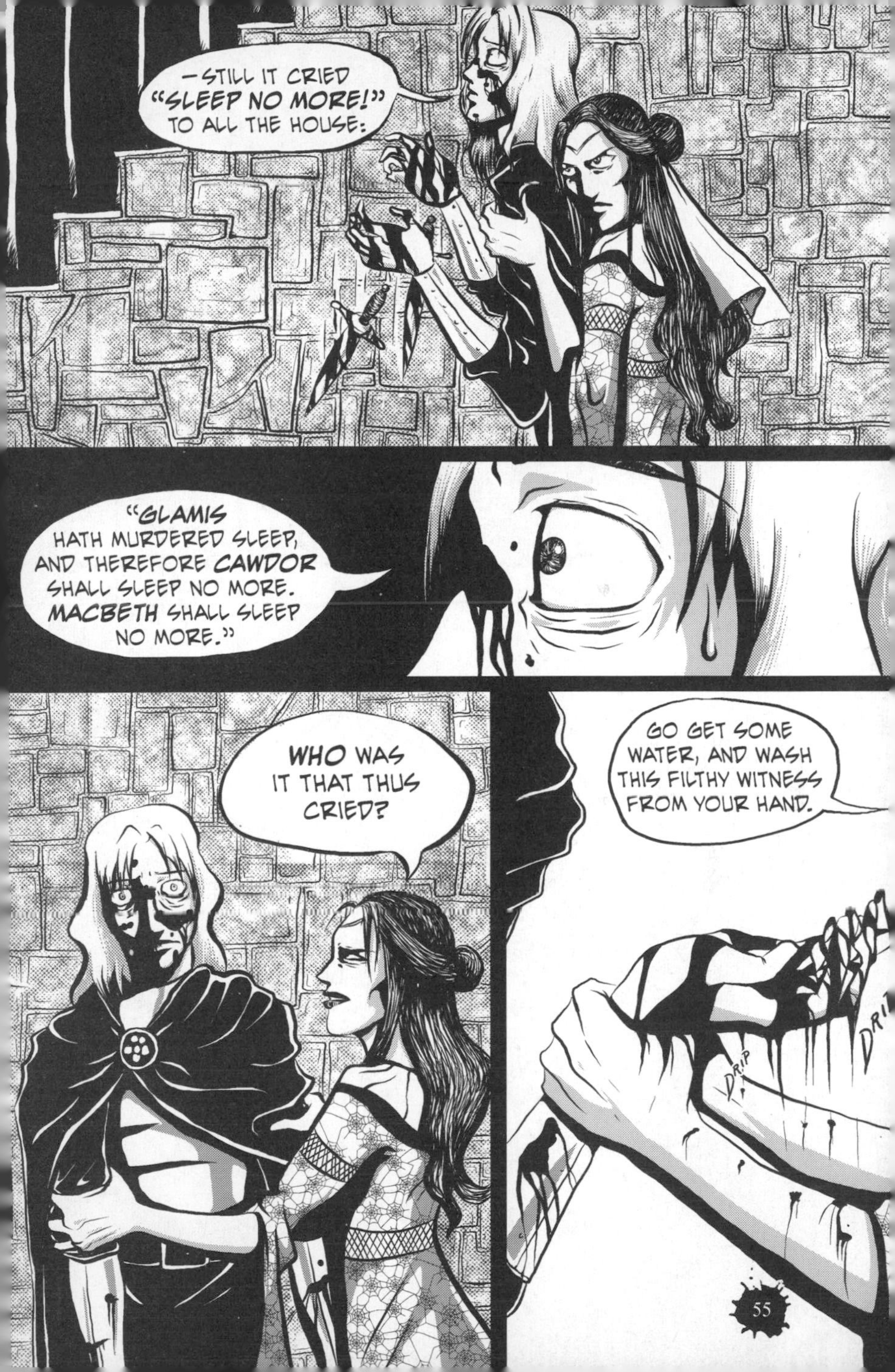

—STILL IT CRIED "SLEEP NO MORE!" TO ALL THE HOUSE:
"GLAMIS HATH MURDERED SLEEP, AND THEREFORE CAWDOR SHALL SLEEP NO MORE. MACBETH SHALL SLEEP NO MORE."
WHO WAS IT THAT THUS CRIED?
GO GET SOME WATER, AND WASH THIS FILTHY WITNESS FROM YOUR HAND.
DRIP

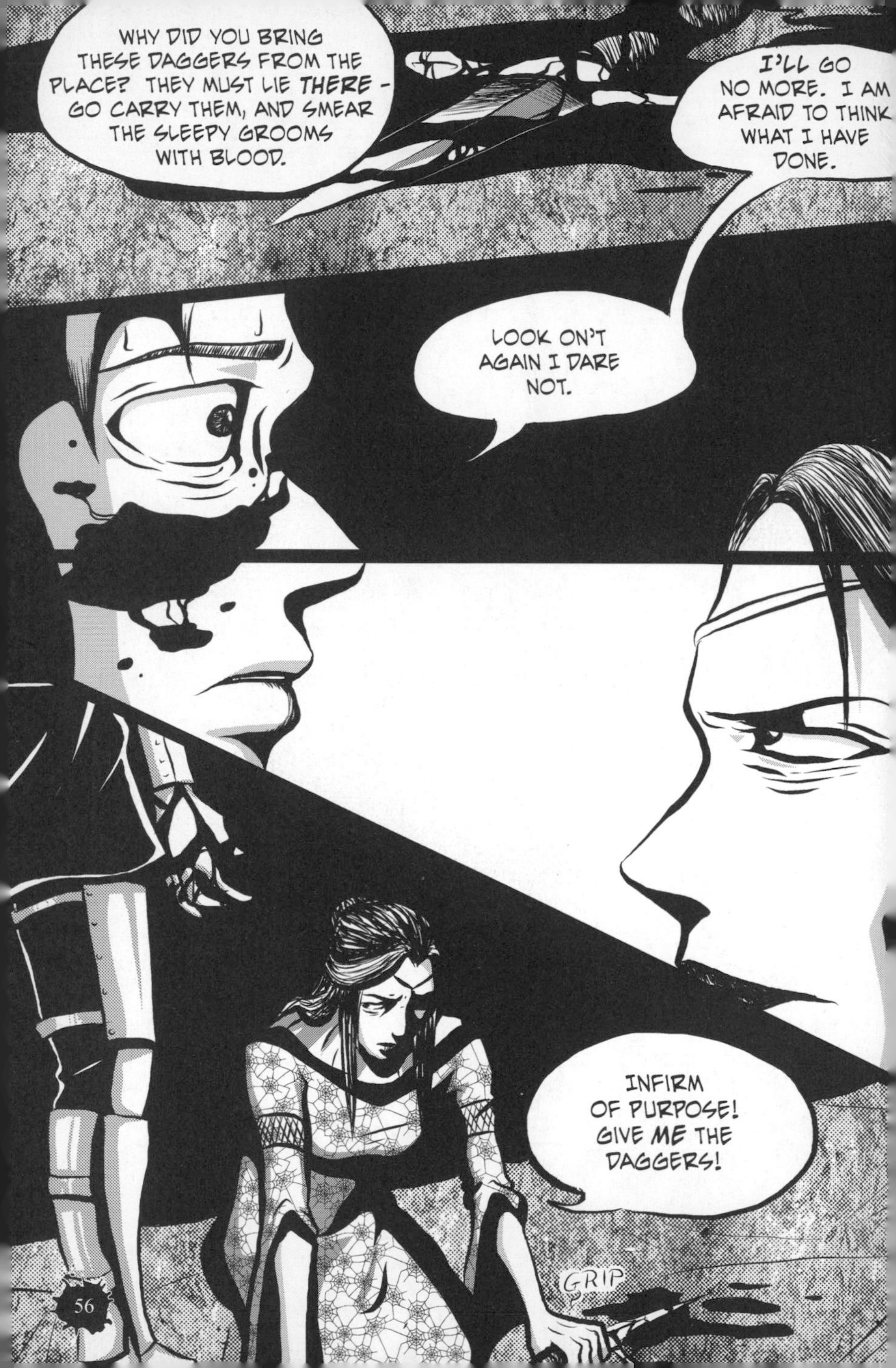
WHY DID YOU BRING THESE DAGGERS FROM THE PLACE? THEY MUST LIE THERE - GO CARRY THEM, AND SMEAR THE SLEEPY GROOMS WITH BLOOD.
I'LL GO NO MORE. I AM AFRAID TO THINK WHAT I HAVE DONE.
LOOK ON'T AGAIN I DARE NOT.
INFIRM OF PURPOSE! GIVE ME THE DAGGERS!
GRIP

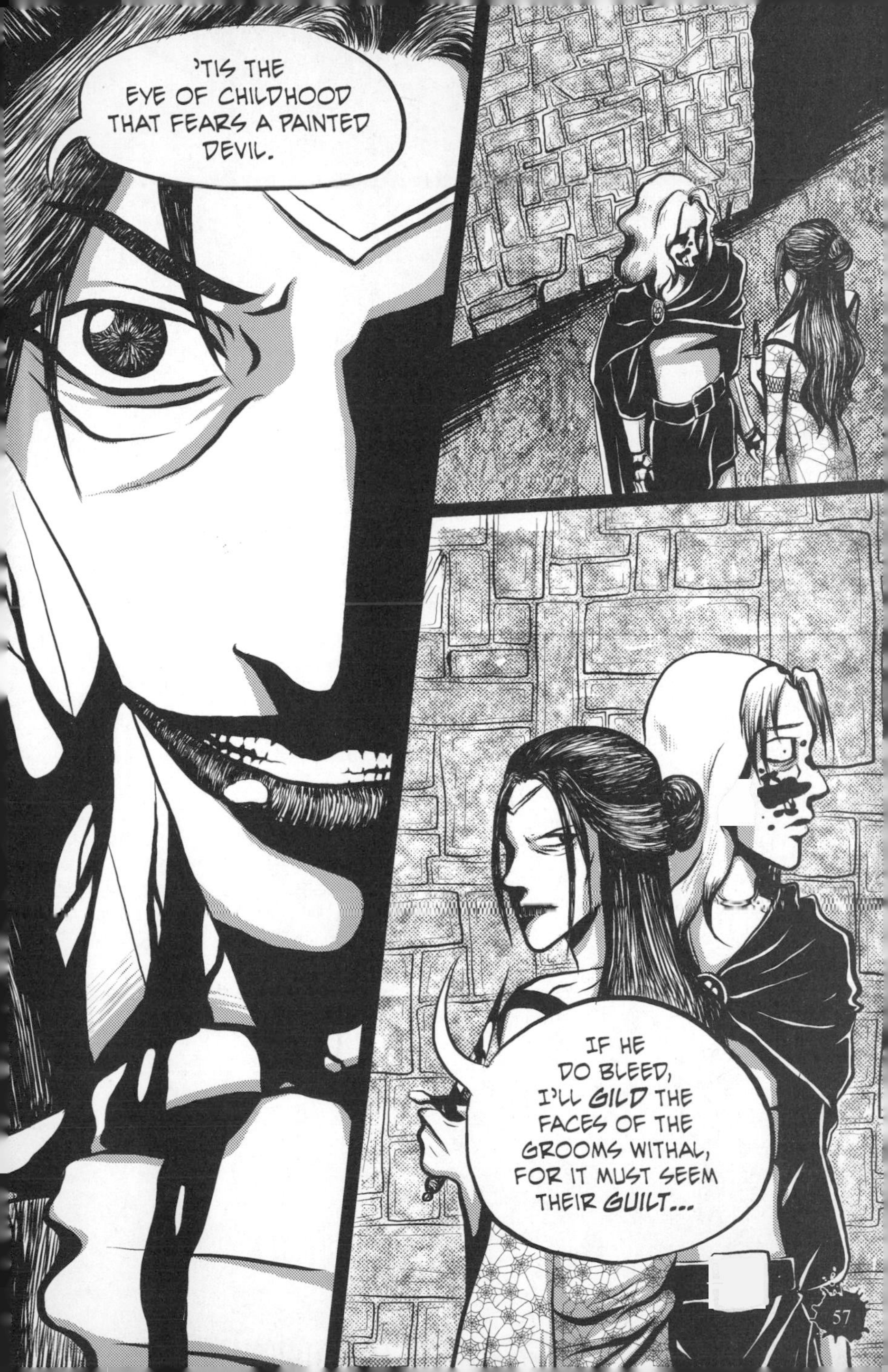
’TIS THE EYE OF CHILDHOOD THAT FEARS A PAINTED DEVIL.
IF HE DO BLEED, I’LL **GILD** THE FACES OF THE GROOMS WITHAL, FOR IT MUST SEEM THEIR **GUILT**...

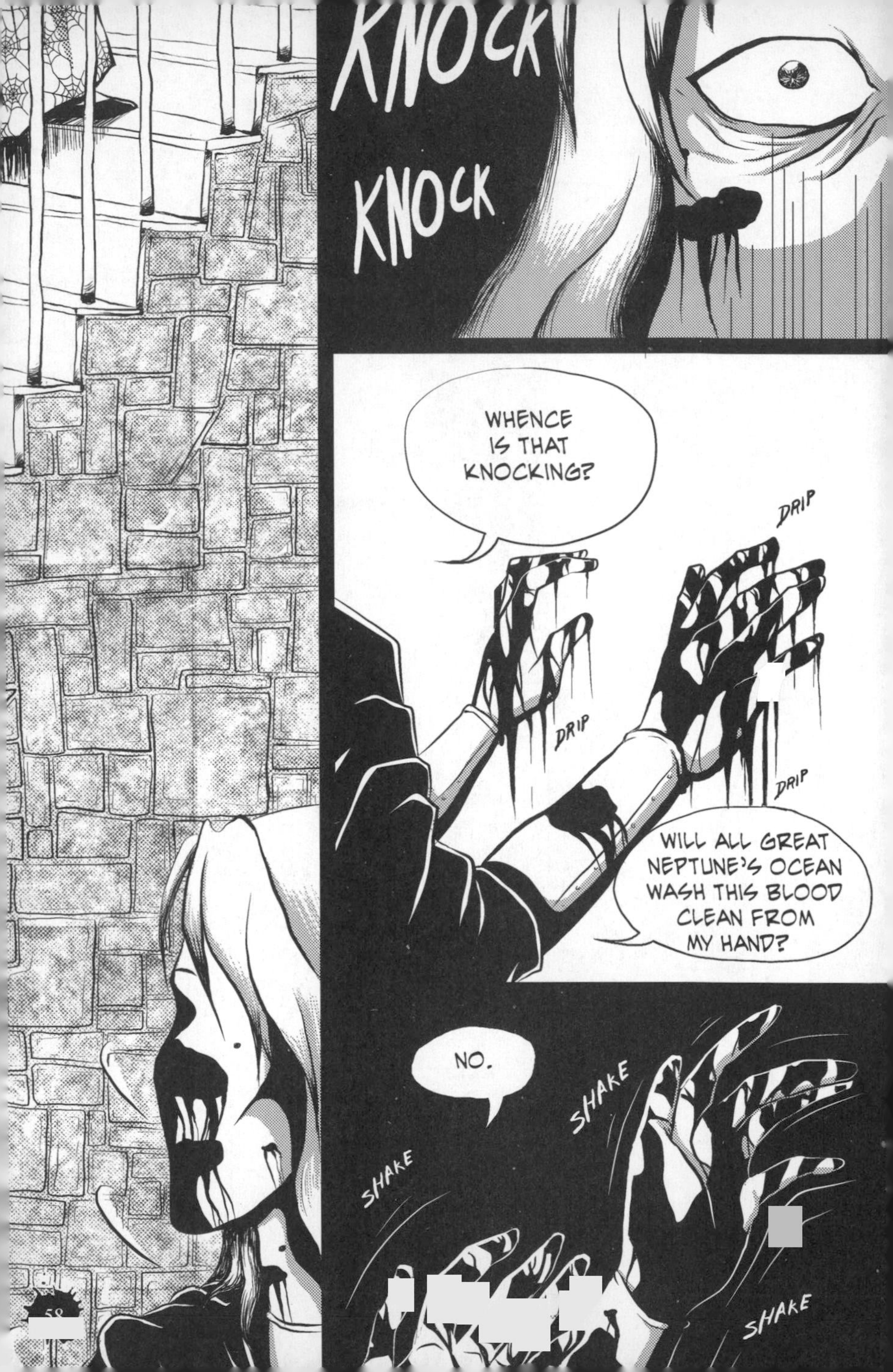
KNOCK
KNOCK
WHENCE IS THAT KNOCKING?
DRIP
DRIP
DRIP
WILL ALL GREAT NEPTUNE'S OCEAN WASH THIS BLOOD CLEAN FROM MY HAND?
NO.
SHAKE
SHAKE
SHAKE

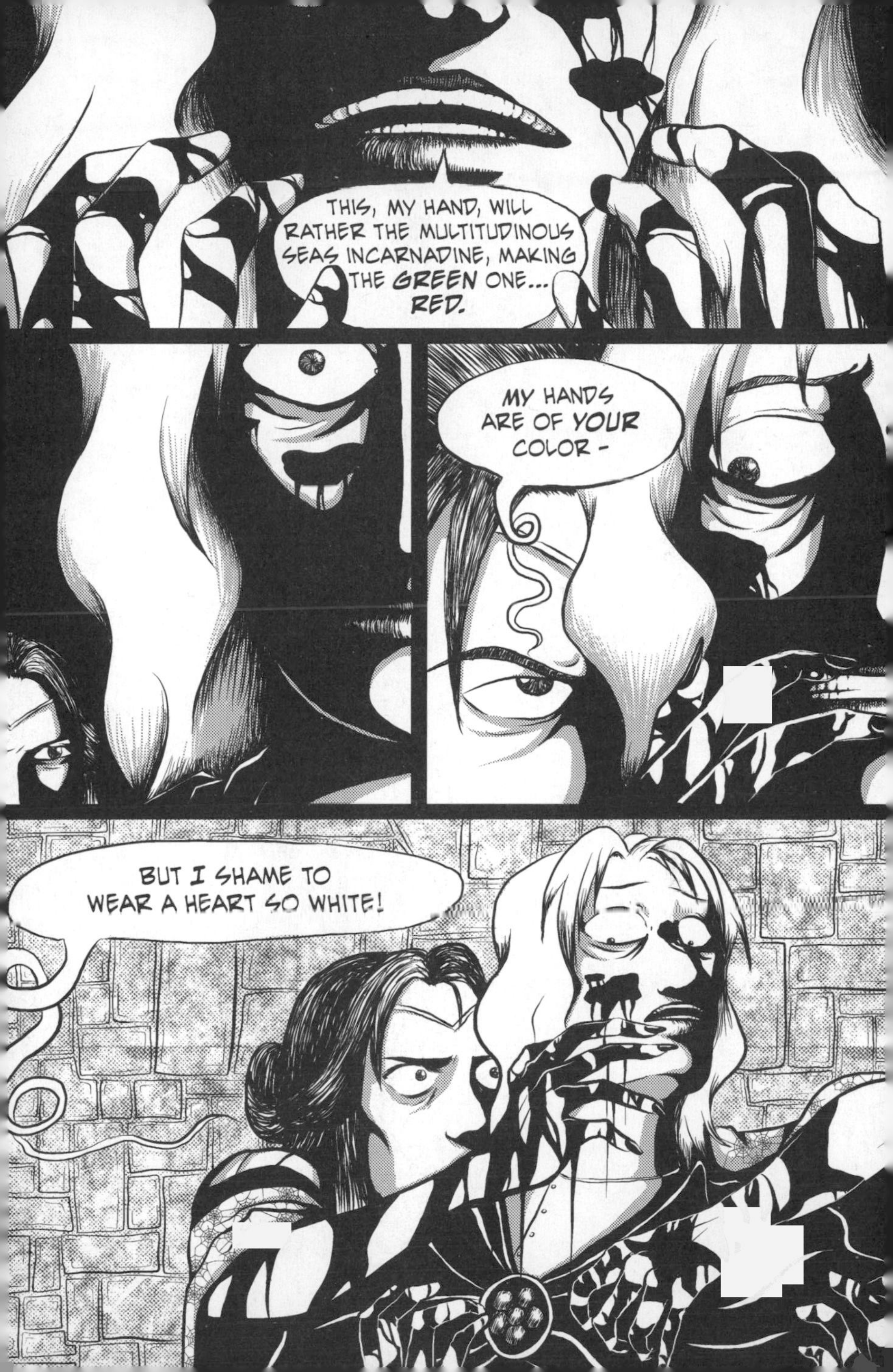
THIS, MY HAND, WILL RATHER THE MULTITUDINOUS SEAS INCARNADINE, MAKING THE GREEN ONE... RED.
MY HANDS ARE OF YOUR COLOR -
BUT I SHAME TO WEAR A HEART SO WHITE!

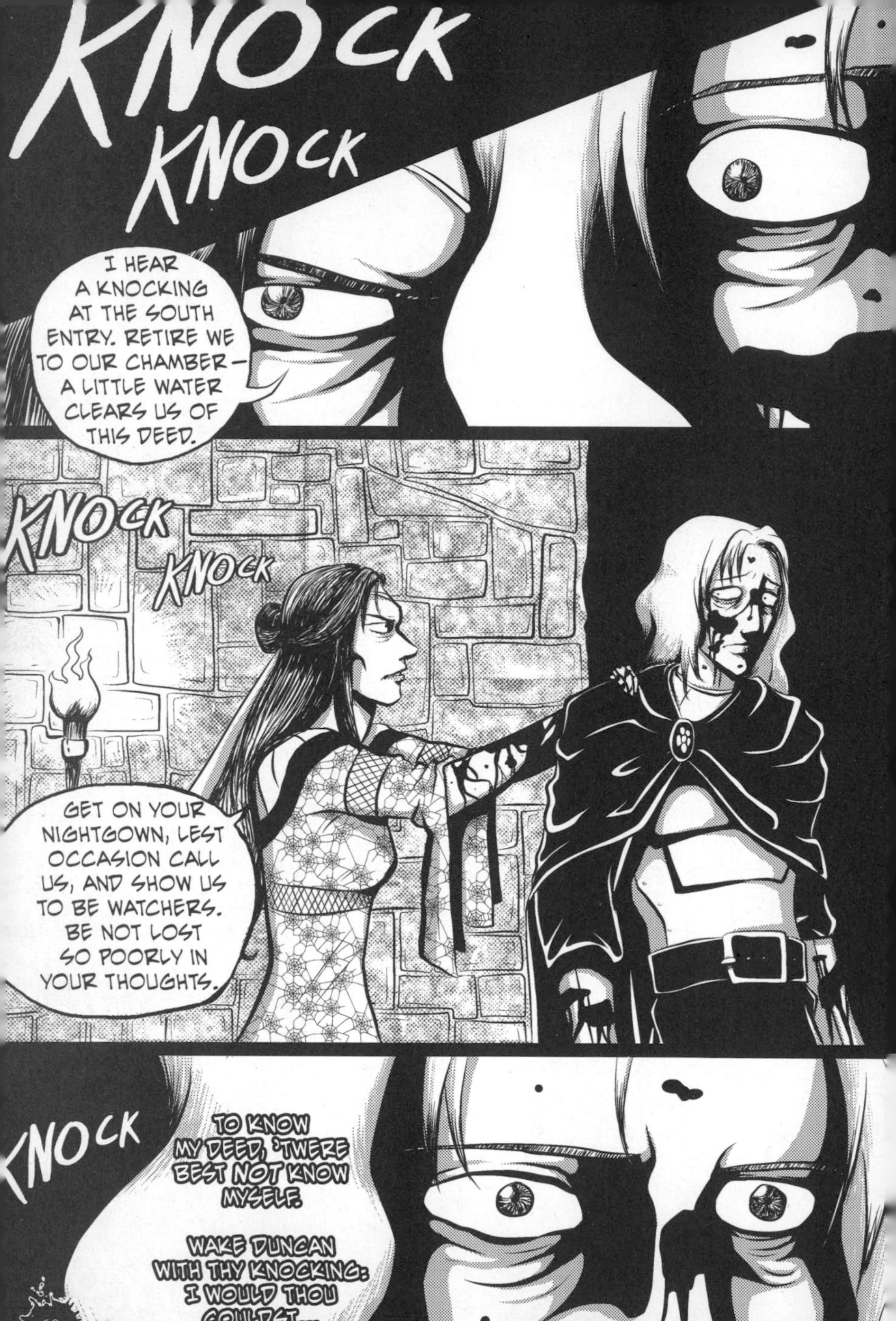
KNOCK KNOCK
I HEAR A KNOCKING AT THE SOUTH ENTRY. RETIRE WE TO OUR CHAMBER— A LITTLE WATER CLEARS US OF THIS DEED.
KNOCK KNOCK
GET ON YOUR NIGHTGOWN, LEST OCCASION CALL US, AND SHOW US TO BE WATCHERS. BE NOT LOST SO POORLY IN YOUR THOUGHTS.
KNOCK
TO KNOW MY DEED, 'TWERE BEST NOT KNOW MYSELF.
WAKE DUNCAN WITH THY KNOCKING: I WOULD THOU COULDST...

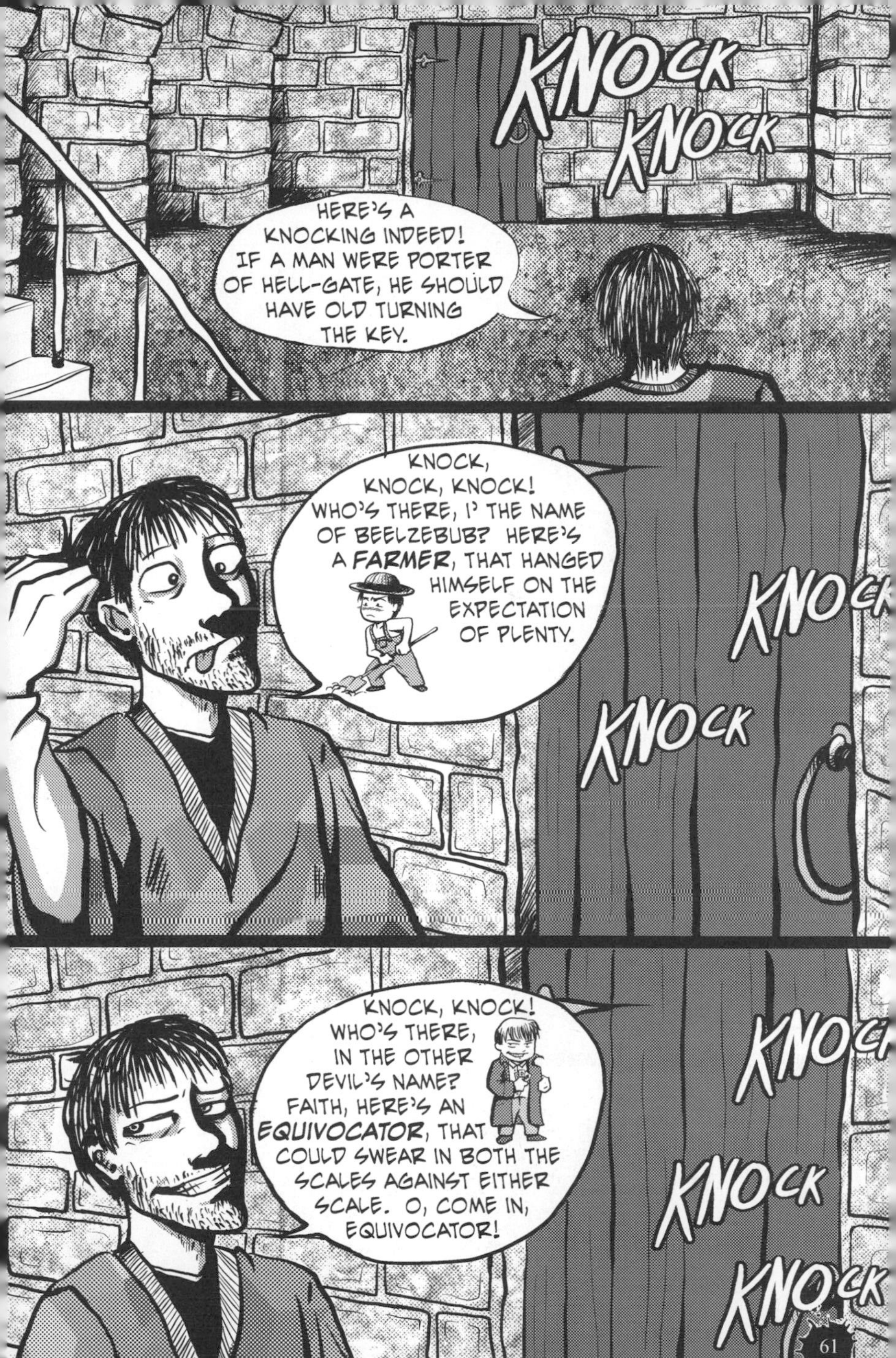
KNOCK KNOCK
HERE'S A KNOCKING INDEED! IF A MAN WERE PORTER OF HELL-GATE, HE SHOULD HAVE OLD TURNING THE KEY.
KNOCK, KNOCK, KNOCK! WHO'S THERE, I' THE NAME OF BEELZEBUB? HERE'S A **FARMER**, THAT HANGED HIMSELF ON THE EXPECTATION OF PLENTY.
KNOCK
KNOCK, KNOCK! WHO'S THERE, IN THE OTHER DEVIL'S NAME? FAITH, HERE'S AN **EQUIVOCATOR**, THAT COULD SWEAR IN BOTH THE SCALES AGAINST EITHER SCALE. O, COME IN, EQUIVOCATOR!
KNOCK
KNOCK

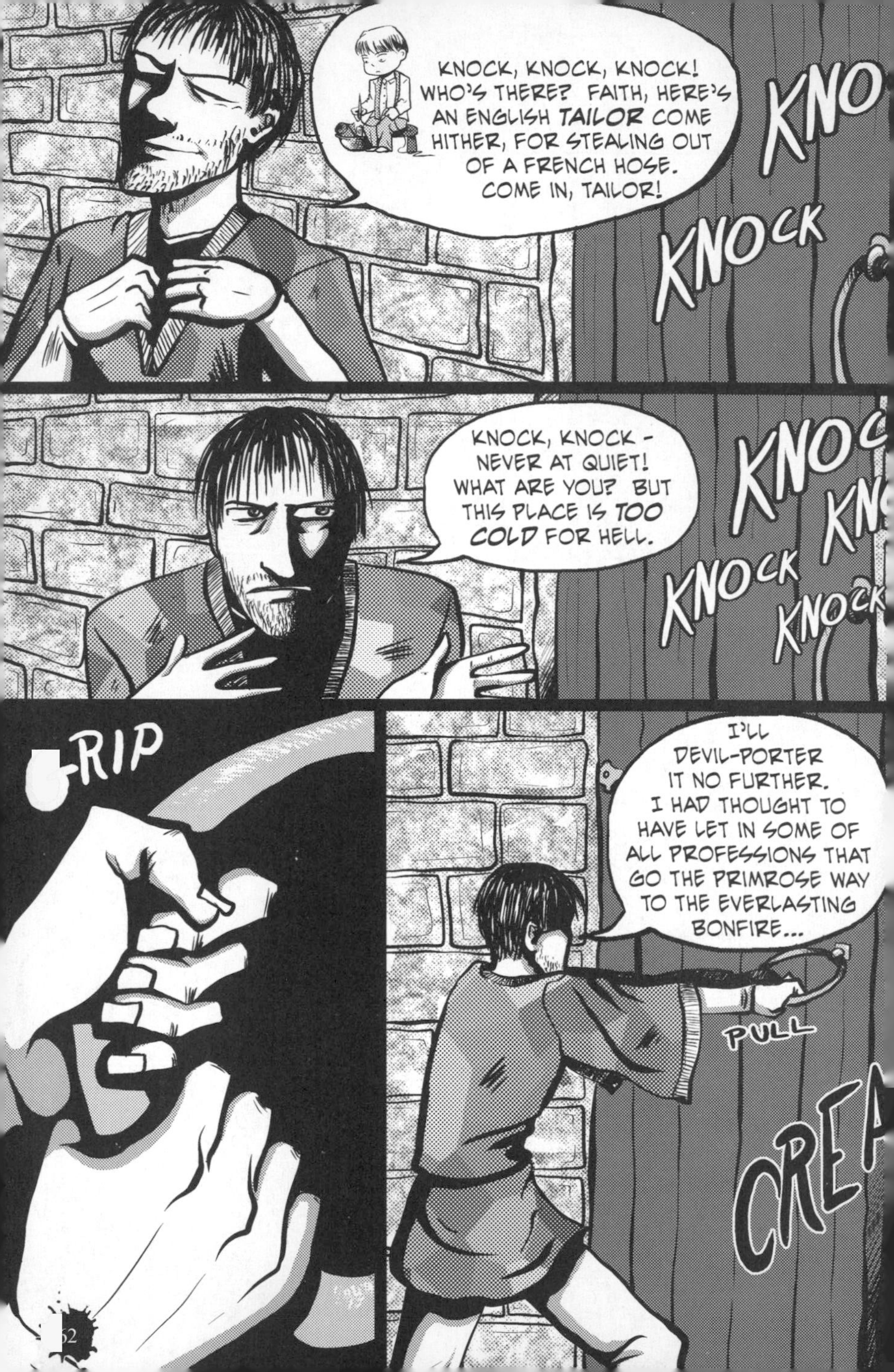
KNOCK, KNOCK, KNOCK! WHO'S THERE? FAITH, HERE'S AN ENGLISH TAILOR COME HITHER, FOR STEALING OUT OF A FRENCH HOSE. COME IN, TAILOR!
KNO
KNOCK
KNOCK, KNOCK - NEVER AT QUIET! WHAT ARE YOU? BUT THIS PLACE IS TOO COLD FOR HELL.
KNOC
KN
KNOCK
KNOCK
RIP
I'LL DEVIL-PORTER IT NO FURTHER. I HAD THOUGHT TO HAVE LET IN SOME OF ALL PROFESSIONS THAT GO THE PRIMROSE WAY TO THE EVERLASTING BONFIRE...
PULL
CREA

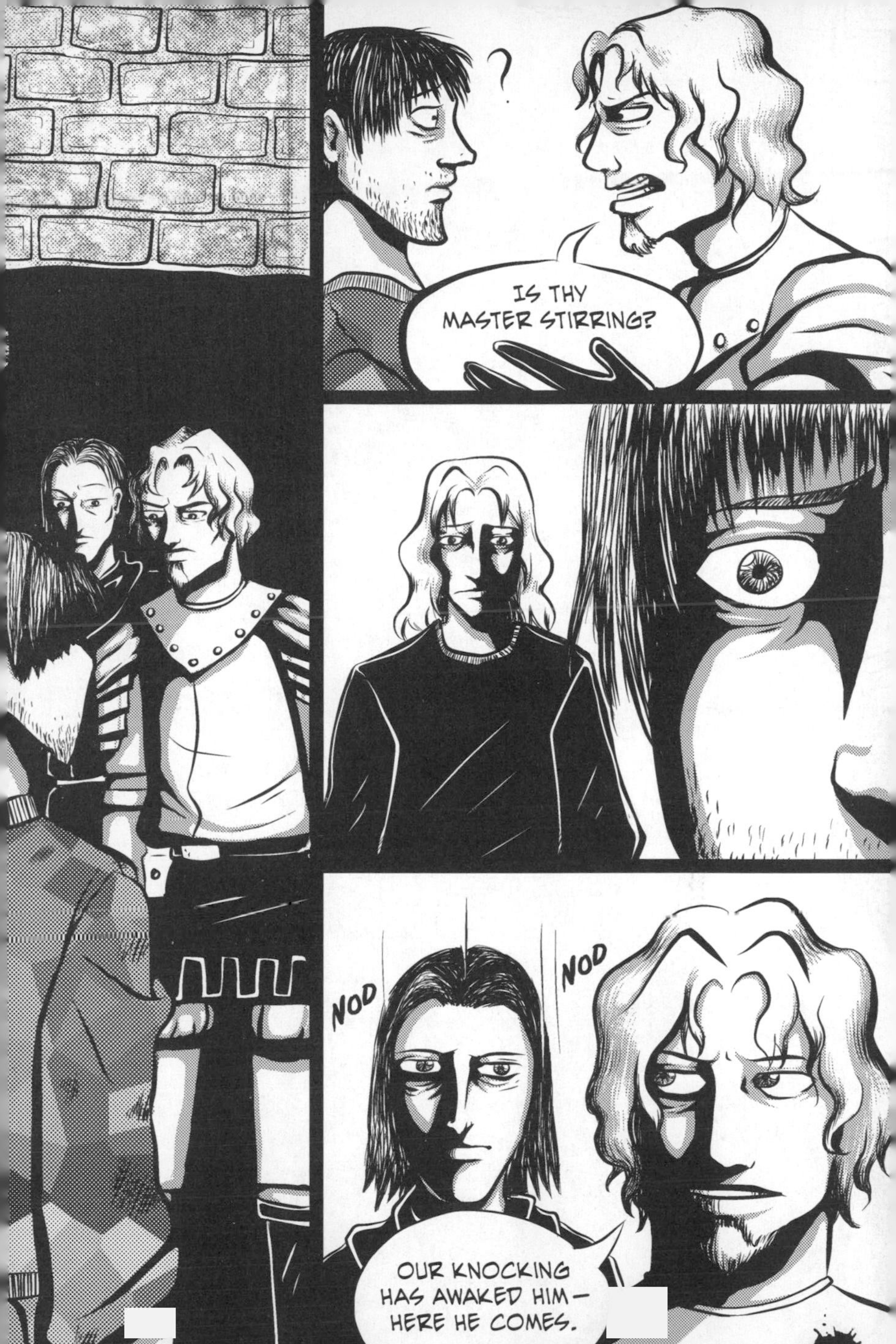
?
IS THY MASTER STIRRING?
NOD
NOD
OUR KNOCKING HAS AWAKED HIM—HERE HE COMES.

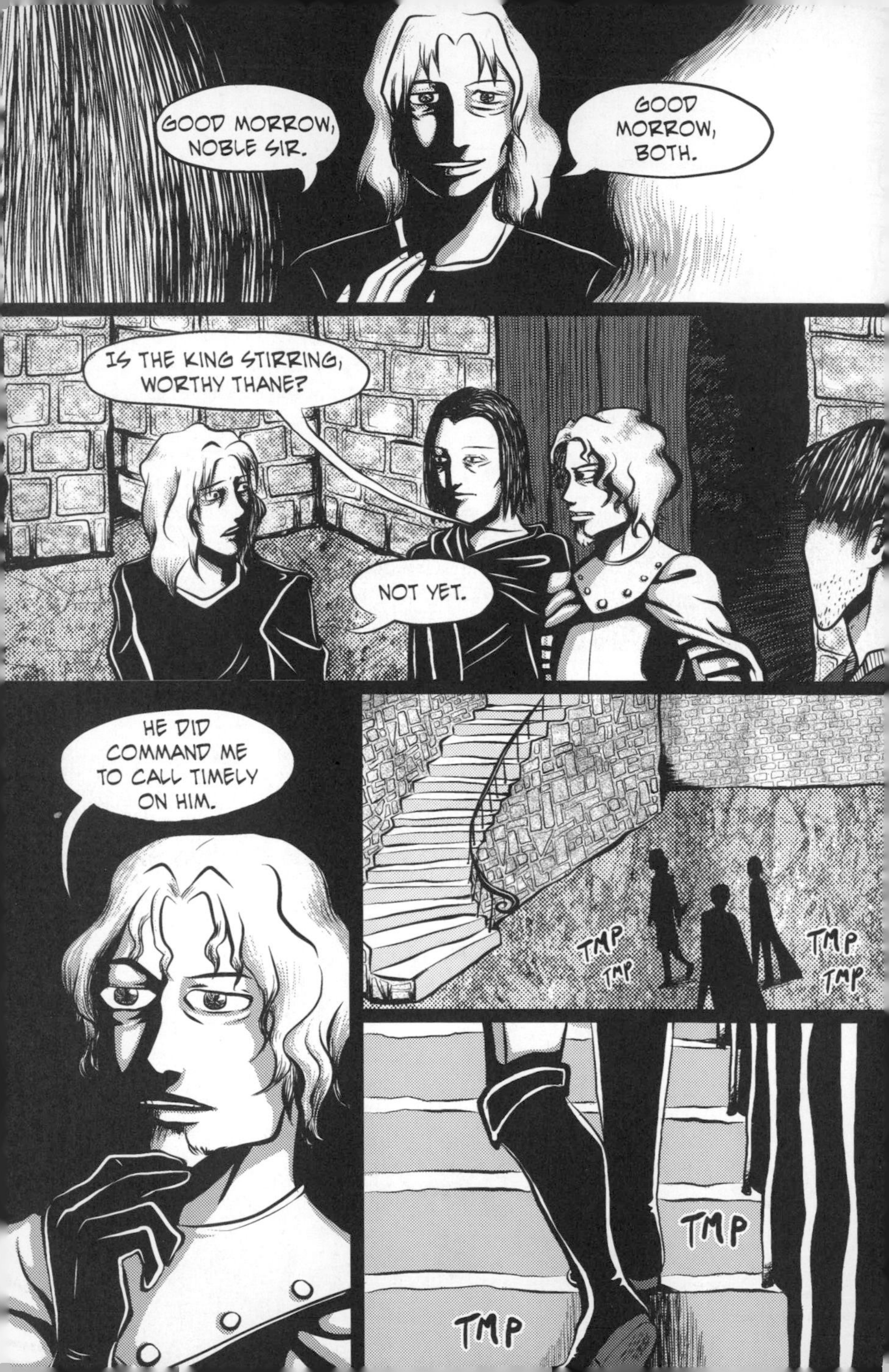
GOOD MORROW, NOBLE SIR.
GOOD MORROW, BOTH.
IS THE KING STIRRING, WORTHY THANE?
NOT YET.
HE DID COMMAND ME TO CALL TIMELY ON HIM.
TMP TMP
TMP TMP
TMP
TMP

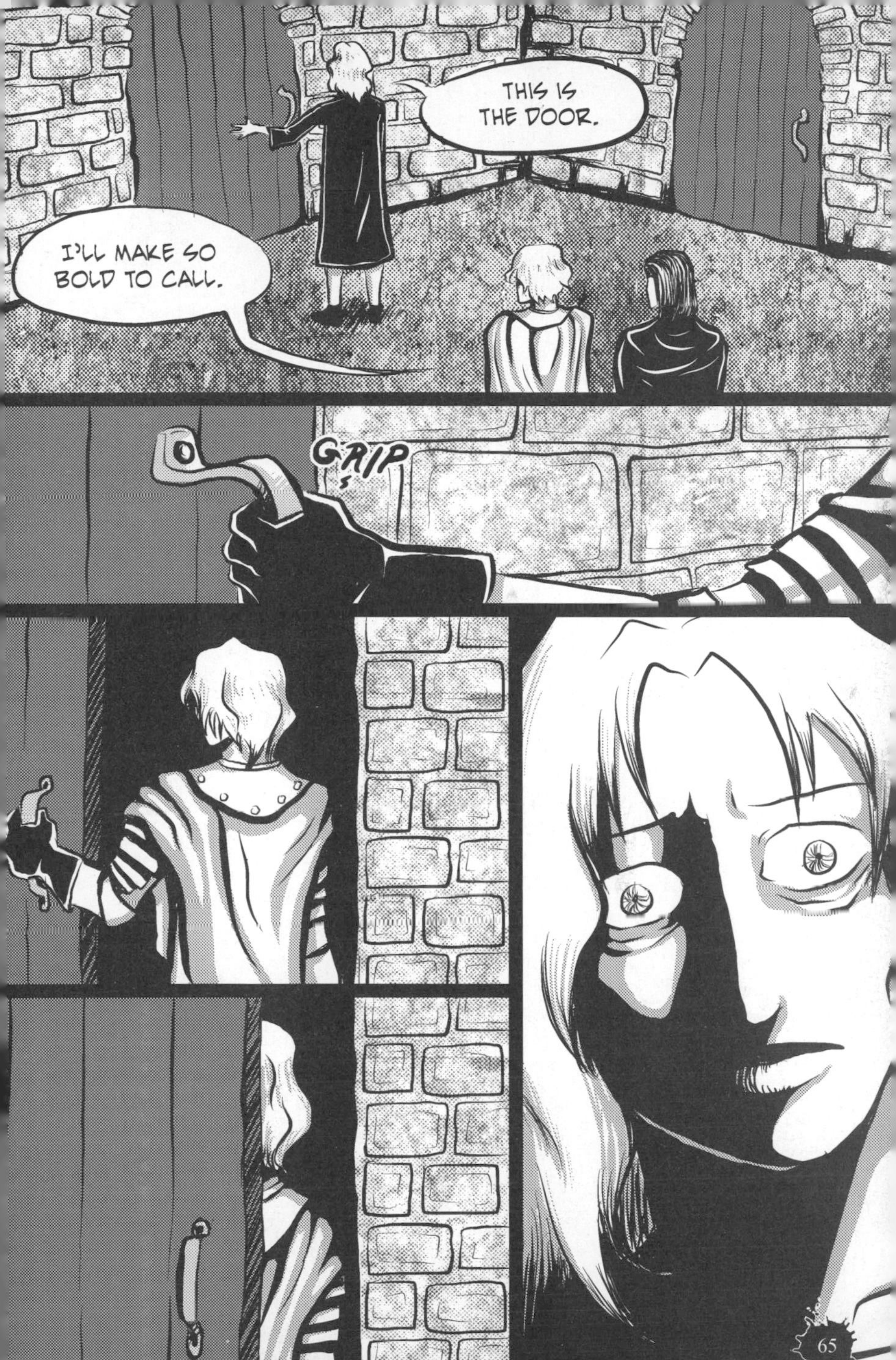

THIS IS THE DOOR.
I'LL MAKE SO BOLD TO CALL.
GRIP

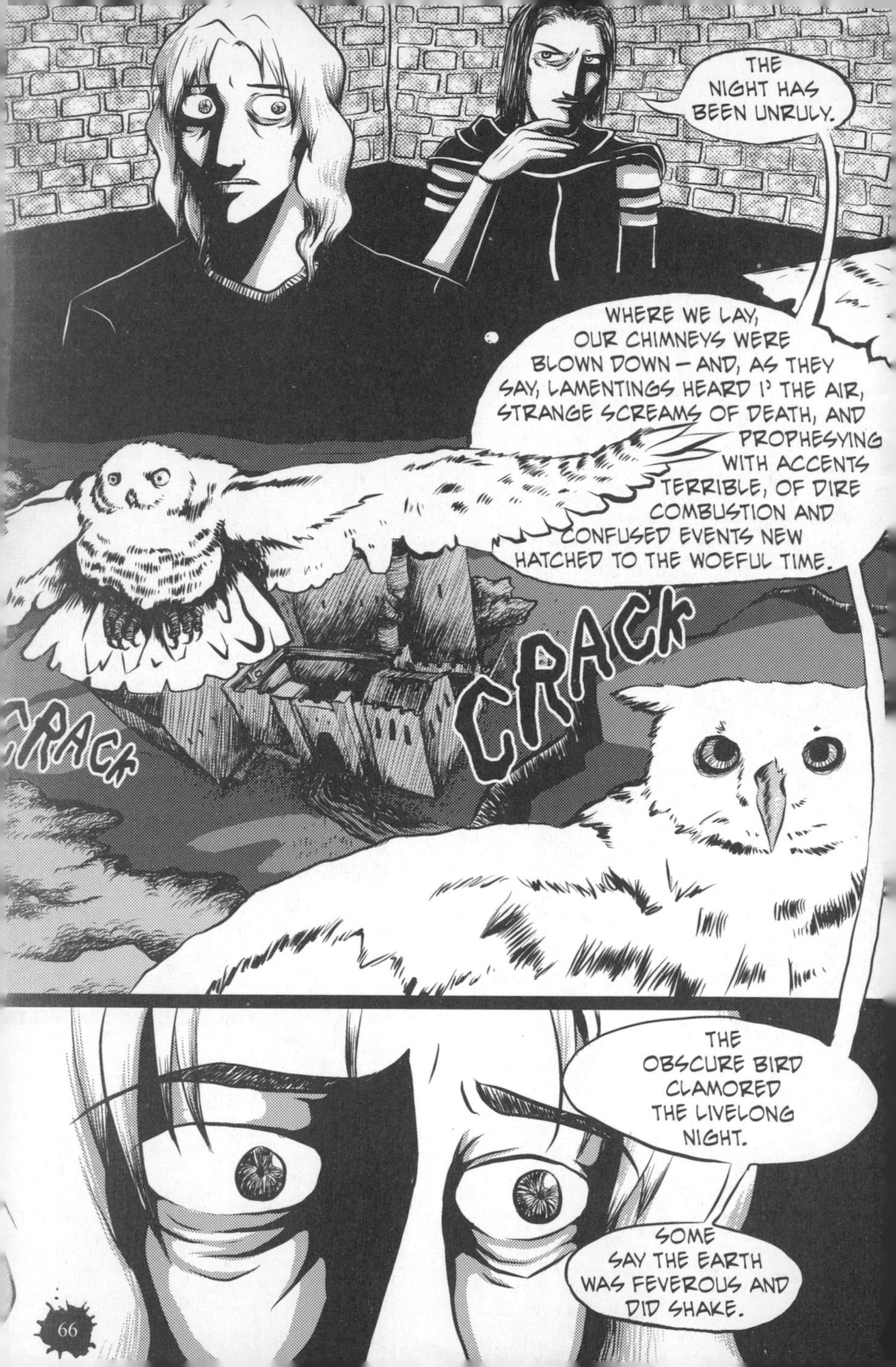

THE NIGHT HAS BEEN UNRULY.
WHERE WE LAY, OUR CHIMNEYS WERE BLOWN DOWN — AND, AS THEY SAY, LAMENTINGS HEARD I' THE AIR, STRANGE SCREAMS OF DEATH, AND PROPHESYING WITH ACCENTS TERRIBLE, OF DIRE COMBUSTION AND CONFUSED EVENTS NEW HATCHED TO THE WOEFUL TIME.
CRACK
CRACK
THE OBSCURE BIRD CLAMORED THE LIVELONG NIGHT.
SOME SAY THE EARTH WAS FEVEROUS AND DID SHAKE.

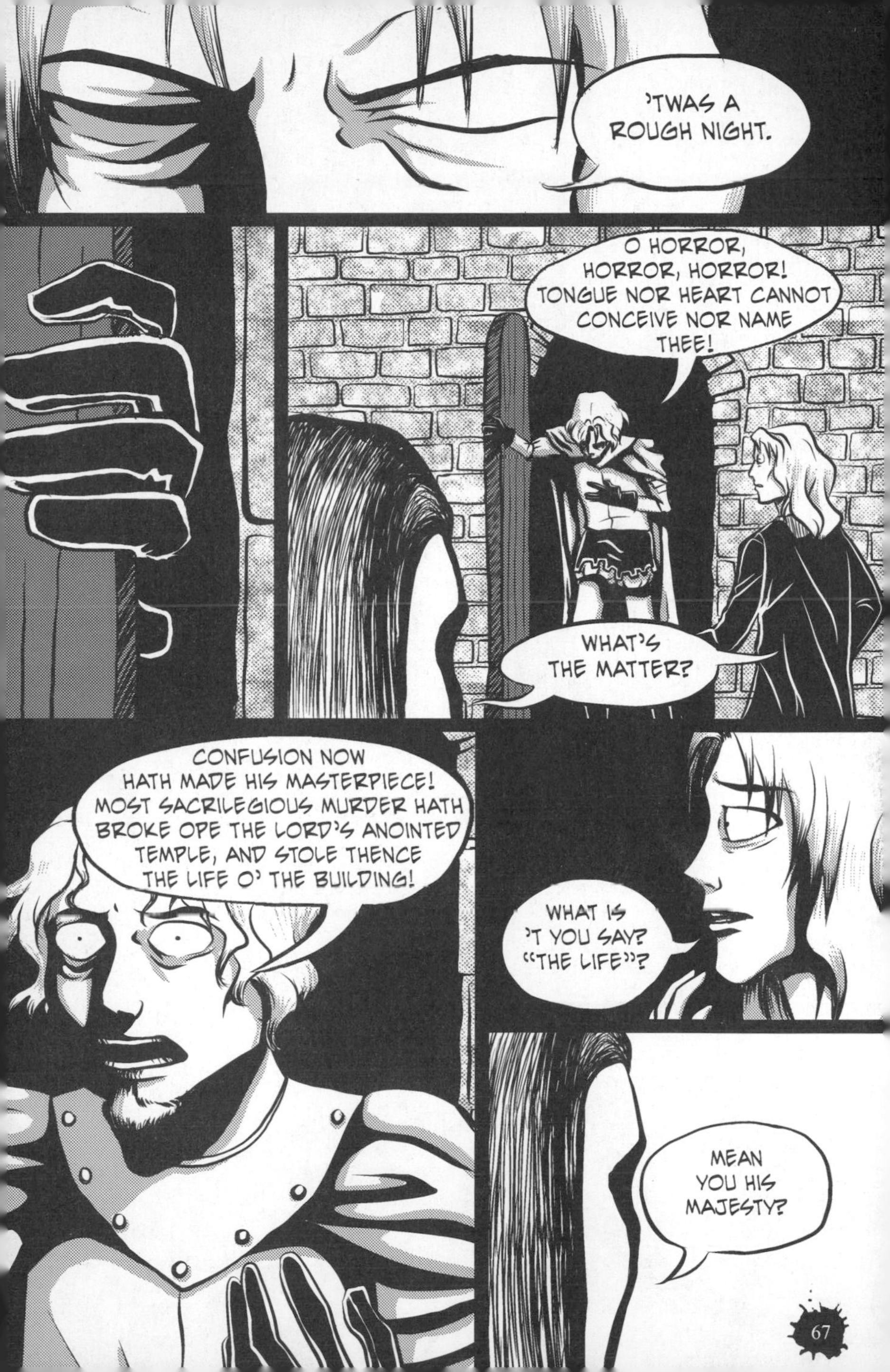
'TWAS A ROUGH NIGHT.
O HORROR, HORROR, HORROR! TONGUE NOR HEART CANNOT CONCEIVE NOR NAME THEE!
WHAT'S THE MATTER?
CONFUSION NOW HATH MADE HIS MASTERPIECE! MOST SACRILEGIOUS MURDER HATH BROKE OPE THE LORD'S ANOINTED TEMPLE, AND STOLE THENCE THE LIFE O' THE BUILDING!
WHAT IS 'T YOU SAY? "THE LIFE"?
MEAN YOU HIS MAJESTY?

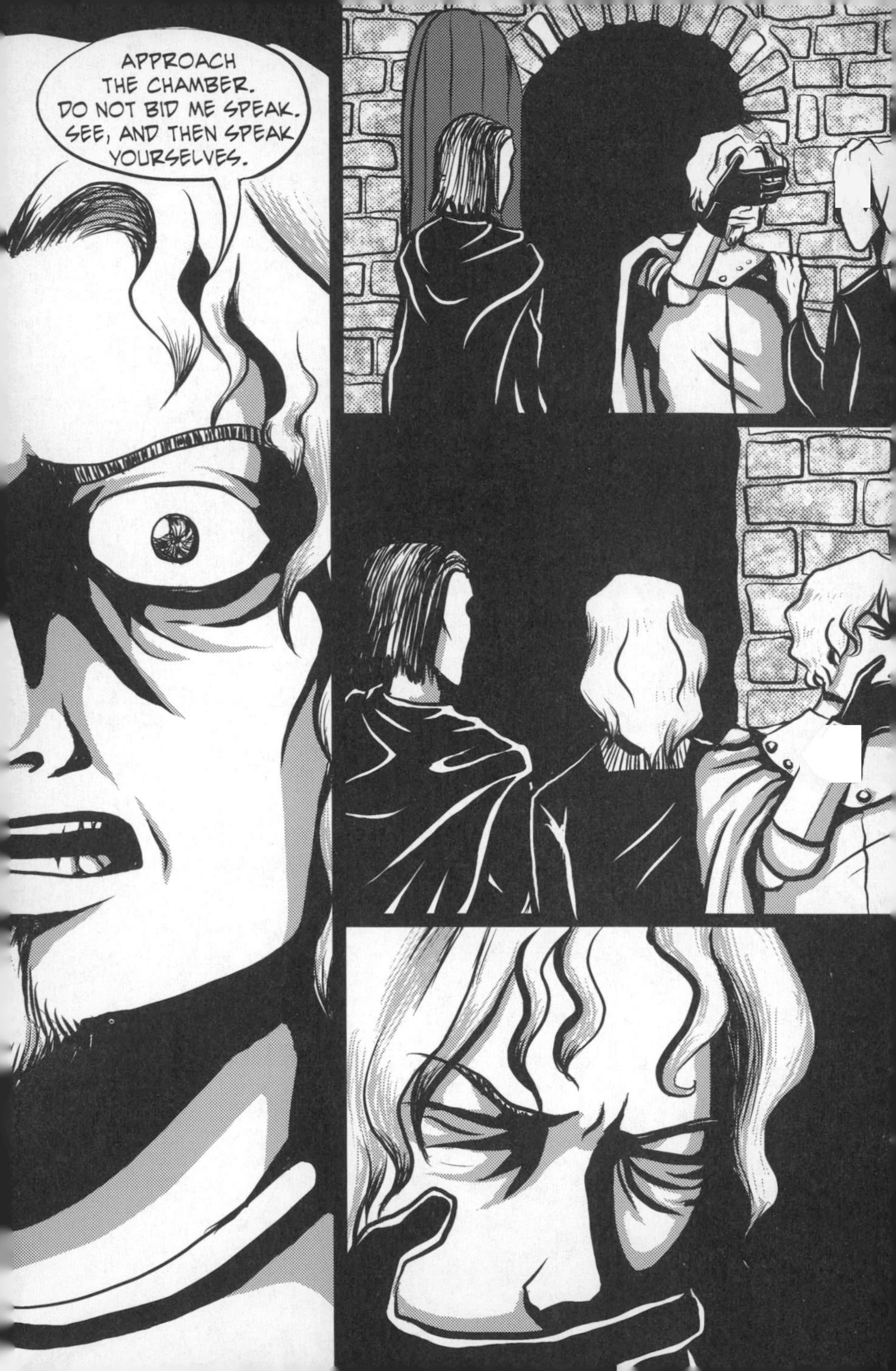
APPROACH THE CHAMBER. DO NOT BID ME SPEAK. SEE, AND THEN SPEAK YOURSELVES.

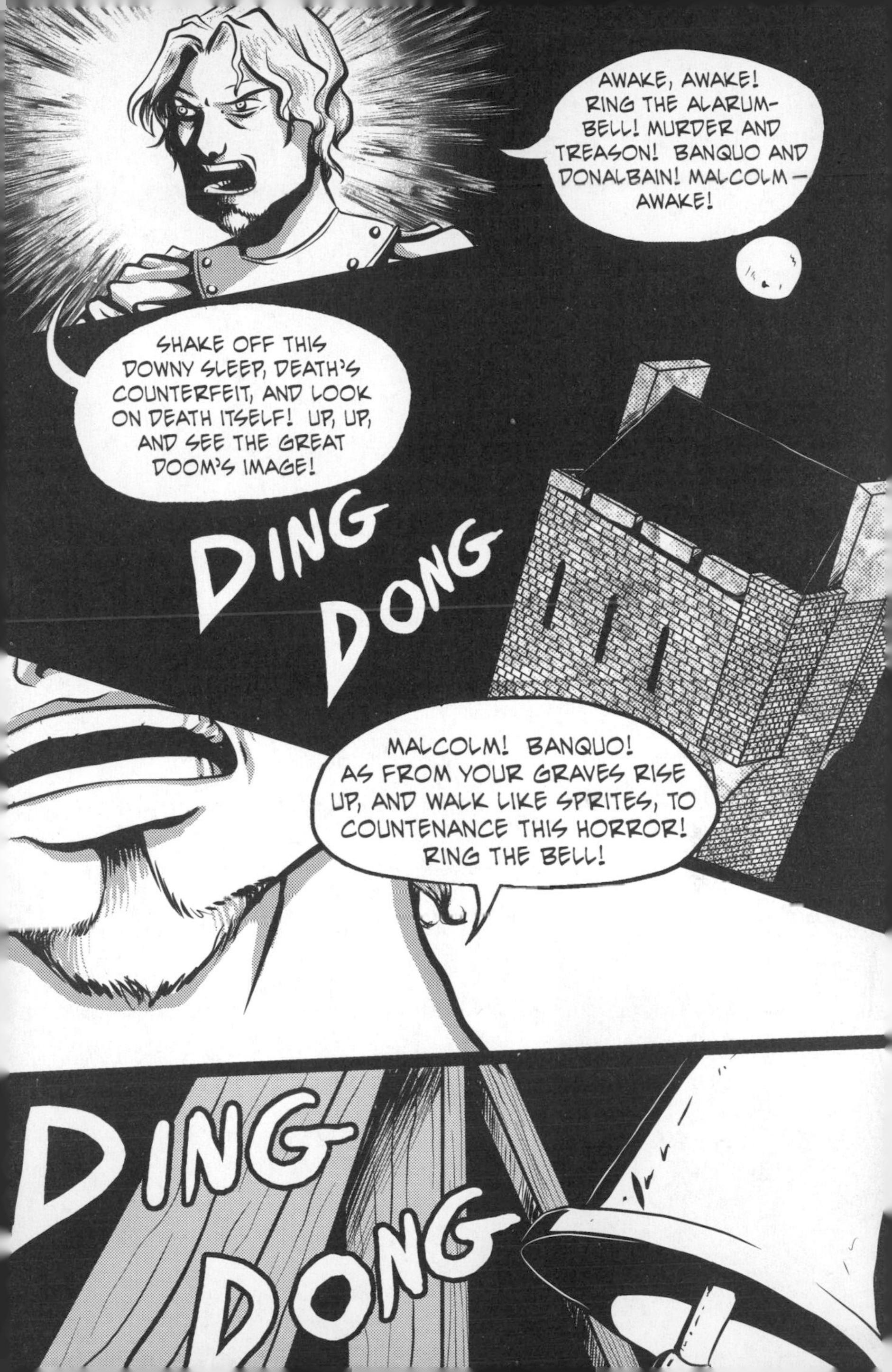
AWAKE, AWAKE! RING THE ALARUM-BELL! MURDER AND TREASON! BANQUO AND DONALBAIN! MALCOLM — AWAKE!
SHAKE OFF THIS DOWNY SLEEP, DEATH'S COUNTERFEIT, AND LOOK ON DEATH ITSELF! UP, UP, AND SEE THE GREAT DOOM'S IMAGE!
DING DONG
MALCOLM! BANQUO! AS FROM YOUR GRAVES RISE UP, AND WALK LIKE SPRITES, TO COUNTENANCE THIS HORROR! RING THE BELL!
DING DONG

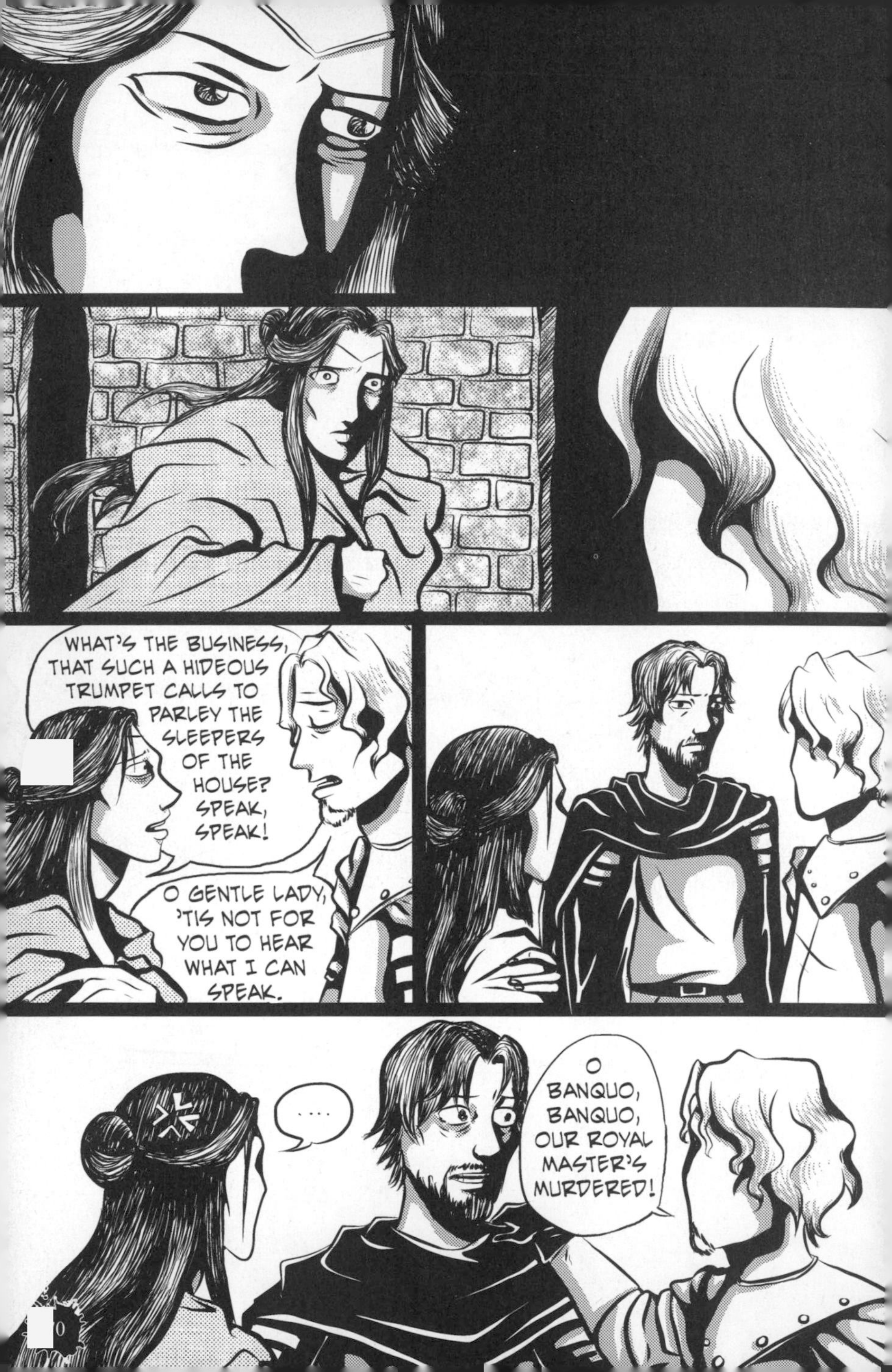
WHAT'S THE BUSINESS, THAT SUCH A HIDEOUS TRUMPET CALLS TO PARLEY THE SLEEPERS OF THE HOUSE? SPEAK, SPEAK!
O GENTLE LADY, 'TIS NOT FOR YOU TO HEAR WHAT I CAN SPEAK.
....
O BANQUO, BANQUO, OUR ROYAL MASTER'S MURDERED!

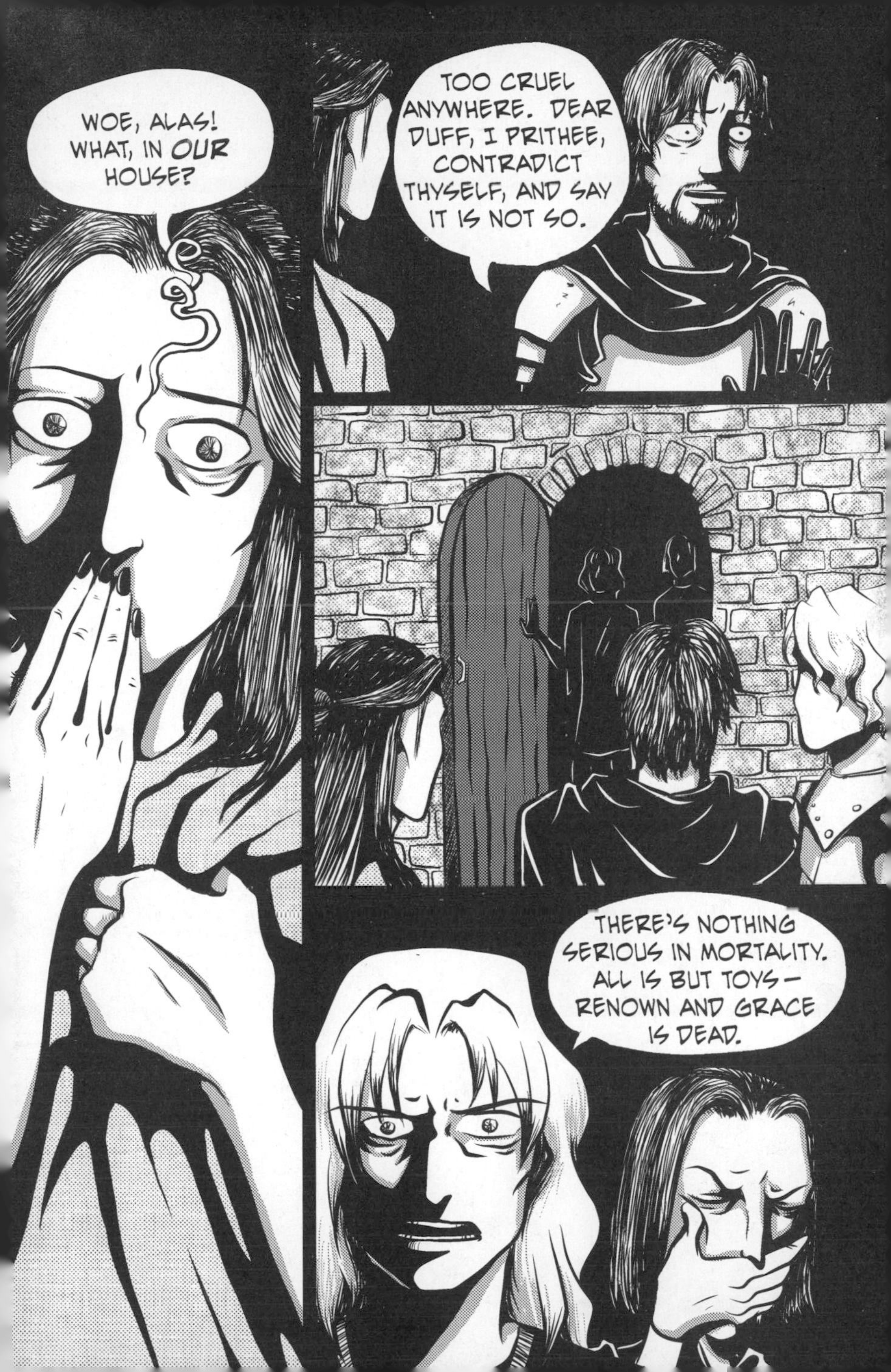
WOE, ALAS! WHAT, IN OUR HOUSE?
TOO CRUEL ANYWHERE. DEAR DUFF, I PRITHEE, CONTRADICT THYSELF, AND SAY IT IS NOT SO.
THERE'S NOTHING SERIOUS IN MORTALITY. ALL IS BUT TOYS— RENOWN AND GRACE IS DEAD.

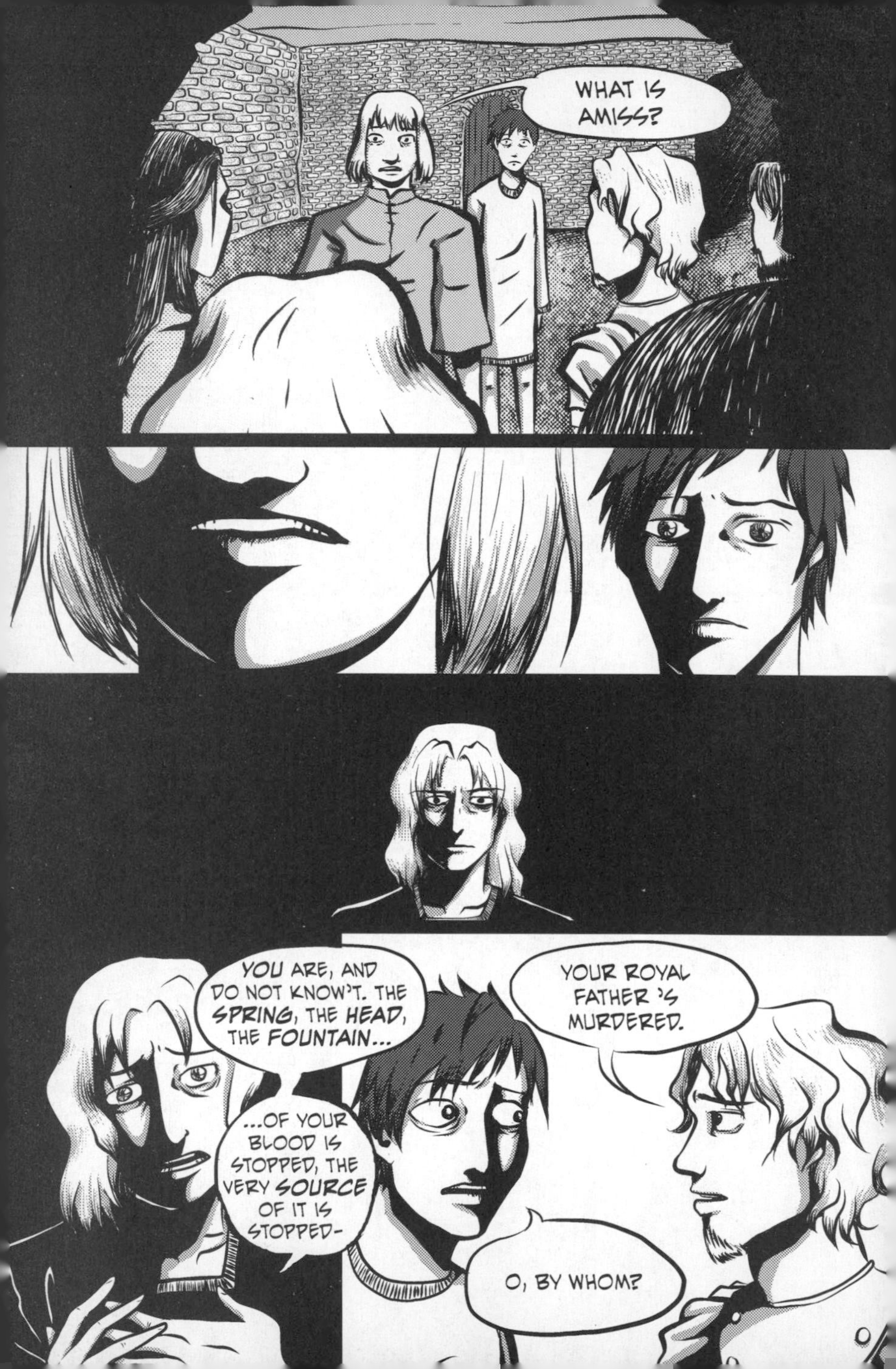
WHAT IS AMISS?
YOU ARE, AND DO NOT KNOW'T. THE SPRING, THE HEAD, THE FOUNTAIN...
...OF YOUR BLOOD IS STOPPED, THE VERY SOURCE OF IT IS STOPPED-
YOUR ROYAL FATHER 'S MURDERED.
O, BY WHOM?

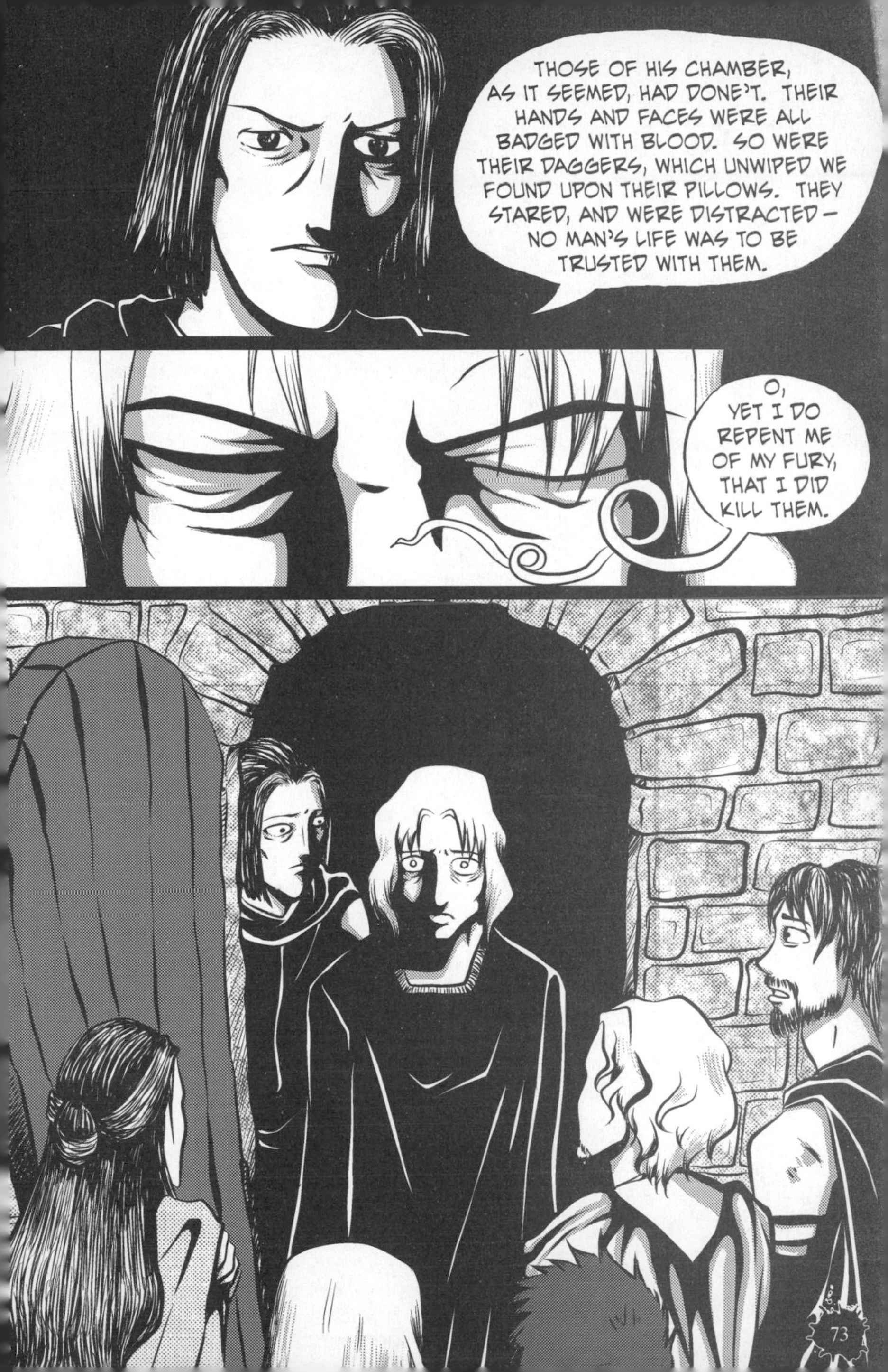
THOSE OF HIS CHAMBER, AS IT SEEMED, HAD DONE'T. THEIR HANDS AND FACES WERE ALL BADGED WITH BLOOD. SO WERE THEIR DAGGERS, WHICH UNWIPED WE FOUND UPON THEIR PILLOWS. THEY STARED, AND WERE DISTRACTED — NO MAN'S LIFE WAS TO BE TRUSTED WITH THEM.
O, YET I DO REPENT ME OF MY FURY, THAT I DID KILL THEM.

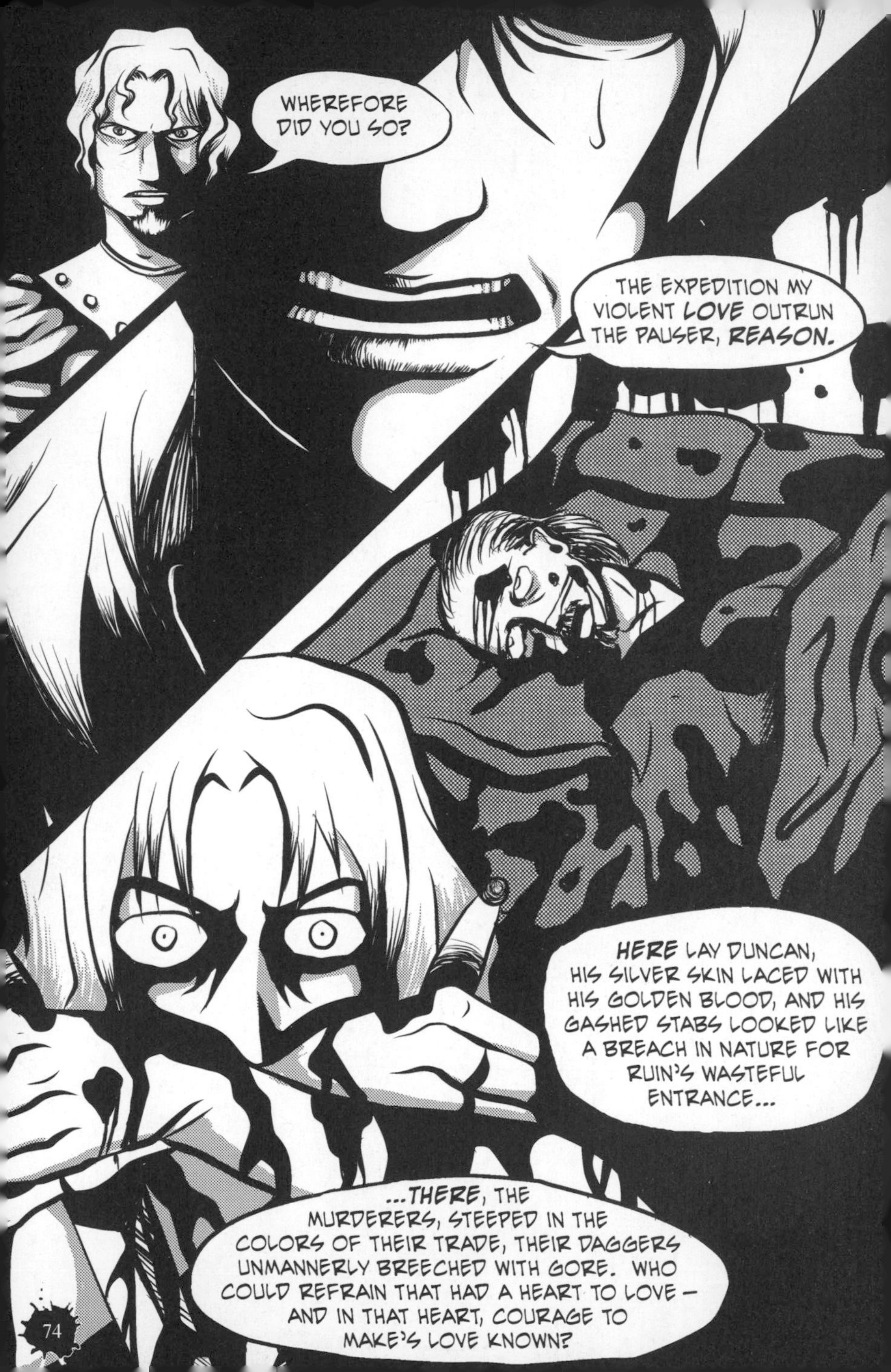
WHEREFORE DID YOU SO?
THE EXPEDITION MY VIOLENT LOVE OUTRUN THE PAUSER, REASON.
HERE LAY DUNCAN, HIS SILVER SKIN LACED WITH HIS GOLDEN BLOOD, AND HIS GASHED STABS LOOKED LIKE A BREACH IN NATURE FOR RUIN'S WASTEFUL ENTRANCE...
...THERE, THE MURDERERS, STEEPED IN THE COLORS OF THEIR TRADE, THEIR DAGGERS UNMANNERLY BREECHED WITH GORE. WHO COULD REFRAIN THAT HAD A HEART TO LOVE – AND IN THAT HEART, COURAGE TO MAKE'S LOVE KNOWN?

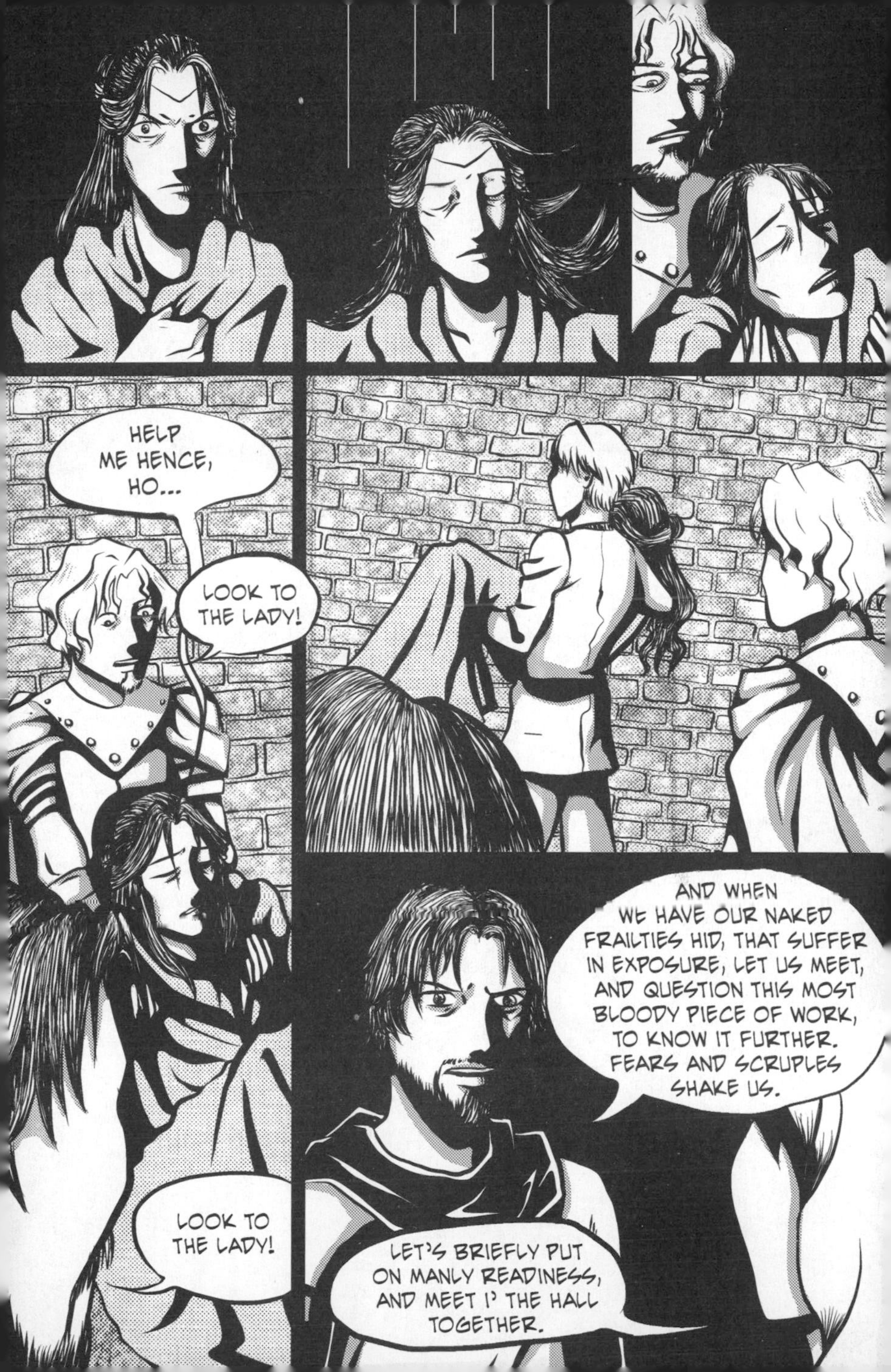
HELP ME HENCE, HO...
LOOK TO THE LADY!
AND WHEN WE HAVE OUR NAKED FRAILTIES HID, THAT SUFFER IN EXPOSURE, LET US MEET, AND QUESTION THIS MOST BLOODY PIECE OF WORK, TO KNOW IT FURTHER. FEARS AND SCRUPLES SHAKE US.
LOOK TO THE LADY!
LET'S BRIEFLY PUT ON MANLY READINESS, AND MEET I' THE HALL TOGETHER.

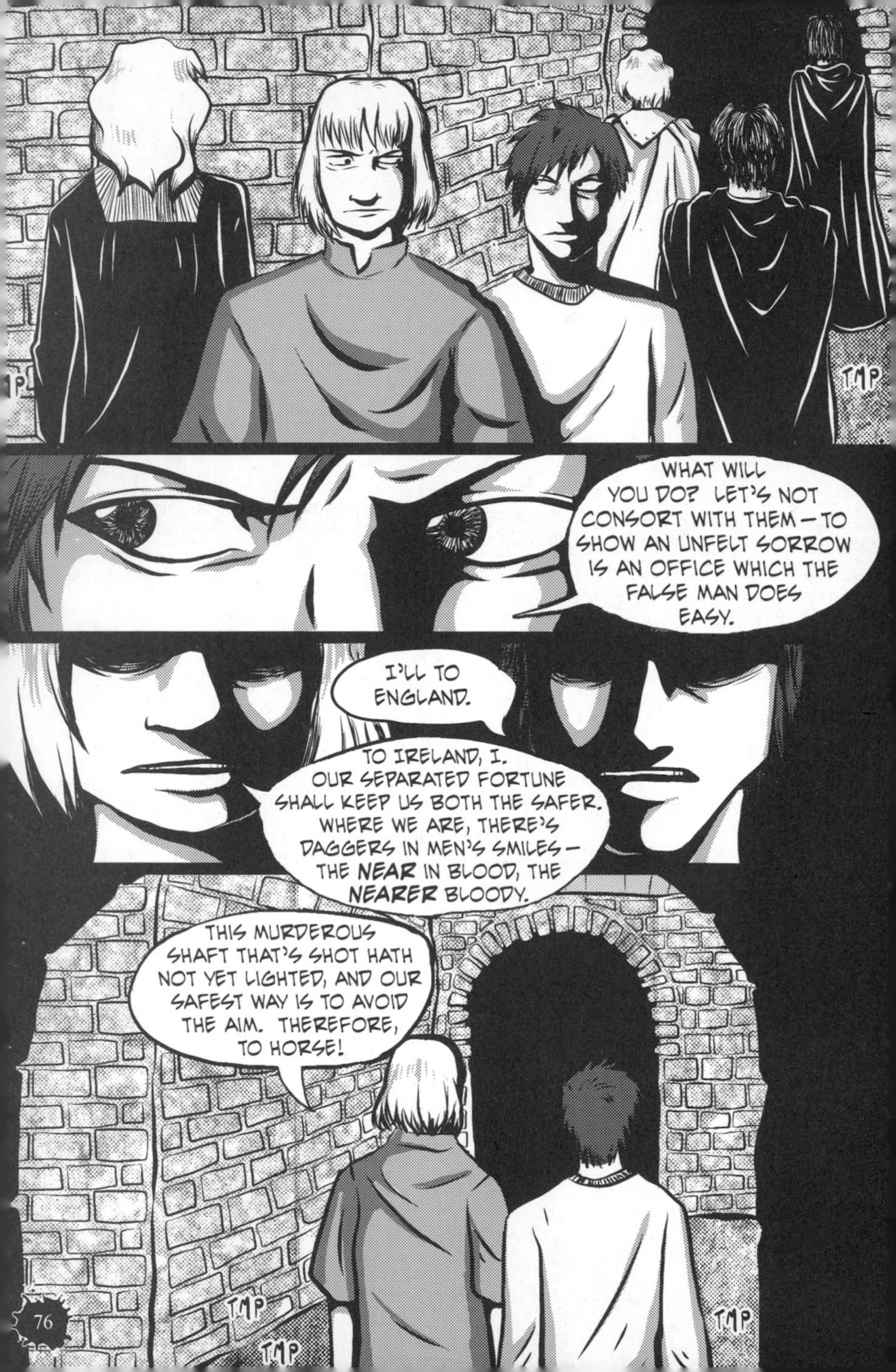
TMP
TMP
WHAT WILL YOU DO? LET'S NOT CONSORT WITH THEM — TO SHOW AN UNFELT SORROW IS AN OFFICE WHICH THE FALSE MAN DOES EASY.
I'LL TO ENGLAND.
TO IRELAND, I. OUR SEPARATED FORTUNE SHALL KEEP US BOTH THE SAFER. WHERE WE ARE, THERE'S DAGGERS IN MEN'S SMILES — THE **NEAR** IN BLOOD, THE **NEARER** BLOODY.
THIS MURDEROUS SHAFT THAT'S SHOT HATH NOT YET LIGHTED, AND OUR SAFEST WAY IS TO AVOID THE AIM. THEREFORE, TO HORSE!
TMP
TMP
TMP

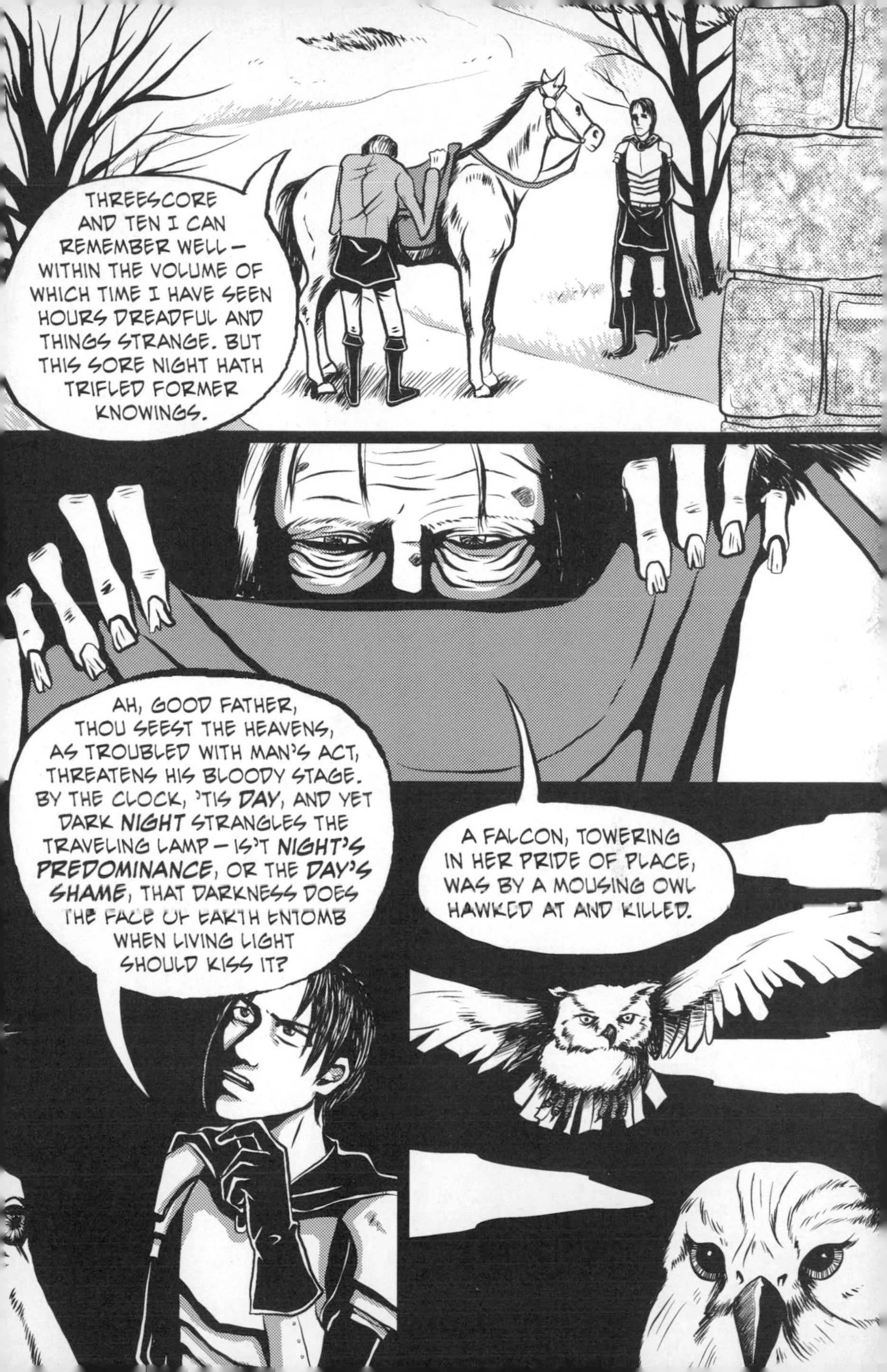
THREESCORE AND TEN I CAN REMEMBER WELL— WITHIN THE VOLUME OF WHICH TIME I HAVE SEEN HOURS DREADFUL AND THINGS STRANGE. BUT THIS SORE NIGHT HATH TRIFLED FORMER KNOWINGS.
AH, GOOD FATHER, THOU SEEST THE HEAVENS, AS TROUBLED WITH MAN'S ACT, THREATENS HIS BLOODY STAGE. BY THE CLOCK, 'TIS *DAY*, AND YET DARK **NIGHT** STRANGLES THE TRAVELING LAMP—IS'T ***NIGHT'S PREDOMINANCE***, OR THE ***DAY'S SHAME***, THAT DARKNESS DOES THE FACE OF EARTH ENTOMB WHEN LIVING LIGHT SHOULD KISS IT?
A FALCON, TOWERING IN HER PRIDE OF PLACE, WAS BY A MOUSING OWL HAWKED AT AND KILLED.

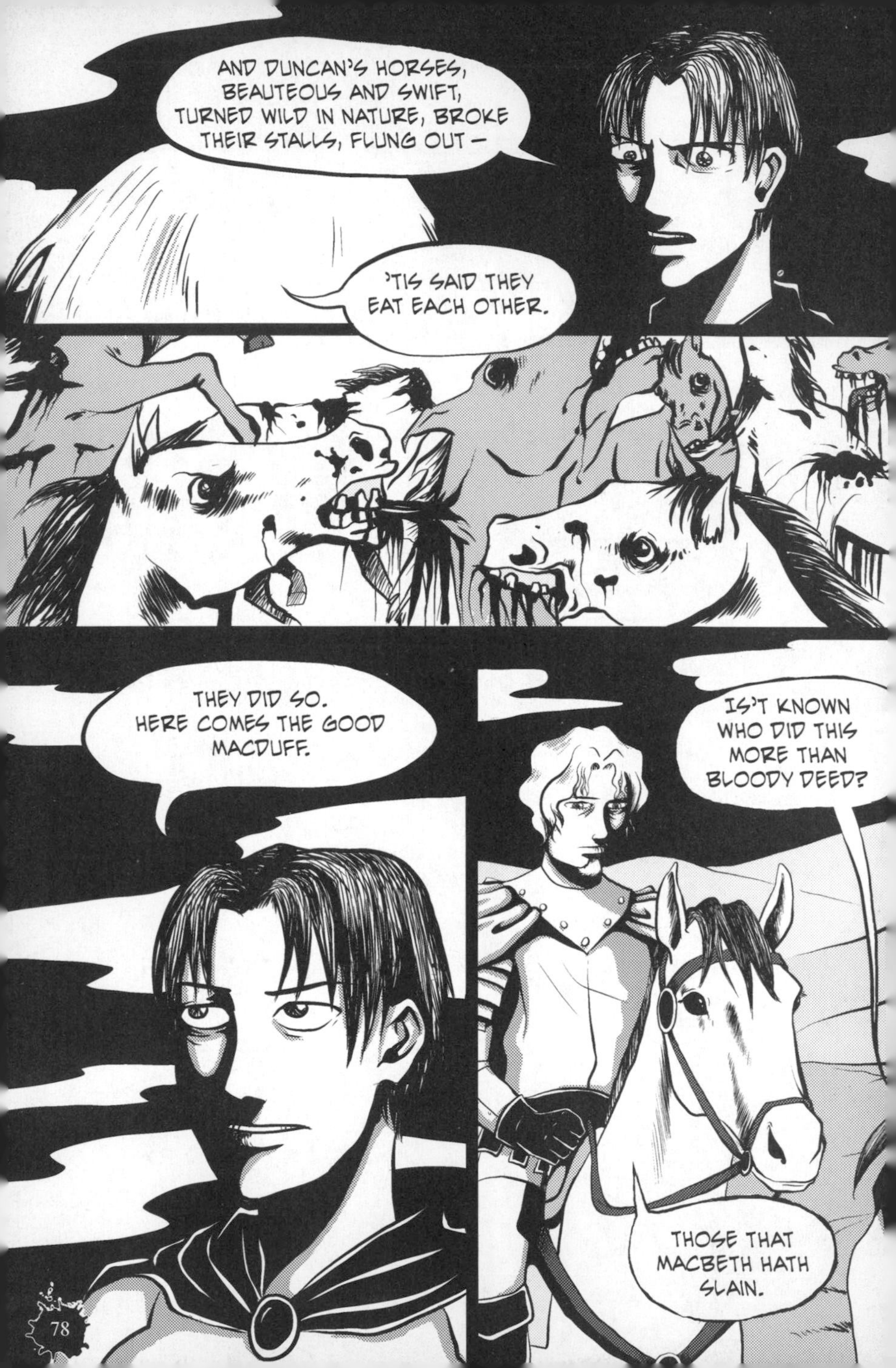
AND DUNCAN'S HORSES, BEAUTEOUS AND SWIFT, TURNED WILD IN NATURE, BROKE THEIR STALLS, FLUNG OUT –
'TIS SAID THEY EAT EACH OTHER.
THEY DID SO. HERE COMES THE GOOD MACDUFF.
IS'T KNOWN WHO DID THIS MORE THAN BLOODY DEED?
THOSE THAT MACBETH HATH SLAIN.

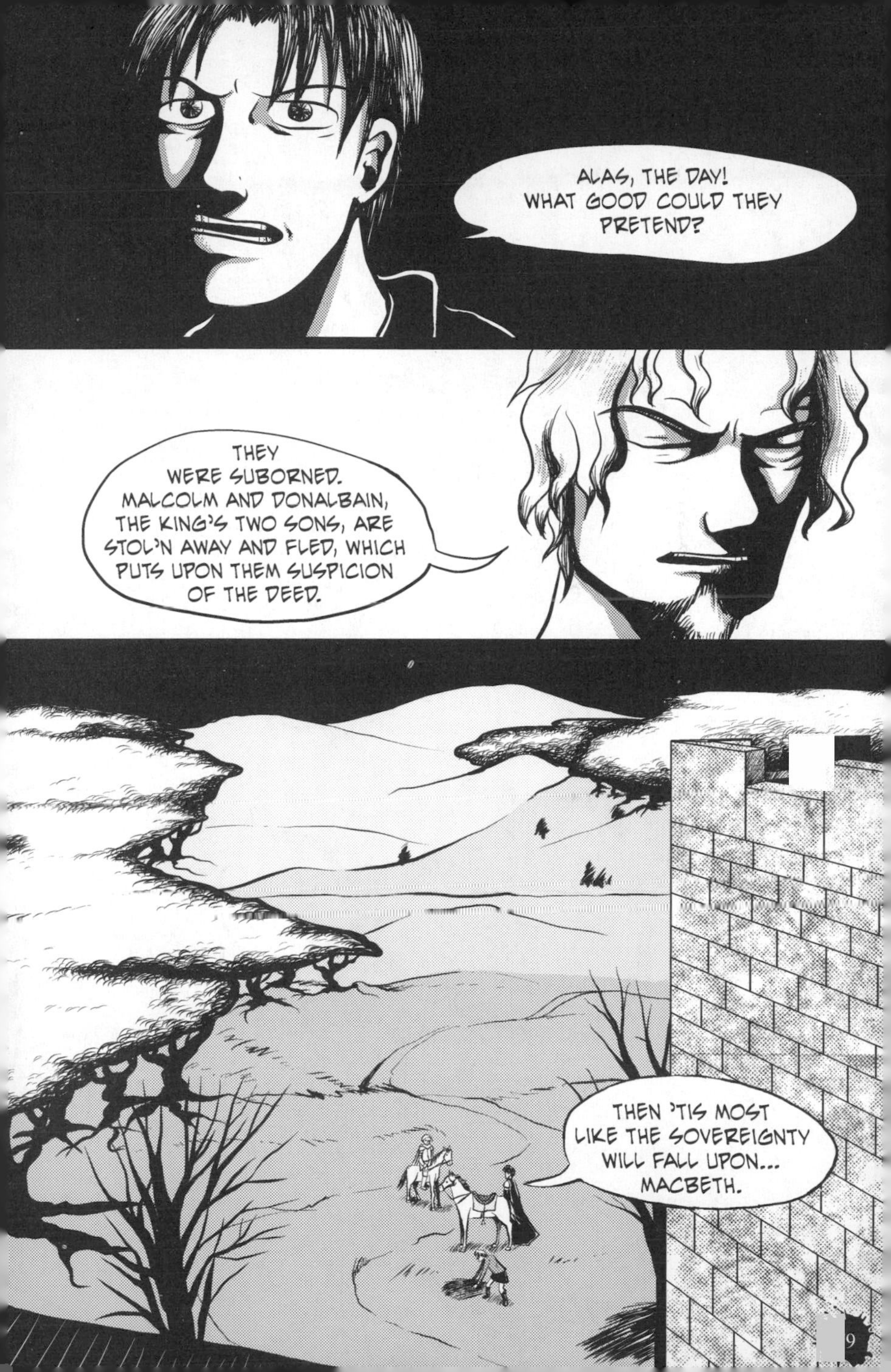
ALAS, THE DAY! WHAT GOOD COULD THEY PRETEND?
THEY WERE SUBORNED. MALCOLM AND DONALBAIN, THE KING'S TWO SONS, ARE STOL'N AWAY AND FLED, WHICH PUTS UPON THEM SUSPICION OF THE DEED.
THEN 'TIS MOST LIKE THE SOVEREIGNTY WILL FALL UPON... MACBETH.

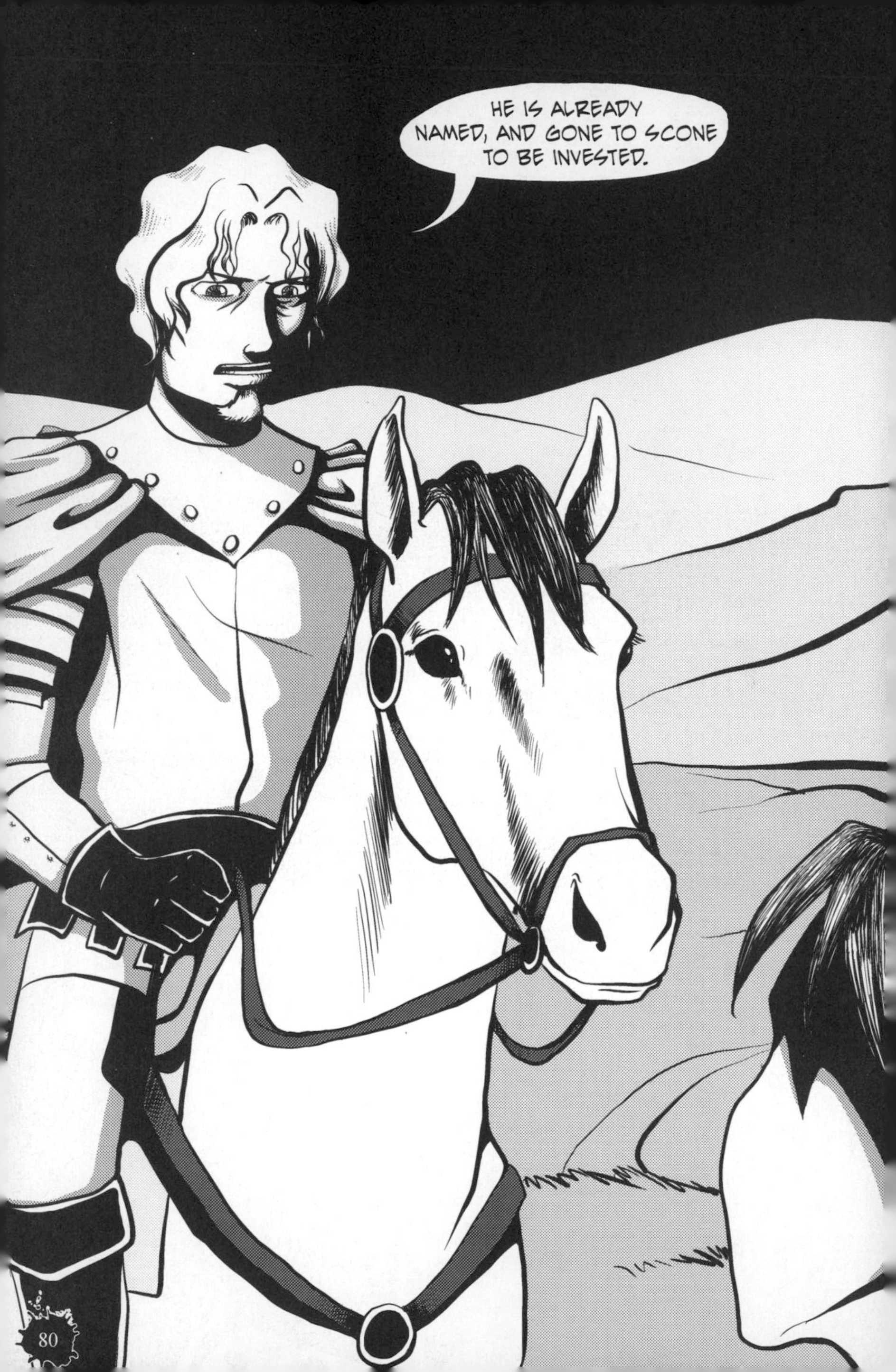
HE IS ALREADY NAMED, AND GONE TO SCONE TO BE INVESTED.

Act III

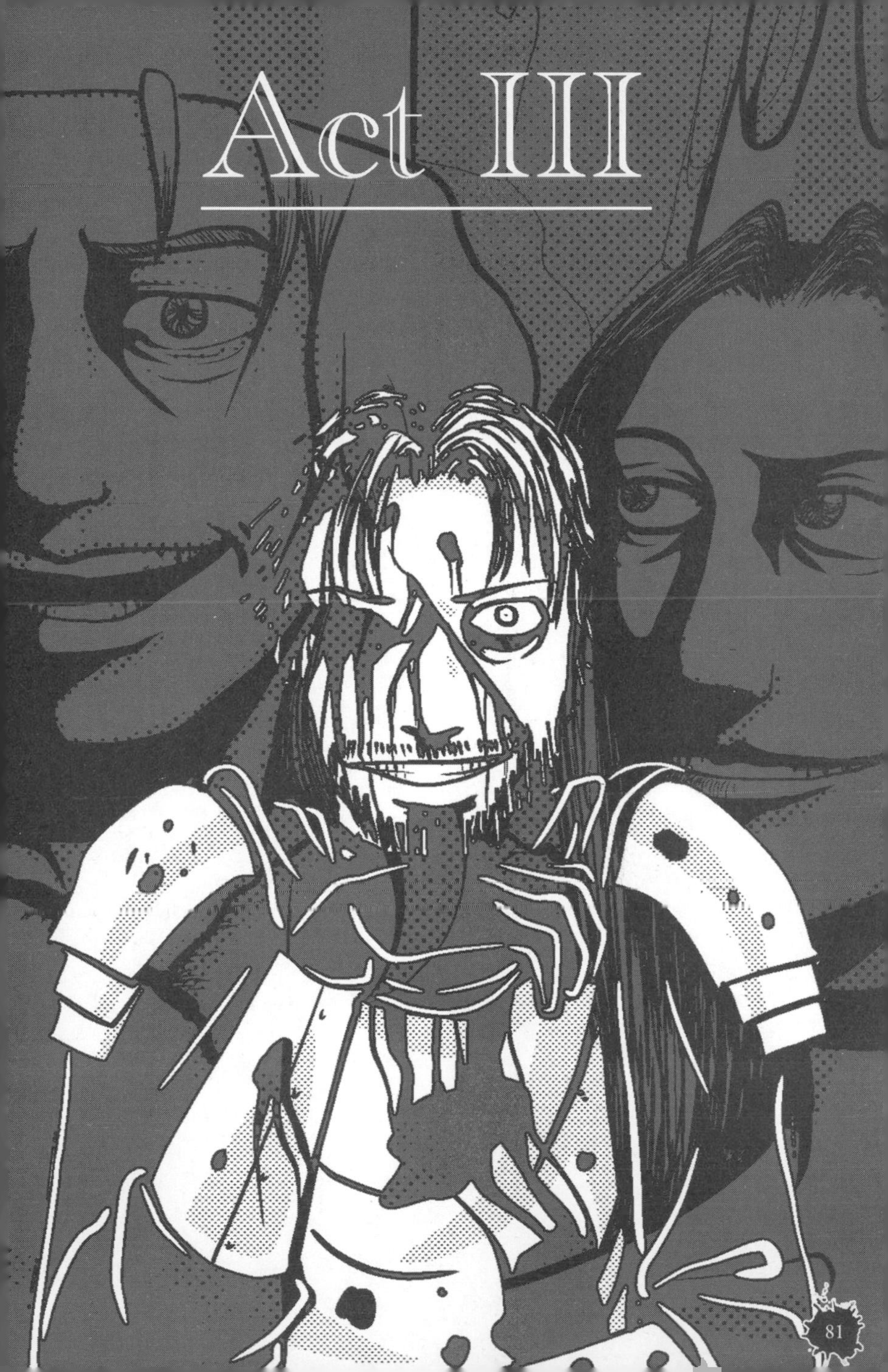

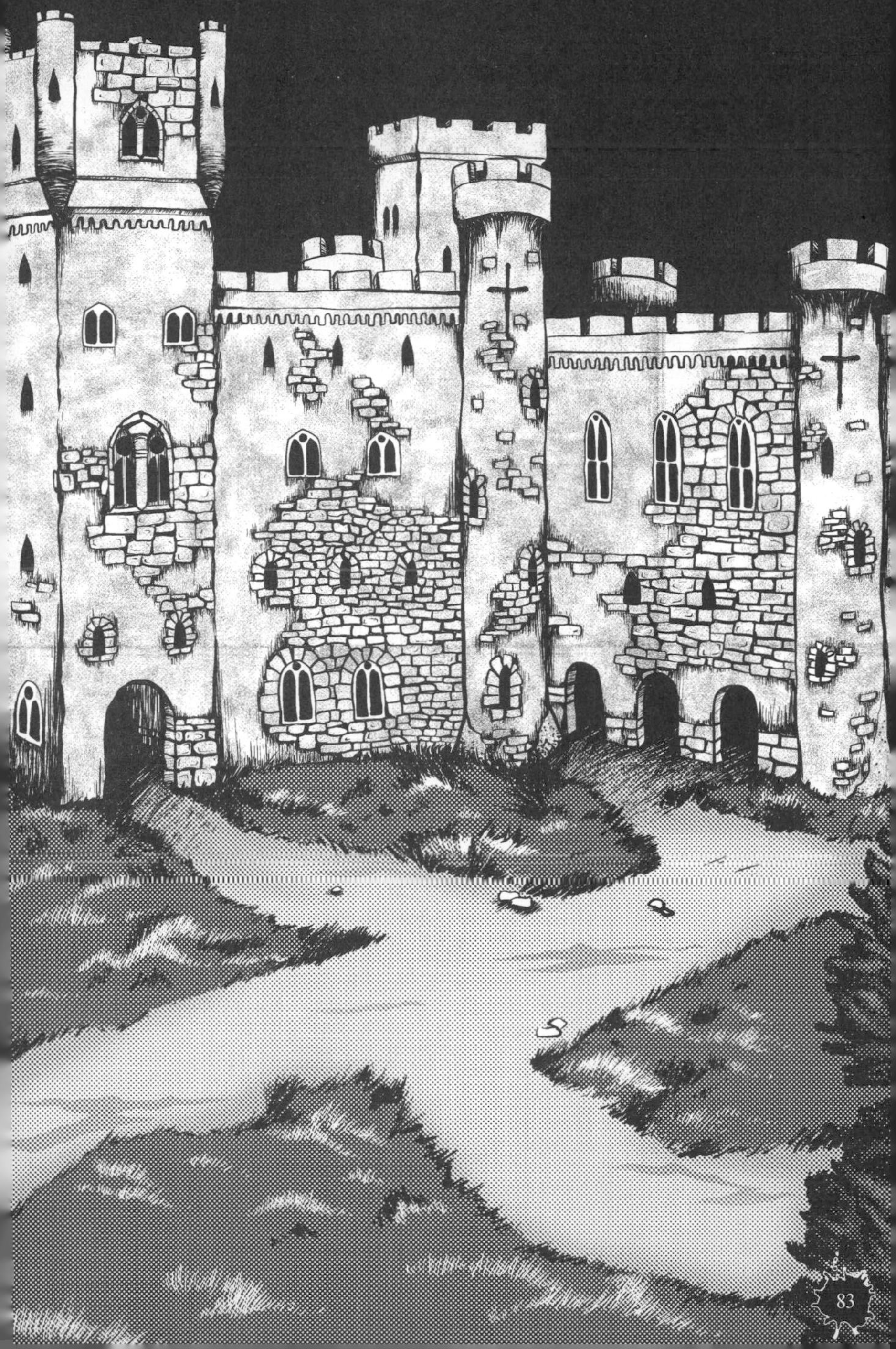

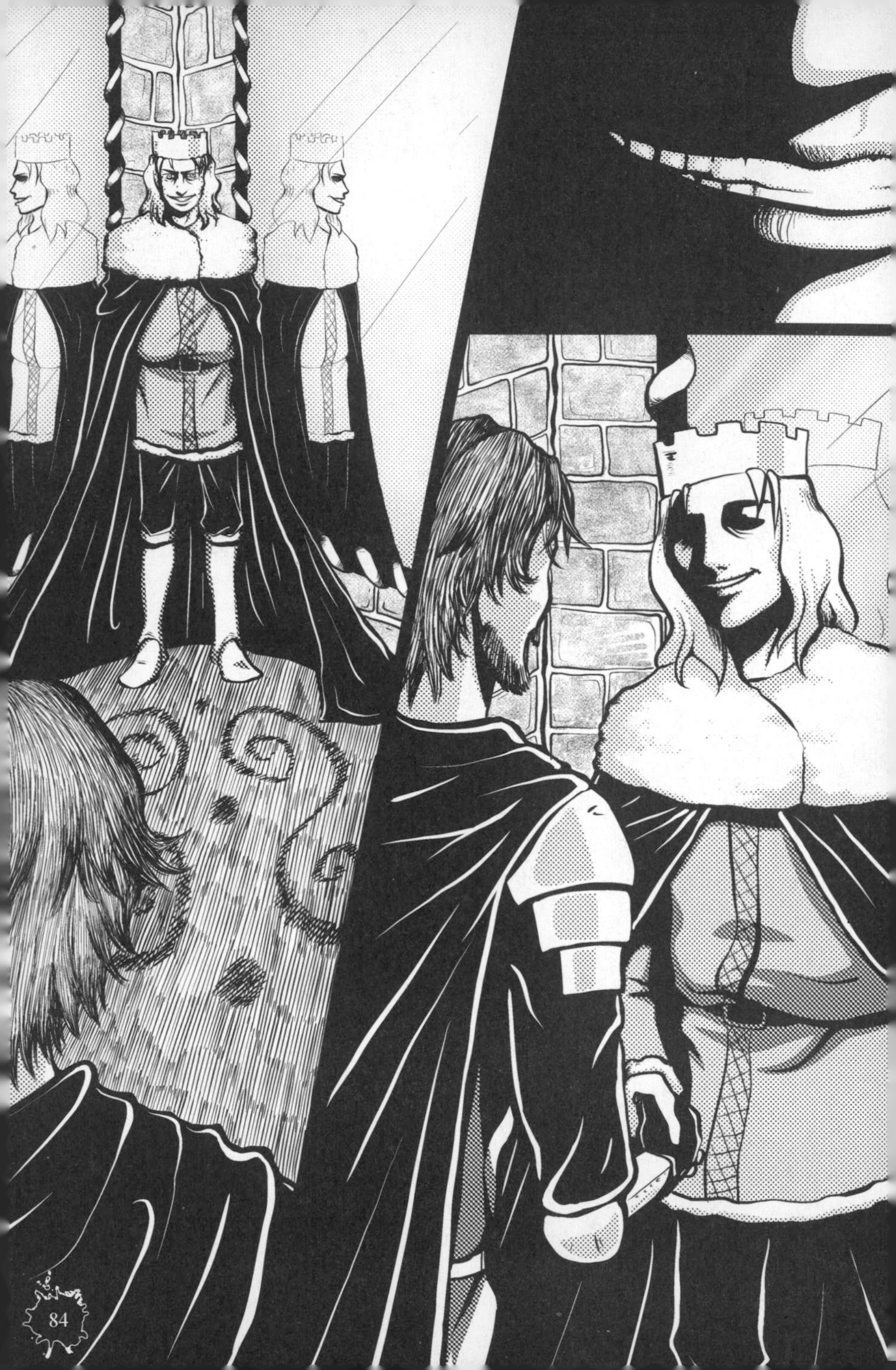

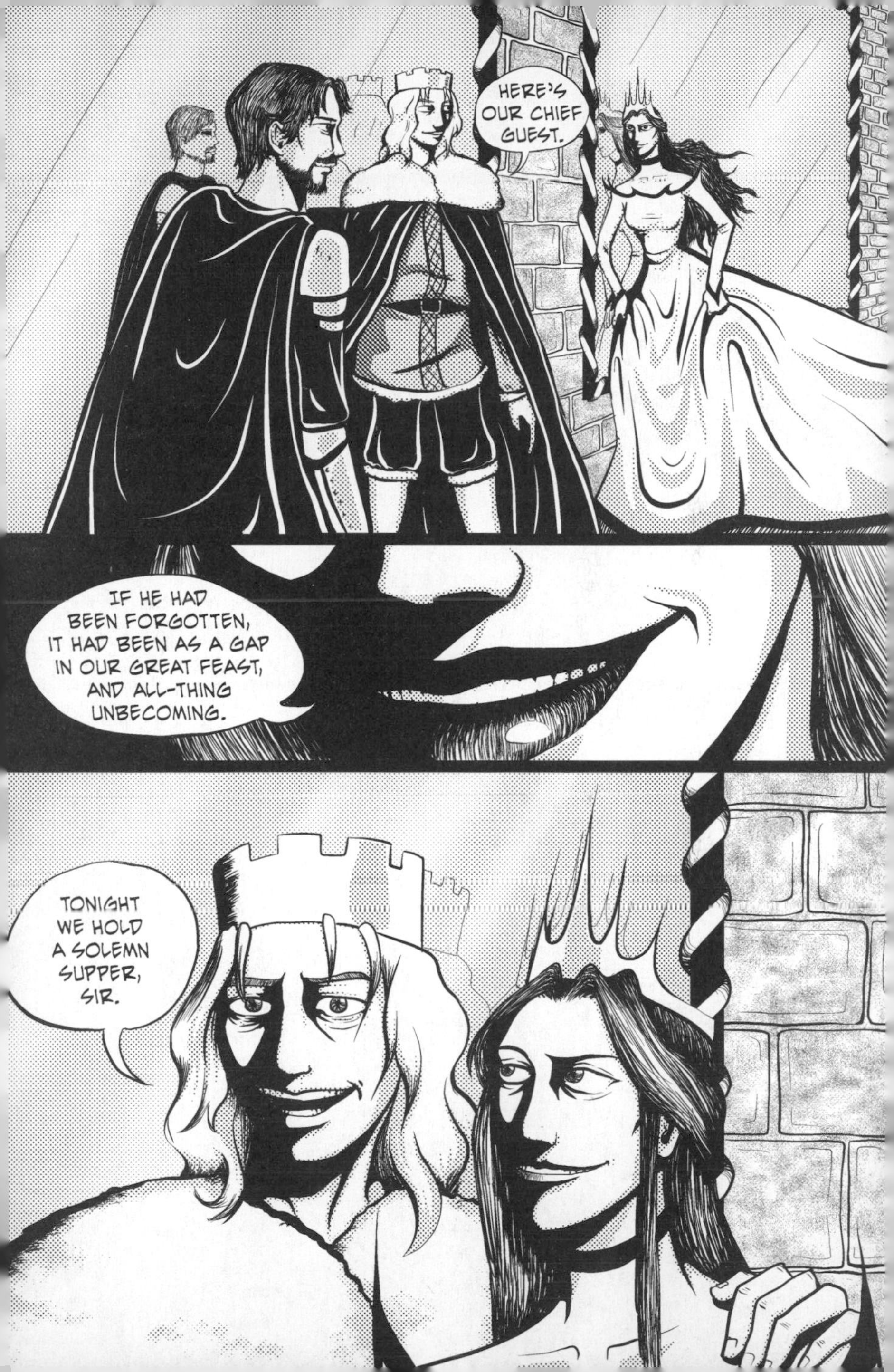
HERE'S OUR CHIEF GUEST.
IF HE HAD BEEN FORGOTTEN, IT HAD BEEN AS A GAP IN OUR GREAT FEAST, AND ALL-THING UNBECOMING.
TONIGHT WE HOLD A SOLEMN SUPPER, SIR.

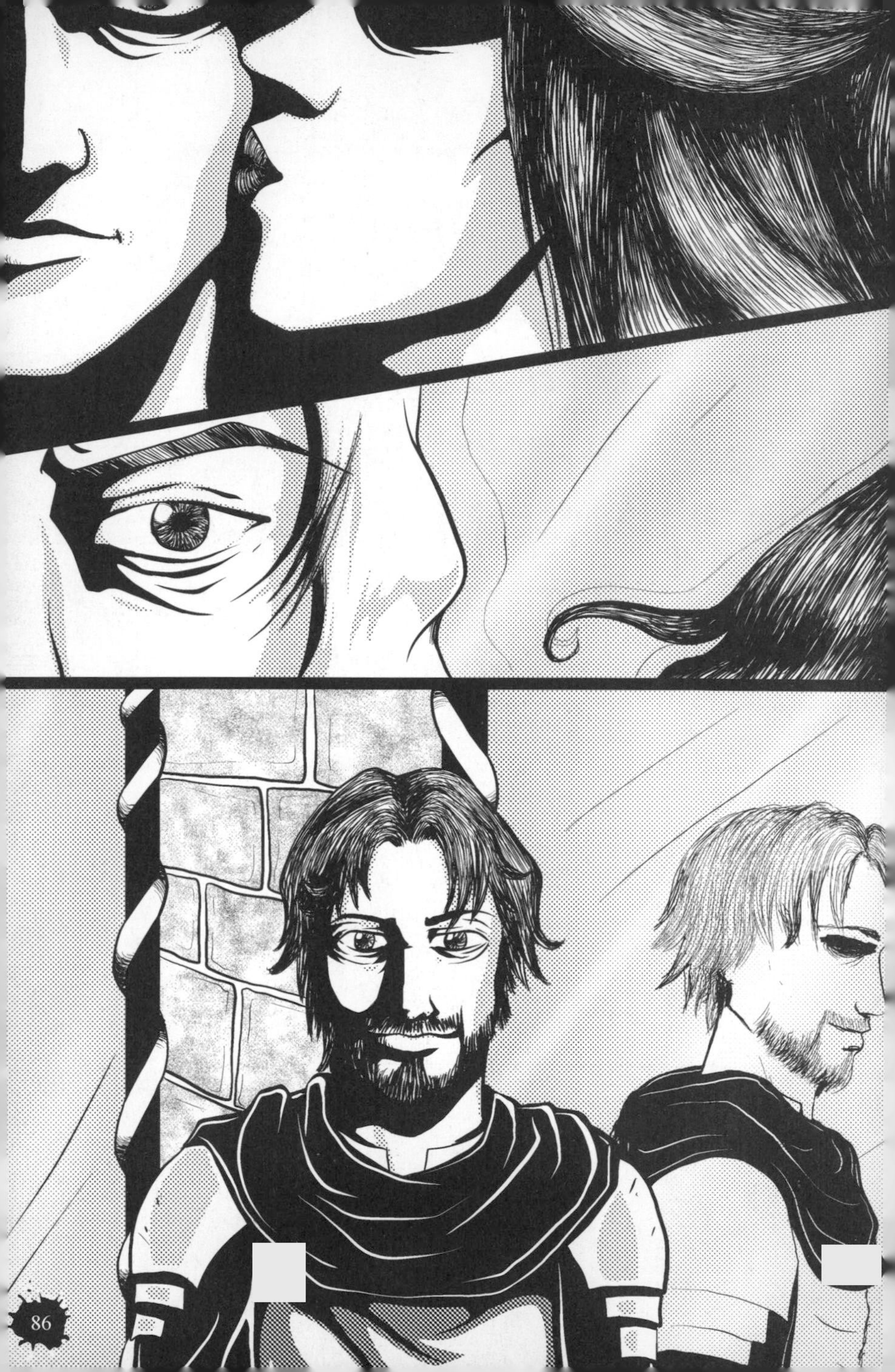

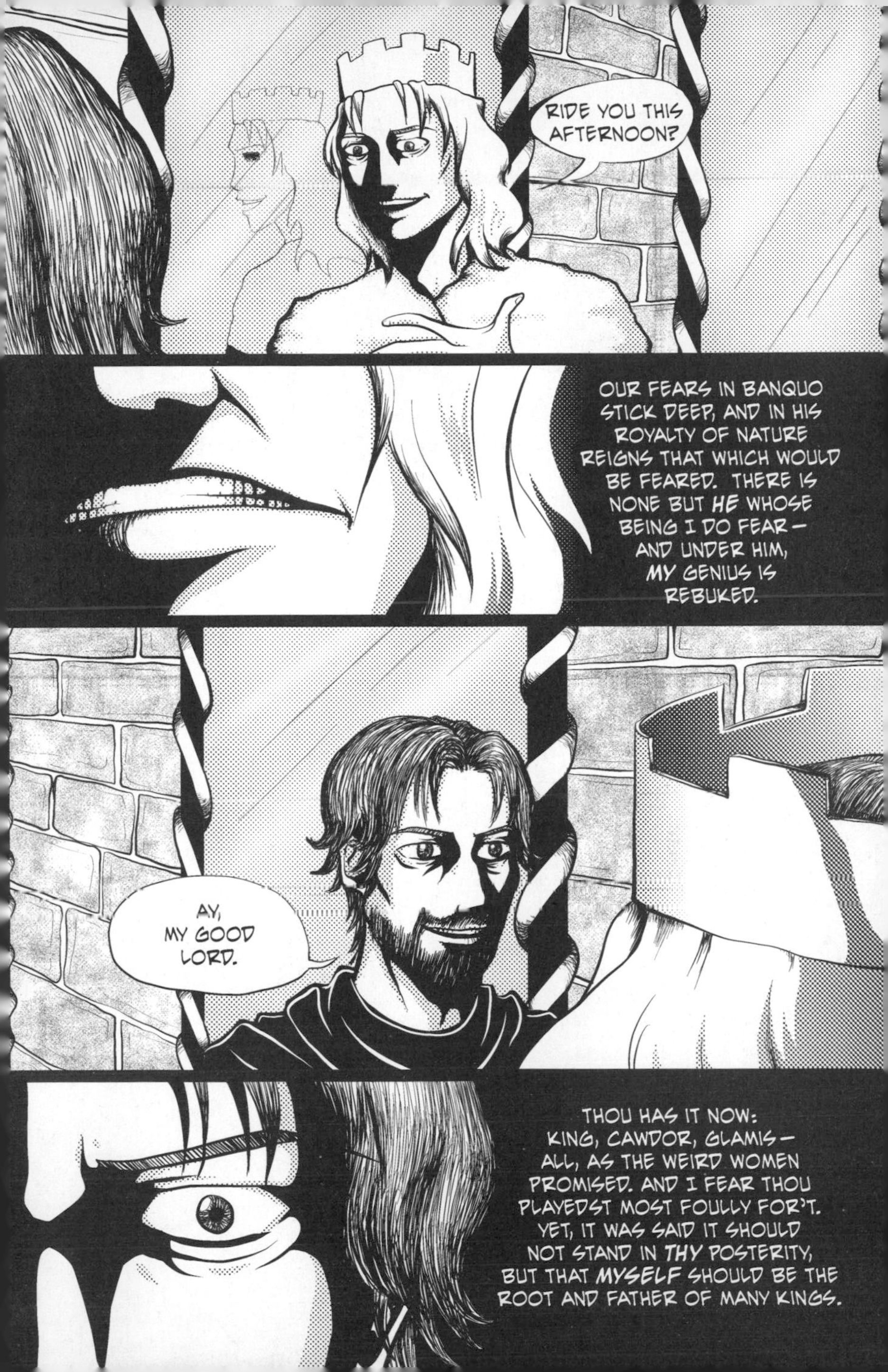
RIDE YOU THIS AFTERNOON?
OUR FEARS IN BANQUO STICK DEEP, AND IN HIS ROYALTY OF NATURE REIGNS THAT WHICH WOULD BE FEARED. THERE IS NONE BUT HE WHOSE BEING I DO FEAR— AND UNDER HIM, MY GENIUS IS REBUKED.
AY, MY GOOD LORD.
THOU HAS IT NOW: KING, CAWDOR, GLAMIS— ALL, AS THE WEIRD WOMEN PROMISED. AND I FEAR THOU PLAYEDST MOST FOULLY FOR'T. YET, IT WAS SAID IT SHOULD NOT STAND IN THY POSTERITY, BUT THAT MYSELF SHOULD BE THE ROOT AND FATHER OF MANY KINGS.

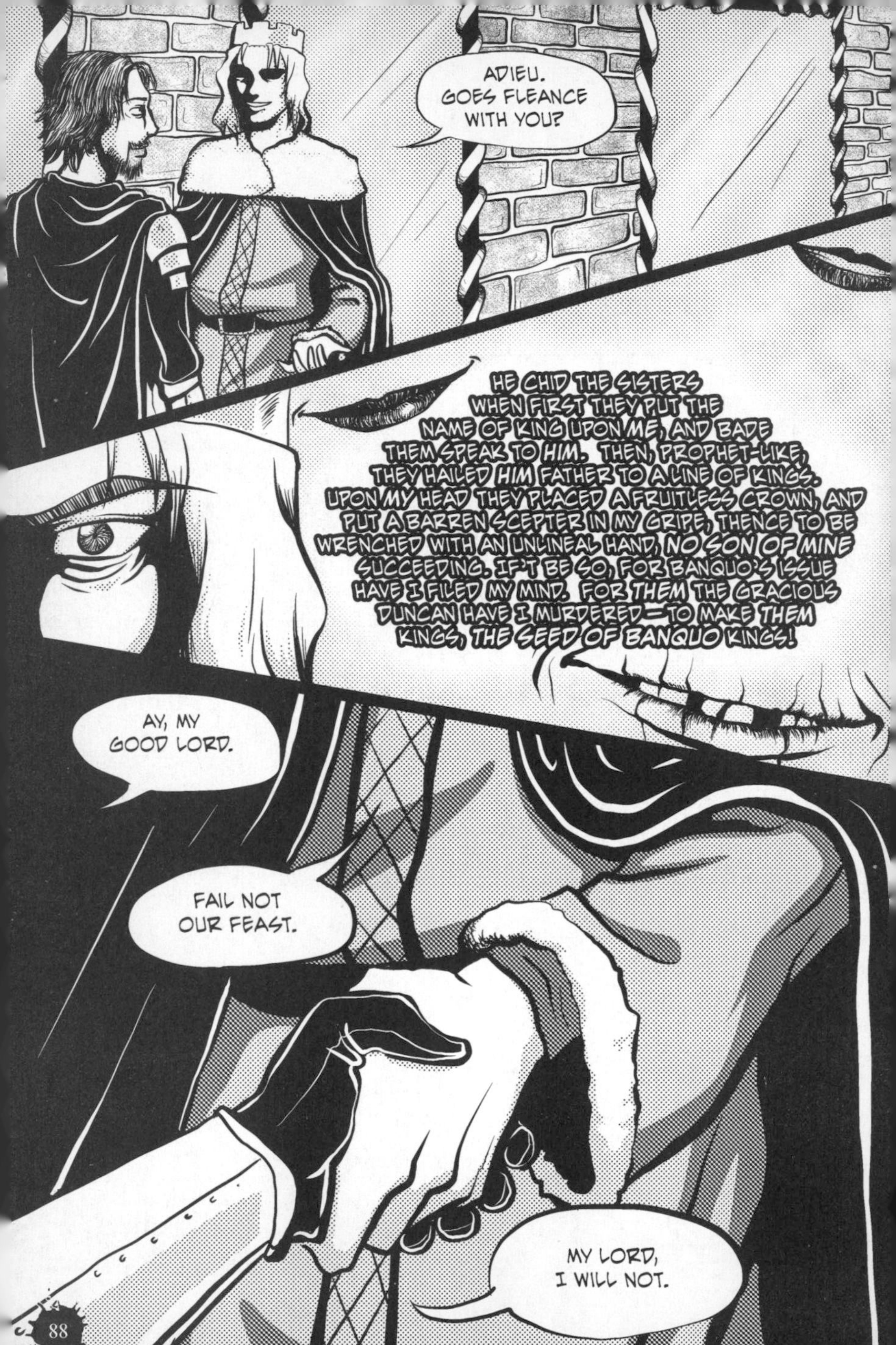
ADIEU. GOES FLEANCE WITH YOU?
HE CHID THE SISTERS WHEN FIRST THEY PUT THE NAME OF KING UPON ME, AND BADE THEM SPEAK TO HIM. THEN, PROPHET-LIKE, THEY HAILED HIM FATHER TO A LINE OF KINGS. UPON MY HEAD THEY PLACED A FRUITLESS CROWN, AND PUT A BARREN SCEPTER IN MY GRIPE, THENCE TO BE WRENCHED WITH AN UNLINEAL HAND, NO SON OF MINE SUCCEEDING. IF'T BE SO, FOR BANQUO'S ISSUE HAVE I FILED MY MIND. FOR THEM THE GRACIOUS DUNCAN HAVE I MURDERED—TO MAKE THEM KINGS, THE SEED OF BANQUO KINGS!
AY, MY GOOD LORD.
FAIL NOT OUR FEAST.
MY LORD, I WILL NOT.

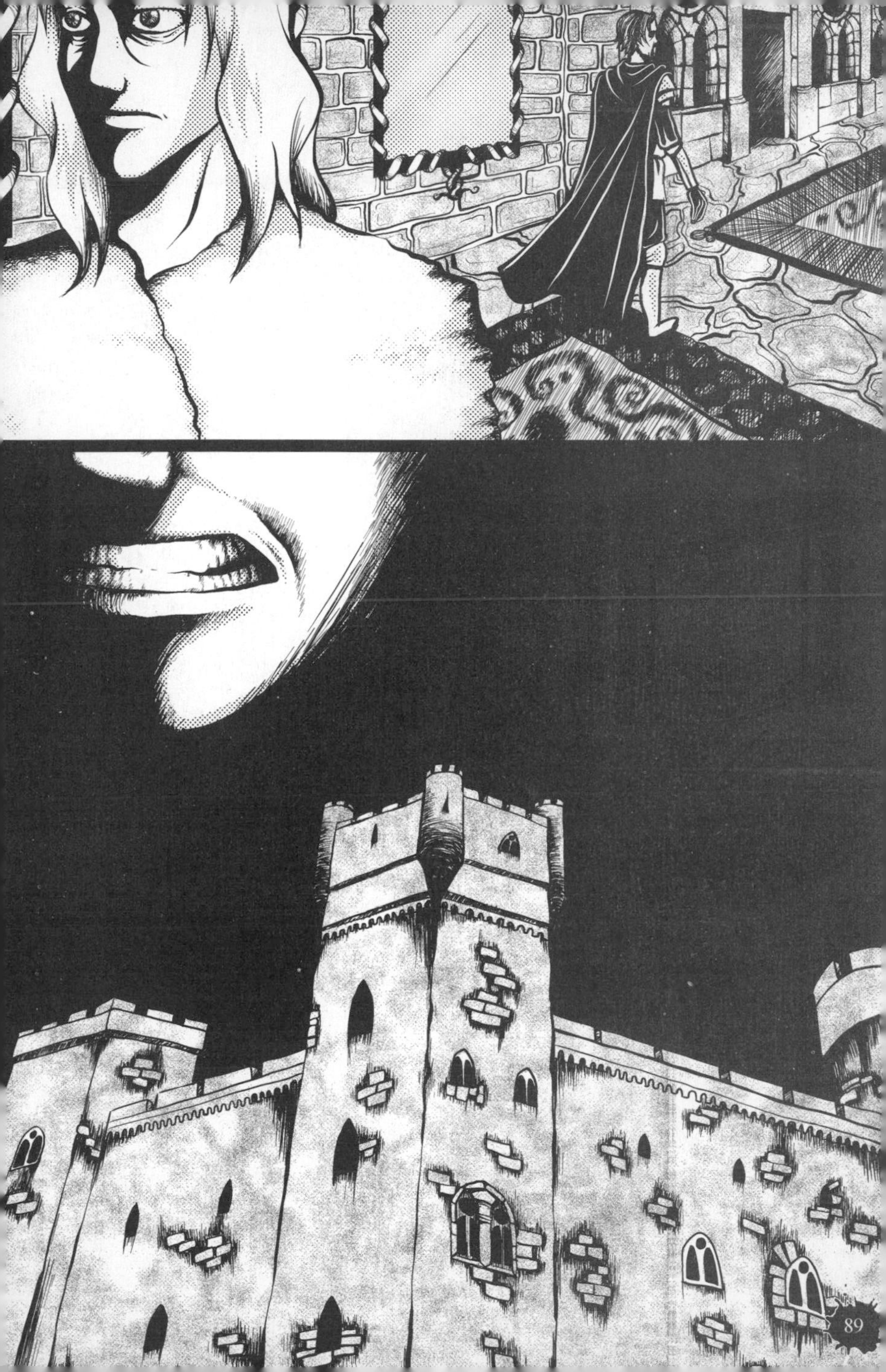

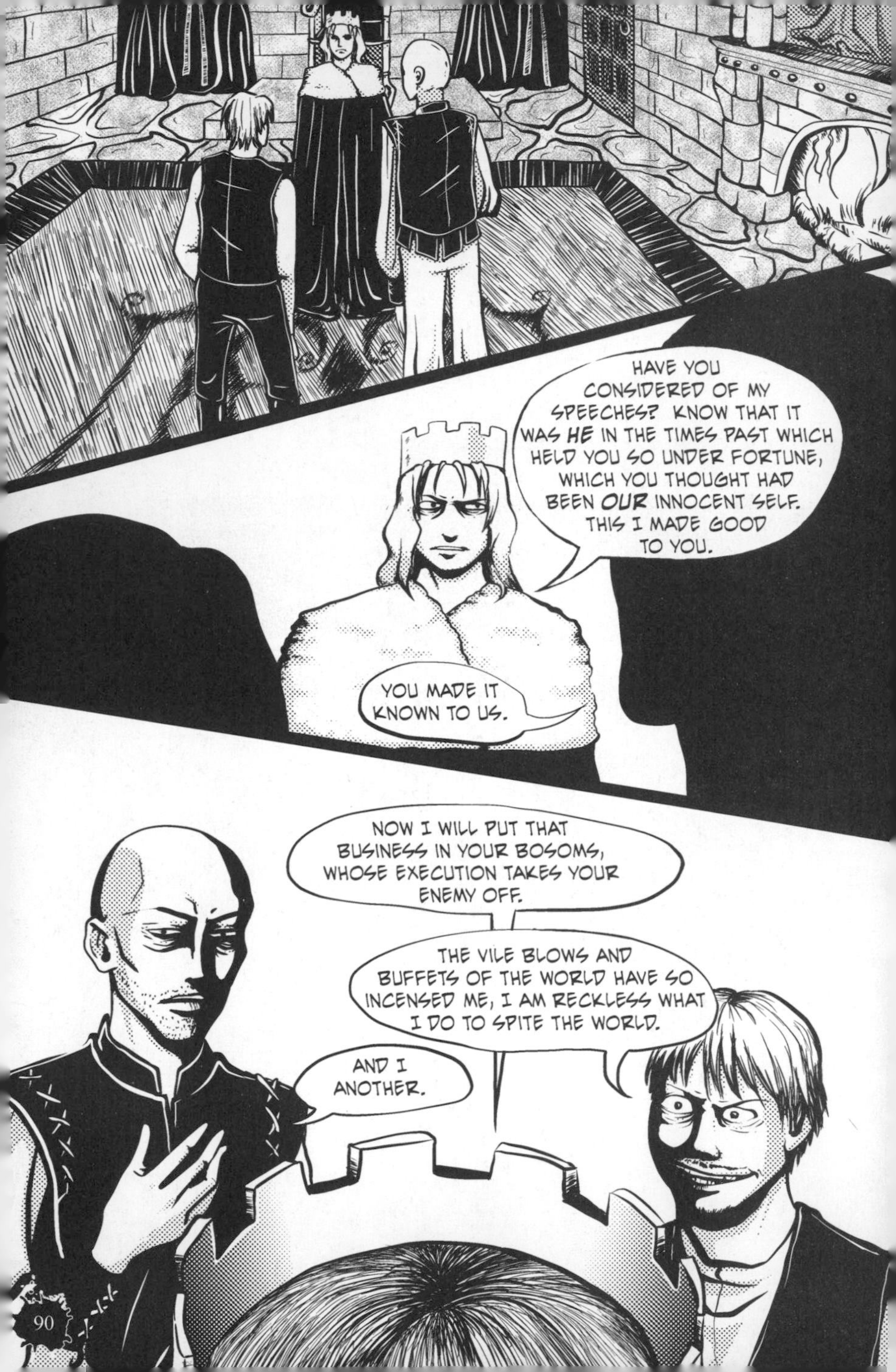
HAVE YOU CONSIDERED OF MY SPEECHES? KNOW THAT IT WAS **HE** IN THE TIMES PAST WHICH HELD YOU SO UNDER FORTUNE, WHICH YOU THOUGHT HAD BEEN **OUR** INNOCENT SELF. THIS I MADE GOOD TO YOU.
YOU MADE IT KNOWN TO US.
NOW I WILL PUT THAT BUSINESS IN YOUR BOSOMS, WHOSE EXECUTION TAKES YOUR ENEMY OFF.
THE VILE BLOWS AND BUFFETS OF THE WORLD HAVE SO INCENSED ME, I AM RECKLESS WHAT I DO TO SPITE THE WORLD.
AND I ANOTHER.

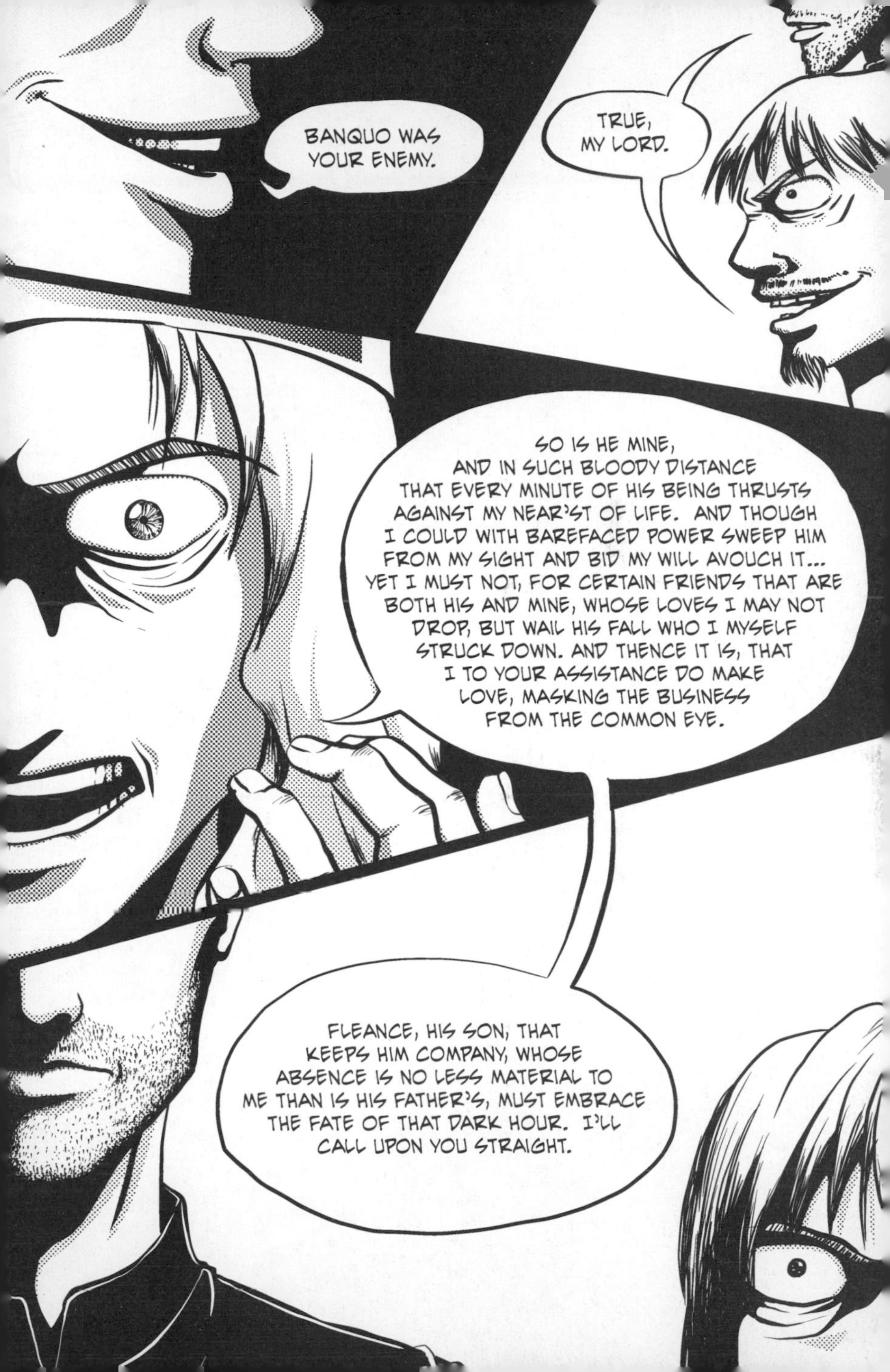
BANQUO WAS YOUR ENEMY.
TRUE, MY LORD.
SO IS HE MINE, AND IN SUCH BLOODY DISTANCE THAT EVERY MINUTE OF HIS BEING THRUSTS AGAINST MY NEAR'ST OF LIFE. AND THOUGH I COULD WITH BAREFACED POWER SWEEP HIM FROM MY SIGHT AND BID MY WILL AVOUCH IT... YET I MUST NOT, FOR CERTAIN FRIENDS THAT ARE BOTH HIS AND MINE, WHOSE LOVES I MAY NOT DROP, BUT WAIL HIS FALL WHO I MYSELF STRUCK DOWN. AND THENCE IT IS, THAT I TO YOUR ASSISTANCE DO MAKE LOVE, MASKING THE BUSINESS FROM THE COMMON EYE.
FLEANCE, HIS SON, THAT KEEPS HIM COMPANY, WHOSE ABSENCE IS NO LESS MATERIAL TO ME THAN IS HIS FATHER'S, MUST EMBRACE THE FATE OF THAT DARK HOUR. I'LL CALL UPON YOU STRAIGHT.

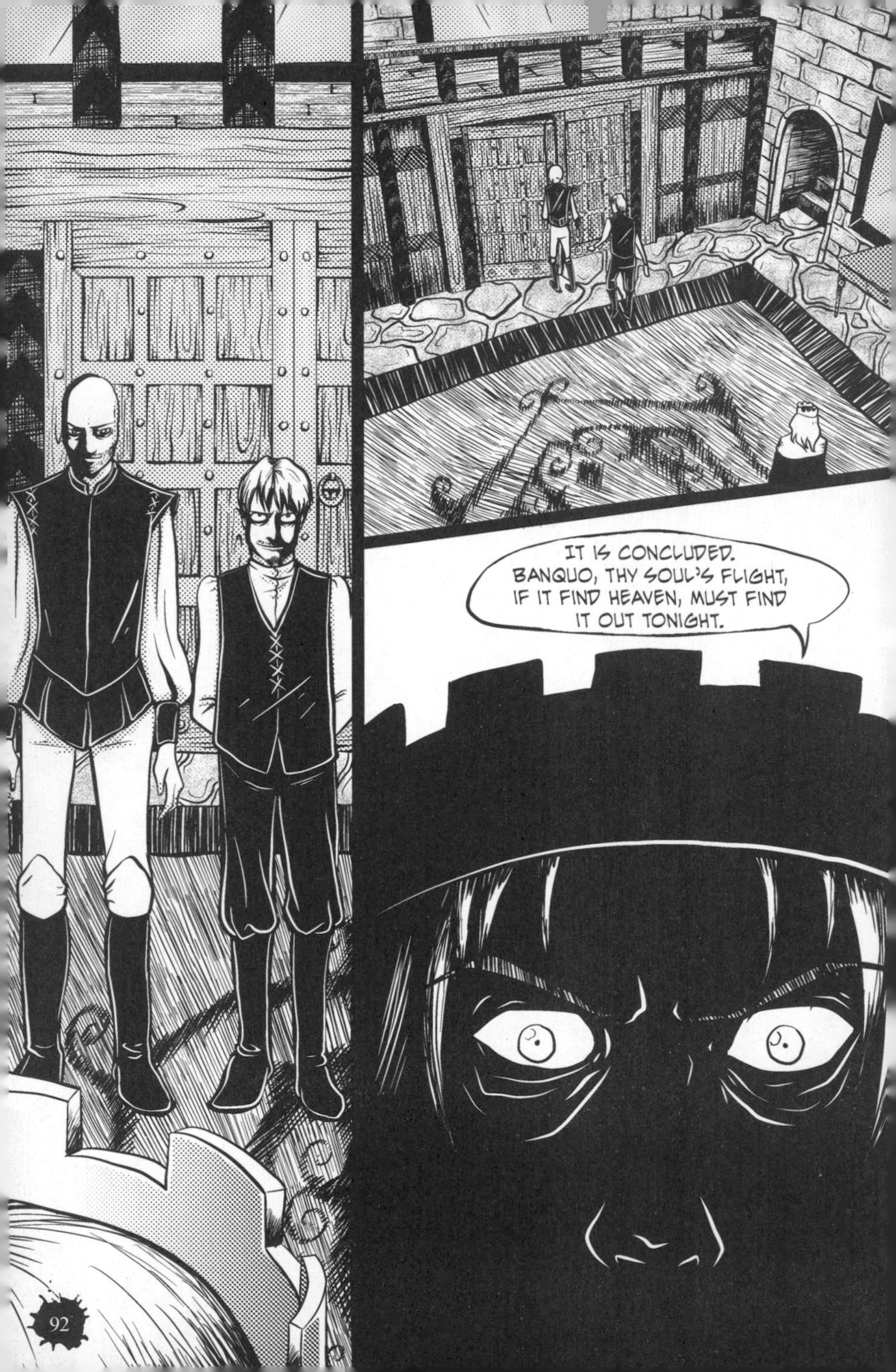
IT IS CONCLUDED. BANQUO, THY SOUL'S FLIGHT, IF IT FIND HEAVEN, MUST FIND IT OUT TONIGHT.

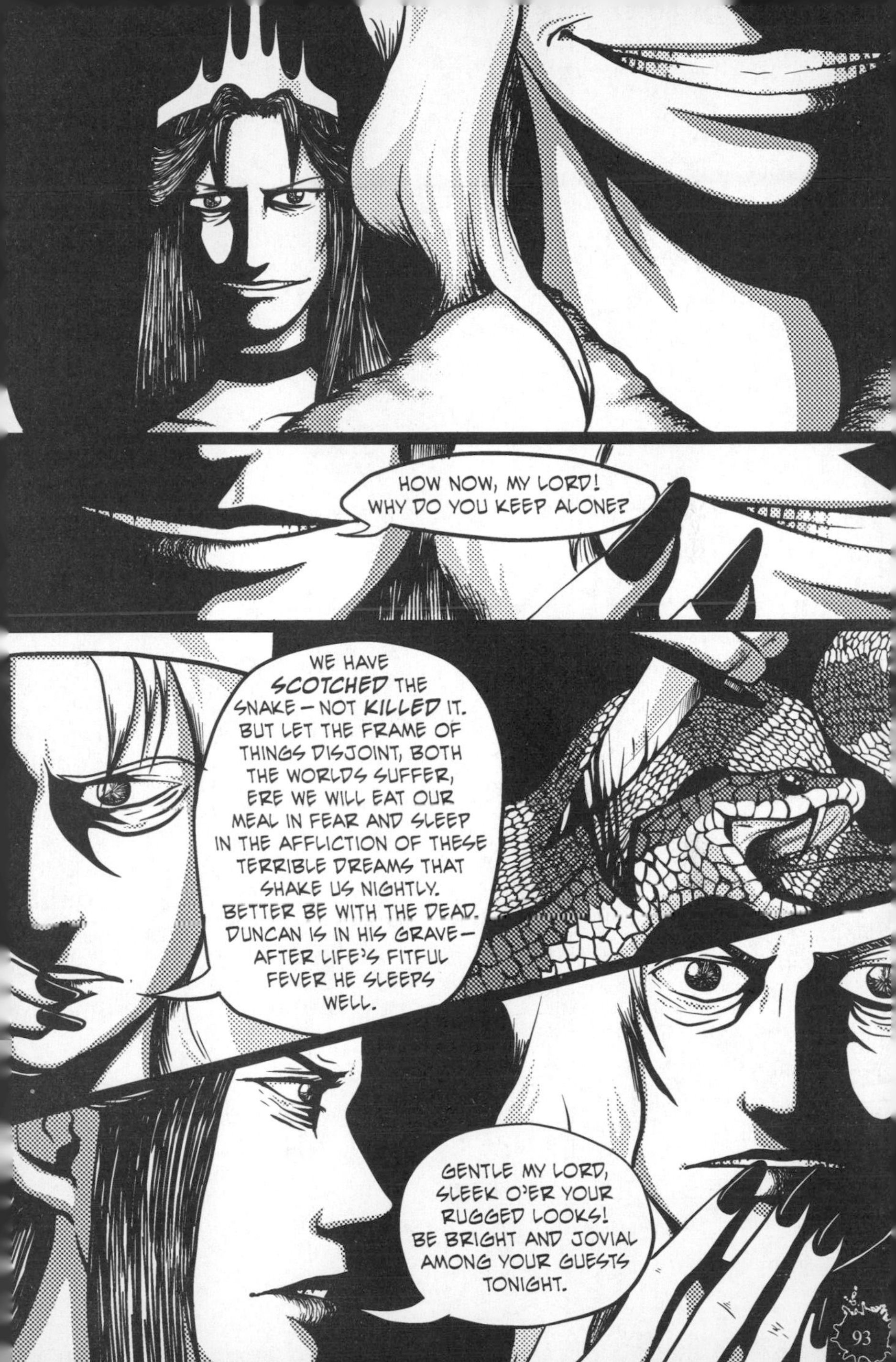
HOW NOW, MY LORD! WHY DO YOU KEEP ALONE?
WE HAVE **SCOTCHED** THE SNAKE—NOT **KILLED** IT. BUT LET THE FRAME OF THINGS DISJOINT, BOTH THE WORLDS SUFFER, ERE WE WILL EAT OUR MEAL IN FEAR AND SLEEP IN THE AFFLICTION OF THESE TERRIBLE DREAMS THAT SHAKE US NIGHTLY. BETTER BE WITH THE DEAD. DUNCAN IS IN HIS GRAVE—AFTER LIFE'S FITFUL FEVER HE SLEEPS WELL.
GENTLE MY LORD, SLEEK O'ER YOUR RUGGED LOOKS! BE BRIGHT AND JOVIAL AMONG YOUR GUESTS TONIGHT.

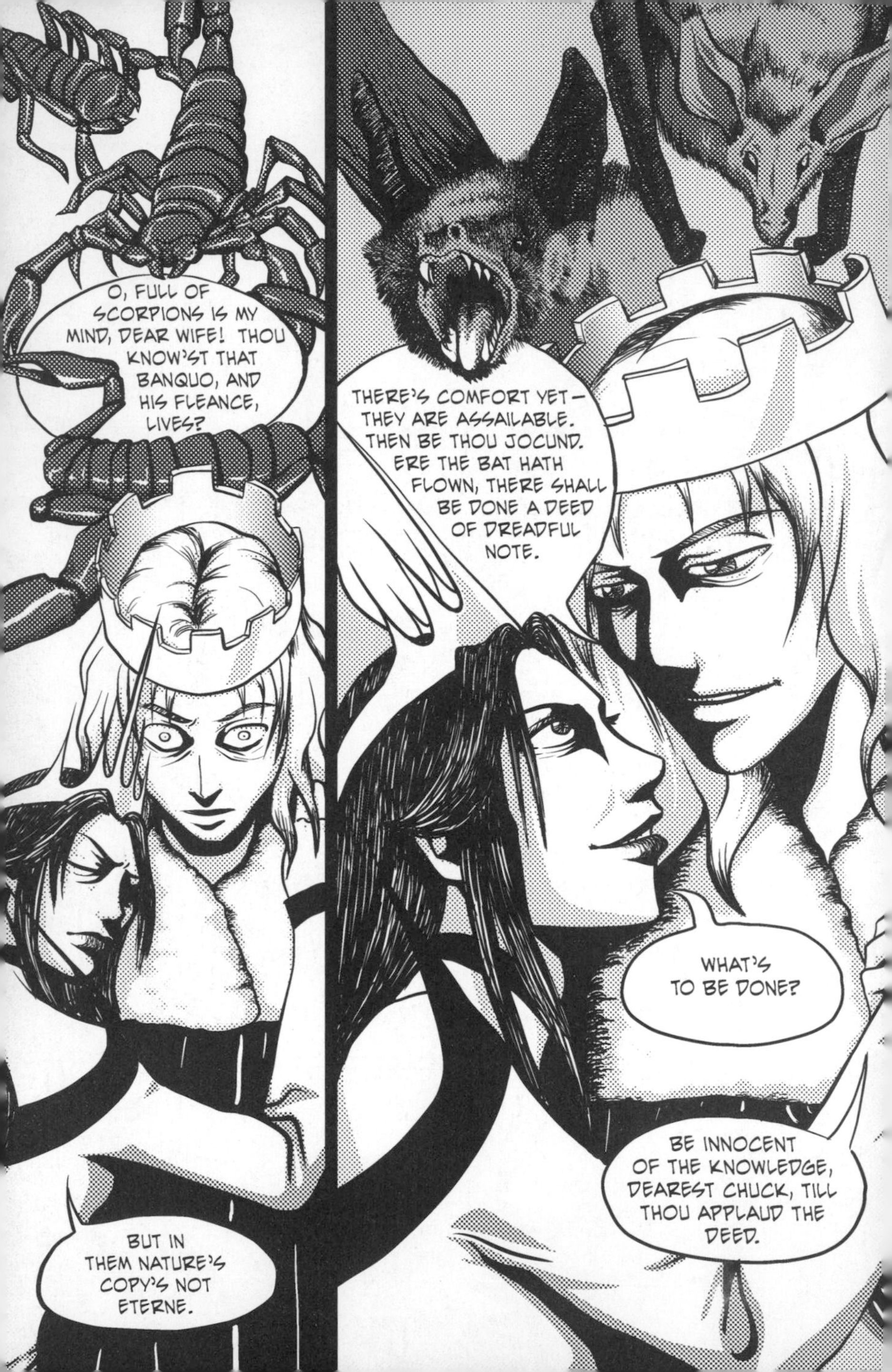
O, FULL OF SCORPIONS IS MY MIND, DEAR WIFE! THOU KNOW'ST THAT BANQUO, AND HIS FLEANCE, LIVES?
BUT IN THEM NATURE'S COPY'S NOT ETERNE.
THERE'S COMFORT YET— THEY ARE ASSAILABLE. THEN BE THOU JOCUND. ERE THE BAT HATH FLOWN, THERE SHALL BE DONE A DEED OF DREADFUL NOTE.
WHAT'S TO BE DONE?
BE INNOCENT OF THE KNOWLEDGE, DEAREST CHUCK, TILL THOU APPLAUD THE DEED.

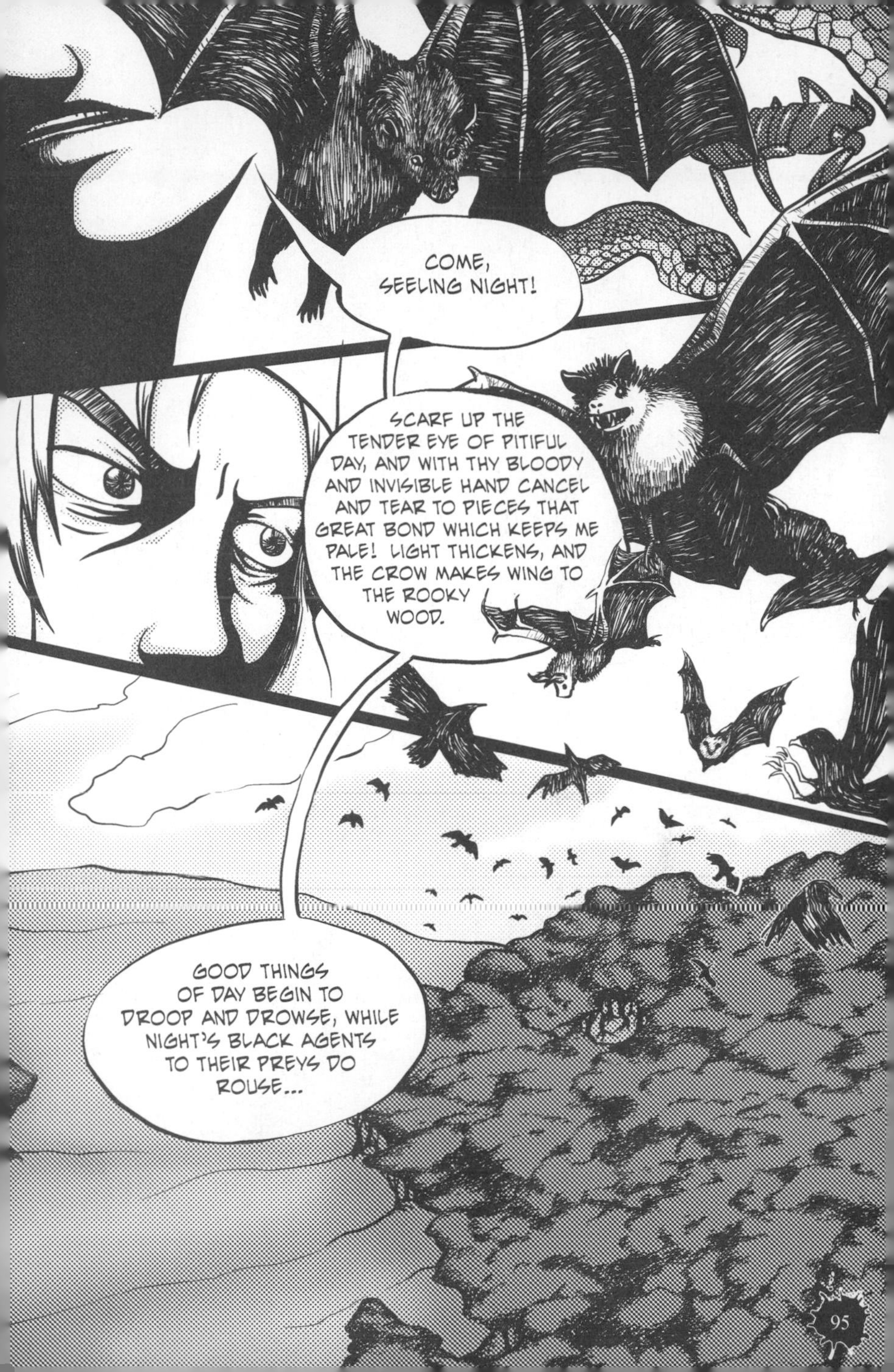
COME, SEELING NIGHT!
SCARF UP THE TENDER EYE OF PITIFUL DAY, AND WITH THY BLOODY AND INVISIBLE HAND CANCEL AND TEAR TO PIECES THAT GREAT BOND WHICH KEEPS ME PALE! LIGHT THICKENS, AND THE CROW MAKES WING TO THE ROOKY WOOD.
GOOD THINGS OF DAY BEGIN TO DROOP AND DROWSE, WHILE NIGHT'S BLACK AGENTS TO THEIR PREYS DO ROUSE...

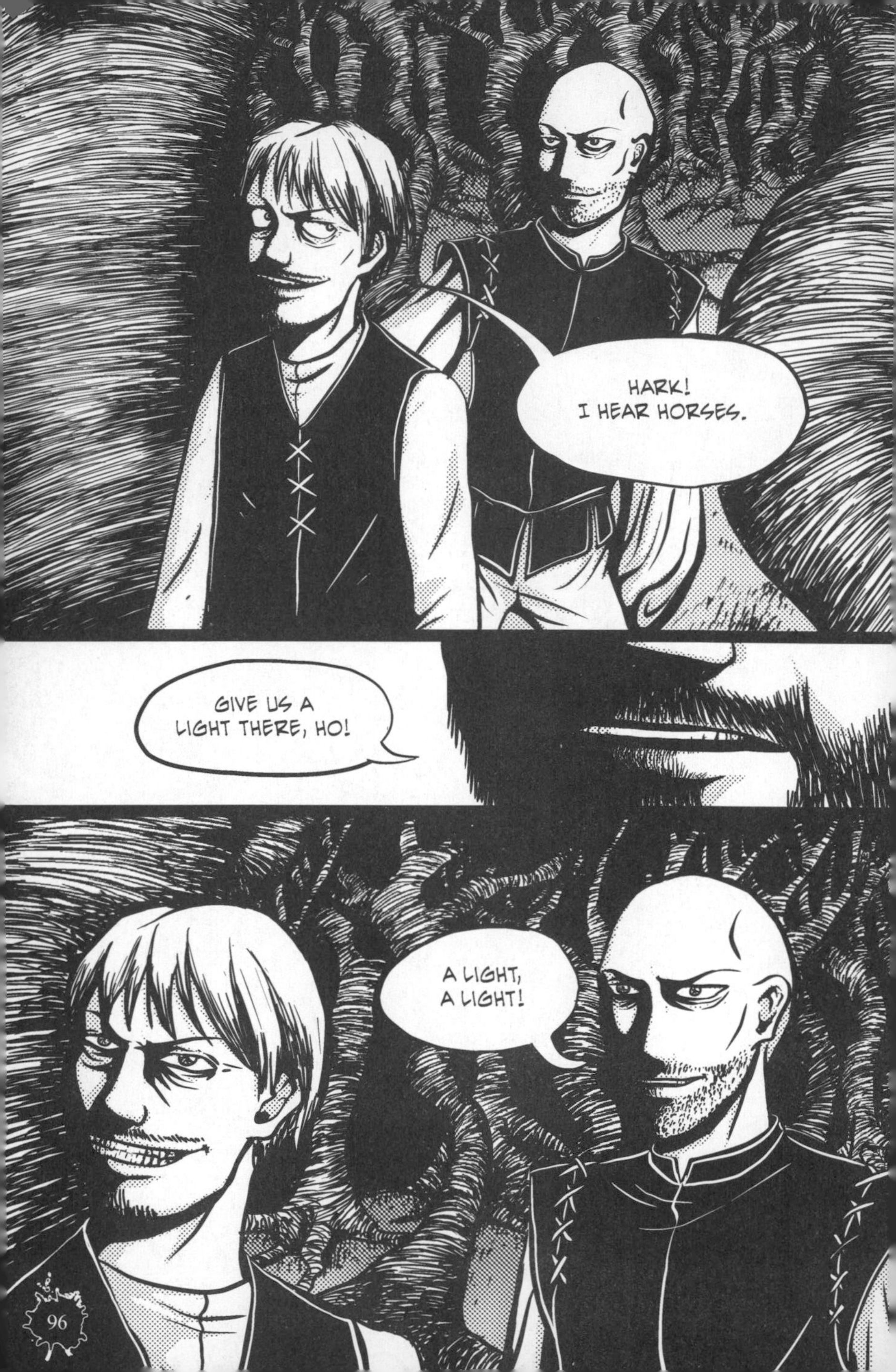
HARK!
I HEAR HORSES.
GIVE US A
LIGHT THERE, HO!
A LIGHT,
A LIGHT!

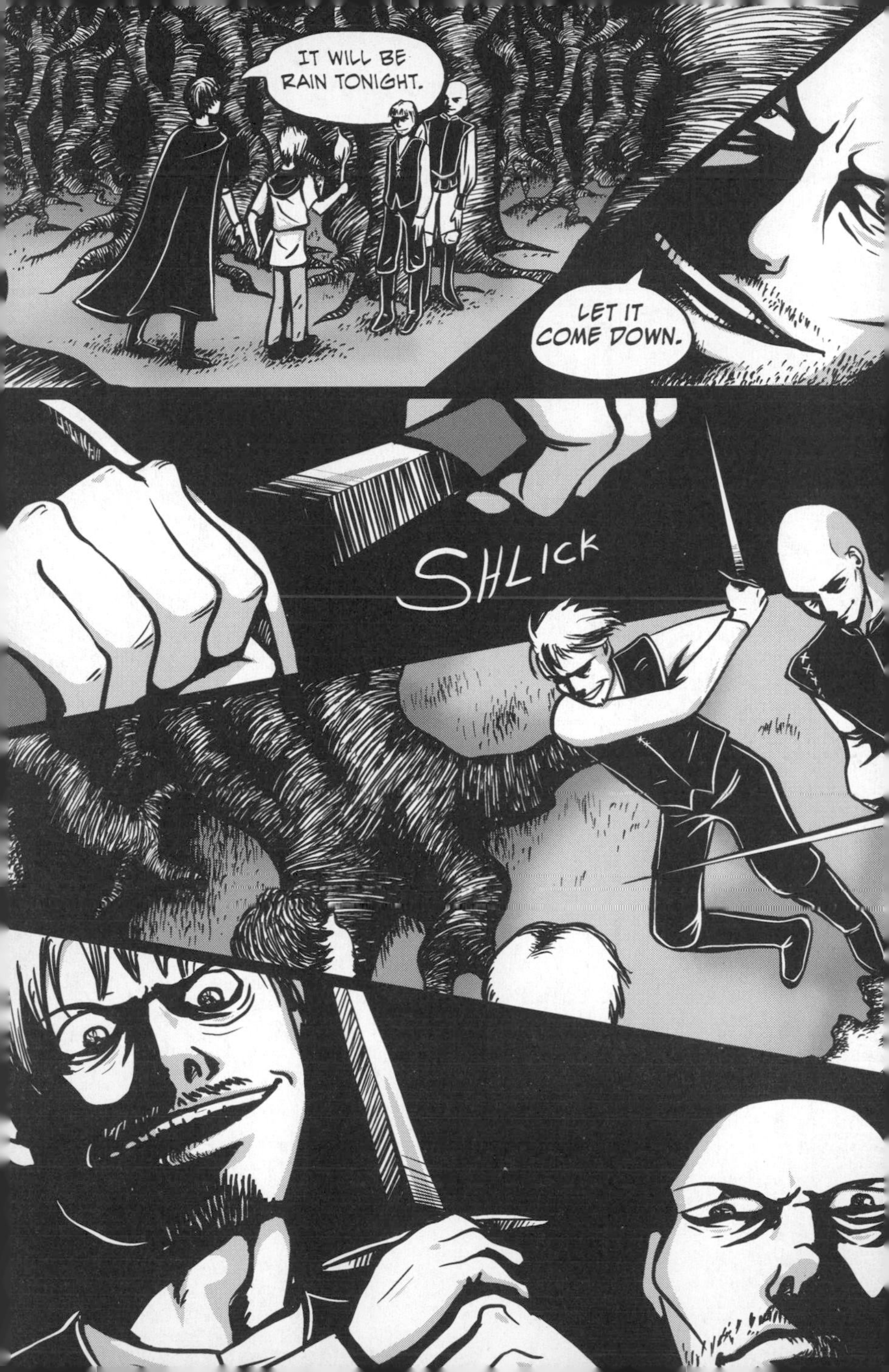
IT WILL BE RAIN TONIGHT.
LET IT COME DOWN.
SHLICK

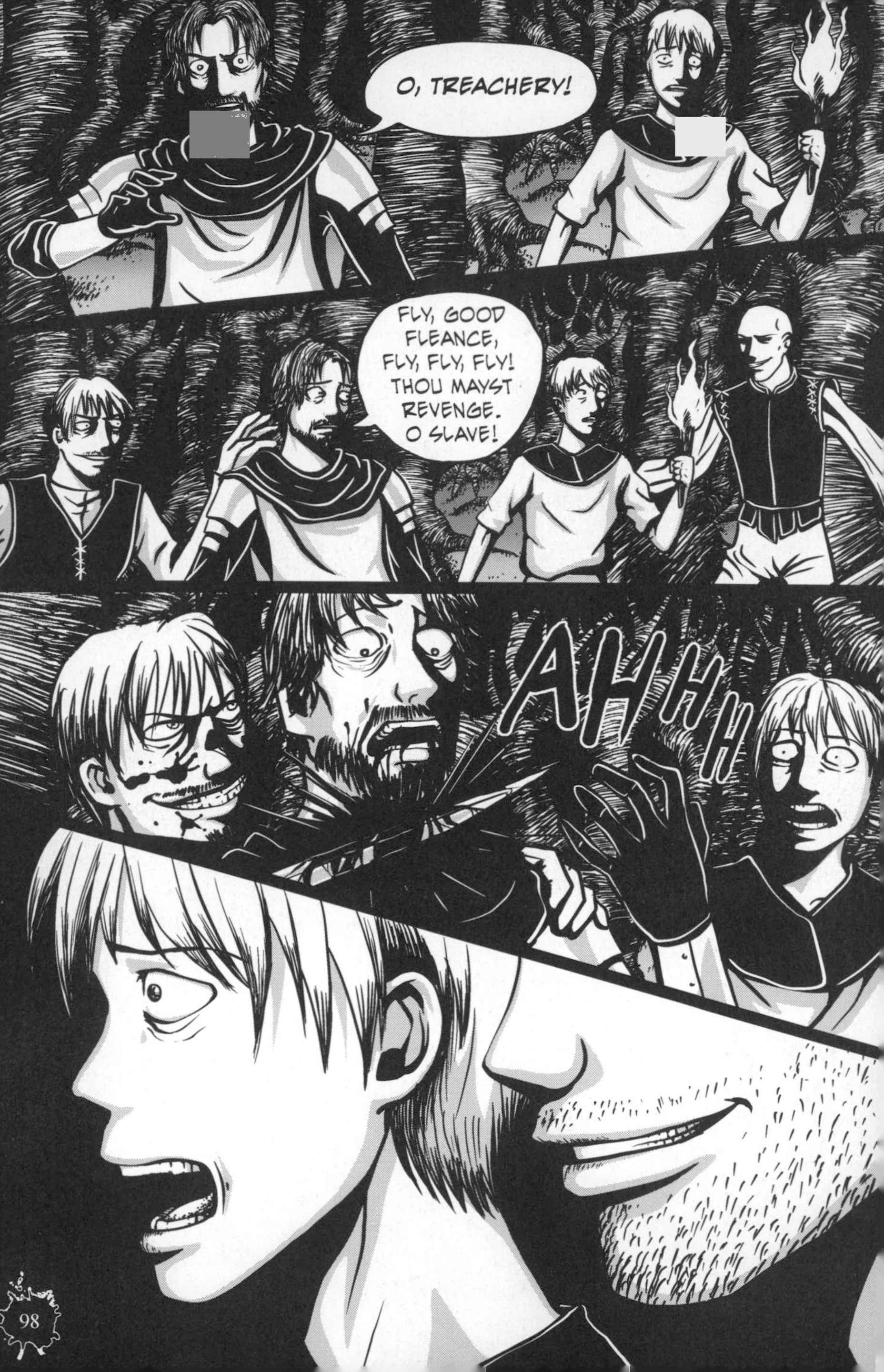
O, TREACHERY!
FLY, GOOD FLEANCE, FLY, FLY, FLY! THOU MAYST REVENGE. O SLAVE!
AHHHH

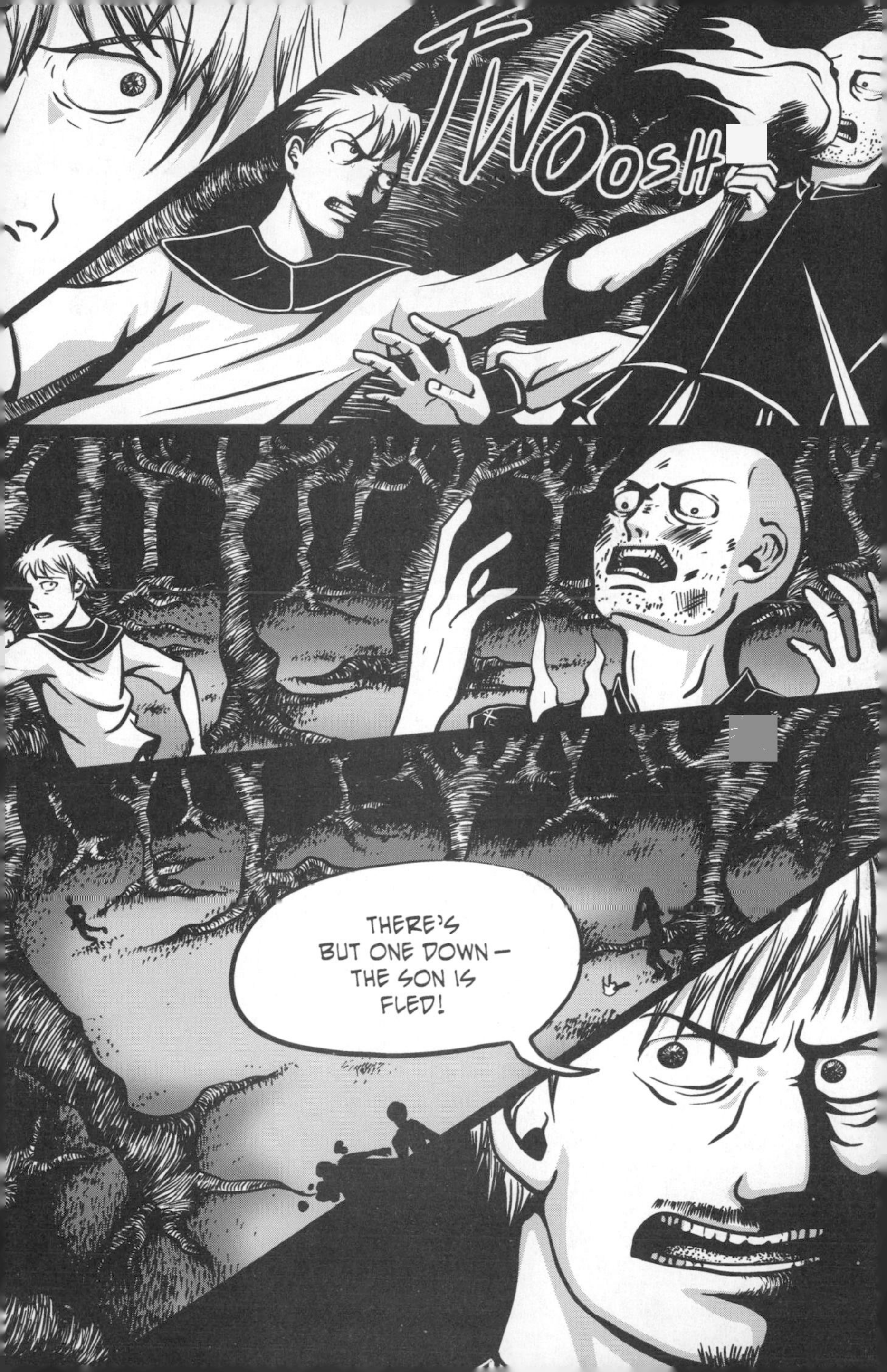
TWOOSH
THERE'S BUT ONE DOWN— THE SON IS FLED!

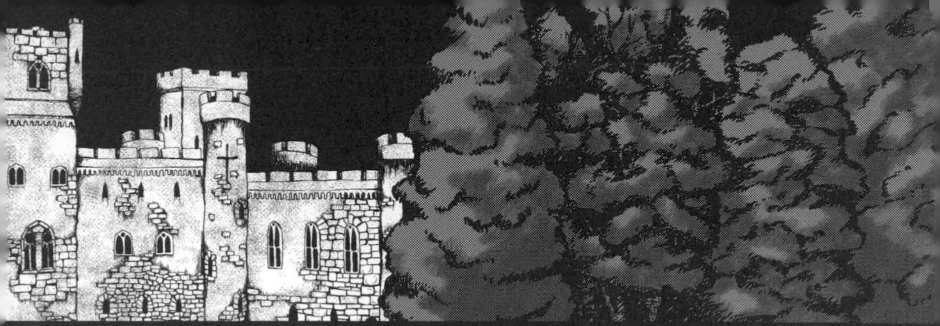
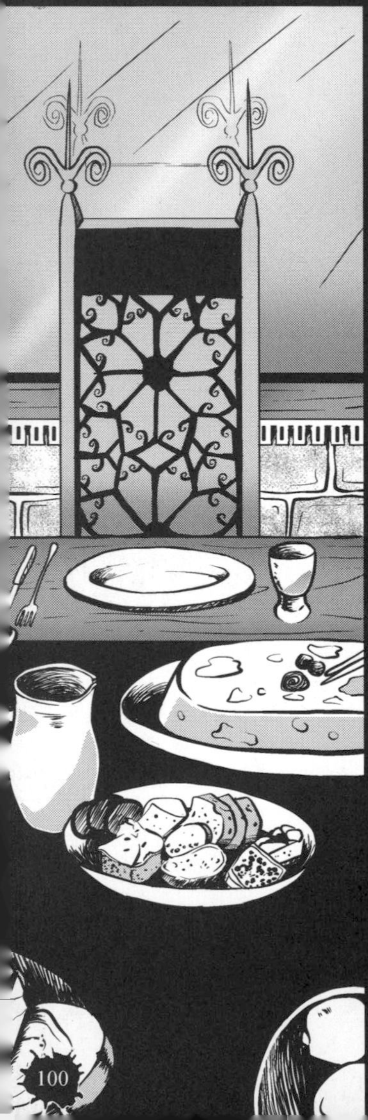
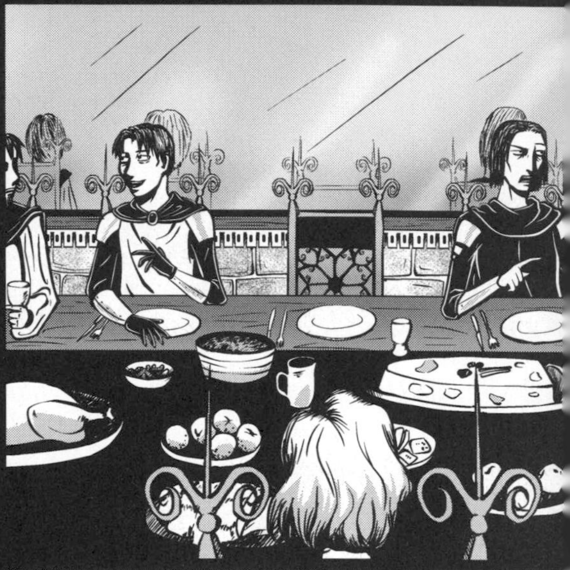
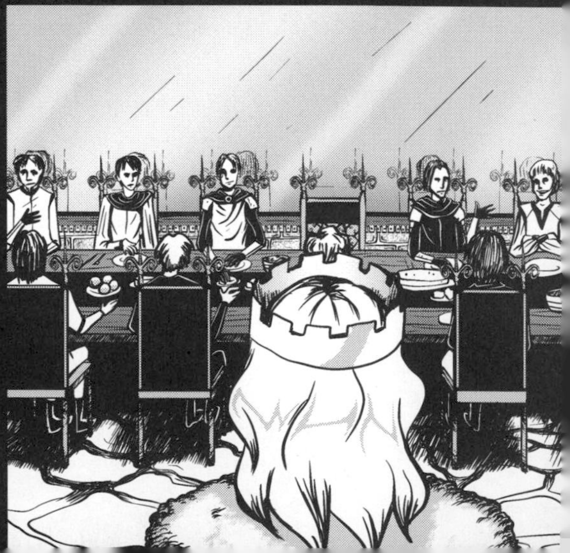

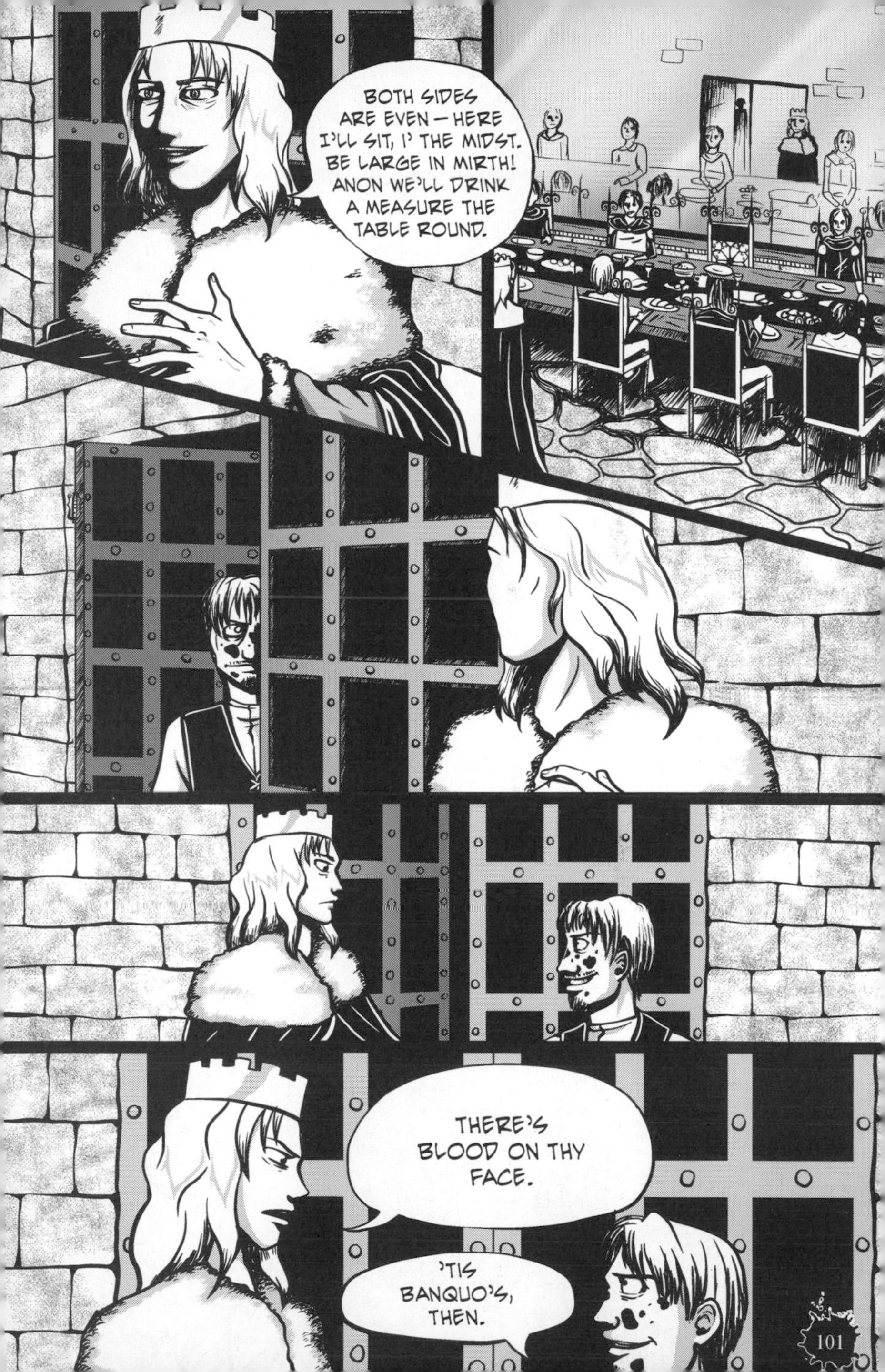
BOTH SIDES ARE EVEN — HERE I'LL SIT, I' THE MIDST. BE LARGE IN MIRTH! ANON WE'LL DRINK A MEASURE THE TABLE ROUND.
THERE'S BLOOD ON THY FACE.
'TIS BANQUO'S, THEN.

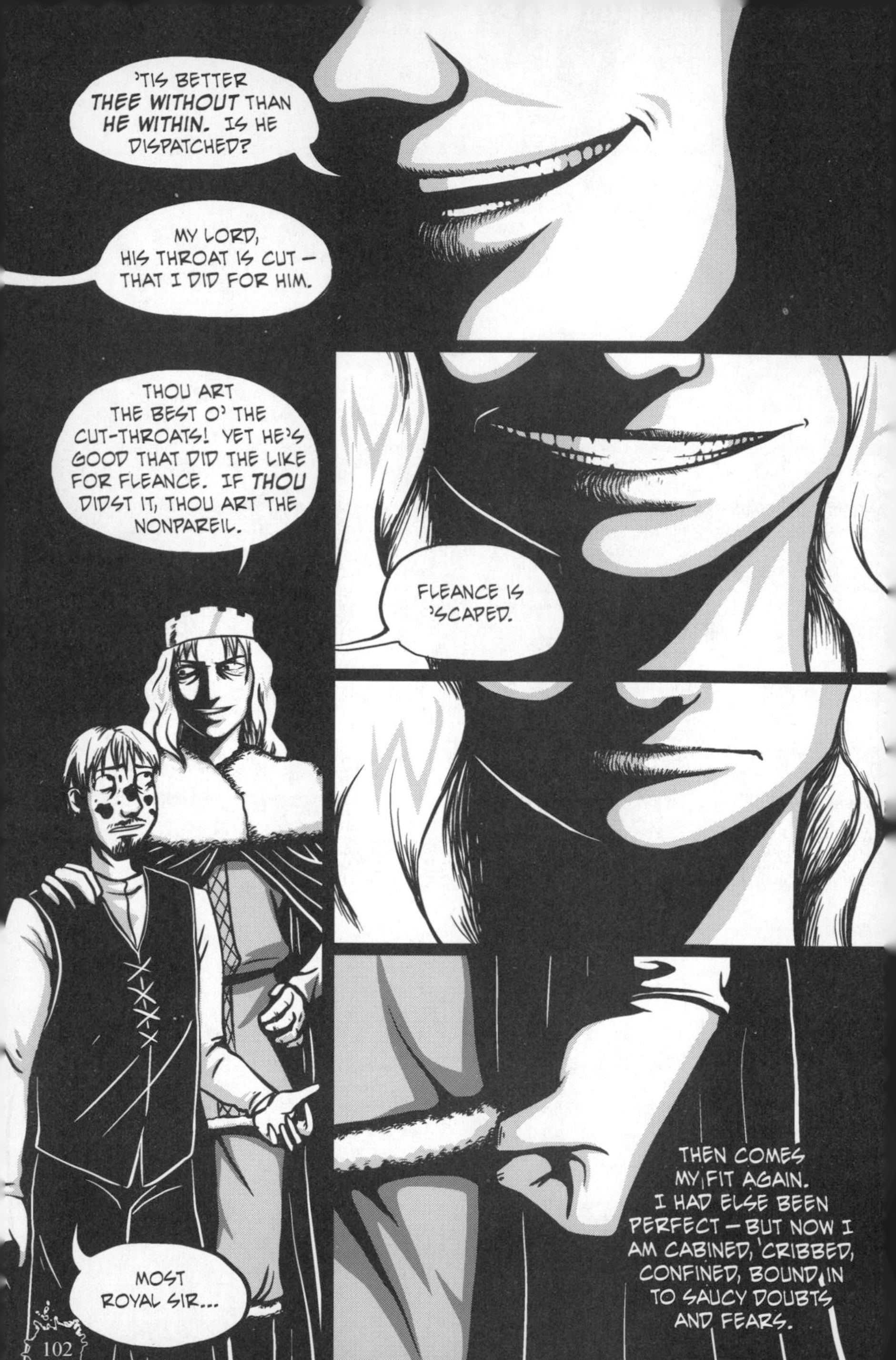
'TIS BETTER THEE WITHOUT THAN HE WITHIN. IS HE DISPATCHED?
MY LORD, HIS THROAT IS CUT — THAT I DID FOR HIM.
THOU ART THE BEST O' THE CUT-THROATS! YET HE'S GOOD THAT DID THE LIKE FOR FLEANCE. IF THOU DIDST IT, THOU ART THE NONPAREIL.
MOST ROYAL SIR...
FLEANCE IS 'SCAPED.
THEN COMES MY FIT AGAIN. I HAD ELSE BEEN PERFECT — BUT NOW I AM CABINED, CRIBBED, CONFINED, BOUND IN TO SAUCY DOUBTS AND FEARS.

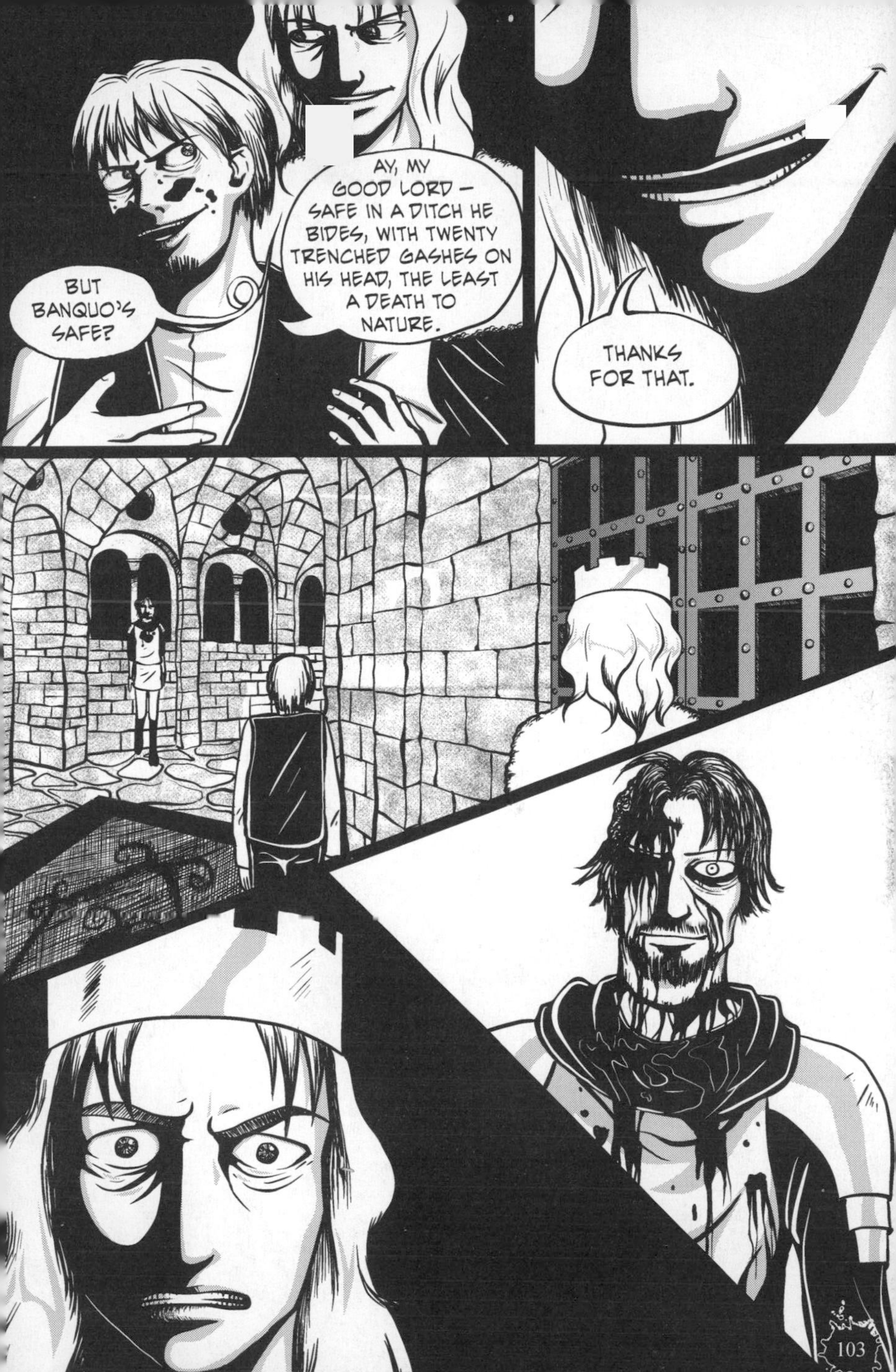
BUT BANQUO'S SAFE?
AY, MY GOOD LORD — SAFE IN A DITCH HE BIDES, WITH TWENTY TRENCHED GASHES ON HIS HEAD, THE LEAST A DEATH TO NATURE.
THANKS FOR THAT.

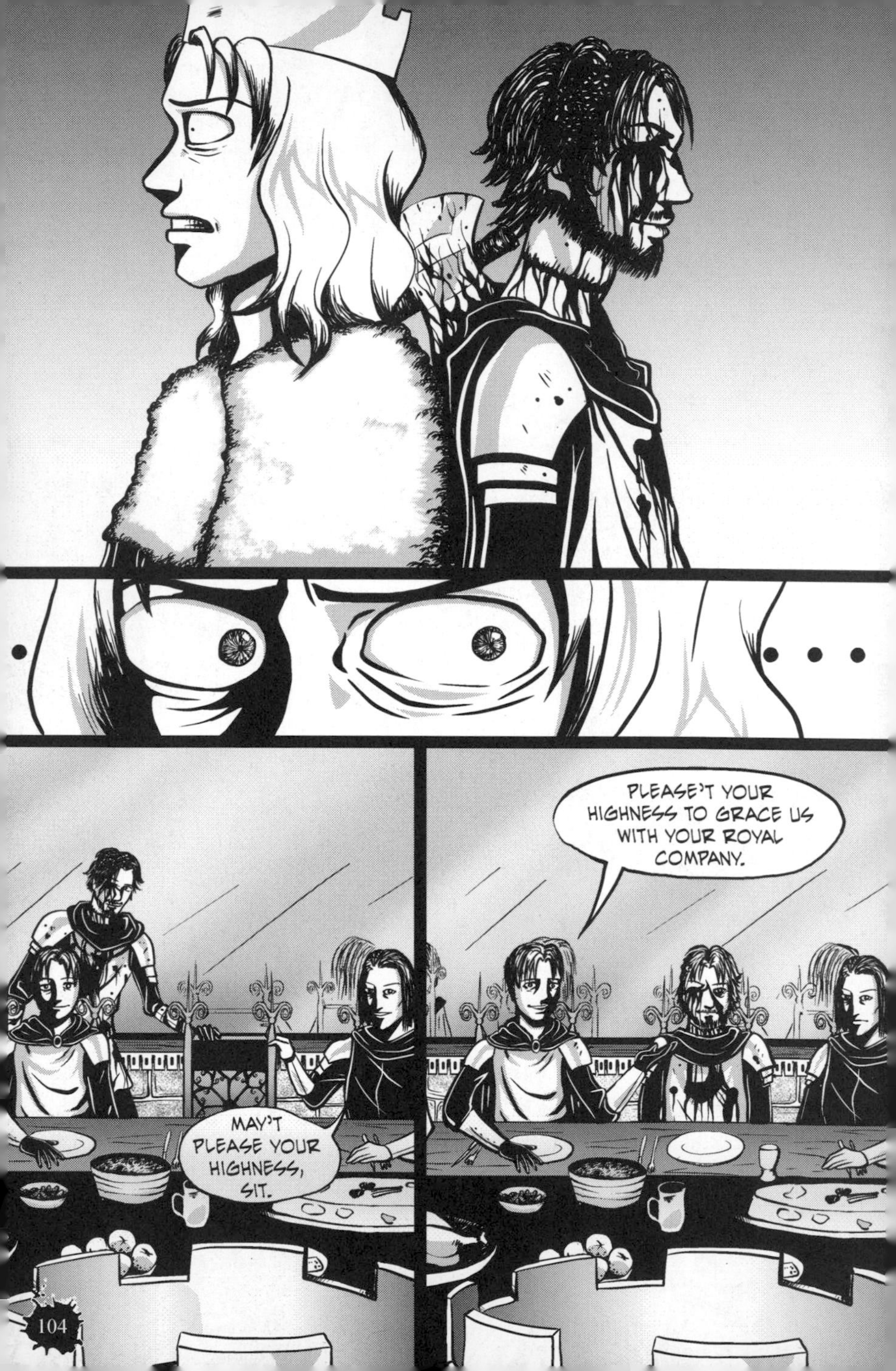
MAY'T PLEASE YOUR HIGHNESS, SIT.
PLEASE'T YOUR HIGHNESS TO GRACE US WITH YOUR ROYAL COMPANY.

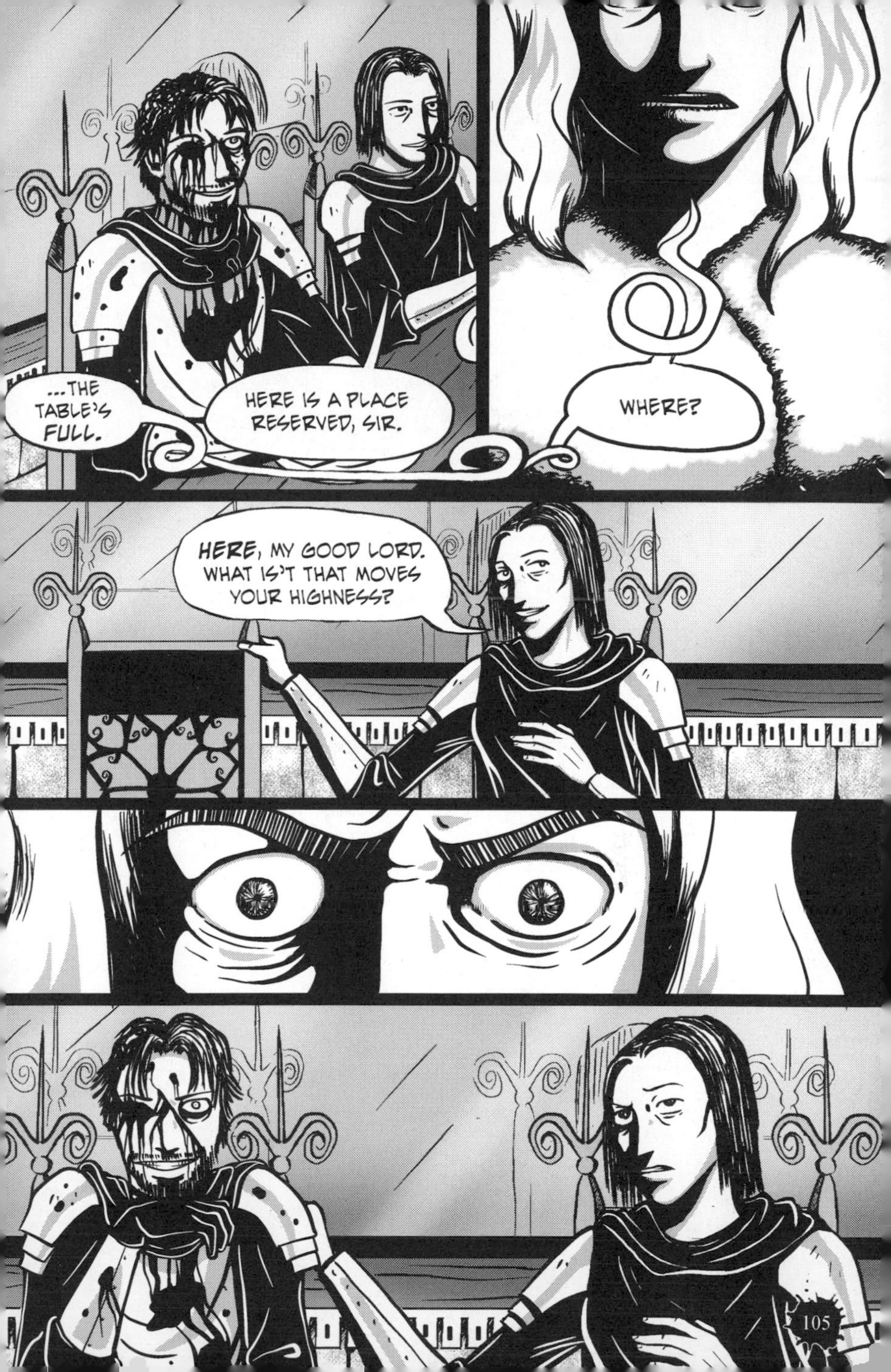
...THE TABLE'S FULL.
HERE IS A PLACE RESERVED, SIR.
WHERE?
HERE, MY GOOD LORD. WHAT IS'T THAT MOVES YOUR HIGHNESS?

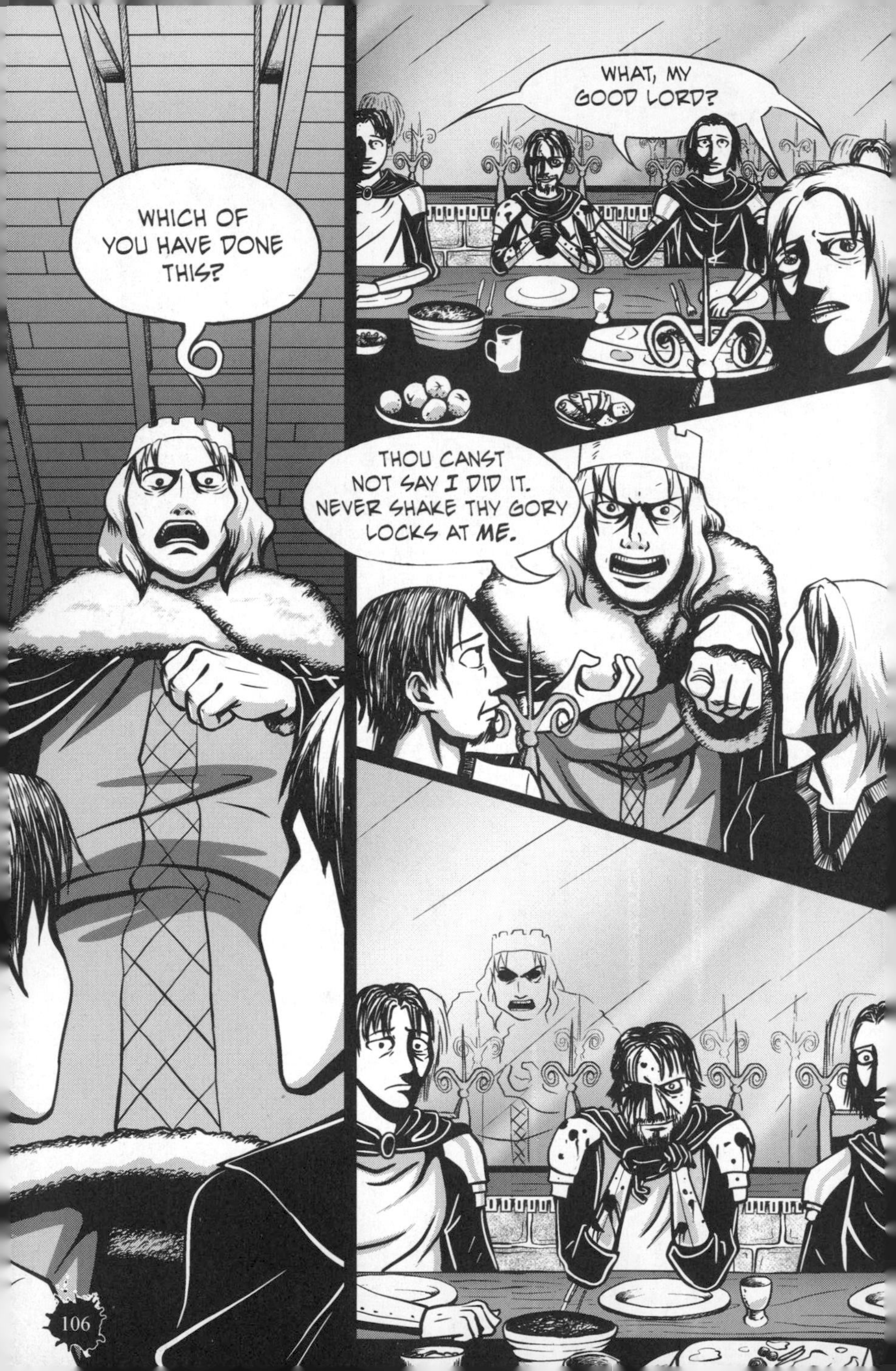
WHICH OF YOU HAVE DONE THIS?
WHAT, MY GOOD LORD?
THOU CANST NOT SAY I DID IT. NEVER SHAKE THY GORY LOCKS AT ME.

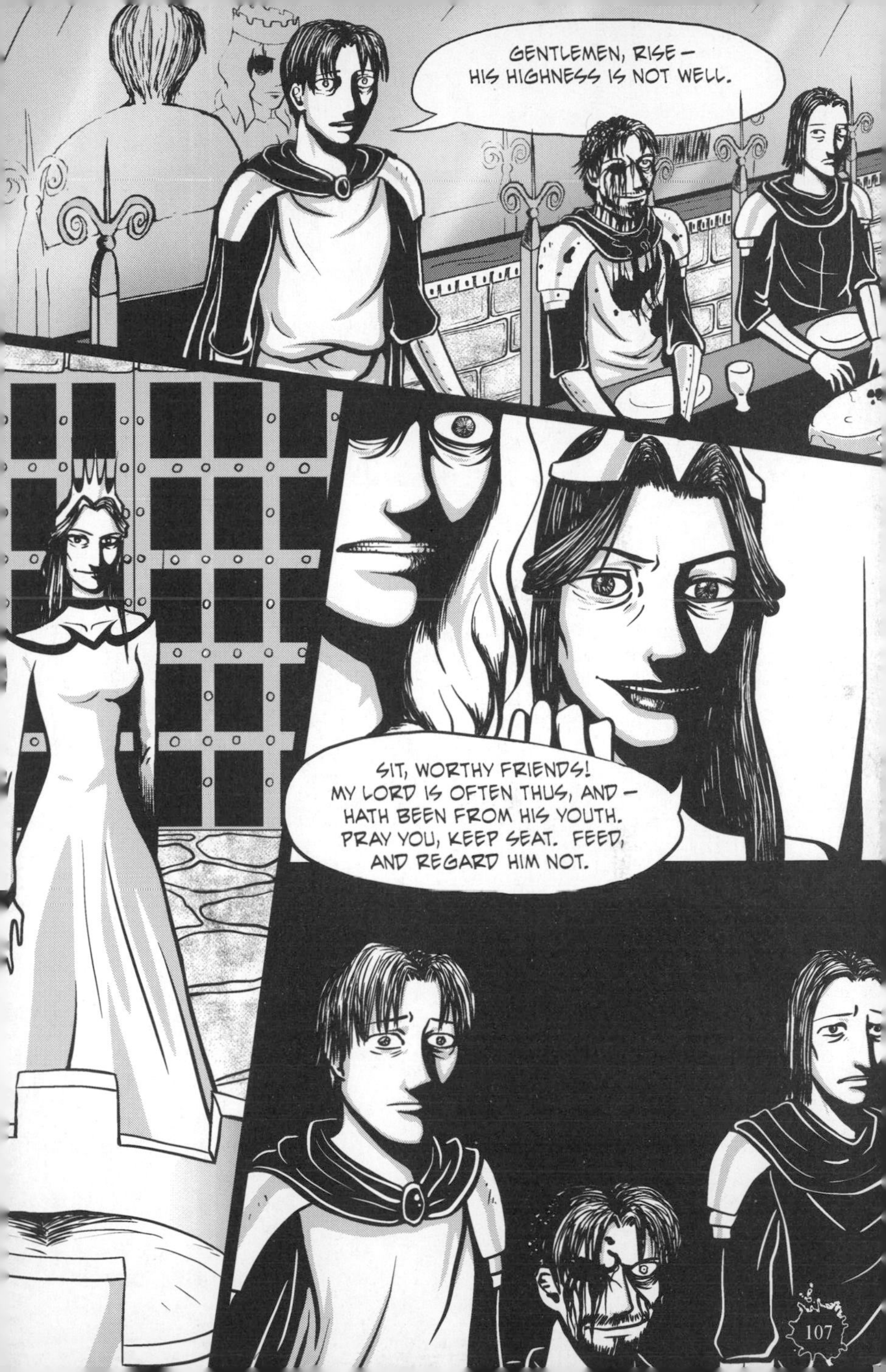
GENTLEMEN, RISE — HIS HIGHNESS IS NOT WELL.
SIT, WORTHY FRIENDS! MY LORD IS OFTEN THUS, AND — HATH BEEN FROM HIS YOUTH. PRAY YOU, KEEP SEAT. FEED, AND REGARD HIM NOT.

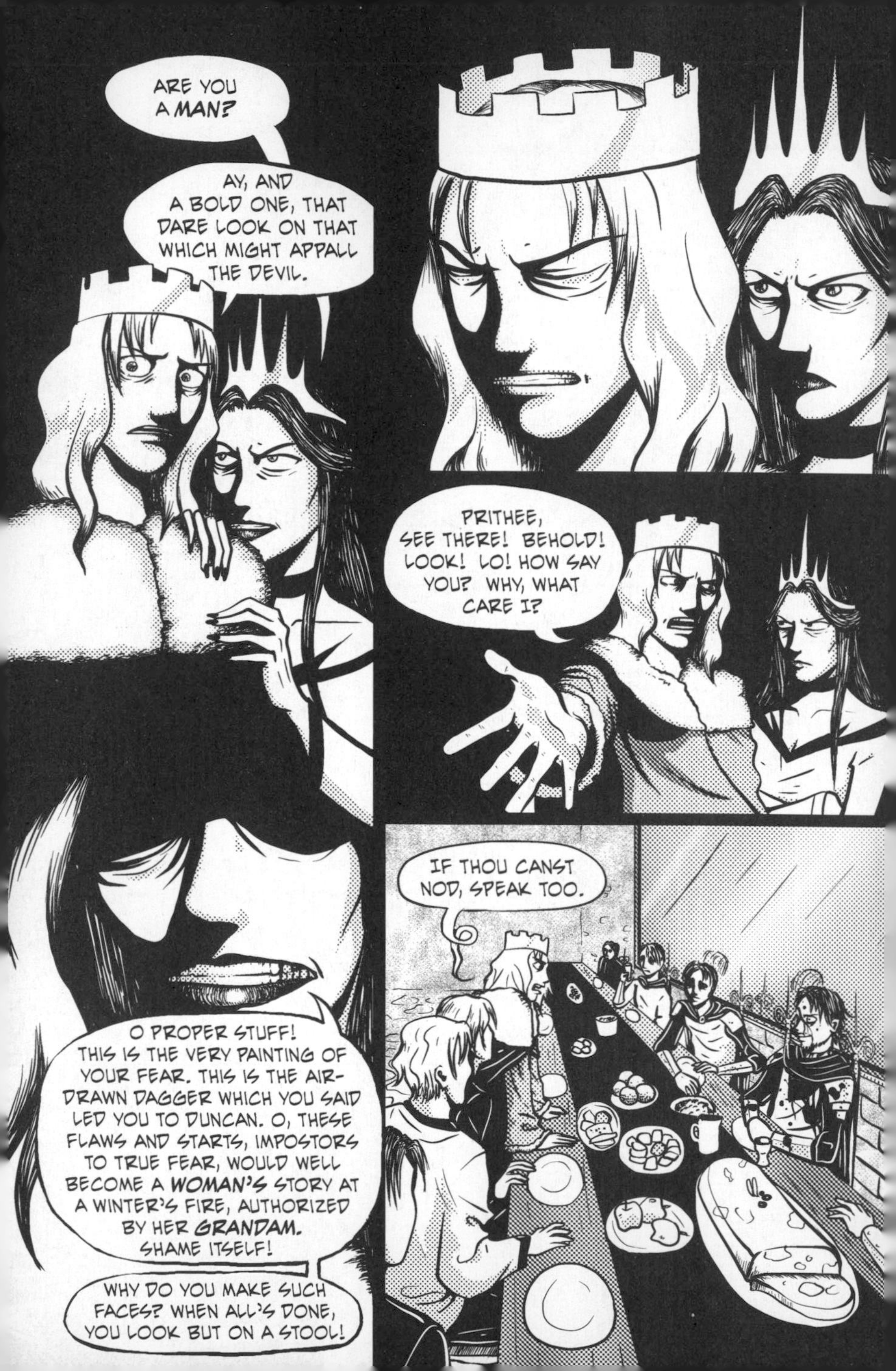
ARE YOU A MAN?
AY, AND A BOLD ONE, THAT DARE LOOK ON THAT WHICH MIGHT APPALL THE DEVIL.
O PROPER STUFF! THIS IS THE VERY PAINTING OF YOUR FEAR. THIS IS THE AIR-DRAWN DAGGER WHICH YOU SAID LED YOU TO DUNCAN. O, THESE FLAWS AND STARTS, IMPOSTORS TO TRUE FEAR, WOULD WELL BECOME A WOMAN'S STORY AT A WINTER'S FIRE, AUTHORIZED BY HER GRANDAM. SHAME ITSELF!
WHY DO YOU MAKE SUCH FACES? WHEN ALL'S DONE, YOU LOOK BUT ON A STOOL!
PRITHEE, SEE THERE! BEHOLD! LOOK! LO! HOW SAY YOU? WHY, WHAT CARE I?
IF THOU CANST NOD, SPEAK TOO.

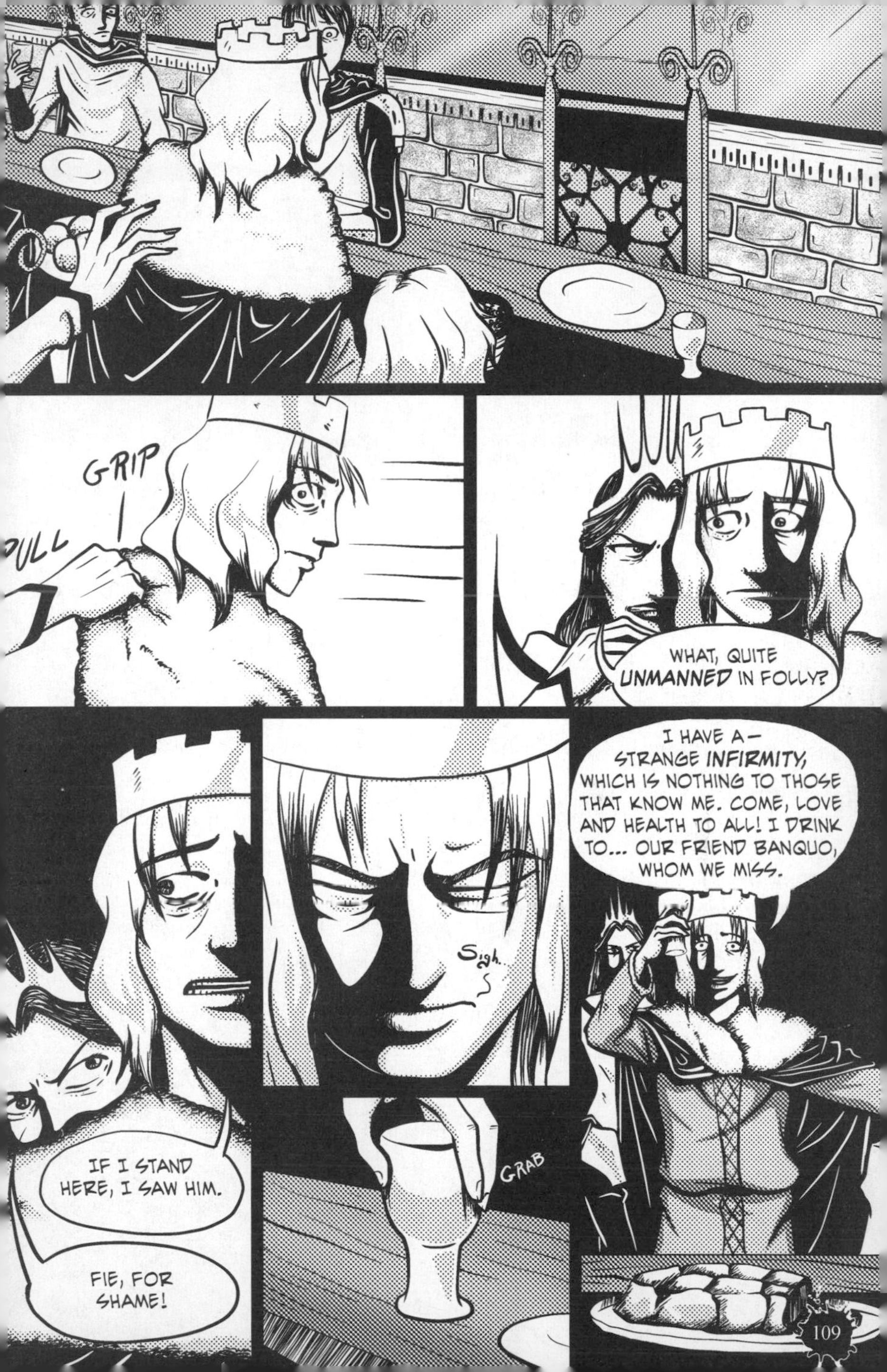
GRIP
PULL
WHAT, QUITE UNMANNED IN FOLLY?
IF I STAND HERE, I SAW HIM.
FIE, FOR SHAME!
Sigh...
GRAB
I HAVE A— STRANGE INFIRMITY, WHICH IS NOTHING TO THOSE THAT KNOW ME. COME, LOVE AND HEALTH TO ALL! I DRINK TO... OUR FRIEND BANQUO, WHOM WE MISS.

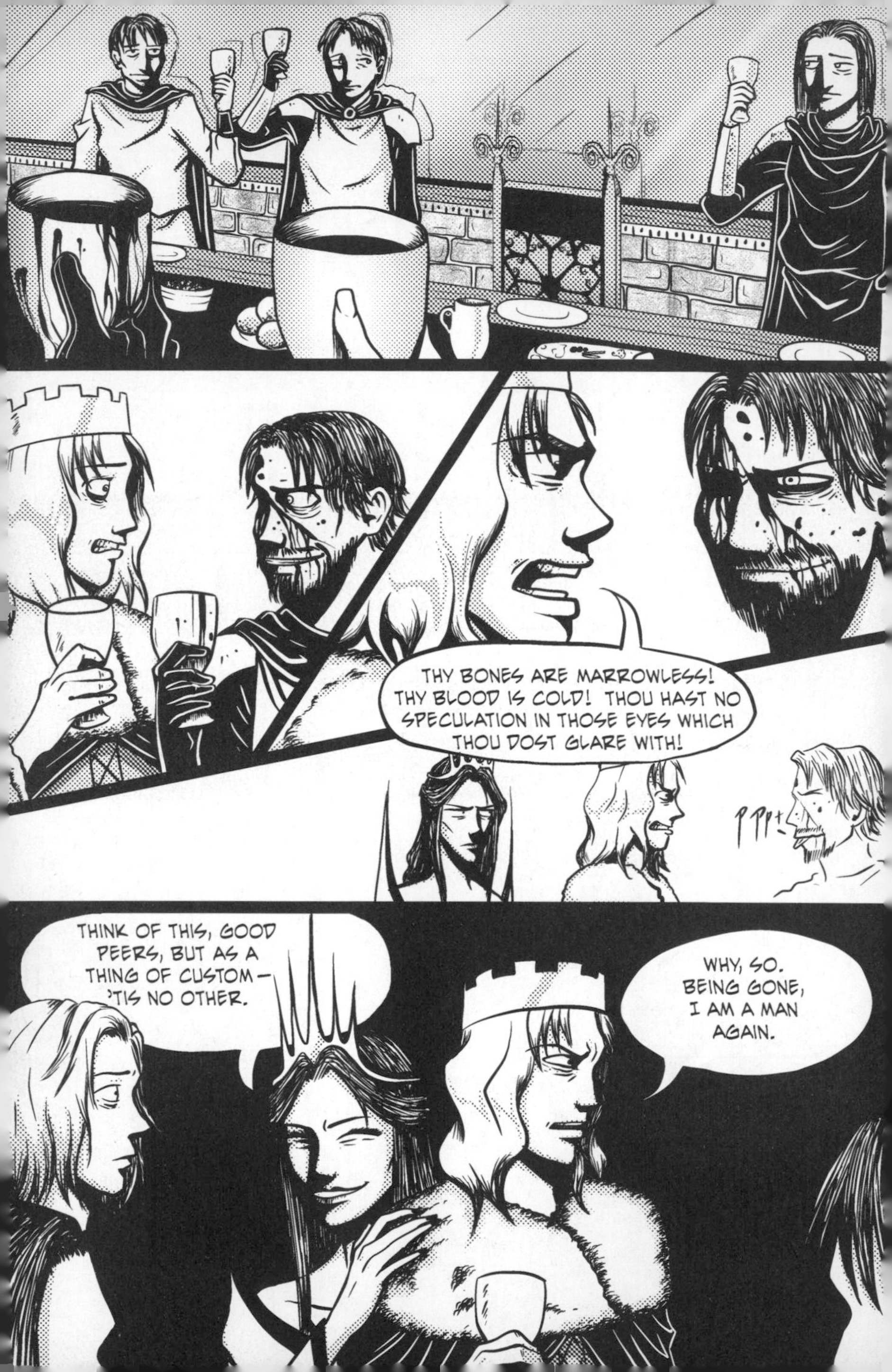
THY BONES ARE MARROWLESS! THY BLOOD IS COLD! THOU HAST NO SPECULATION IN THOSE EYES WHICH THOU DOST GLARE WITH!
PPpt
THINK OF THIS, GOOD PEERS, BUT AS A THING OF CUSTOM — 'TIS NO OTHER.
WHY, SO. BEING GONE, I AM A MAN AGAIN.

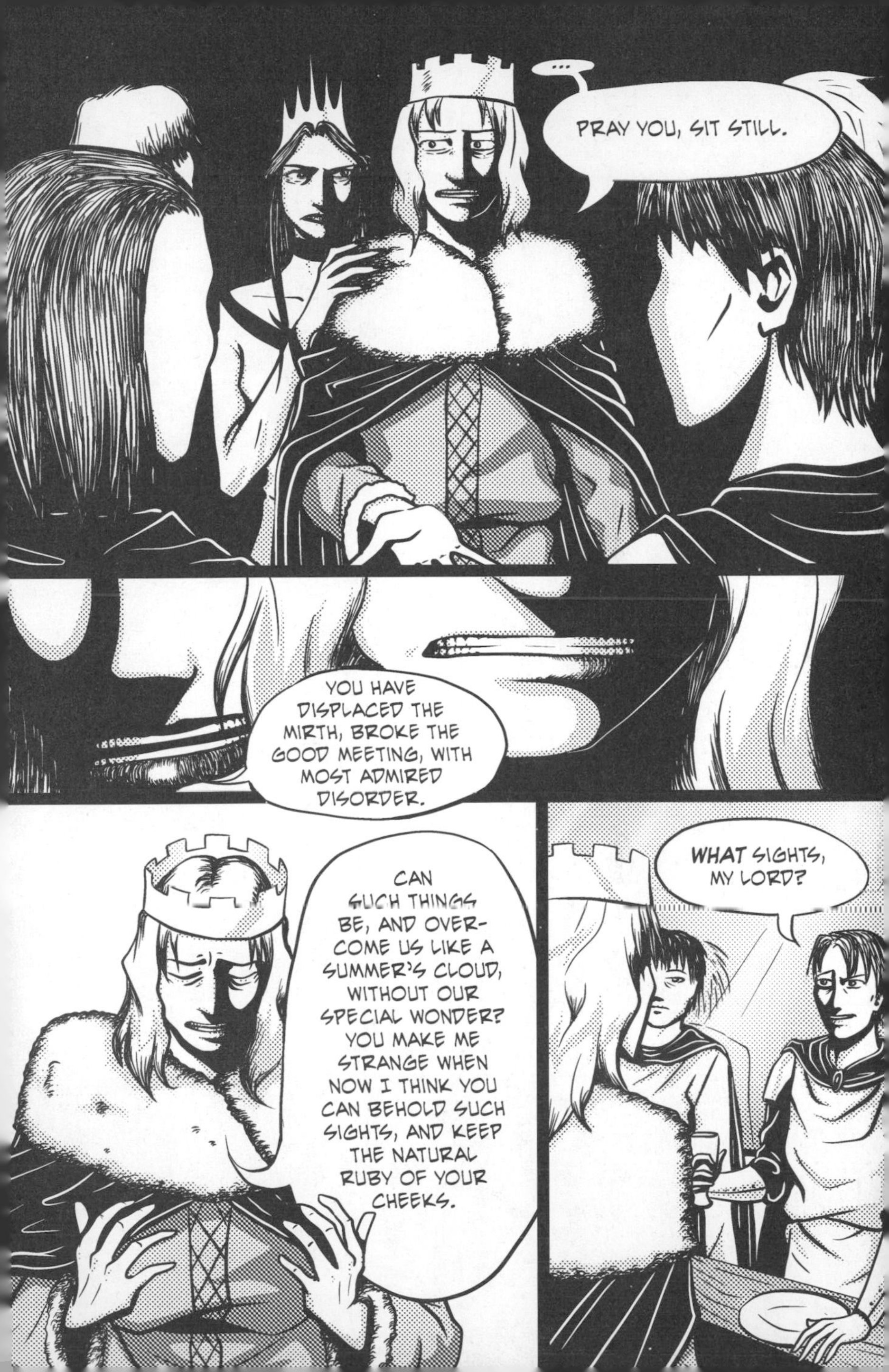
...
PRAY YOU, SIT STILL.
YOU HAVE DISPLACED THE MIRTH, BROKE THE GOOD MEETING, WITH MOST ADMIRED DISORDER.
CAN SUCH THINGS BE, AND OVER-COME US LIKE A SUMMER'S CLOUD, WITHOUT OUR SPECIAL WONDER? YOU MAKE ME STRANGE WHEN NOW I THINK YOU CAN BEHOLD SUCH SIGHTS, AND KEEP THE NATURAL RUBY OF YOUR CHEEKS.
WHAT SIGHTS, MY LORD?

I PRAY YOU, SPEAK NOT — HE GROWS WORSE AND WORSE. QUESTION ENRAGES HIM. AT ONCE, GOOD NIGHT.

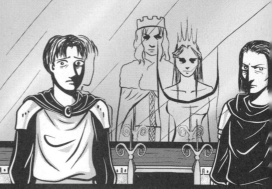

GOOD NIGHT, AND BETTER HEALTH ATTEND HIS MAJESTY!

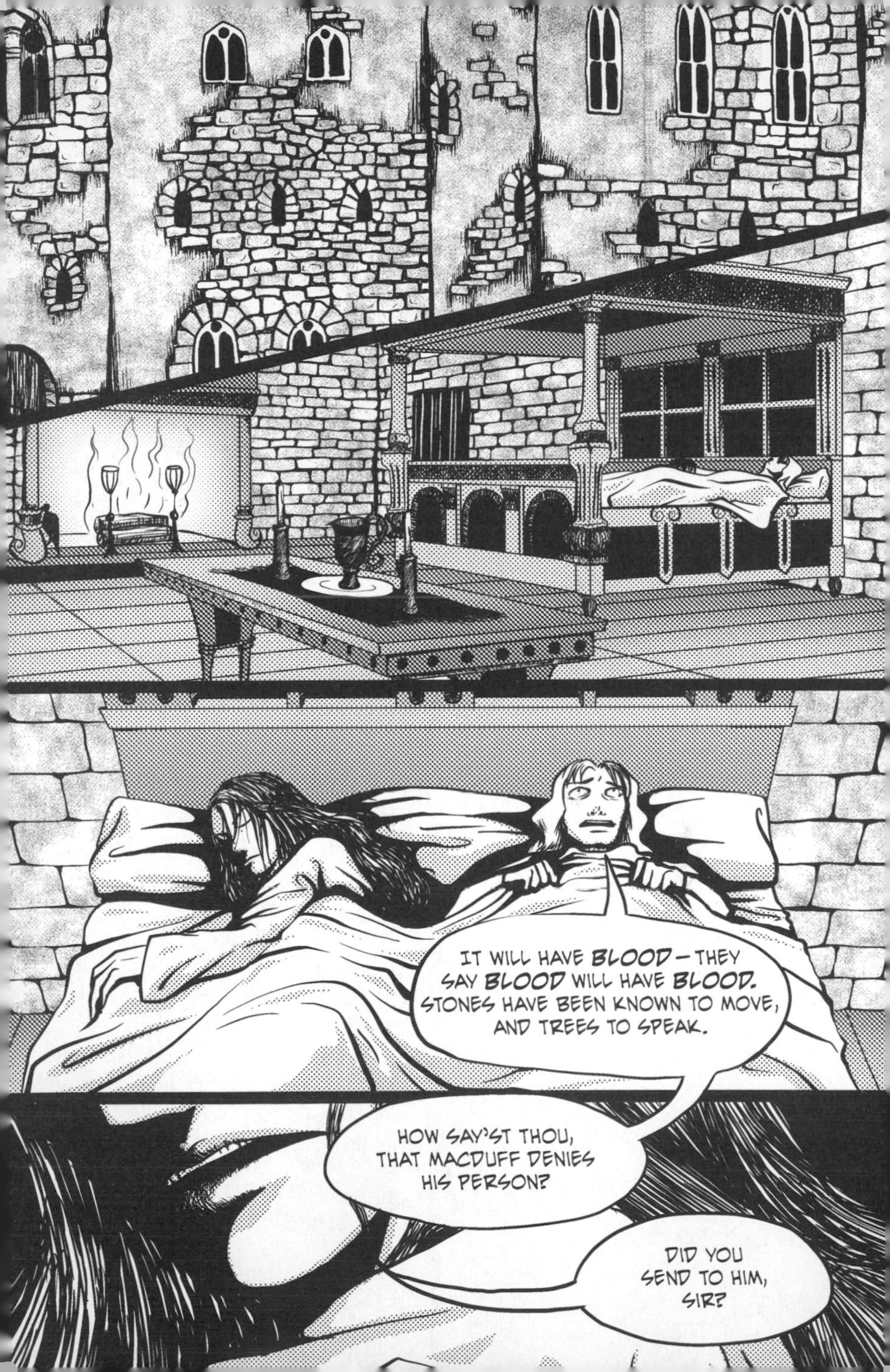
IT WILL HAVE BLOOD — THEY SAY BLOOD WILL HAVE BLOOD. STONES HAVE BEEN KNOWN TO MOVE, AND TREES TO SPEAK.
HOW SAY'ST THOU, THAT MACDUFF DENIES HIS PERSON?
DID YOU SEND TO HIM, SIR?

I WILL TOMORROW, AND BETIMES I WILL TO THE WEIRD SISTERS. MORE SHALL THEY SPEAK, FOR NOW I AM BENT TO KNOW, BY THE WORST MEANS THE WORST. FOR MINE OWN GOOD, ALL CAUSES SHALL GIVE WAY. I AM IN BLOOD STEPPED IN SO FAR THAT, SHOULD I WADE NO MORE, RETURNING WERE AS TEDIOUS AS GO O'ER.
YOU LACK THE SEASON OF ALL NATURES, SLEEP.
COME, WE'LL TO SLEEP.
KISS

THINGS HAVE BEEN... STRANGELY BORNE. THE GRACIOUS DUNCAN WAS PITIED OF MACBETH. MARRY, HE WAS DEAD! AND THE RIGHT-VALIANT BANQUO WALKED TOO LATE, WHOM, YOU MAY SAY (IF'T PLEASE YOU) FLEANCE KILLED — FOR FLEANCE FLED. MEN MUST NOT WALK TOO LATE. WHO CANNOT WANT THE THOUGHT HOW MONSTROUS IT WAS FOR MALCOLM AND FOR DONALBAIN TO KILL THEIR GRACIOUS FATHER? DAMNED FACT!
MACBETH BORNE ALL THINGS WELL — AND I DO THINK THAT HAD HE DUNCAN'S SONS UNDER HIS KEY (AS, AN'T PLEASE HEAVEN, HE SHALL NOT), THEY SHOULD FIND WHAT 'TWERE TO KILL A FATHER. SO SHOULD FLEANCE. BUT, PEACE! FOR FROM BROAD WORDS AND 'CAUSE HE FAILED HIS PRESENCE AT THE TYRANT'S FEAST, I HEAR MACDUFF LIVES IN DISGRACE. SIR, CAN YOU TELL WHERE HE BESTOWS HIMSELF?

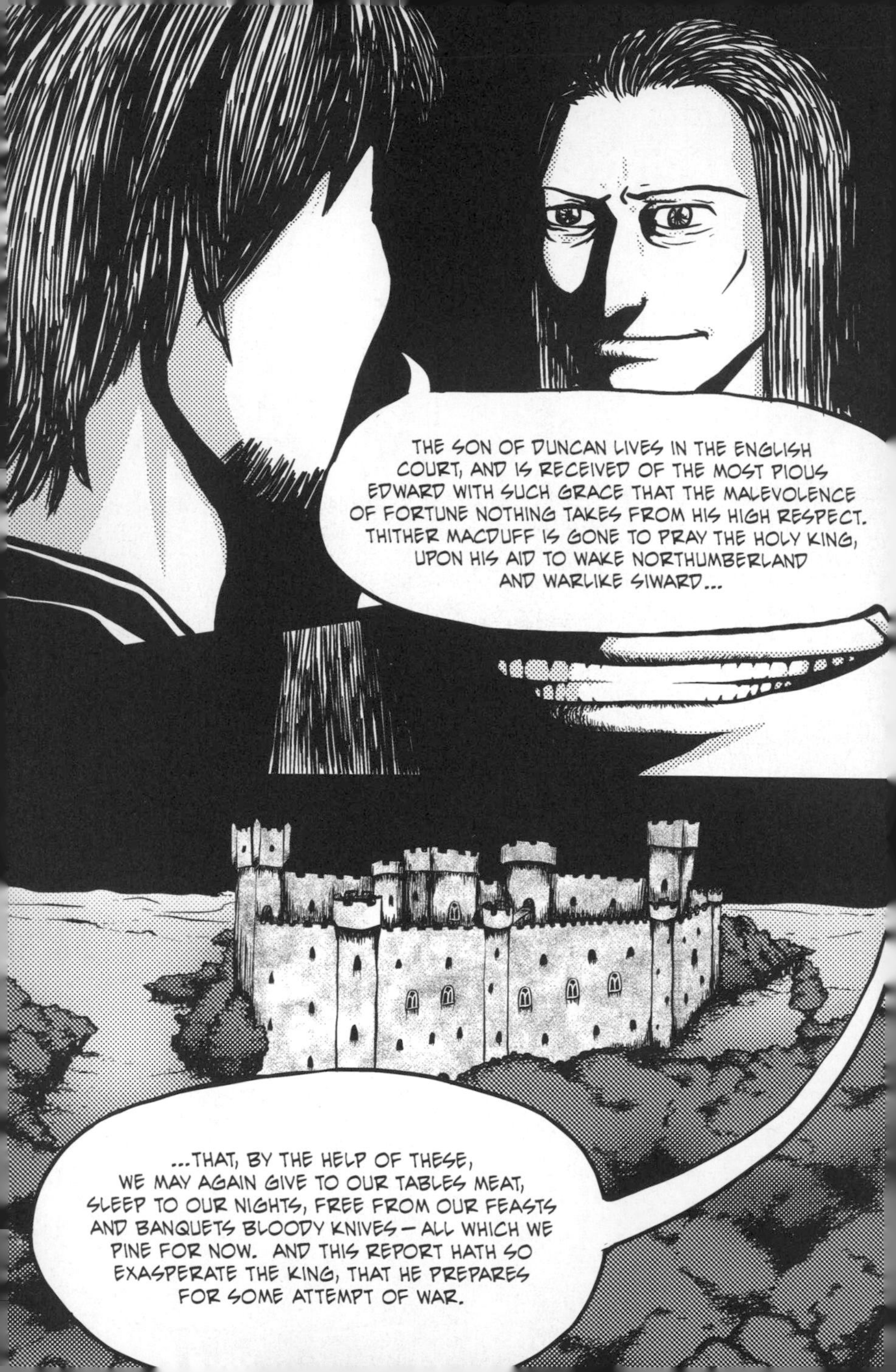
THE SON OF DUNCAN LIVES IN THE ENGLISH COURT, AND IS RECEIVED OF THE MOST PIOUS EDWARD WITH SUCH GRACE THAT THE MALEVOLENCE OF FORTUNE NOTHING TAKES FROM HIS HIGH RESPECT. THITHER MACDUFF IS GONE TO PRAY THE HOLY KING, UPON HIS AID TO WAKE NORTHUMBERLAND AND WARLIKE SIWARD...
...THAT, BY THE HELP OF THESE, WE MAY AGAIN GIVE TO OUR TABLES MEAT, SLEEP TO OUR NIGHTS, FREE FROM OUR FEASTS AND BANQUETS BLOODY KNIVES—ALL WHICH WE PINE FOR NOW. AND THIS REPORT HATH SO EXASPERATE THE KING, THAT HE PREPARES FOR SOME ATTEMPT OF WAR.

Act IV

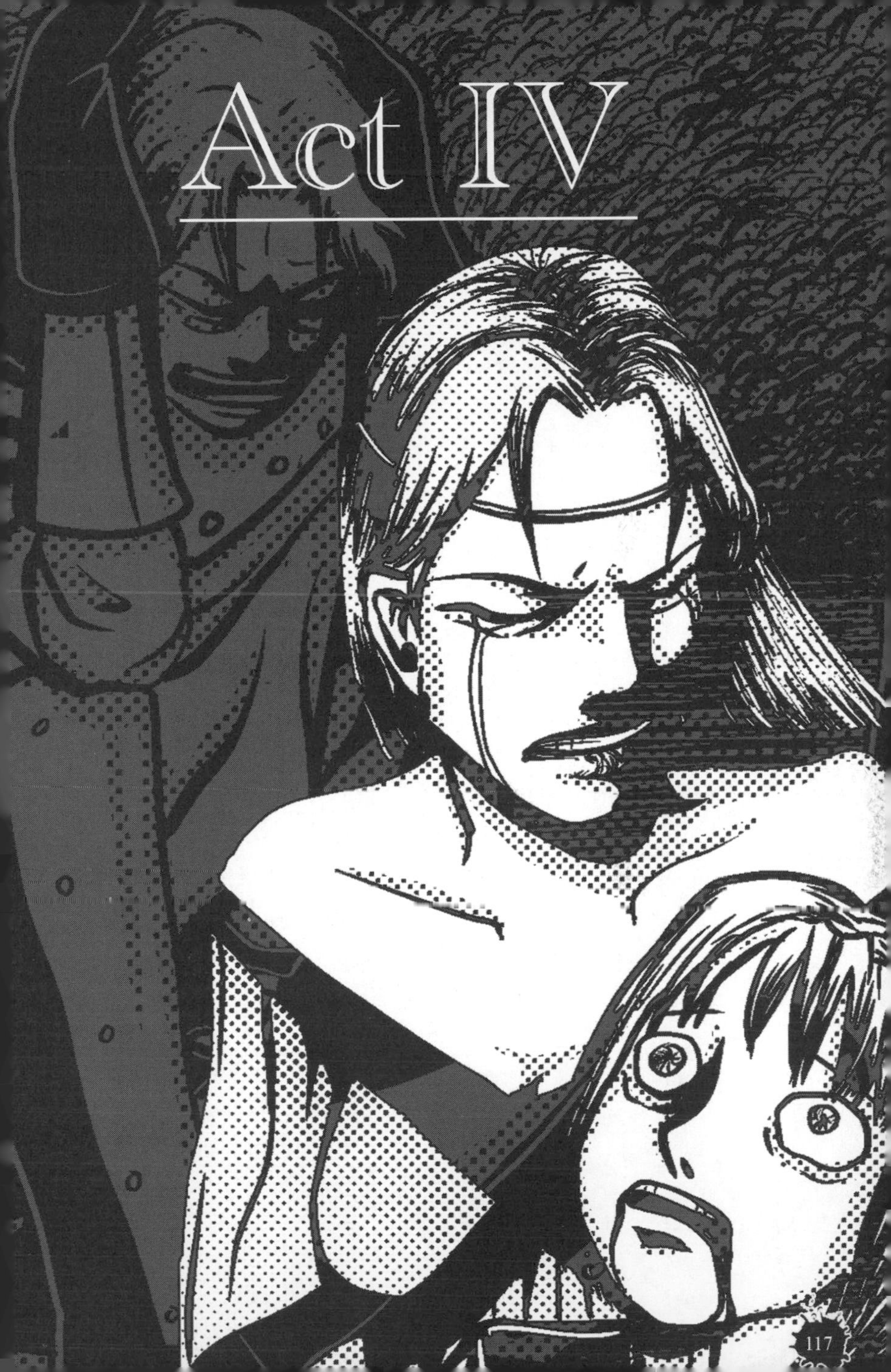

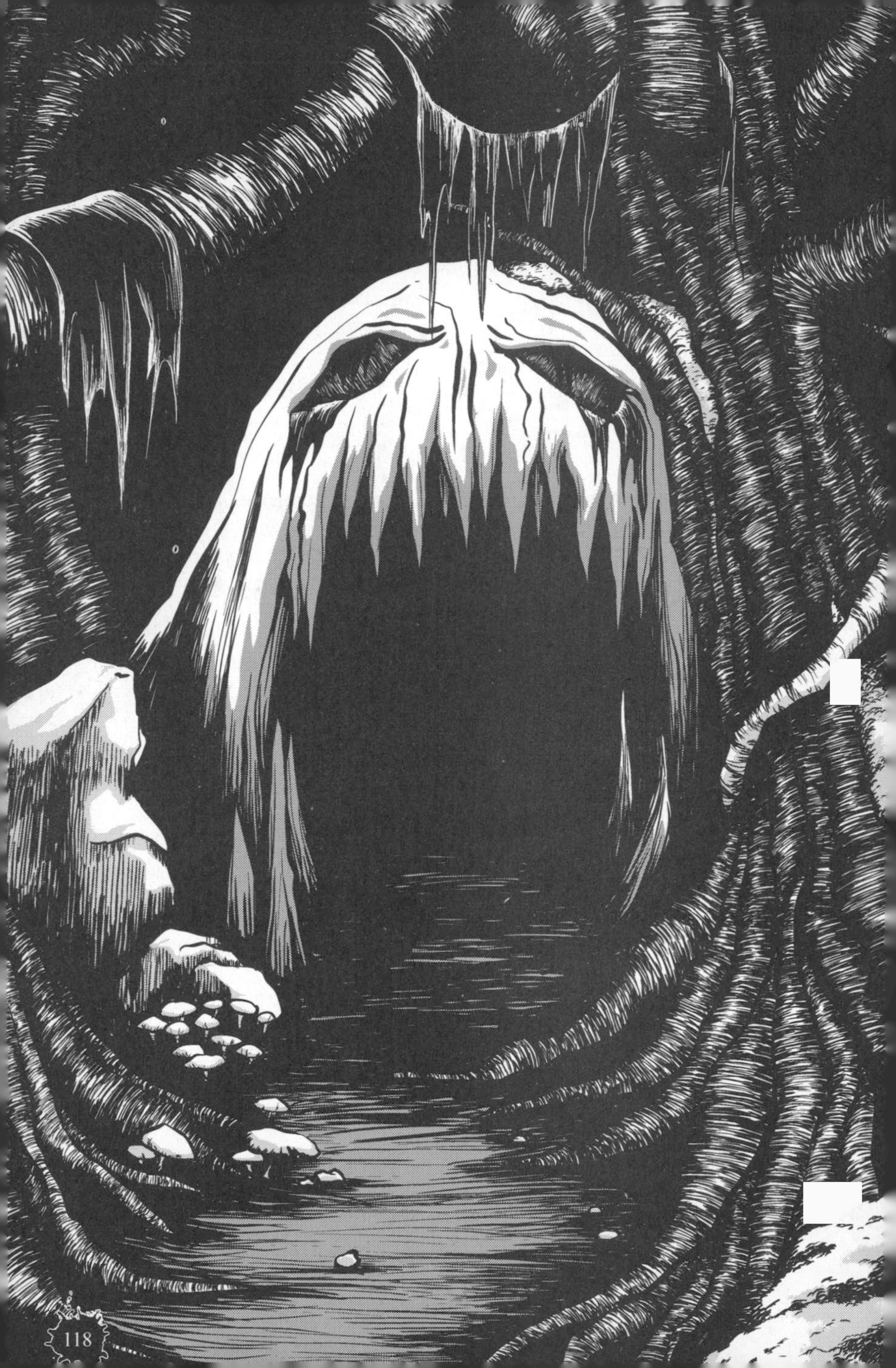

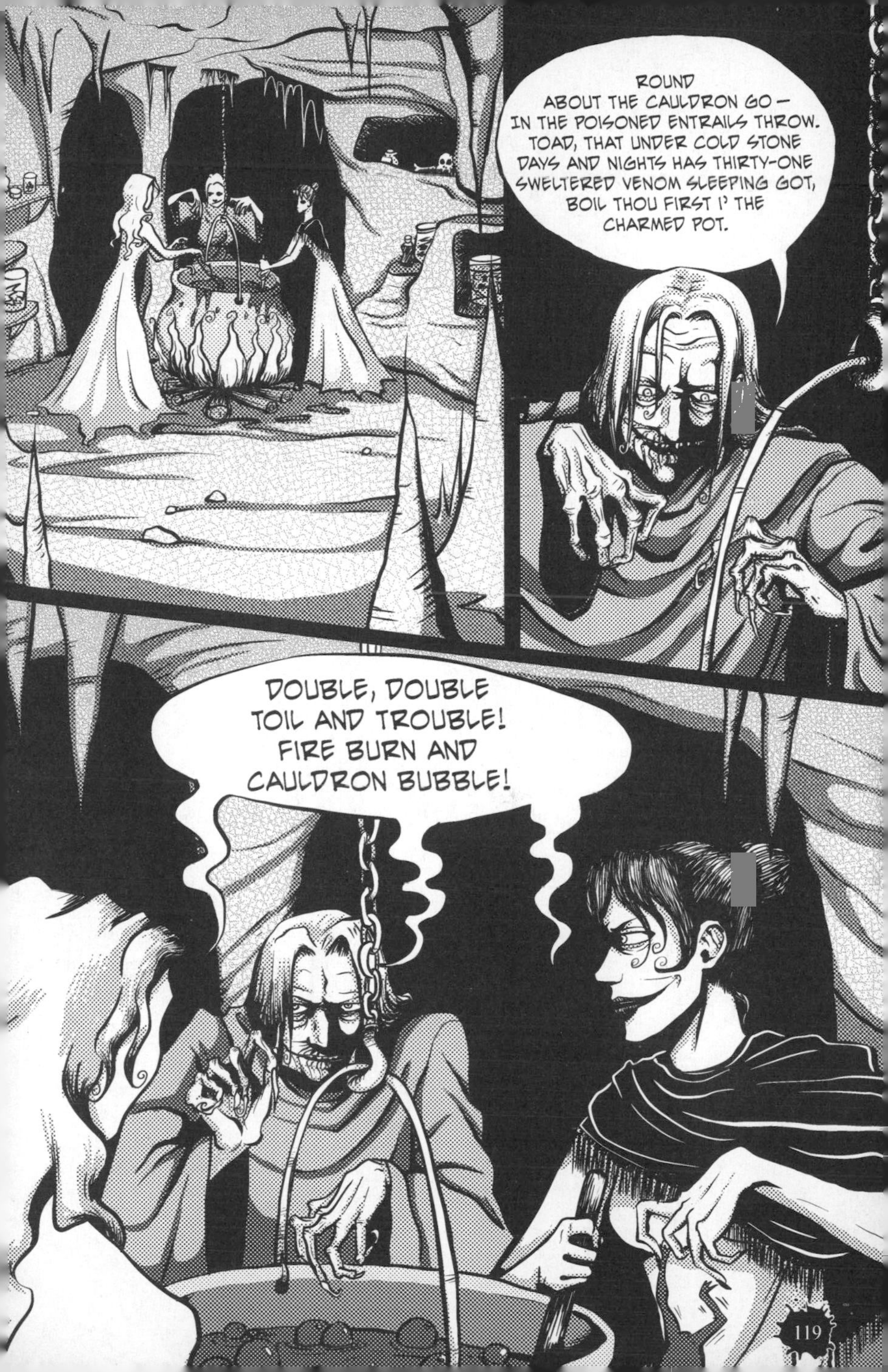
ROUND ABOUT THE CAULDRON GO — IN THE POISONED ENTRAILS THROW. TOAD, THAT UNDER COLD STONE DAYS AND NIGHTS HAS THIRTY-ONE SWELTERED VENOM SLEEPING GOT, BOIL THOU FIRST I' THE CHARMED POT.
DOUBLE, DOUBLE TOIL AND TROUBLE! FIRE BURN AND CAULDRON BUBBLE!

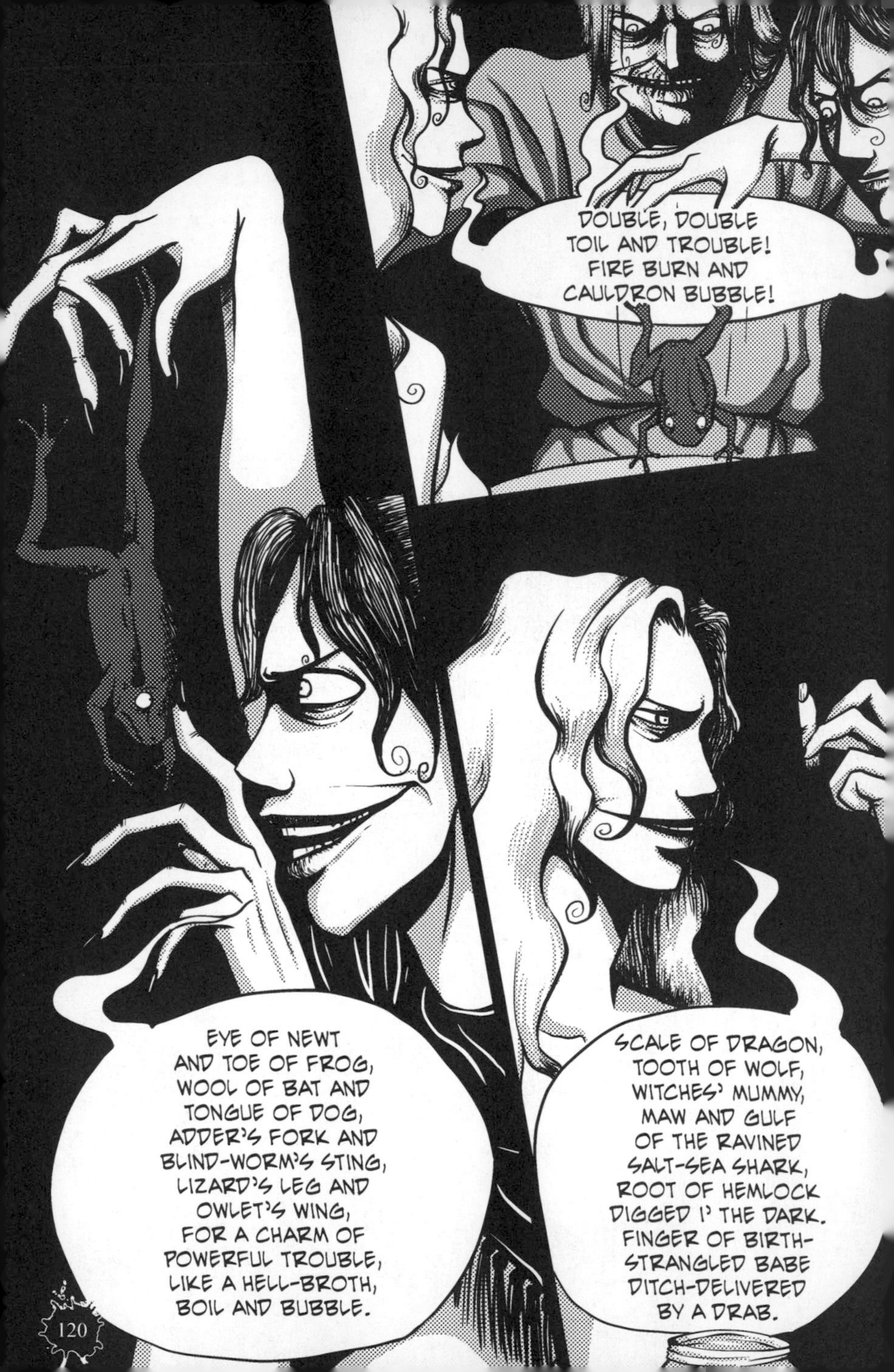
DOUBLE, DOUBLE TOIL AND TROUBLE! FIRE BURN AND CAULDRON BUBBLE!
EYE OF NEWT AND TOE OF FROG, WOOL OF BAT AND TONGUE OF DOG, ADDER'S FORK AND BLIND-WORM'S STING, LIZARD'S LEG AND OWLET'S WING, FOR A CHARM OF POWERFUL TROUBLE, LIKE A HELL-BROTH, BOIL AND BUBBLE.
SCALE OF DRAGON, TOOTH OF WOLF, WITCHES' MUMMY, MAW AND GULF OF THE RAVINED SALT-SEA SHARK, ROOT OF HEMLOCK DIGGED I' THE DARK. FINGER OF BIRTH-STRANGLED BABE DITCH-DELIVERED BY A DRAB.

DOUBLE, DOUBLE TOIL AND TROUBLE! FIRE BURN AND CAULDRON BUBBLE!
COOL IT WITH A BABOON'S BLOOD— THEN THE CHARM IS FIRM AND GOOD.
— BY THE PRICKING OF MY THUMBS, SOMETHING WICKED THIS WAY COMES. OPEN, LOCKS, WHOEVER KNOCKS!

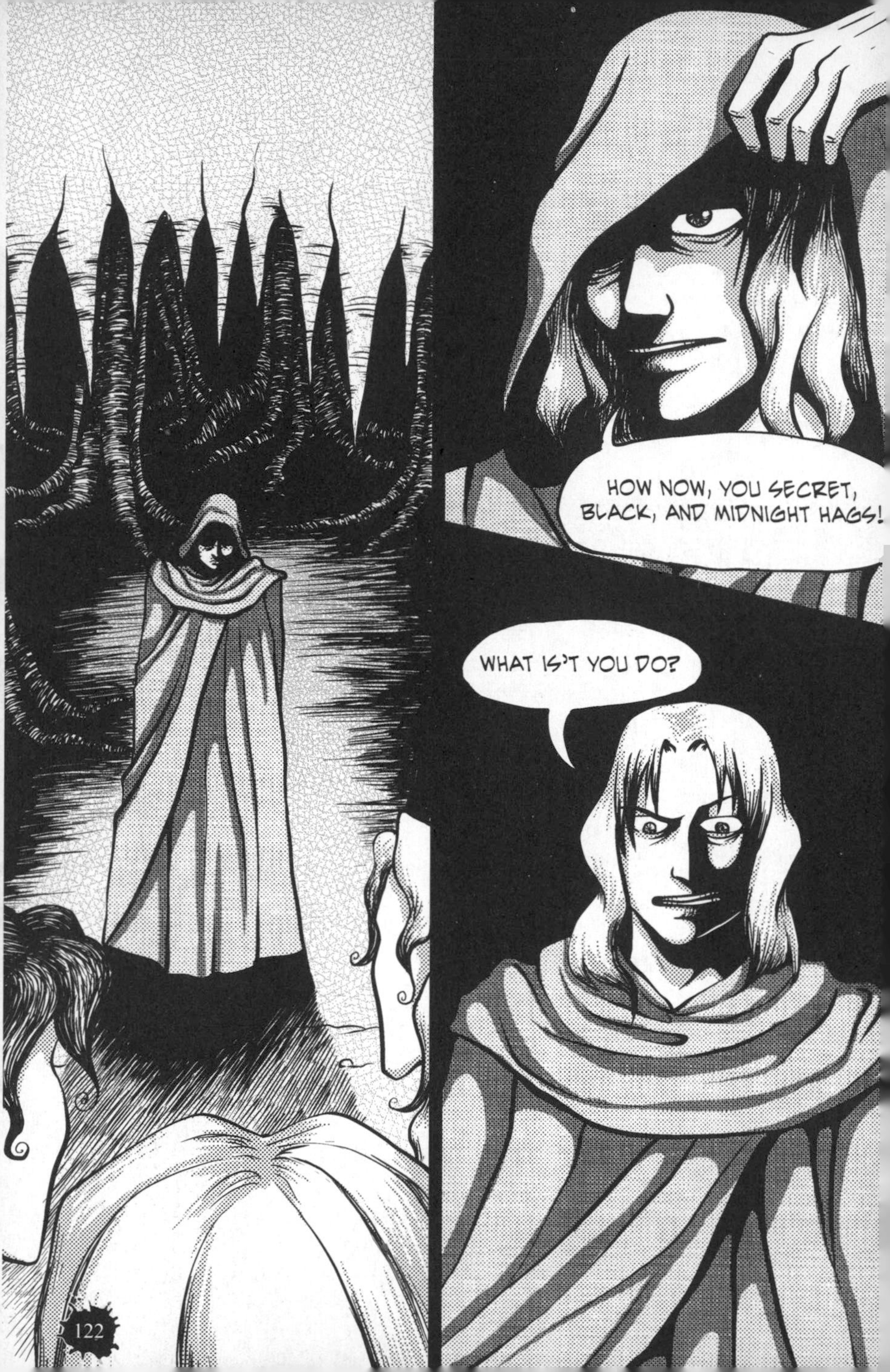
HOW NOW, YOU SECRET, BLACK, AND MIDNIGHT HAGS!
WHAT IS'T YOU DO?

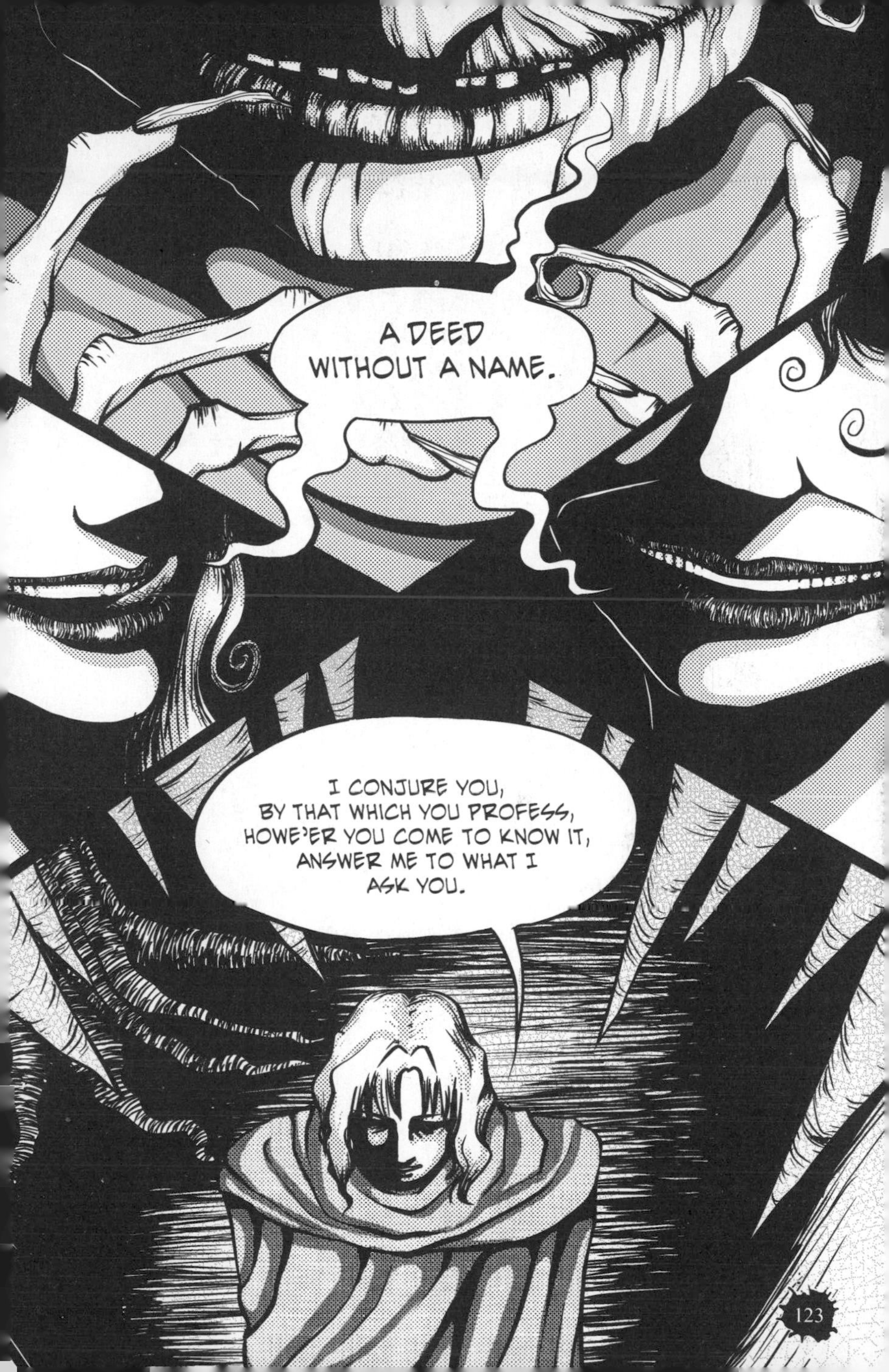
A DEED WITHOUT A NAME.
I CONJURE YOU, BY THAT WHICH YOU PROFESS, HOWE'ER YOU COME TO KNOW IT, ANSWER ME TO WHAT I ASK YOU.

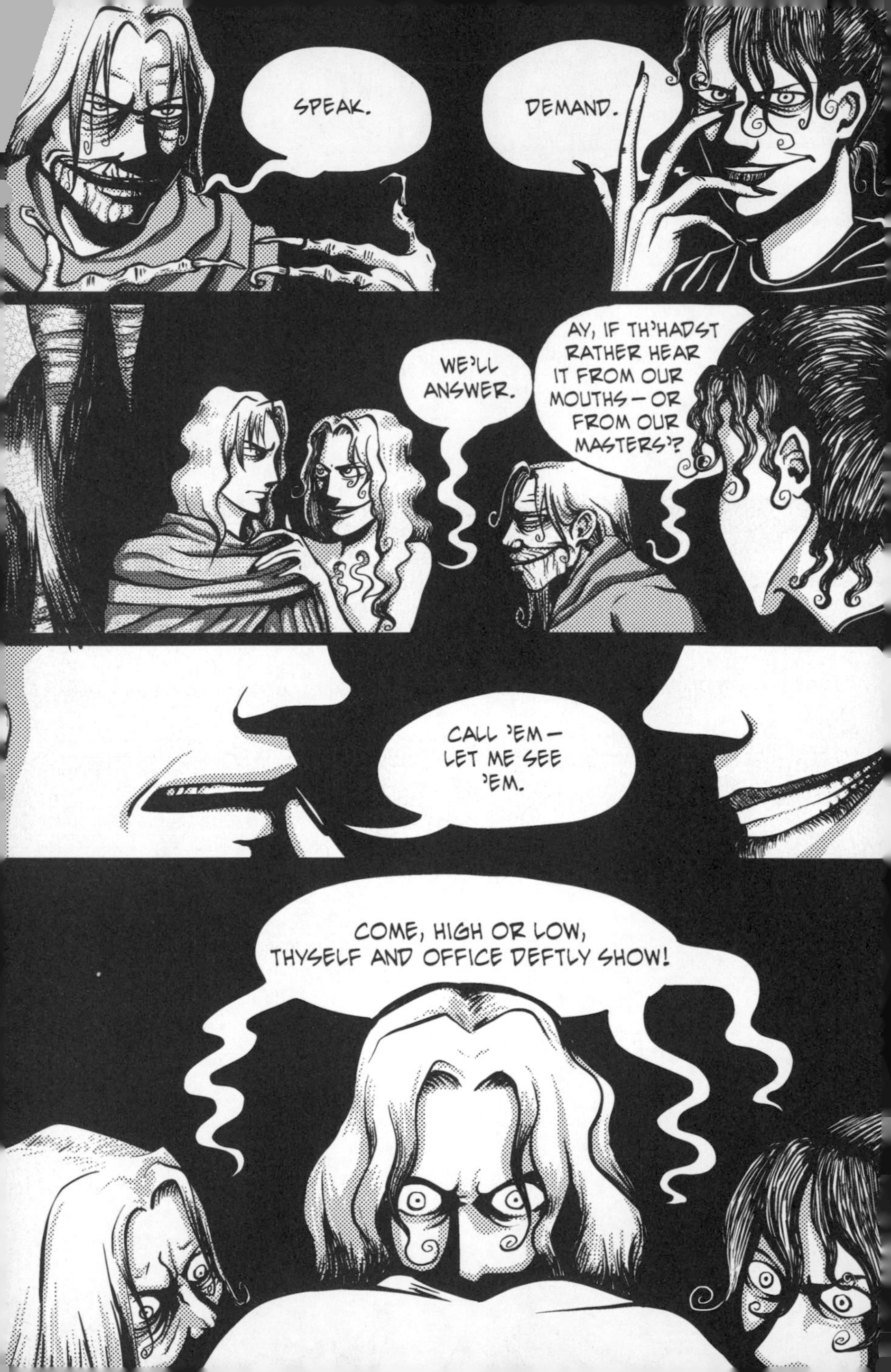
SPEAK.
DEMAND.
WE'LL ANSWER.
AY, IF TH'HADST RATHER HEAR IT FROM OUR MOUTHS—OR FROM OUR MASTERS'?
CALL 'EM—LET ME SEE 'EM.
COME, HIGH OR LOW, THYSELF AND OFFICE DEFTLY SHOW!

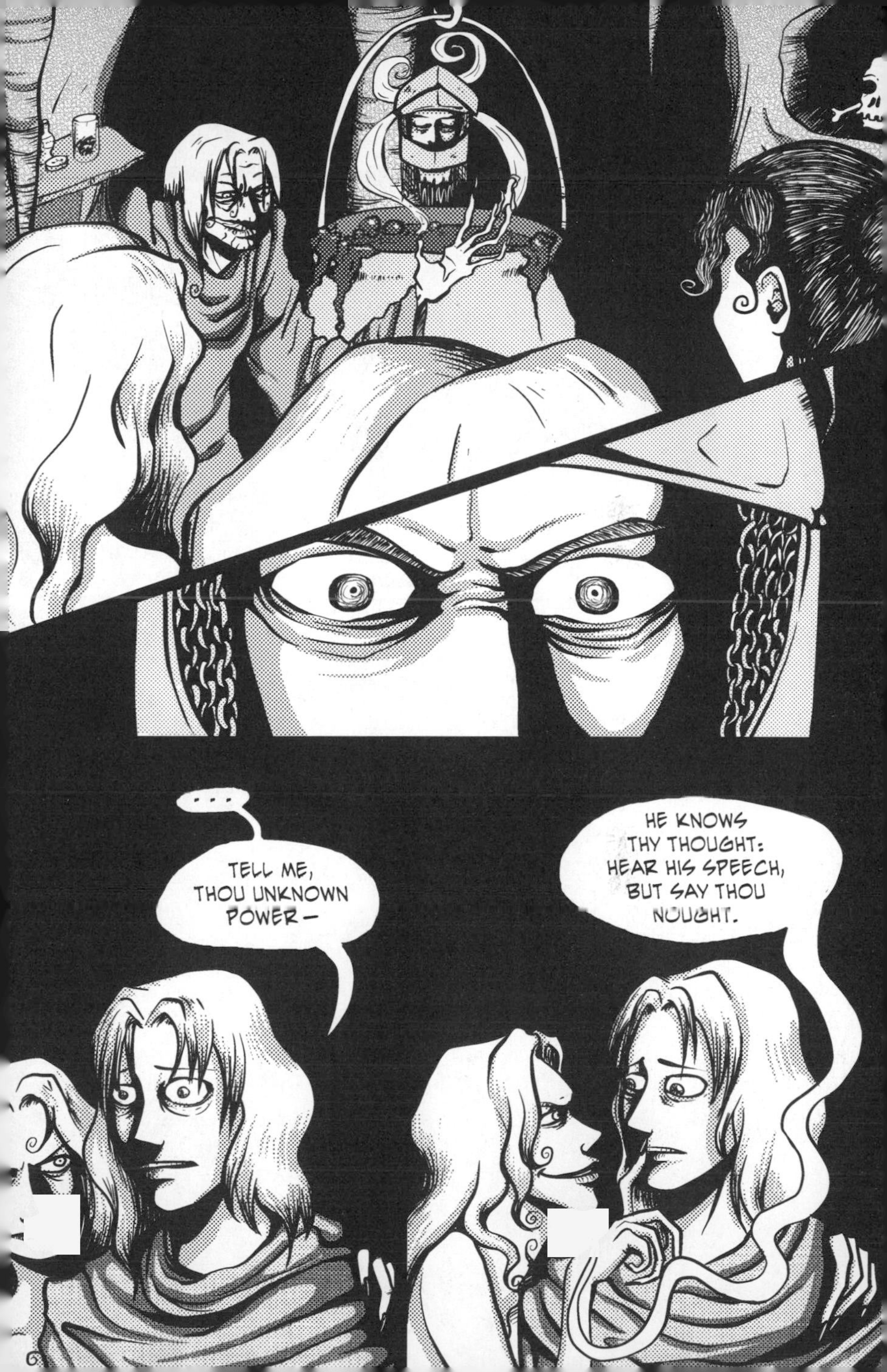
...
TELL ME, THOU UNKNOWN POWER—
HE KNOWS THY THOUGHT: HEAR HIS SPEECH, BUT SAY THOU NOUGHT.

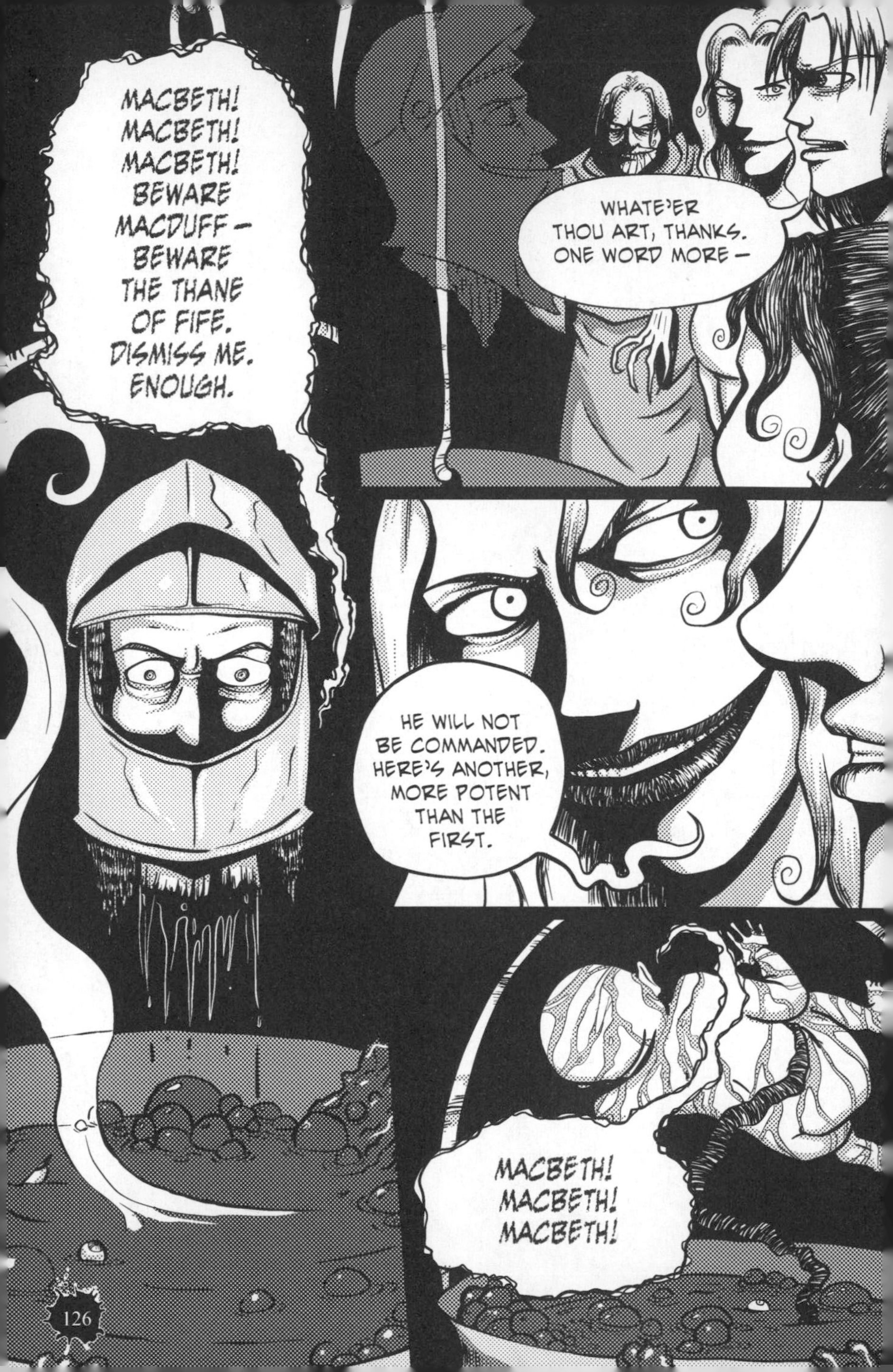
MACBETH! MACBETH! MACBETH! BEWARE MACDUFF – BEWARE THE THANE OF FIFE. DISMISS ME. ENOUGH.
WHATE'ER THOU ART, THANKS. ONE WORD MORE –
HE WILL NOT BE COMMANDED. HERE'S ANOTHER, MORE POTENT THAN THE FIRST.
MACBETH! MACBETH! MACBETH!

...
HAD I THREE EARS, I'D HEAR THEE.
BE BLOODY, BOLD, AND RESOLUTE—LAUGH TO SCORN THE POWER OF MAN, FOR NONE OF WOMAN BORN SHALL HARM...
...MACBETH.
THEN LIVE, MACDUFF—WHAT NEED I FEAR OF THEE? BUT YET I'LL MAKE ASSURANCE DOUBLE SURE, AND TAKE A BOND OF FATE: THOU SHALT NOT LIVE!

WHAT IS THIS THAT RISES LIKE THE ISSUE OF A KING, AND WEARS UPON HIS BABY-BROW THE ROUND AND TOP OF SOVEREIGNTY?
LISTEN, BUT SPEAK NOT TO'T.

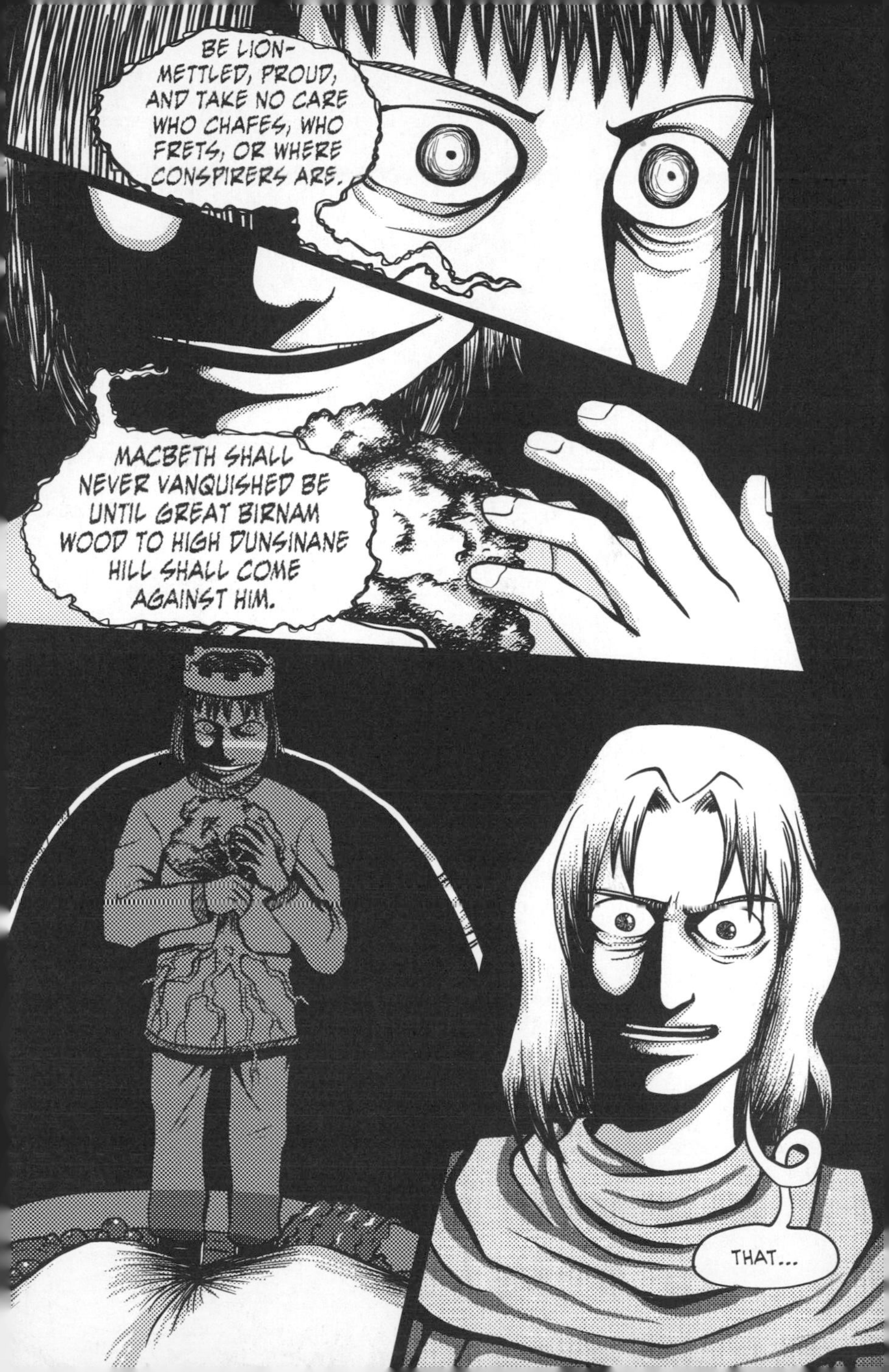
BE LION-METTLED, PROUD, AND TAKE NO CARE WHO CHAFES, WHO FRETS, OR WHERE CONSPIRERS ARE.
MACBETH SHALL NEVER VANQUISHED BE UNTIL GREAT BIRNAM WOOD TO HIGH DUNSINANE HILL SHALL COME AGAINST HIM.
THAT...

YET MY HEART THROBS TO KNOW ONE THING. TELL ME, IF YOUR ART CAN TELL SO MUCH: SHALL BANQUO'S ISSUE EVER REIGN IN THIS KINGDOM?
SEEK TO KNOW NO MORE.
THAT WILL NEVER BE. WHO CAN IMPRESS THE FOREST, BID THE TREE UNFIX HIS EARTH-BOUND ROOT? SWEET BODEMENTS! GOOD! REBELLION'S HEAD, RISE NEVER TILL THE WOOD OF BIRNAM RISE, AND OUR HIGH-PLACED MACBETH SHALL LIVE THE LEASE OF NATURE, PAY HIS BREATH TO TIME AND MORTAL CUSTOM.
I WILL BE SATISFIED—
DENY ME THIS, AND AN ETERNAL CURSE FALL ON YOU. LET ME KNOW!

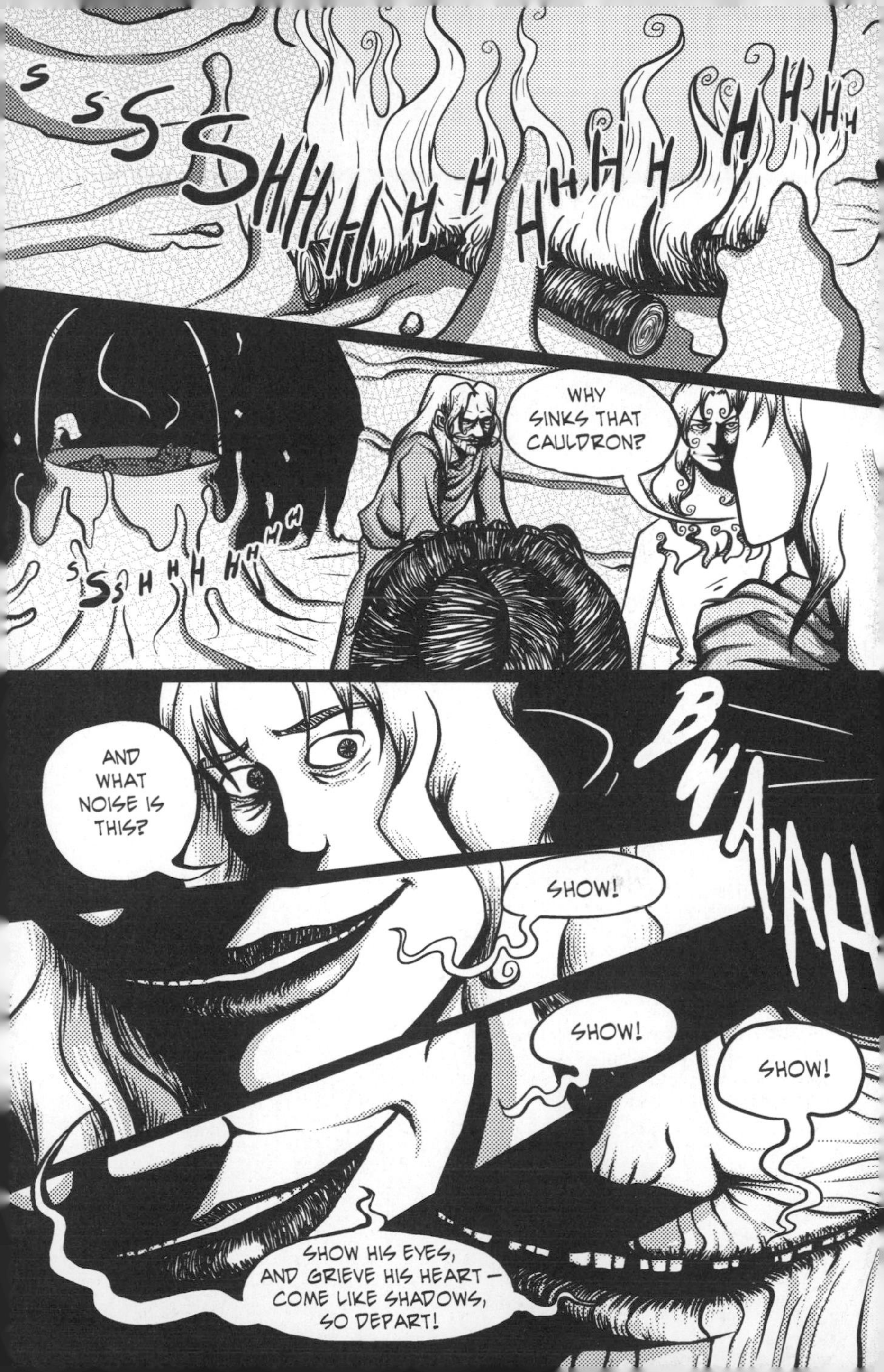
SSSSHHHHHHHHHHHHHHHHH
SSSHHHHHHHH
WHY SINKS THAT CAULDRON?
AND WHAT NOISE IS THIS?
BWAAAH
SHOW!
SHOW!
SHOW!
SHOW HIS EYES, AND GRIEVE HIS HEART — COME LIKE SHADOWS, SO DEPART!

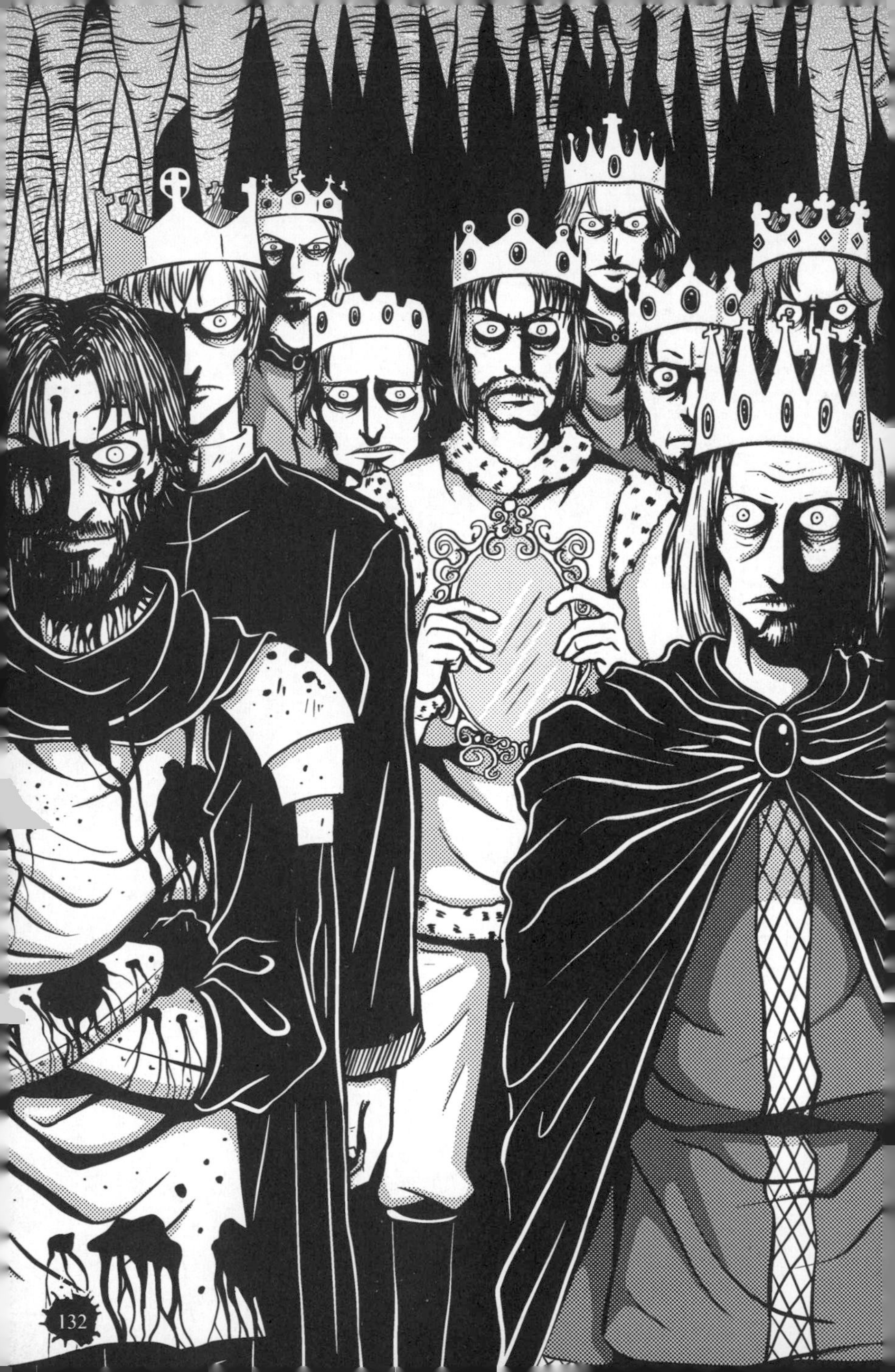

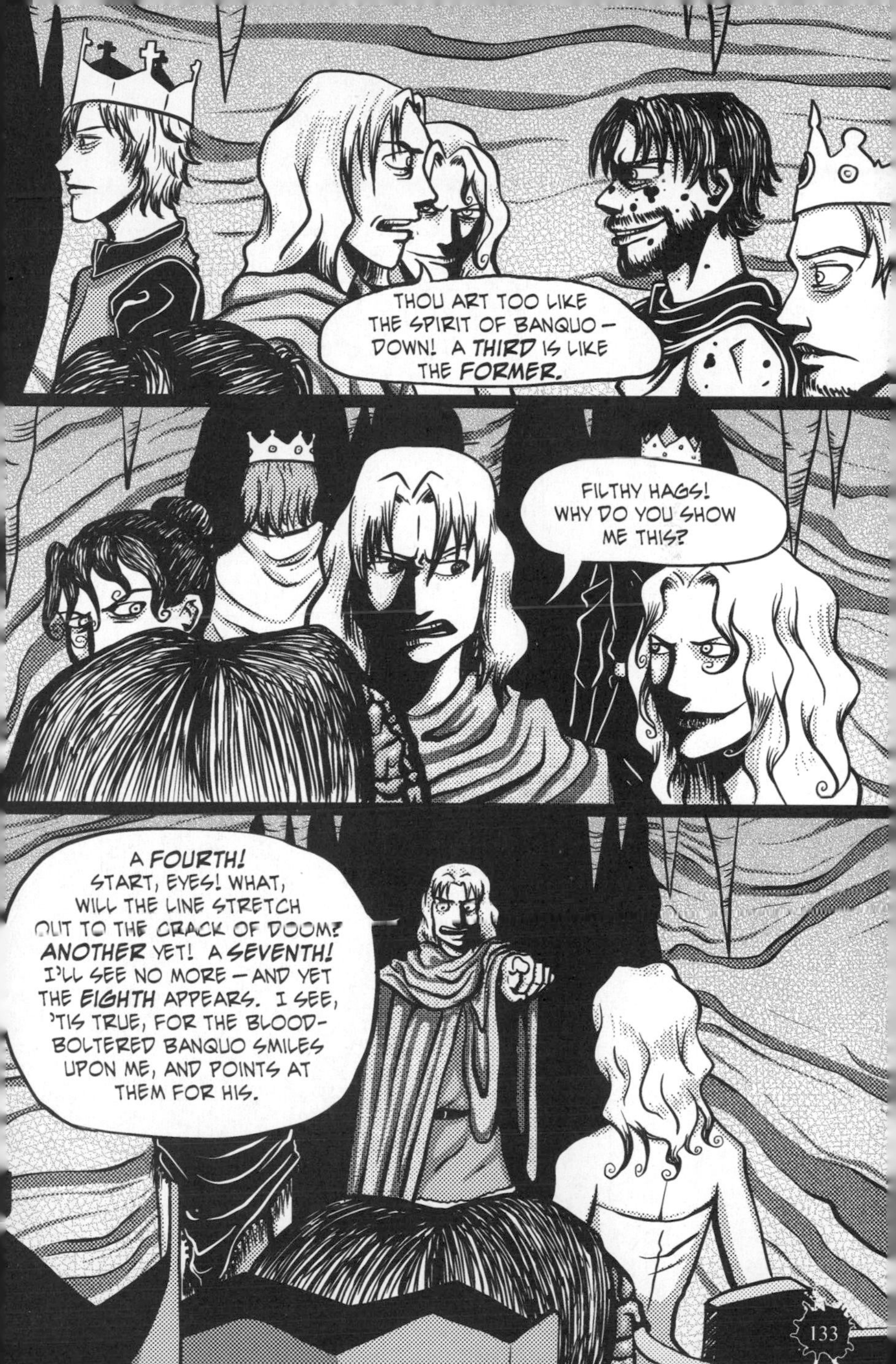
THOU ART TOO LIKE THE SPIRIT OF BANQUO — DOWN! A THIRD IS LIKE THE FORMER.
FILTHY HAGS! WHY DO YOU SHOW ME THIS?
A FOURTH! START, EYES! WHAT, WILL THE LINE STRETCH OUT TO THE CRACK OF DOOM? ANOTHER YET! A SEVENTH! I'LL SEE NO MORE — AND YET THE EIGHTH APPEARS. I SEE, 'TIS TRUE, FOR THE BLOOD-BOLTERED BANQUO SMILES UPON ME, AND POINTS AT THEM FOR HIS.

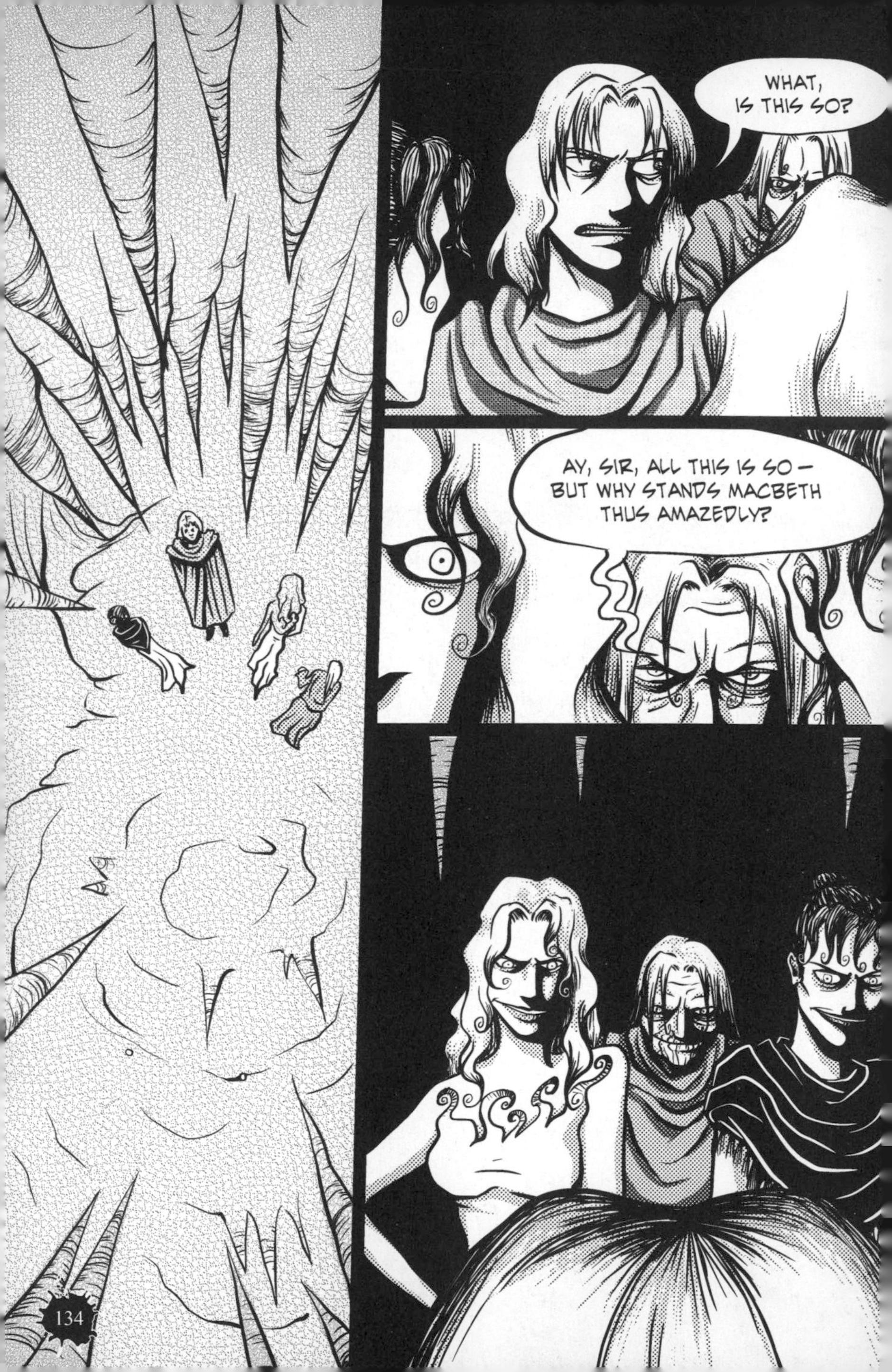
WHAT, IS THIS SO?
AY, SIR, ALL THIS IS SO — BUT WHY STANDS MACBETH THUS AMAZEDLY?

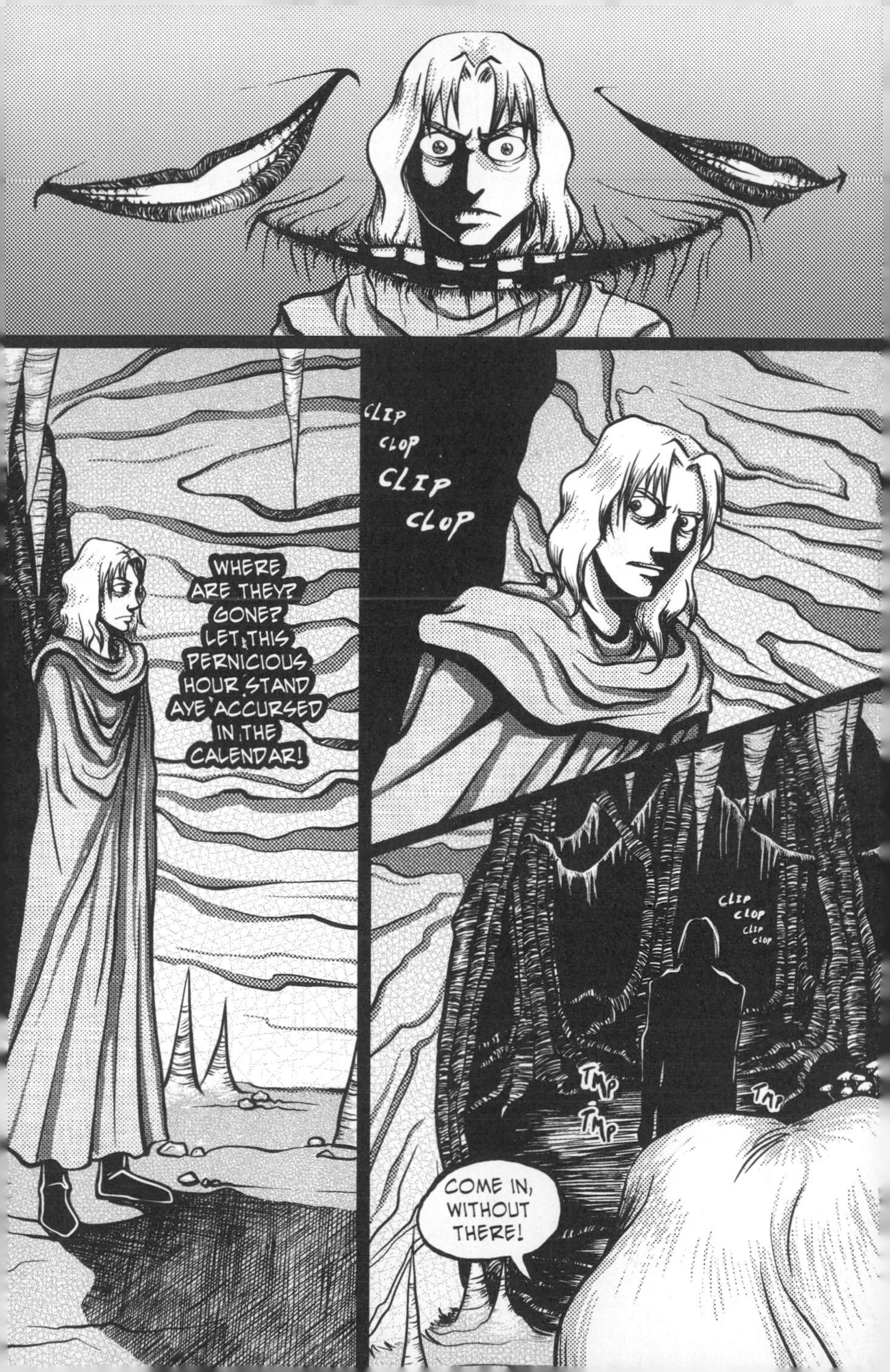
WHERE ARE THEY? GONE? LET THIS PERNICIOUS HOUR STAND AYE ACCURSED IN THE CALENDAR!
CLIP
CLOP
CLIP
CLOP
CLIP
CLOP
CLIP
CLOP
TMP
TMP
TMP
COME IN, WITHOUT THERE!

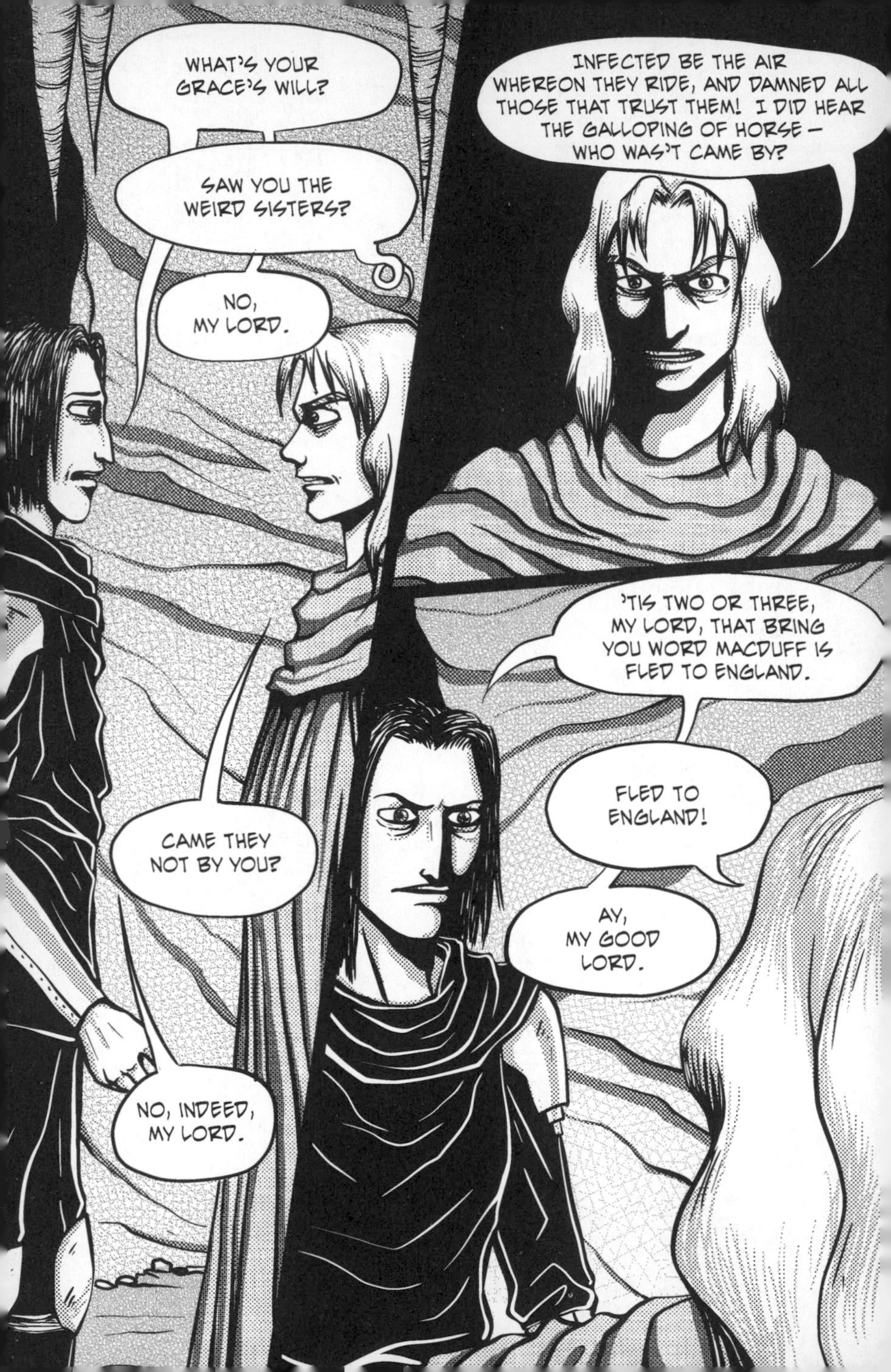
WHAT'S YOUR GRACE'S WILL?
SAW YOU THE WEIRD SISTERS?
NO, MY LORD.
CAME THEY NOT BY YOU?
NO, INDEED, MY LORD.
INFECTED BE THE AIR WHEREON THEY RIDE, AND DAMNED ALL THOSE THAT TRUST THEM! I DID HEAR THE GALLOPING OF HORSE — WHO WAS'T CAME BY?
'TIS TWO OR THREE, MY LORD, THAT BRING YOU WORD MACDUFF IS FLED TO ENGLAND.
FLED TO ENGLAND!
AY, MY GOOD LORD.

THE CASTLE OF MACDUFF I WILL SURPRISE, SEIZE UPON FIFE, GIVE TO THE EDGE O' THE SWORD HIS WIFE, HIS BABES, AND ALL UNFORTUNATE SOULS THAT TRACE HIM IN HIS LINE. NO BOASTING LIKE A FOOL! THIS DEED I'LL DO BEFORE THIS PURPOSE COOL...

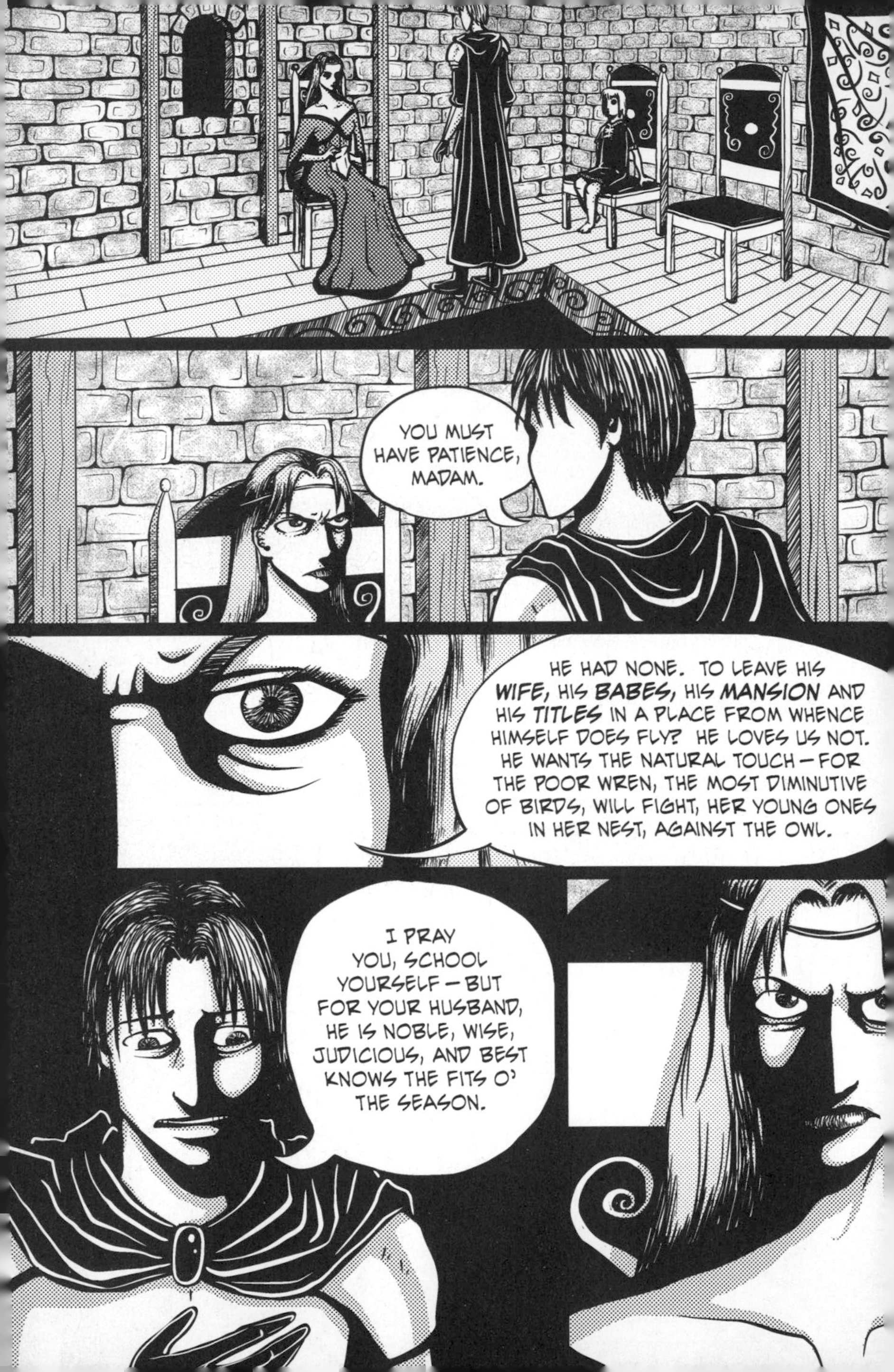
YOU MUST HAVE PATIENCE, MADAM.
HE HAD NONE. TO LEAVE HIS WIFE, HIS BABES, HIS MANSION AND HIS TITLES IN A PLACE FROM WHENCE HIMSELF DOES FLY? HE LOVES US NOT. HE WANTS THE NATURAL TOUCH — FOR THE POOR WREN, THE MOST DIMINUTIVE OF BIRDS, WILL FIGHT, HER YOUNG ONES IN HER NEST, AGAINST THE OWL.
I PRAY YOU, SCHOOL YOURSELF — BUT FOR YOUR HUSBAND, HE IS NOBLE, WISE, JUDICIOUS, AND BEST KNOWS THE FITS O' THE SEASON.

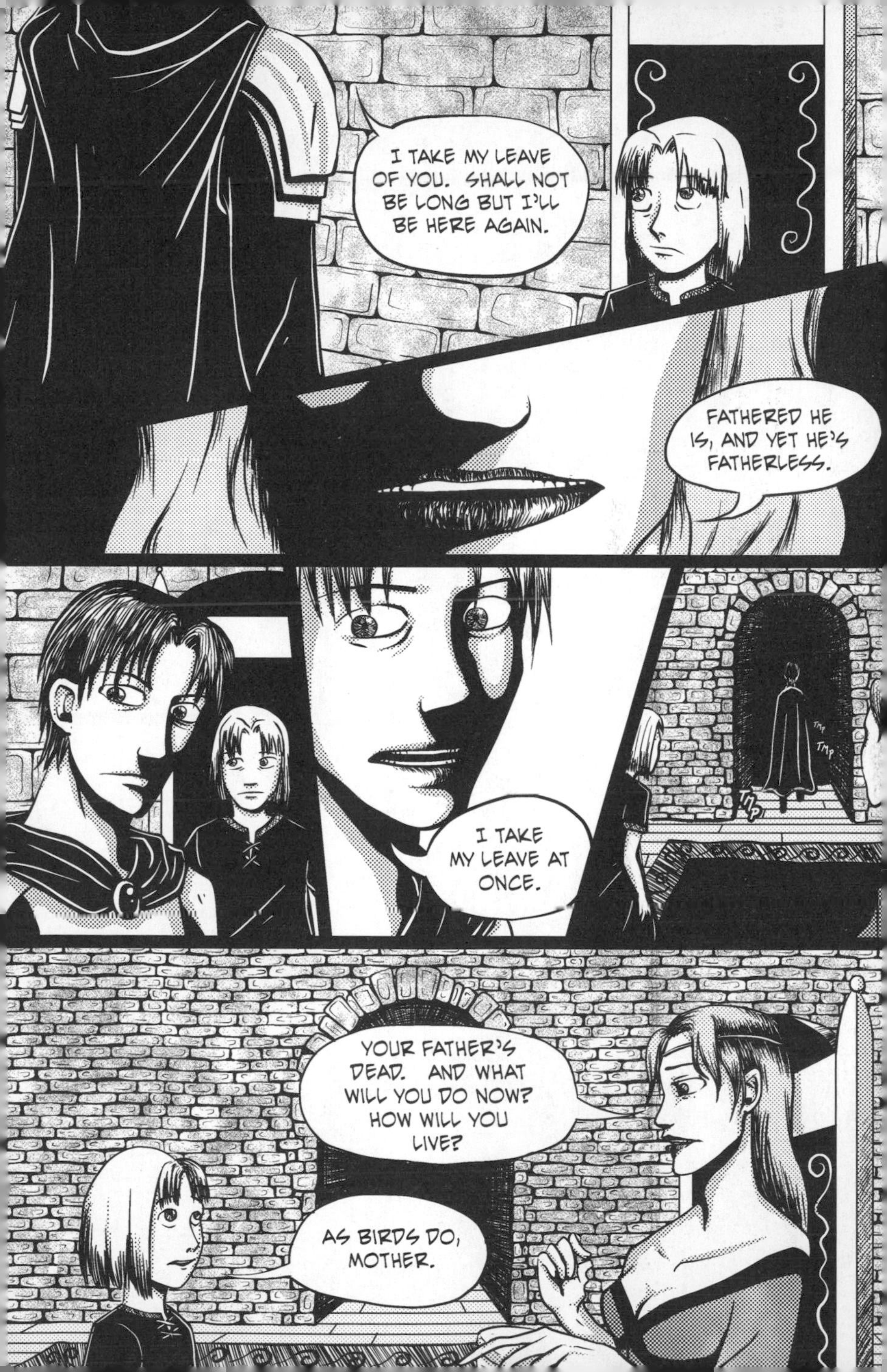
I TAKE MY LEAVE OF YOU. SHALL NOT BE LONG BUT I'LL BE HERE AGAIN.
FATHERED HE IS, AND YET HE'S FATHERLESS.
I TAKE MY LEAVE AT ONCE.
TMP
TMP
TMP
YOUR FATHER'S DEAD. AND WHAT WILL YOU DO NOW? HOW WILL YOU LIVE?
AS BIRDS DO, MOTHER.

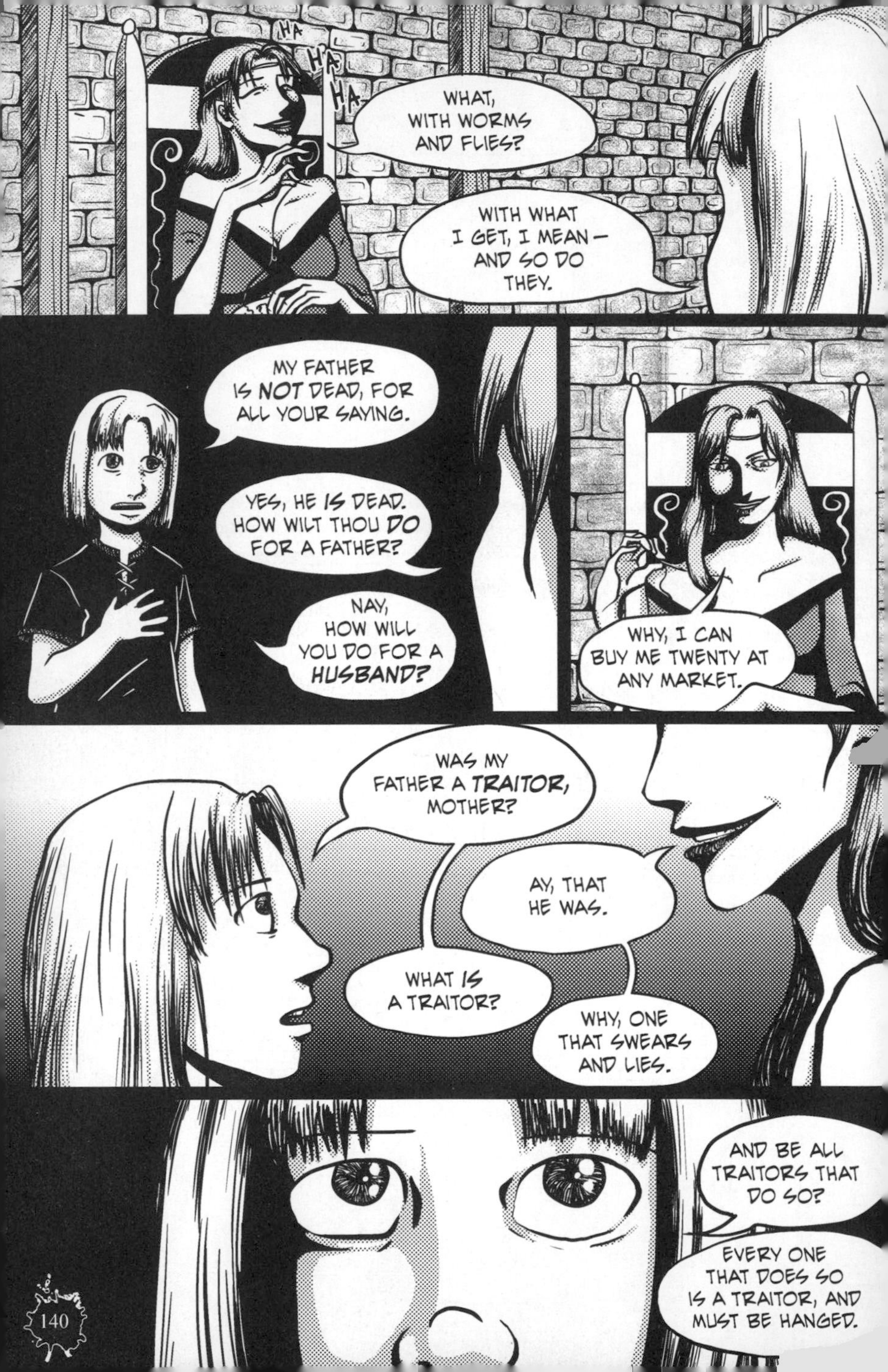
HA HA HA
WHAT, WITH WORMS AND FLIES?
WITH WHAT I GET, I MEAN — AND SO DO THEY.
MY FATHER IS **NOT** DEAD, FOR ALL YOUR SAYING.
YES, HE *IS* DEAD. HOW WILT THOU *DO* FOR A FATHER?
NAY, HOW WILL YOU DO FOR A ***HUSBAND?***
WHY, I CAN BUY ME TWENTY AT ANY MARKET.
WAS MY FATHER A ***TRAITOR,*** MOTHER?
AY, THAT HE WAS.
WHAT *IS* A TRAITOR?
WHY, ONE THAT SWEARS AND LIES.
AND BE ALL TRAITORS THAT DO SO?
EVERY ONE THAT DOES SO IS A TRAITOR, AND MUST BE HANGED.

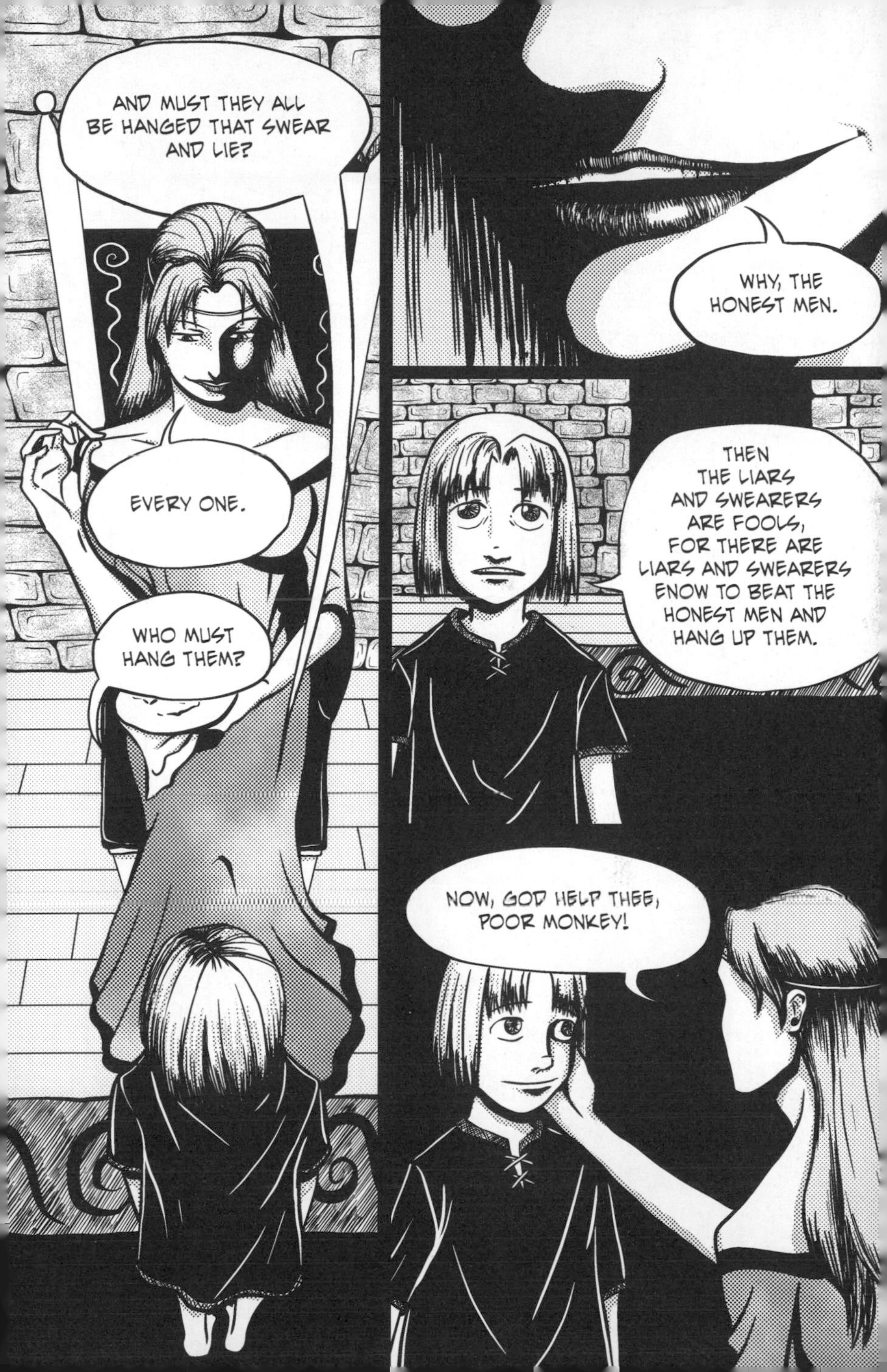
AND MUST THEY ALL BE HANGED THAT SWEAR AND LIE?
EVERY ONE.
WHO MUST HANG THEM?
WHY, THE HONEST MEN.
THEN THE LIARS AND SWEARERS ARE FOOLS, FOR THERE ARE LIARS AND SWEARERS ENOW TO BEAT THE HONEST MEN AND HANG UP THEM.
NOW, GOD HELP THEE, POOR MONKEY!

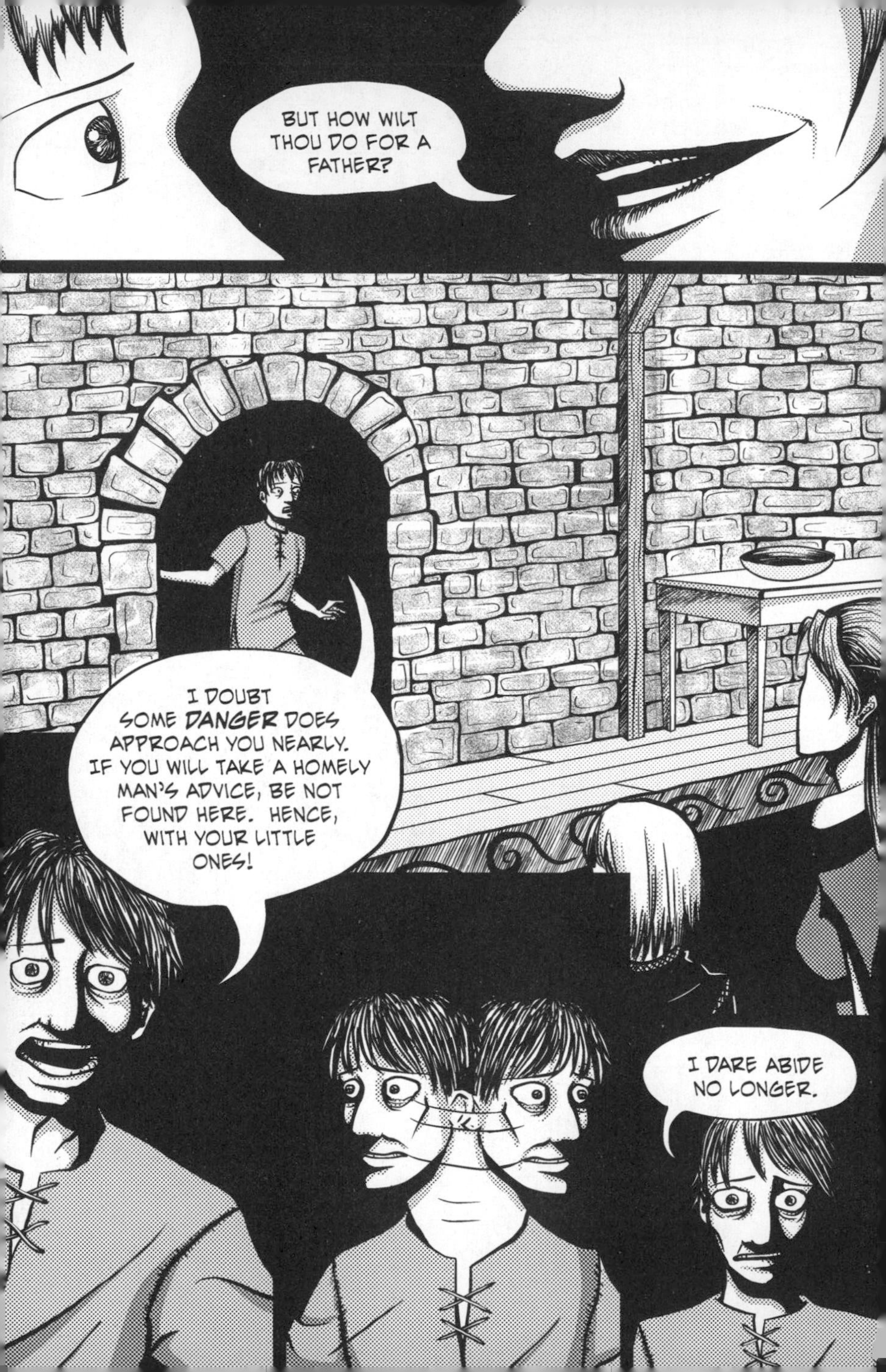
BUT HOW WILT THOU DO FOR A FATHER?
I DOUBT SOME DANGER DOES APPROACH YOU NEARLY. IF YOU WILL TAKE A HOMELY MAN'S ADVICE, BE NOT FOUND HERE. HENCE, WITH YOUR LITTLE ONES!
I DARE ABIDE NO LONGER.

TMP
TMp
TMp
TMp
TMp
WHITHER SHOULD I FLY? I HAVE DONE NO HARM. BUT I REMEMBER NOW: I AM IN THIS EARTHLY WORLD, WHERE TO DO HARM IS OFTEN LAUDABLE, TO DO GOOD SOMETIME ACCOUNTED DANGEROUS FOLLY.
TOMP
TOMP
TOMP
TOMP
TOMP
WHAT ARE THESE FACES?

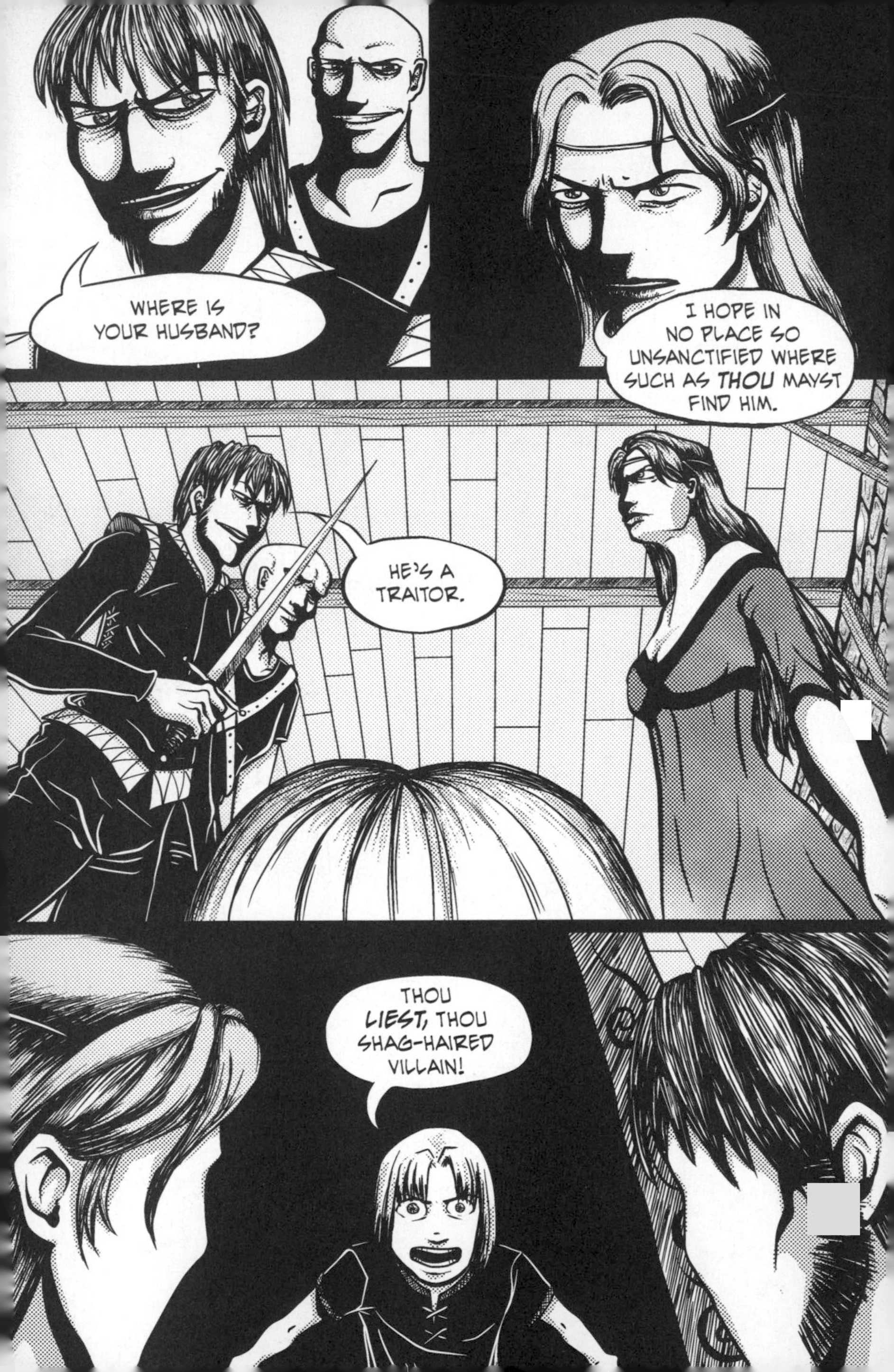
WHERE IS YOUR HUSBAND?
I HOPE IN NO PLACE SO UNSANCTIFIED WHERE SUCH AS THOU MAYST FIND HIM.
HE'S A TRAITOR.
THOU LIEST, THOU SHAG-HAIRED VILLAIN!

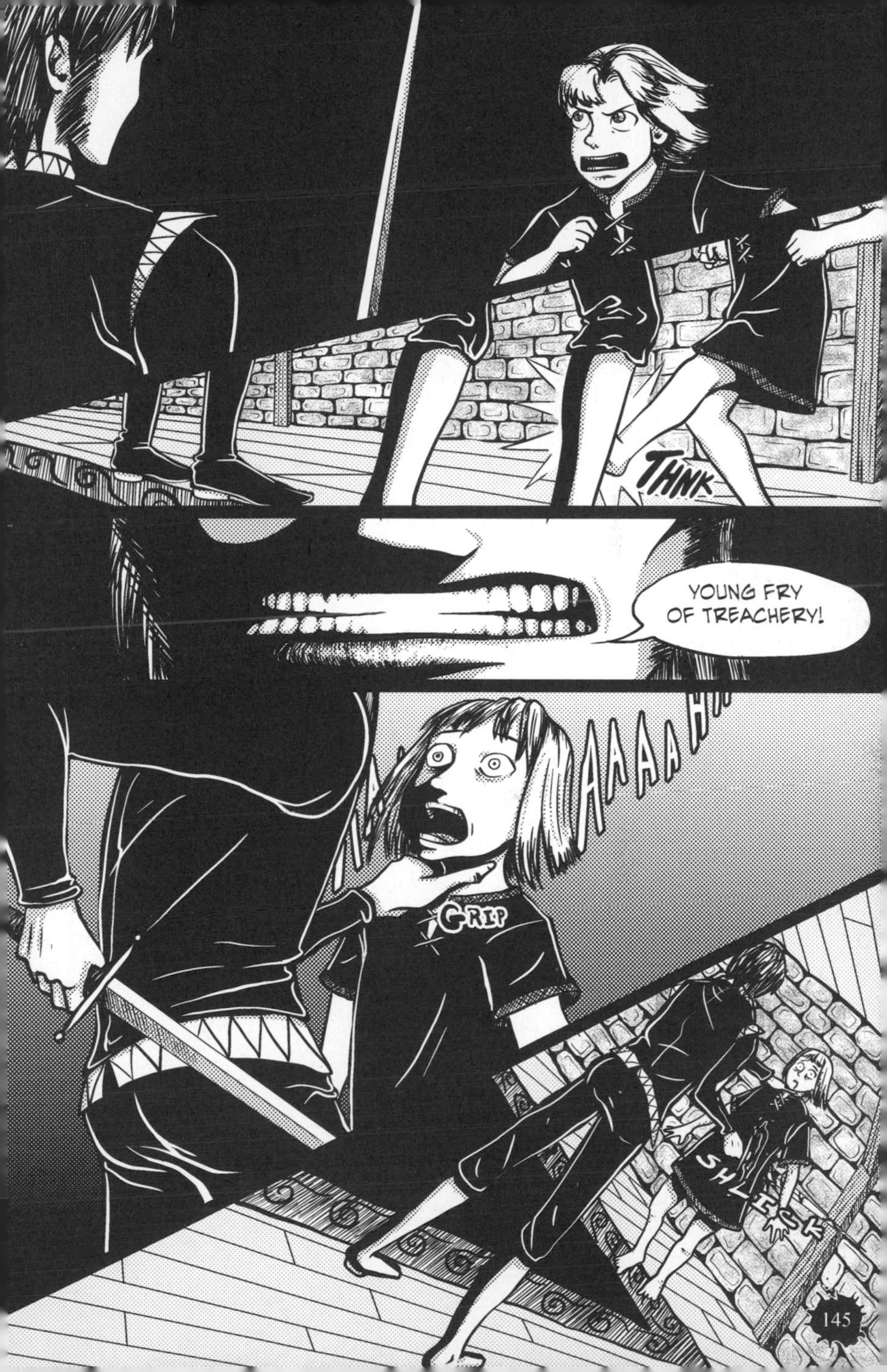
THNK
YOUNG FRY OF TREACHERY!
AAAAH
GRIP
SHLISK

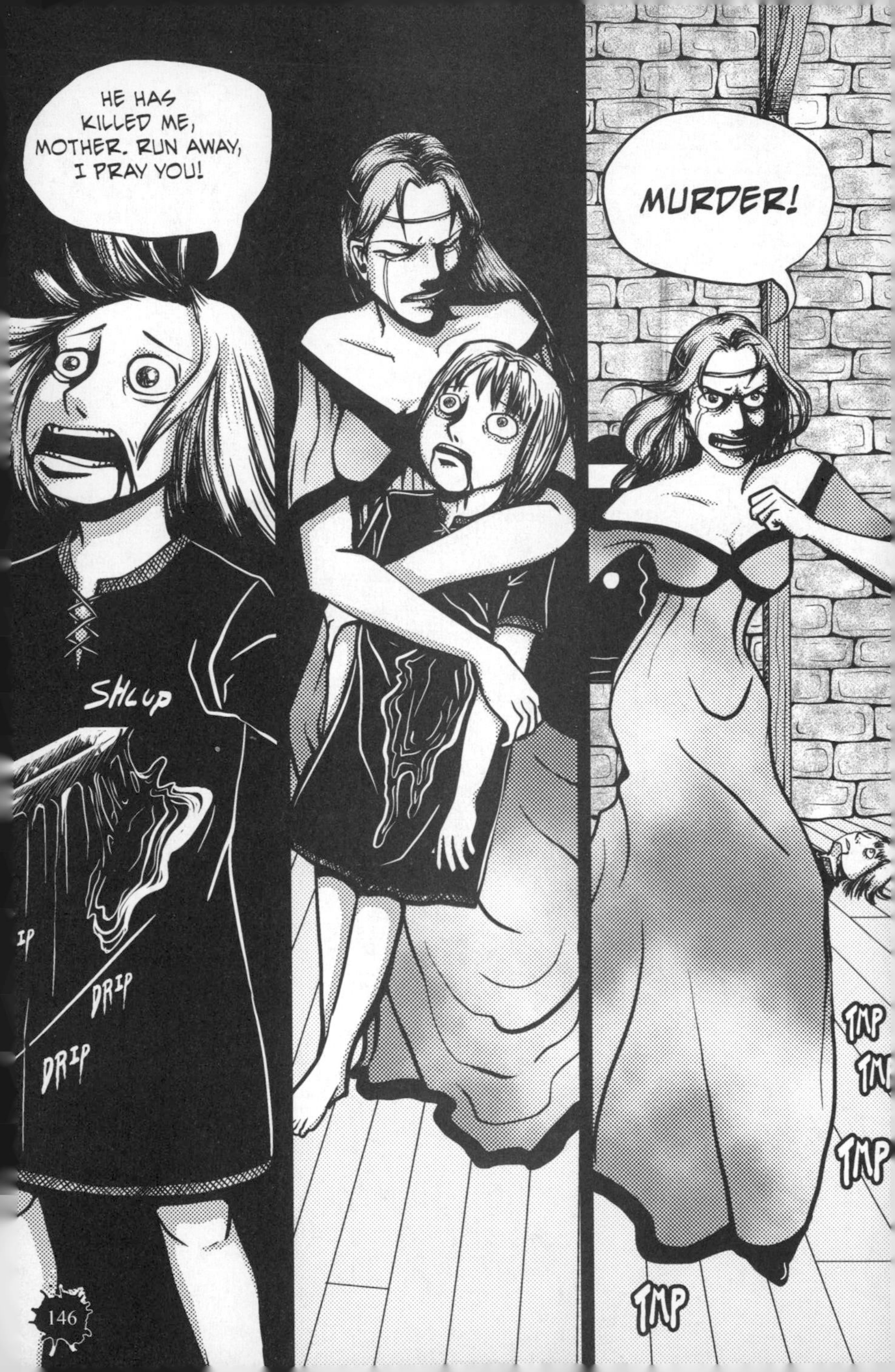
HE HAS KILLED ME, MOTHER. RUN AWAY, I PRAY YOU!
SHLUP
DRIP
DRIP
MURDER!
TMP
TMP
TMP
TMP

I AM NOT TREACHEROUS.
BUT MACBETH IS.
WHY IN THAT RAWNESS LEFT YOU WIFE AND CHILD – THOSE PRECIOUS MOTIVES, THOSE STRONG KNOTS OF LOVE?
I WOULD NOT BE THE VILLAIN THAT THOU THINK'ST FOR THE WHOLE SPACE THAT'S IN THE TYRANT'S GRASP.

I THINK OUR COUNTRY SINKS BENEATH THE YOKE, AND HERE FROM GRACIOUS ENGLAND HAVE I OFFER OF GOODLY THOUSANDS.
BUT, FOR ALL THIS, WHEN I SHALL TREAD UPON THE TYRANT'S HEAD, OR WEAR IT ON MY SWORD, YET MY POOR COUNTRY SHALL HAVE MORE VICES THAN IT HAD BEFORE, BY HIM THAT SHALL SUCCEED.
WHAT SHOULD HE BE?
IT IS MYSELF I MEAN, IN WHOM I KNOW ALL THE PARTICULARS OF VICE SO GRAFTED THAT, WHEN THEY SHALL BE OPENED, BLACK MACBETH WILL SEEM AS PURE AS SNOW, AND THE POOR STATE ESTEEM HIM AS A LAMB.
NOT IN THE LEGIONS OF HORRID HELL CAN COME A DEVIL MORE DAMNED IN EVILS TO TOP MACBETH.
I GRANT HIM BLOODY, LUXURIOUS, AVARICIOUS, FALSE, DECEITFUL, SUDDEN, MALICIOUS—SMACKING OF EVERY SIN THAT HAS A NAME. BUT THERE'S NO BOTTOM—NONE—IN MY... VOLUPTUOUSNESS. YOUR WIVES, YOUR DAUGHTERS, YOUR MATRONS AND YOUR MAIDS, COULD NOT FILL UP THE CISTERN OF MY LUST—BETTER MACBETH THAN SUCH AN ONE TO REIGN.
WITH THIS THERE GROWS IN MY MOST ILL-COMPOSED AFFECTION SUCH A STANCHLESS AVARICE THAT, WERE I KING, I SHOULD CUT OFF THE NOBLES FOR THEIR LANDS—DESIRE HIS JEWELS, AND THIS OTHER'S HOUSE...

O SCOTLAND, SCOTLAND!
IF SUCH A ONE BE FIT TO GOVERN, SPEAK. I AM AS I HAVE SPOKEN.
"FIT TO GOVERN"? NO — NOT TO LIVE! O NATION MISERABLE, WITH AN UNTITLED TYRANT BLOODY-SCEPTERED, WHEN SHALT THOU SEE THY WHOLESOME DAYS AGAIN?
MACDUFF, DEVLISH MACBETH HATH SOUGHT TO WIN ME INTO HIS POWER, AND MODEST WISDOM PLUCKS ME FROM OVER-CREDULOUS HASTE. BUT EVEN NOW I PUT MYSELF TO THY DIRECTION, AND UNSPEAK MINE OWN DETRACTION, HERE ABJURE THE TAINTS AND BLAMES I LAID UPON MYSELF, FOR STRANGERS TO MY NATURE.
WHAT I AM TRULY IS THINE AND MY POOR COUNTRY'S TO COMMAND: WHITHER INDEED, BEFORE THY HERE-APPROACH, OLD SIWARD, WITH TEN THOUSAND WARLIKE MEN, ALREADY AT A POINT, WAS SETTING FORTH.

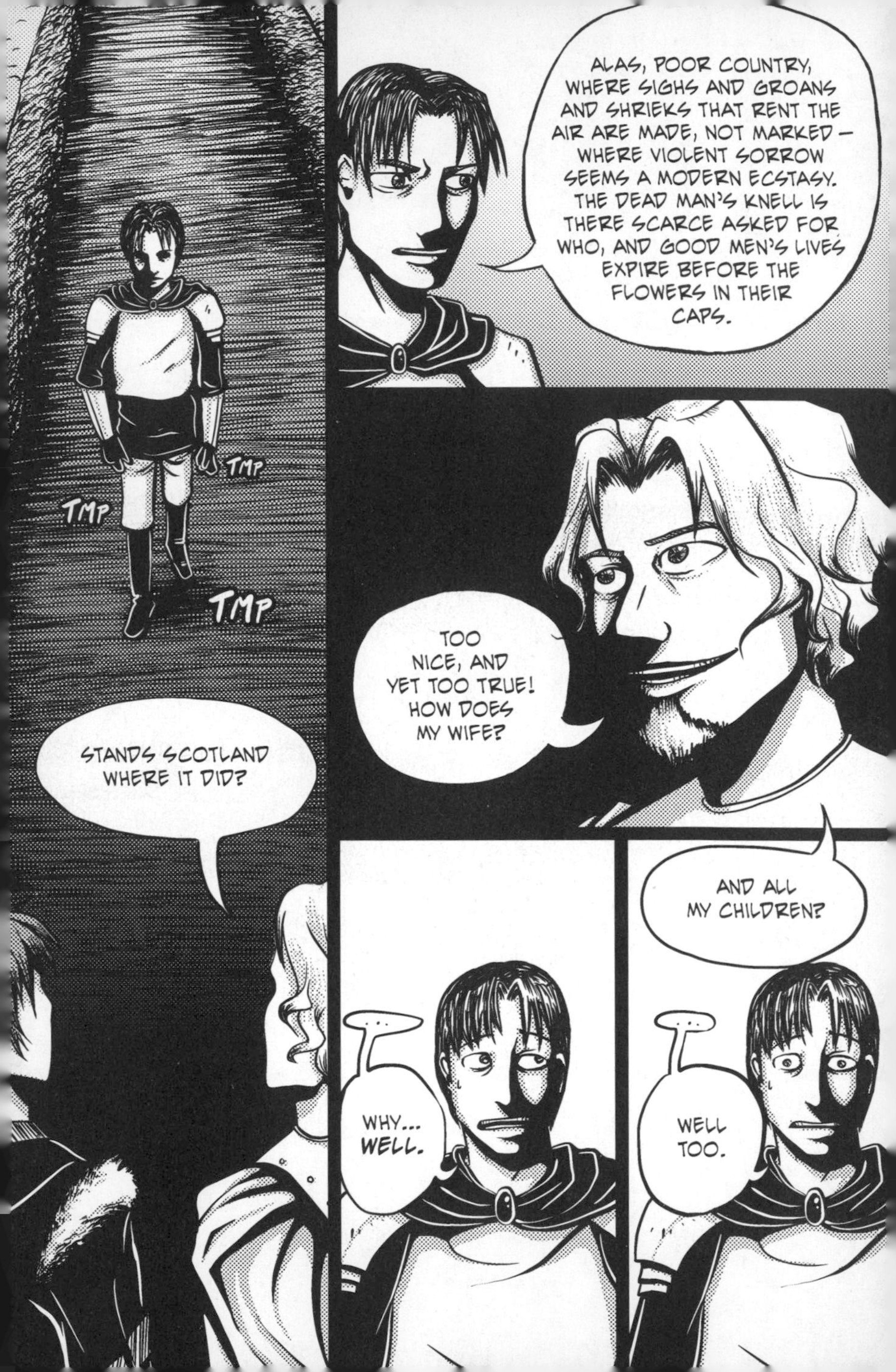
TMP
TMP
TMP
STANDS SCOTLAND WHERE IT DID?
ALAS, POOR COUNTRY, WHERE SIGHS AND GROANS AND SHRIEKS THAT RENT THE AIR ARE MADE, NOT MARKED— WHERE VIOLENT SORROW SEEMS A MODERN ECSTASY. THE DEAD MAN'S KNELL IS THERE SCARCE ASKED FOR WHO, AND GOOD MEN'S LIVES EXPIRE BEFORE THE FLOWERS IN THEIR CAPS.
TOO NICE, AND YET TOO TRUE! HOW DOES MY WIFE?
...
WHY... **WELL.**
AND ALL MY CHILDREN?
...
WELL TOO.

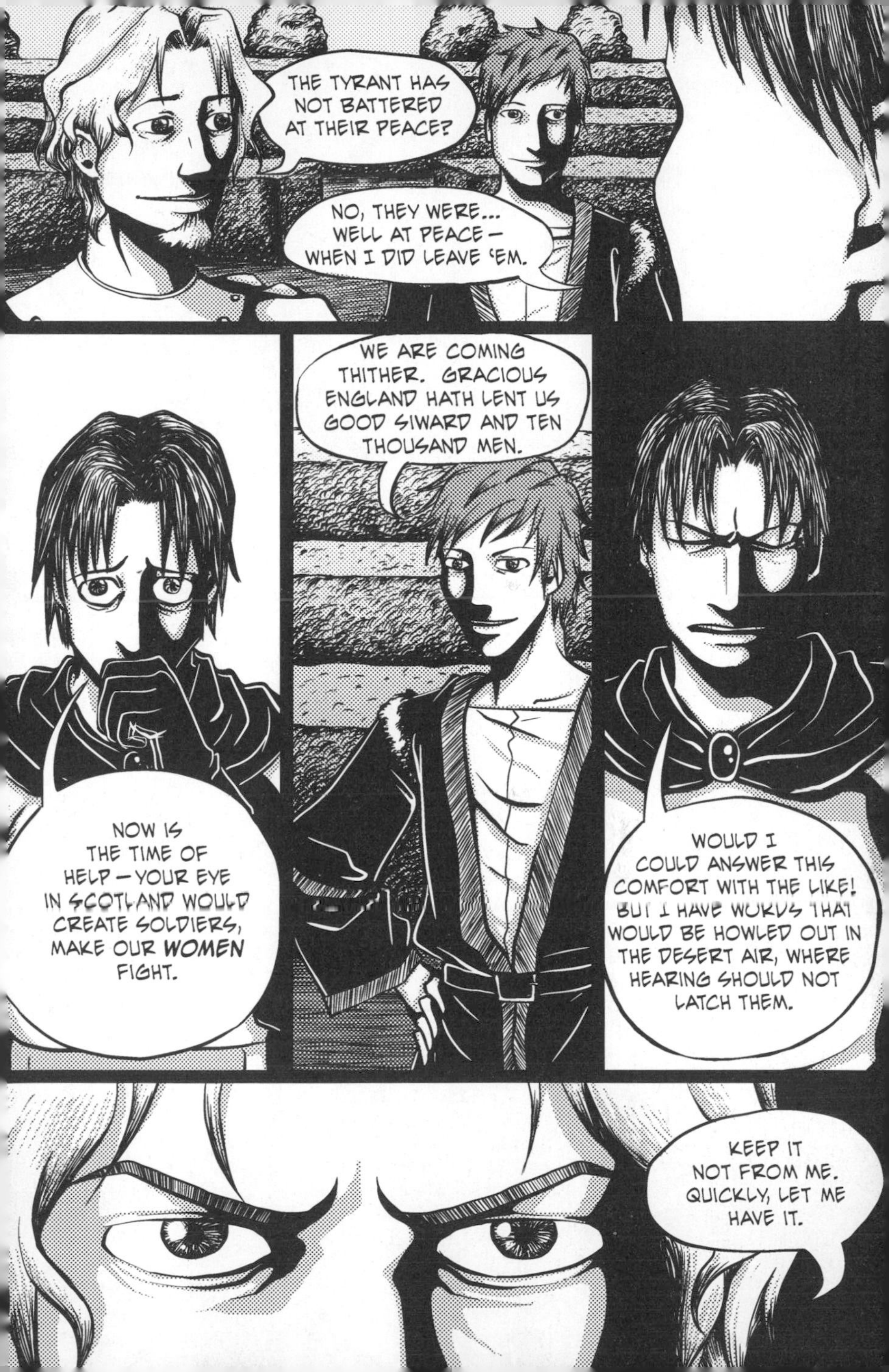
THE TYRANT HAS NOT BATTERED AT THEIR PEACE?
NO, THEY WERE... WELL AT PEACE — WHEN I DID LEAVE 'EM.
NOW IS THE TIME OF HELP — YOUR EYE IN SCOTLAND WOULD CREATE SOLDIERS, MAKE OUR **WOMEN** FIGHT.
WE ARE COMING THITHER. GRACIOUS ENGLAND HATH LENT US GOOD SIWARD AND TEN THOUSAND MEN.
WOULD I COULD ANSWER THIS COMFORT WITH THE LIKE! BUT I HAVE WORDS THAT WOULD BE HOWLED OUT IN THE DESERT AIR, WHERE HEARING SHOULD NOT LATCH THEM.
KEEP IT NOT FROM ME. QUICKLY, LET ME HAVE IT.

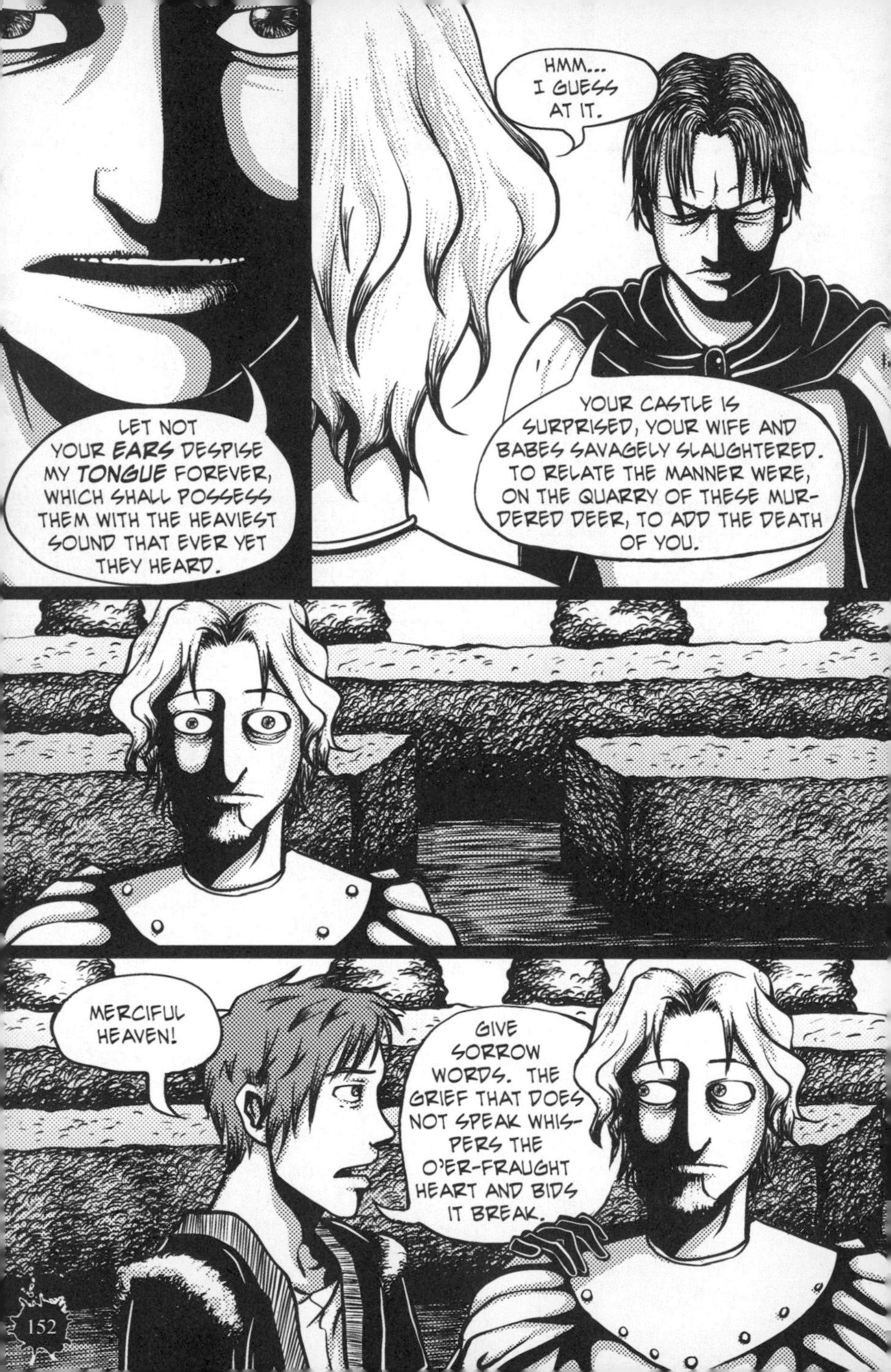
HMM... I GUESS AT IT.
LET NOT YOUR EARS DESPISE MY TONGUE FOREVER, WHICH SHALL POSSESS THEM WITH THE HEAVIEST SOUND THAT EVER YET THEY HEARD.
YOUR CASTLE IS SURPRISED, YOUR WIFE AND BABES SAVAGELY SLAUGHTERED. TO RELATE THE MANNER WERE, ON THE QUARRY OF THESE MURDERED DEER, TO ADD THE DEATH OF YOU.
MERCIFUL HEAVEN!
GIVE SORROW WORDS. THE GRIEF THAT DOES NOT SPEAK WHISPERS THE O'ER-FRAUGHT HEART AND BIDS IT BREAK.

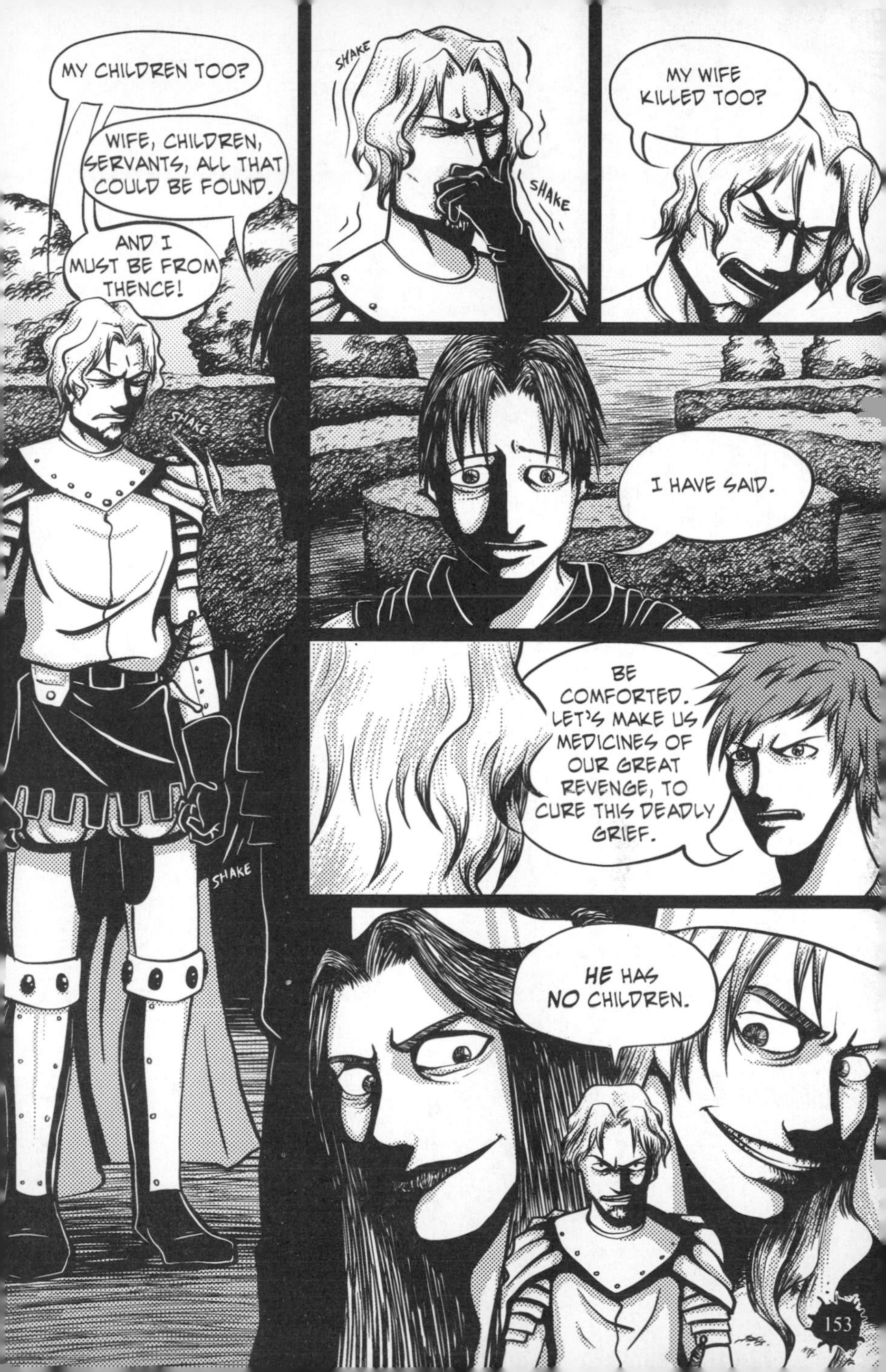
MY CHILDREN TOO?
WIFE, CHILDREN, SERVANTS, ALL THAT COULD BE FOUND.
AND I MUST BE FROM THENCE!
SHAKE
SHAKE
SHAKE
SHAKE
MY WIFE KILLED TOO?
I HAVE SAID.
BE COMFORTED. LET'S MAKE US MEDICINES OF OUR GREAT REVENGE, TO CURE THIS DEADLY GRIEF.
HE HAS NO CHILDREN.

ALL MY PRETTY ONES? DID YOU SAY ALL? O HELL-KITE! ALL? WHAT, ALL MY PRETTY CHICKENS AND THEIR DAM AT ONE FELL
DISPUTE IT LIKE A MAN.
I SHALL DO SO.
BUT I MUST ALSO FEEL IT AS A MAN. I CANNOT BUT REMEMBER SUCH THINGS WERE, THAT WERE MOST PRE-CIOUS TO ME. DID HEAVEN LOOK ON, AND WOULD NOT TAKE THEIR PART? SINFUL MACDUFF! NOT FOR THEIR OWN DEMERITS, BUT FOR MINE, FELL SLAUGHTER ON THEIR SOULS. HEAVEN REST THEM NOW!
BE THIS THE WHETSTONE OF YOUR SWORD—LET GRIEF CONVERT TO ANGER. BLUNT NOT THE HEART, ENRAGE IT.
O, I COULD PLAY THE WOMAN WITH MINE EYES AND BRAGGART WITH MY TONGUE! BUT, FRONT TO FRONT BRING THOU THIS FIEND OF SCOTLAND AND MYSELF. WITHIN MY SWORD'S LENGTH SET HIM—IF HE 'SCAPE, HEAVEN FOR-GIVE HIM, TOO!

Act V

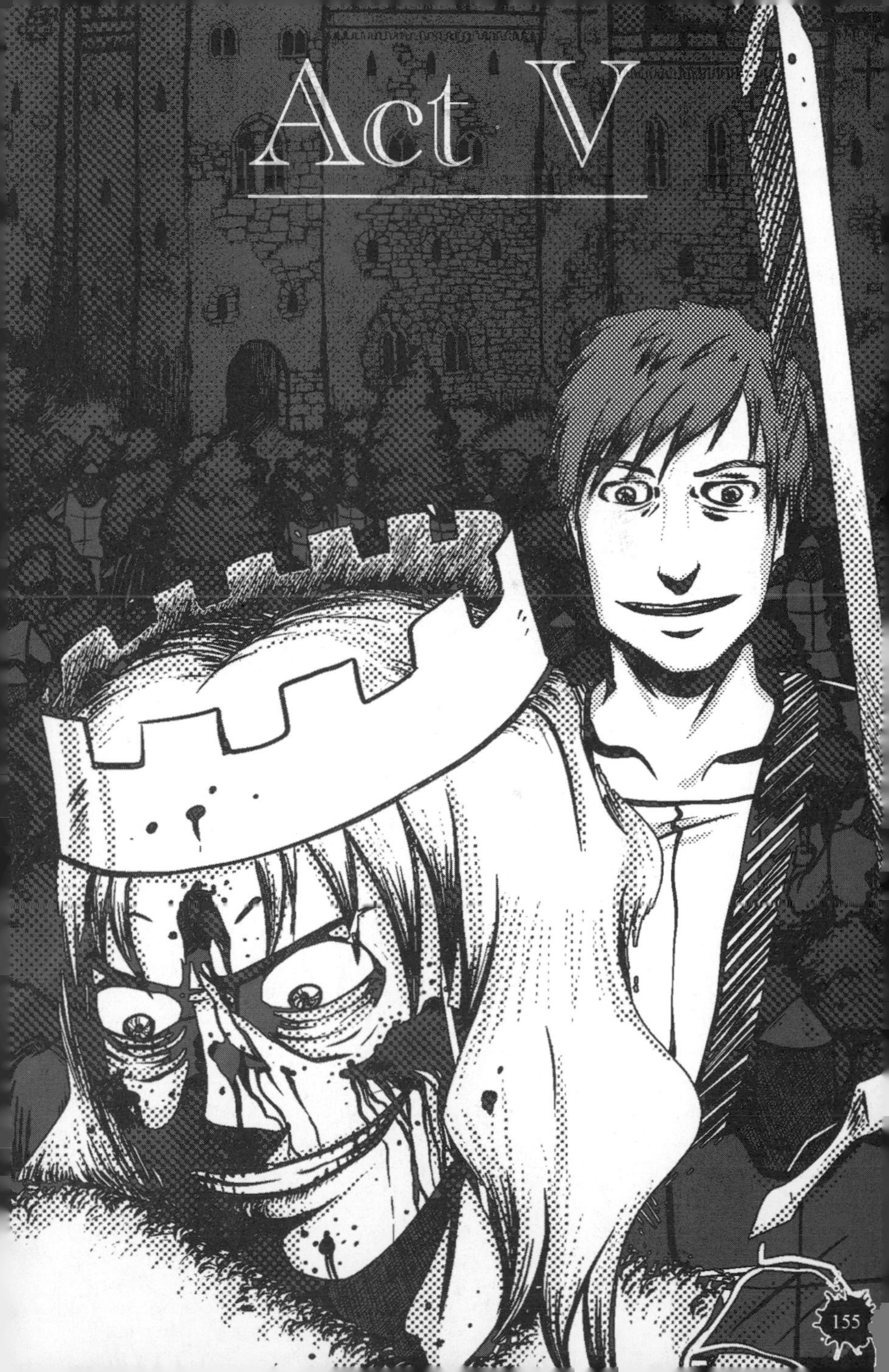

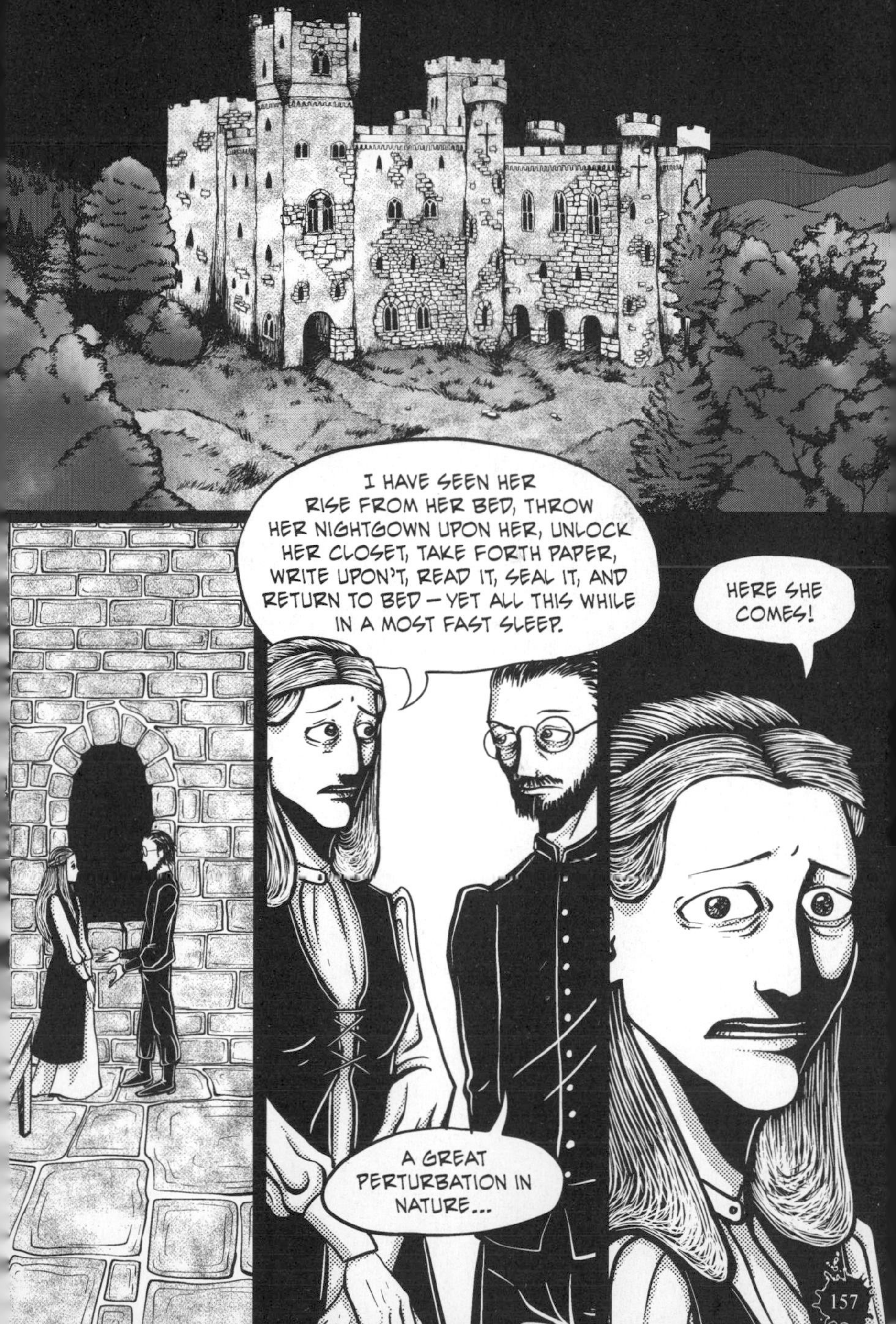
I HAVE SEEN HER RISE FROM HER BED, THROW HER NIGHTGOWN UPON HER, UNLOCK HER CLOSET, TAKE FORTH PAPER, WRITE UPON'T, READ IT, SEAL IT, AND RETURN TO BED—YET ALL THIS WHILE IN A MOST FAST SLEEP.
A GREAT PERTURBATION IN NATURE...
HERE SHE COMES!

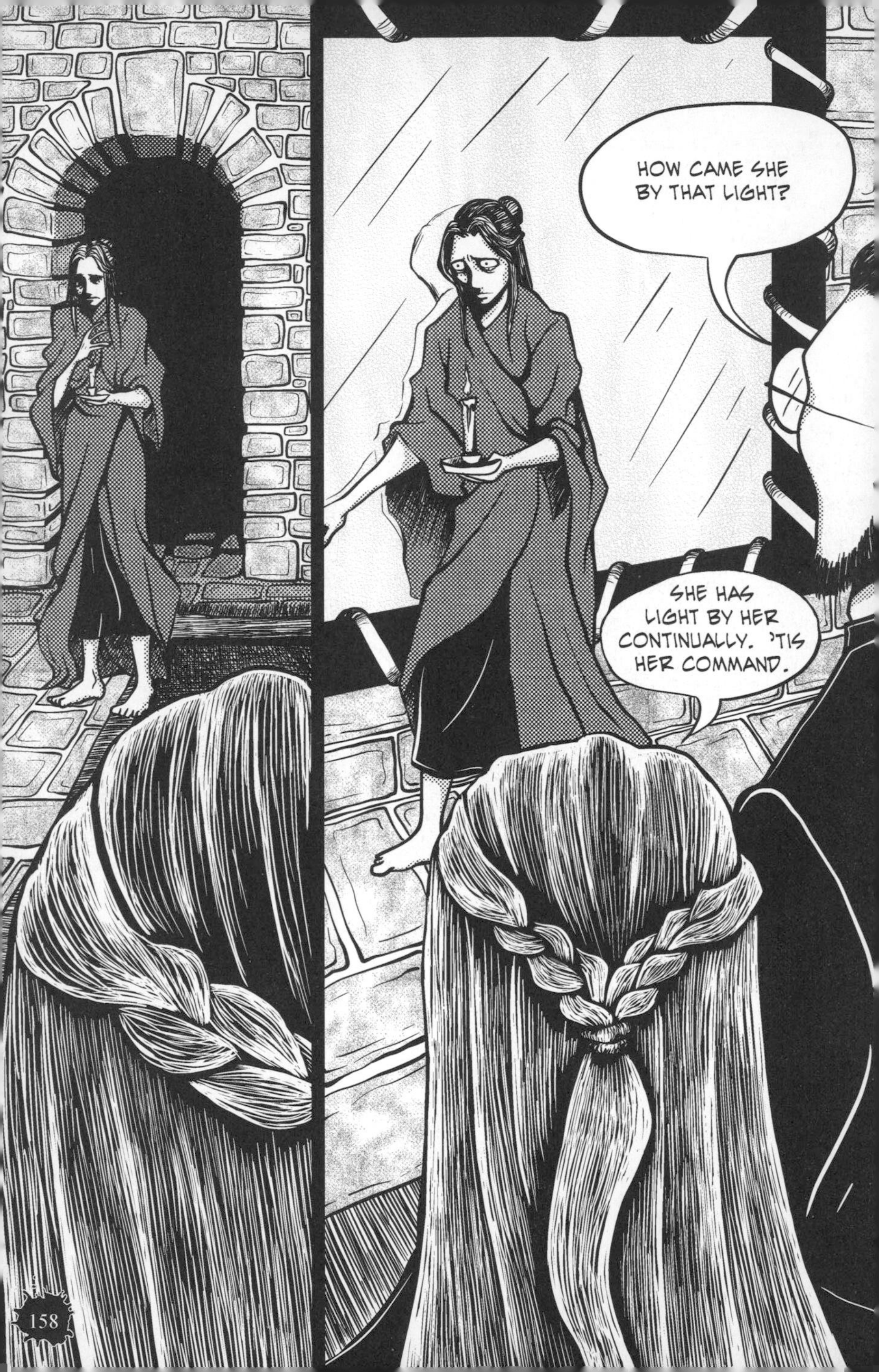
HOW CAME SHE BY THAT LIGHT?
SHE HAS LIGHT BY HER CONTINUALLY. 'TIS HER COMMAND.

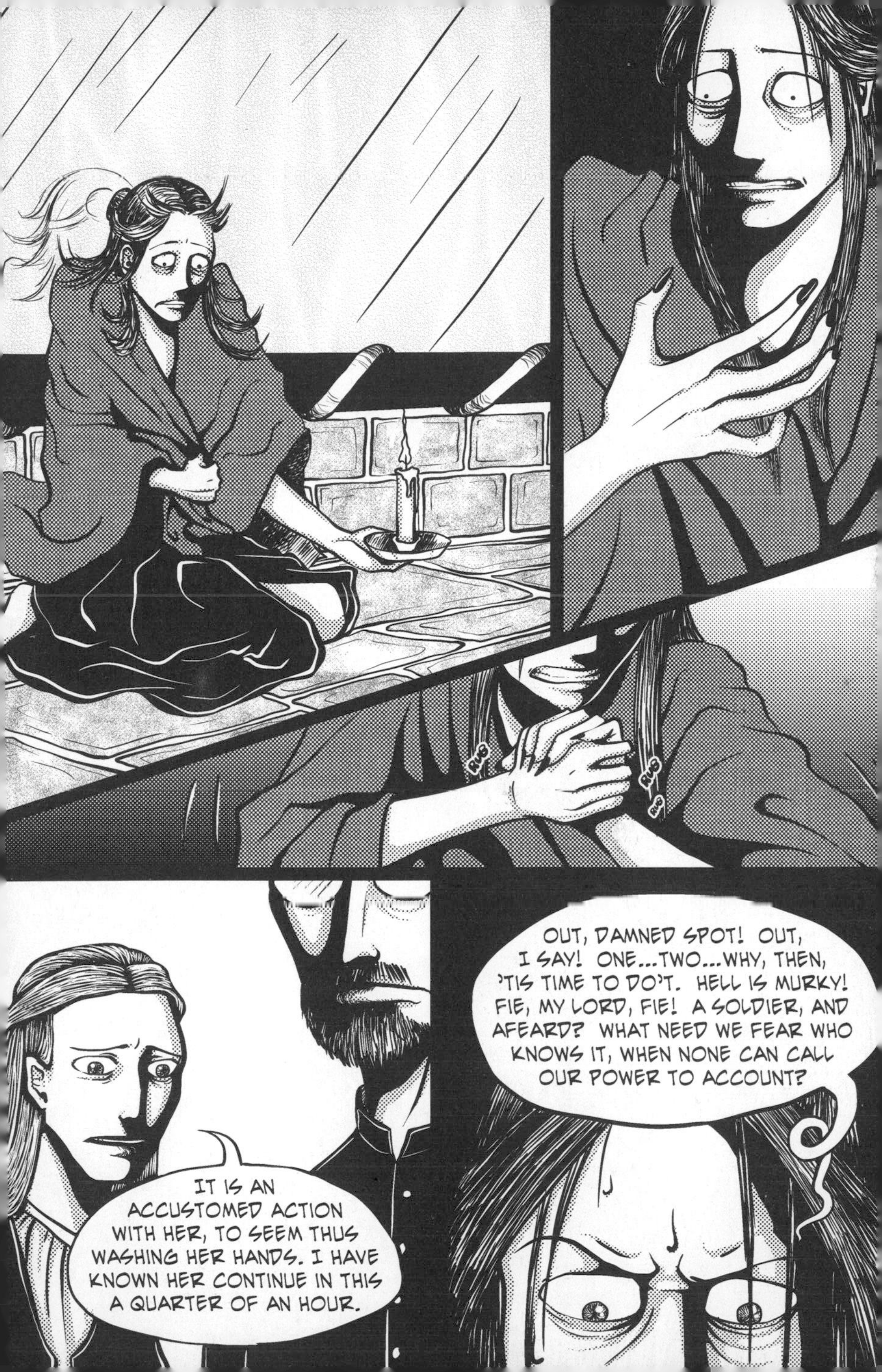
RUB
RUB
RUB
OUT, DAMNED SPOT! OUT, I SAY! ONE...TWO...WHY, THEN, 'TIS TIME TO DO'T. HELL IS MURKY! FIE, MY LORD, FIE! A SOLDIER, AND AFEARD? WHAT NEED WE FEAR WHO KNOWS IT, WHEN NONE CAN CALL OUR POWER TO ACCOUNT?
IT IS AN ACCUSTOMED ACTION WITH HER, TO SEEM THUS WASHING HER HANDS. I HAVE KNOWN HER CONTINUE IN THIS A QUARTER OF AN HOUR.

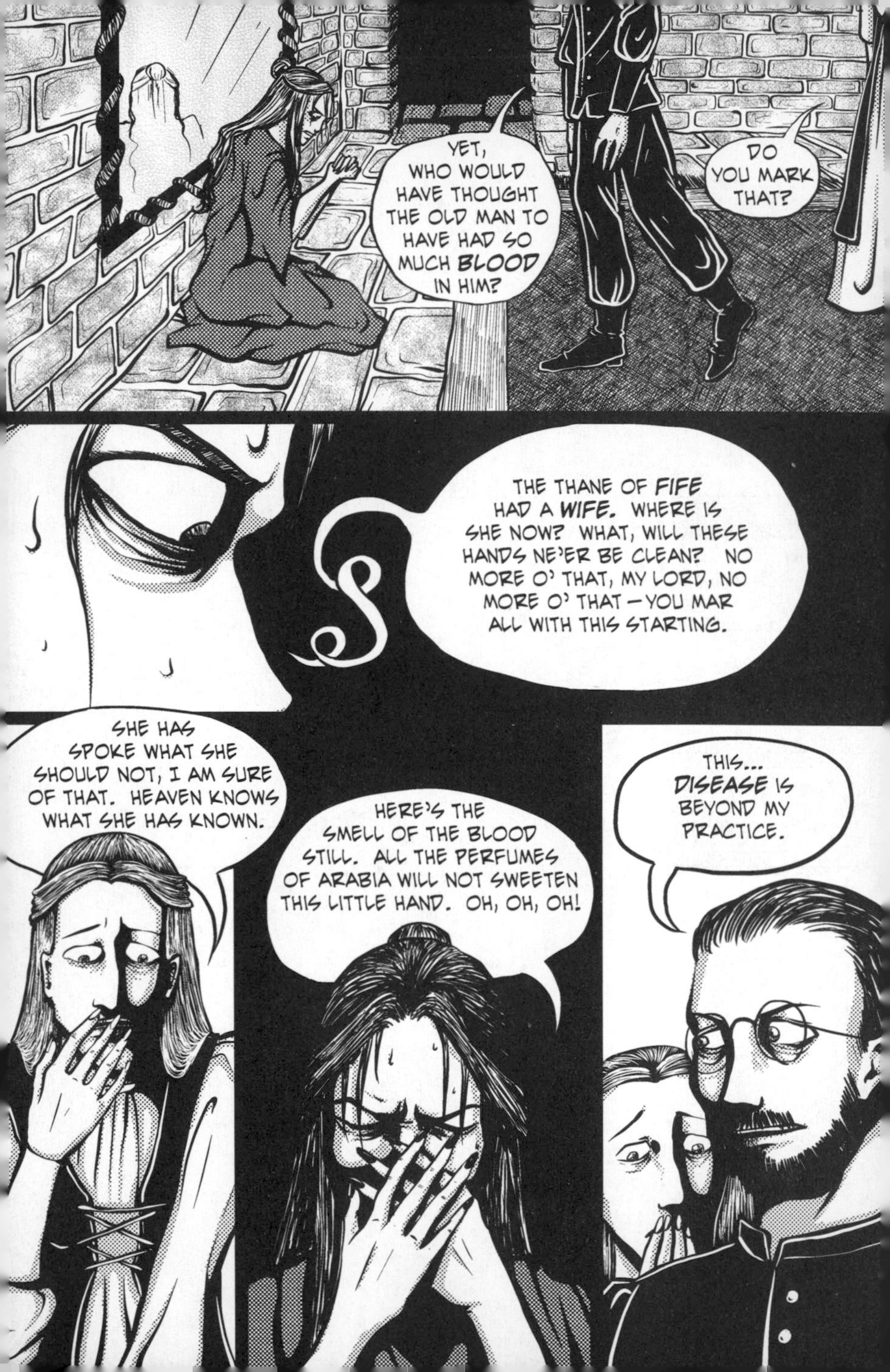

YET, WHO WOULD HAVE THOUGHT THE OLD MAN TO HAVE HAD SO MUCH **BLOOD** IN HIM?
DO YOU MARK THAT?
THE THANE OF **FIFE** HAD A **WIFE**. WHERE IS SHE NOW? WHAT, WILL THESE HANDS NE'ER BE CLEAN? NO MORE O' THAT, MY LORD, NO MORE O' THAT—YOU MAR ALL WITH THIS STARTING.
SHE HAS SPOKE WHAT SHE SHOULD NOT, I AM SURE OF THAT. HEAVEN KNOWS WHAT SHE HAS KNOWN.
HERE'S THE SMELL OF THE BLOOD STILL. ALL THE PERFUMES OF ARABIA WILL NOT SWEETEN THIS LITTLE HAND. OH, OH, OH!
THIS... **DISEASE** IS BEYOND MY PRACTICE.

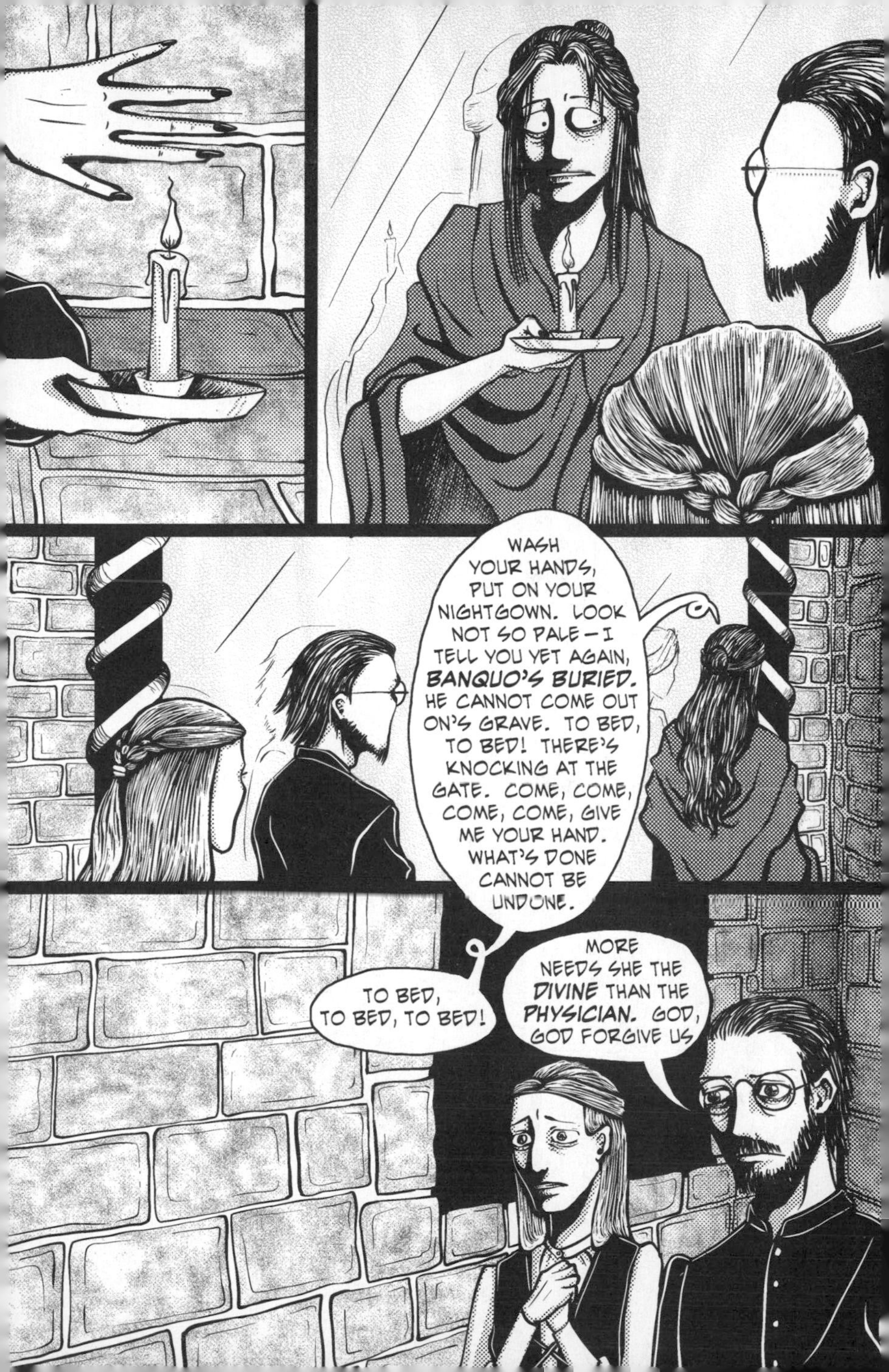
WASH YOUR HANDS, PUT ON YOUR NIGHTGOWN. LOOK NOT SO PALE — I TELL YOU YET AGAIN, BANQUO'S BURIED. HE CANNOT COME OUT ON'S GRAVE. TO BED, TO BED! THERE'S KNOCKING AT THE GATE. COME, COME, COME, COME, GIVE ME YOUR HAND. WHAT'S DONE CANNOT BE UNDONE.
TO BED, TO BED, TO BED!
MORE NEEDS SHE THE DIVINE THAN THE PHYSICIAN. GOD, GOD FORGIVE US

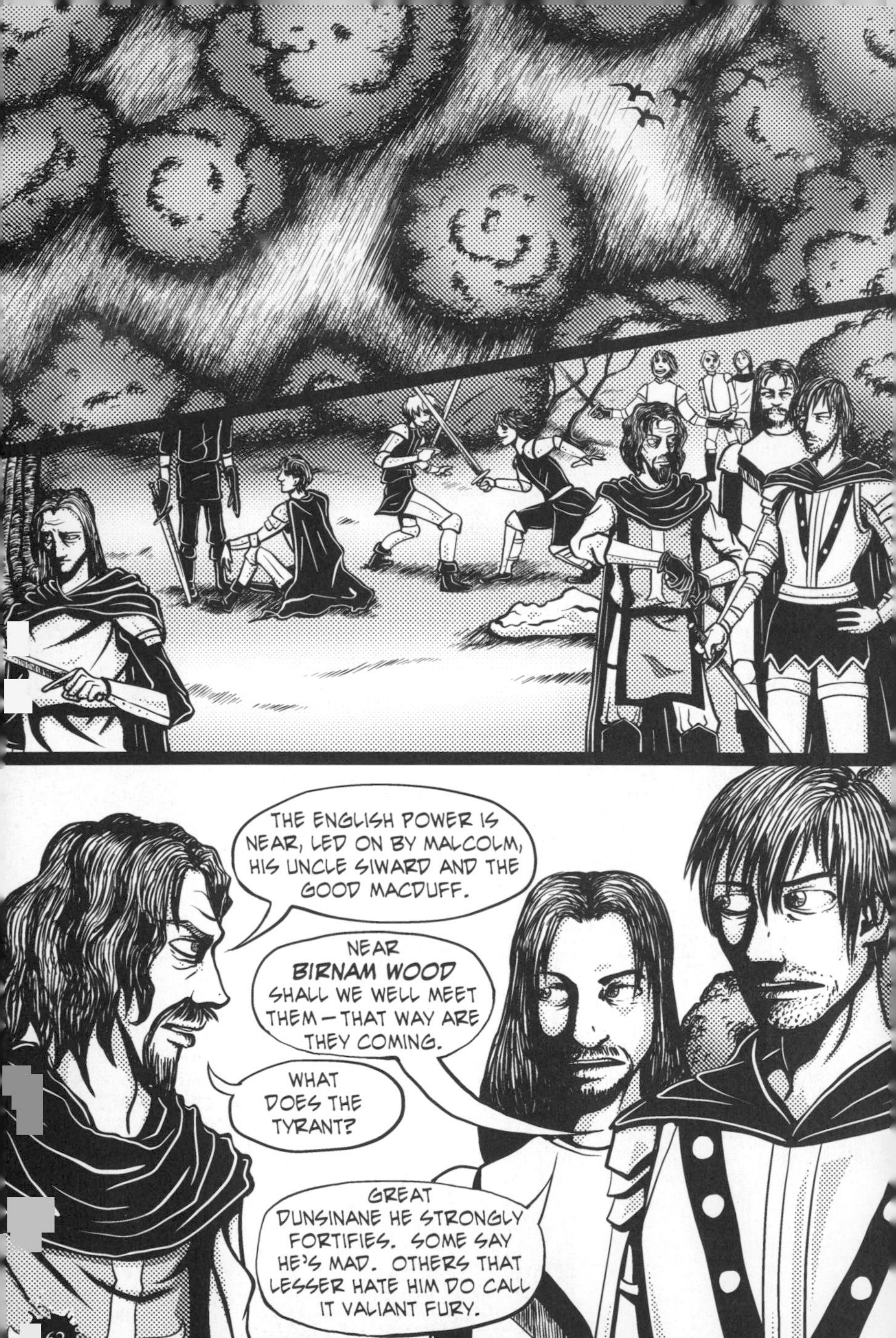
THE ENGLISH POWER IS NEAR, LED ON BY MALCOLM, HIS UNCLE SIWARD AND THE GOOD MACDUFF.
NEAR **BIRNAM WOOD** SHALL WE WELL MEET THEM — THAT WAY ARE THEY COMING.
WHAT DOES THE TYRANT?
GREAT DUNSINANE HE STRONGLY FORTIFIES. SOME SAY HE'S MAD. OTHERS THAT LESSER HATE HIM DO CALL IT VALIANT FURY.

NOW HE FEELS HIS SECRET MURDERS STICKING ON HIS HANDS. THOSE HE COMMANDS MOVE ONLY IN COMMAND, NOTHING IN LOVE. NOW DOES HE FEEL HIS TITLE HANG LOOSE ABOUT HIM, LIKE A GIANT'S ROBE UPON A DWARFISH THIEF...
TILL BIRNAM WOOD REMOVE TO DUNSINANE, I CANNOT TAINT WITH FEAR. WHAT'S THE BOY MALCOLM? WAS HE NOT BORN OF WOMAN? THE SPIRITS THAT KNOW ALL MORTAL CONSEQUENCES HAVE PRONOUNCED ME THUS: "FEAR NOT, MACBETH—NO MAN THAT'S BORN OF WOMAN SHALL E'ER HAVE POWER UPON THEE." THEN FLY, FALSE THANES!

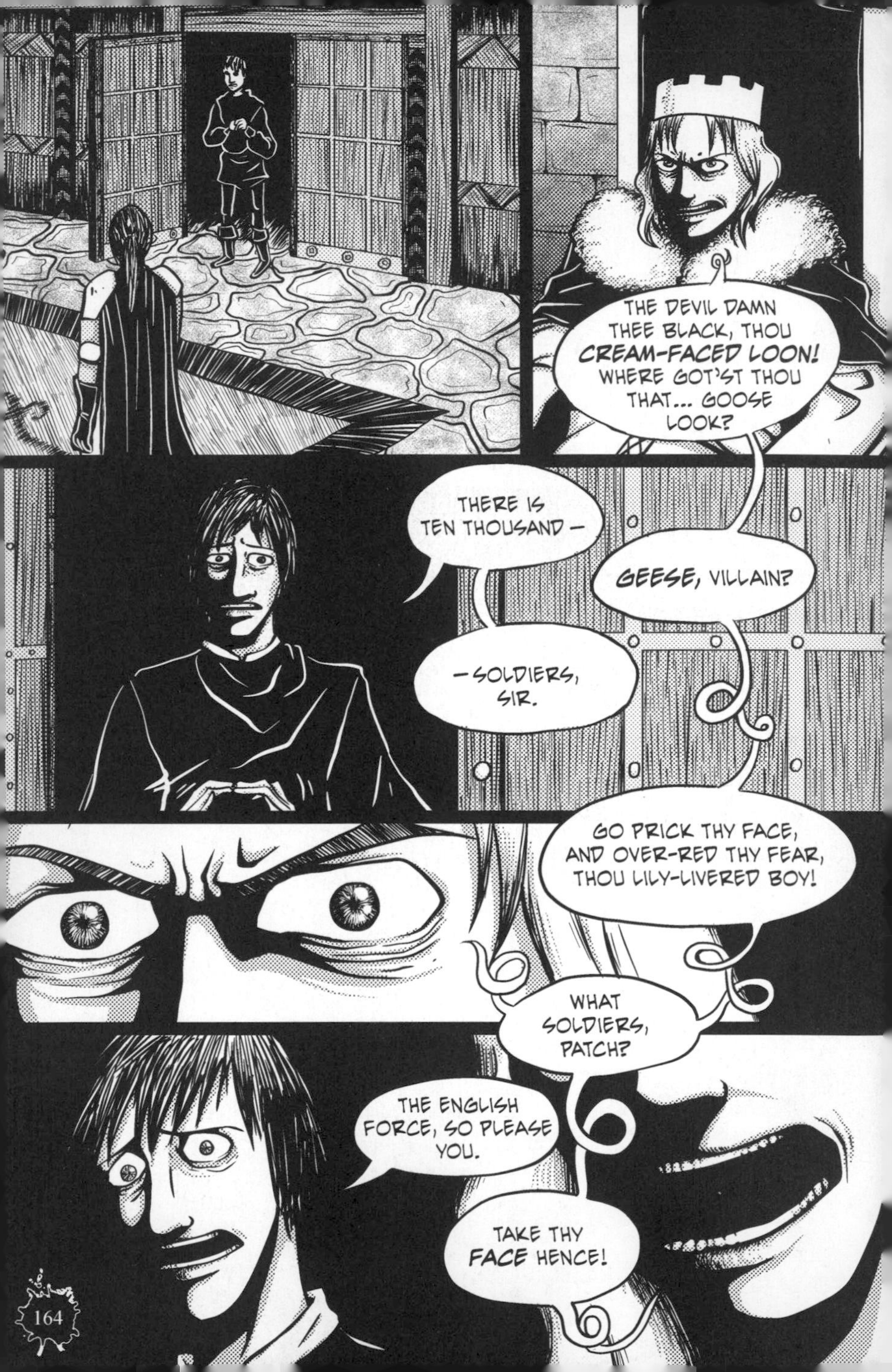
THE DEVIL DAMN THEE BLACK, THOU CREAM-FACED LOON! WHERE GOT'ST THOU THAT... GOOSE LOOK?
THERE IS TEN THOUSAND —
GEESE, VILLAIN?
—SOLDIERS, SIR.
GO PRICK THY FACE, AND OVER-RED THY FEAR, THOU LILY-LIVERED BOY!
WHAT SOLDIERS, PATCH?
THE ENGLISH FORCE, SO PLEASE YOU.
TAKE THY FACE HENCE!

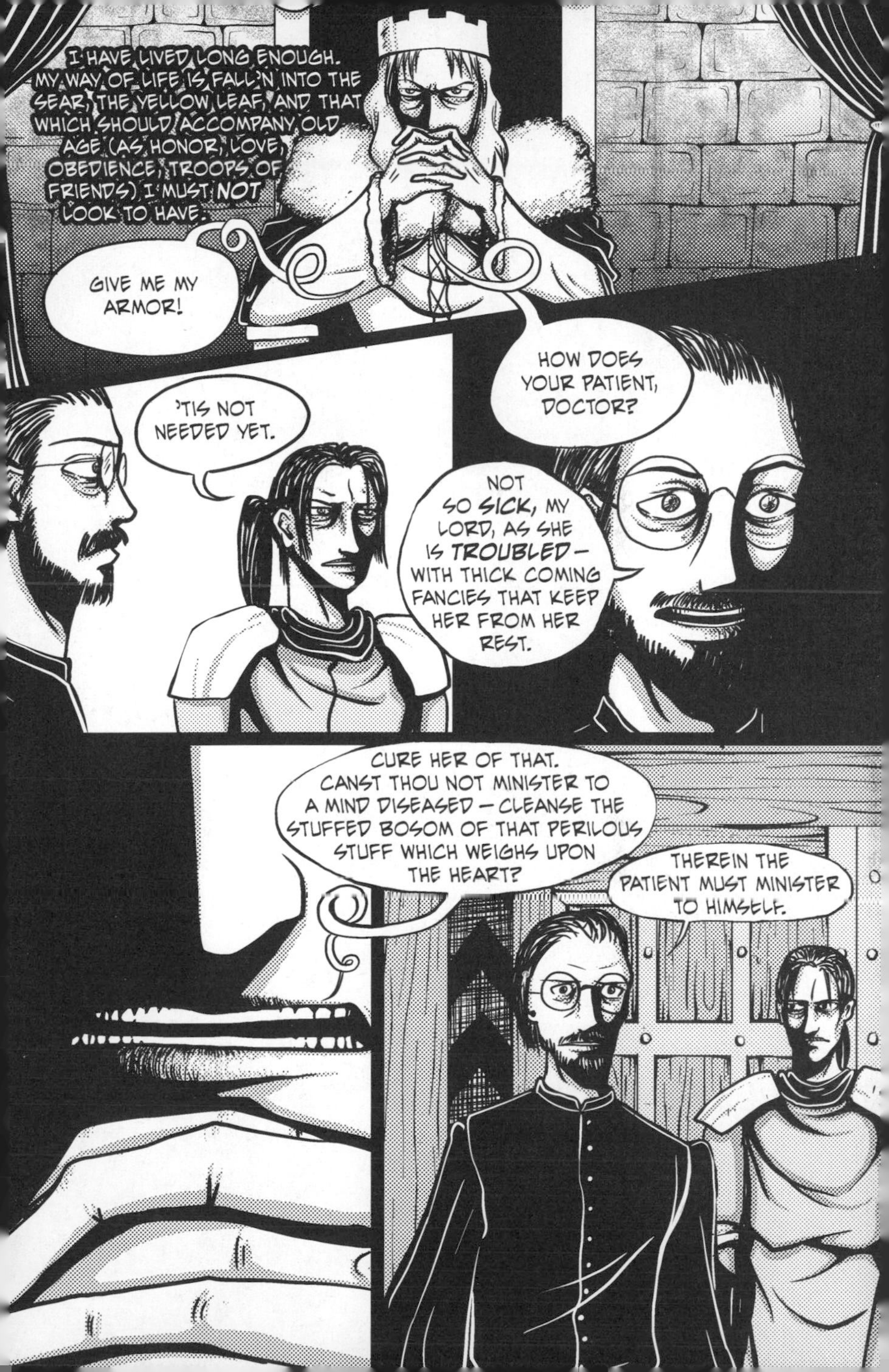
I HAVE LIVED LONG ENOUGH. MY WAY OF LIFE IS FALL'N INTO THE SEAR, THE YELLOW LEAF, AND THAT WHICH SHOULD ACCOMPANY OLD AGE (AS HONOR, LOVE, OBEDIENCE, TROOPS OF FRIENDS) I MUST NOT LOOK TO HAVE.
GIVE ME MY ARMOR!
'TIS NOT NEEDED YET.
HOW DOES YOUR PATIENT, DOCTOR?
NOT SO SICK, MY LORD, AS SHE IS TROUBLED— WITH THICK COMING FANCIES THAT KEEP HER FROM HER REST.
CURE HER OF THAT. CANST THOU NOT MINISTER TO A MIND DISEASED— CLEANSE THE STUFFED BOSOM OF THAT PERILOUS STUFF WHICH WEIGHS UPON THE HEART?
THEREIN THE PATIENT MUST MINISTER TO HIMSELF.

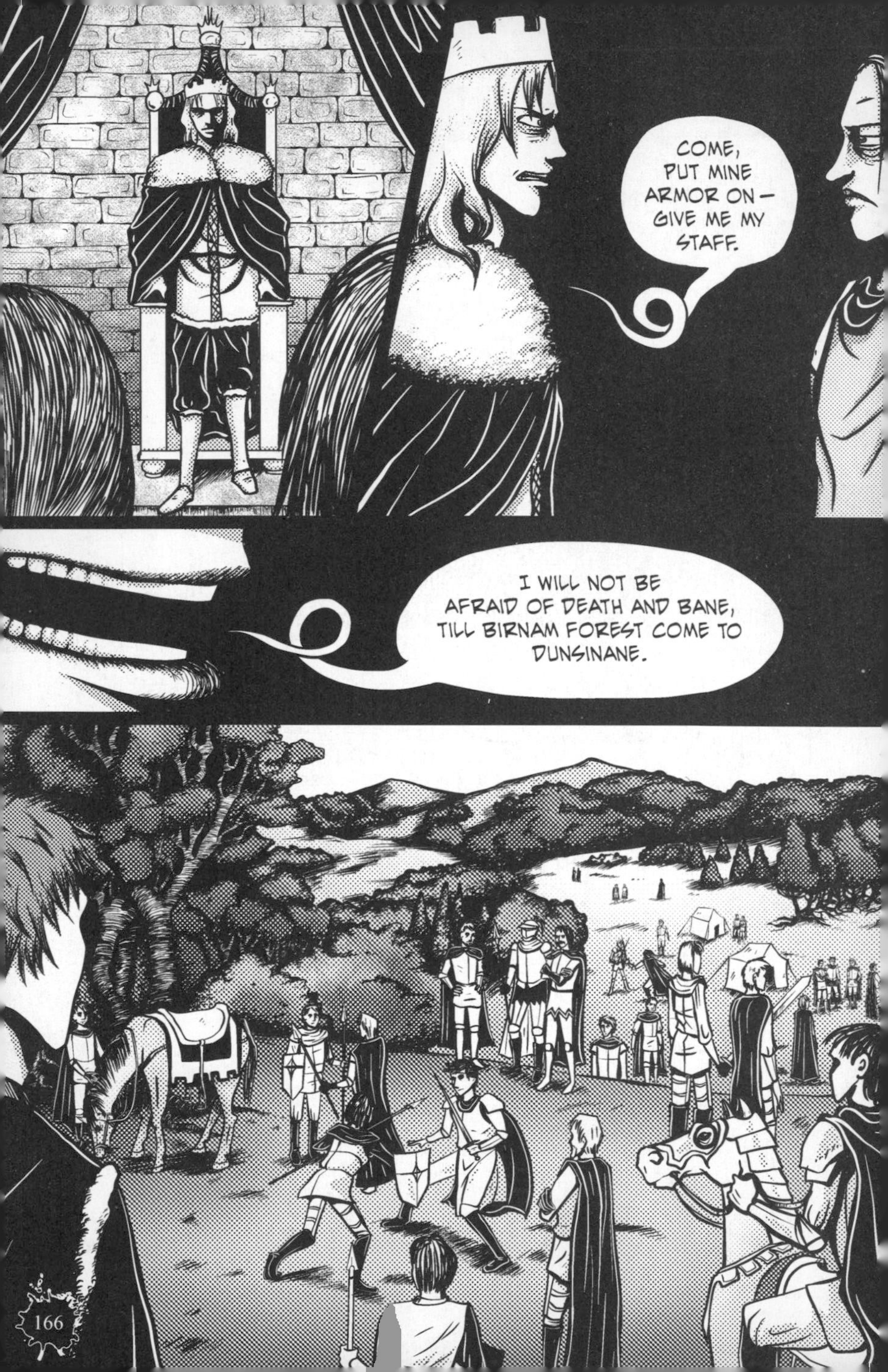
COME, PUT MINE ARMOR ON— GIVE ME MY STAFF.
I WILL NOT BE AFRAID OF DEATH AND BANE, TILL BIRNAM FOREST COME TO DUNSINANE.

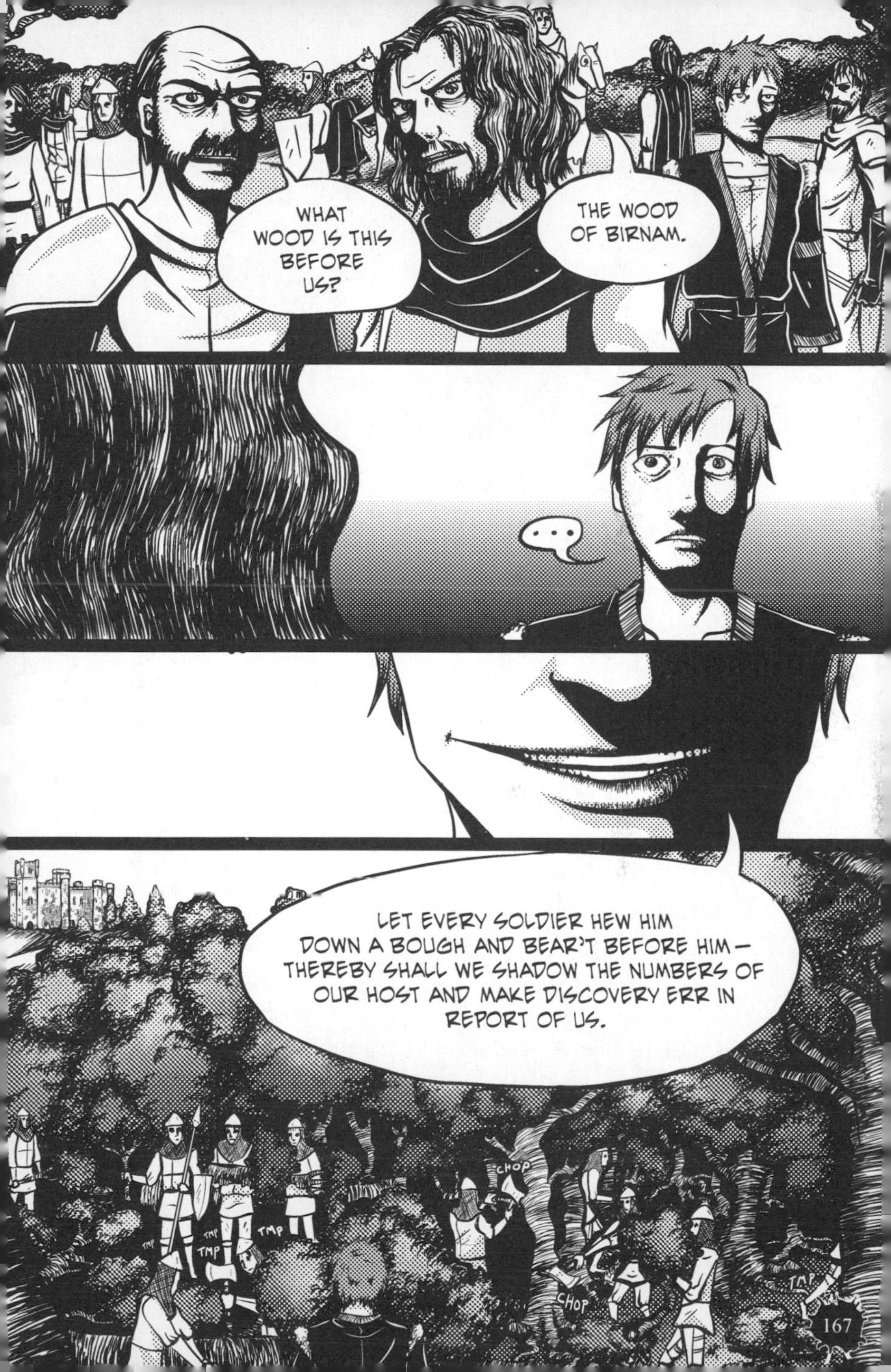
WHAT WOOD IS THIS BEFORE US?
THE WOOD OF BIRNAM.
...
LET EVERY SOLDIER HEW HIM DOWN A BOUGH AND BEAR'T BEFORE HIM— THEREBY SHALL WE SHADOW THE NUMBERS OF OUR HOST AND MAKE DISCOVERY ERR IN REPORT OF US.
CHOP
TMP
TMP
TMP
TMP
CHOP
TMP

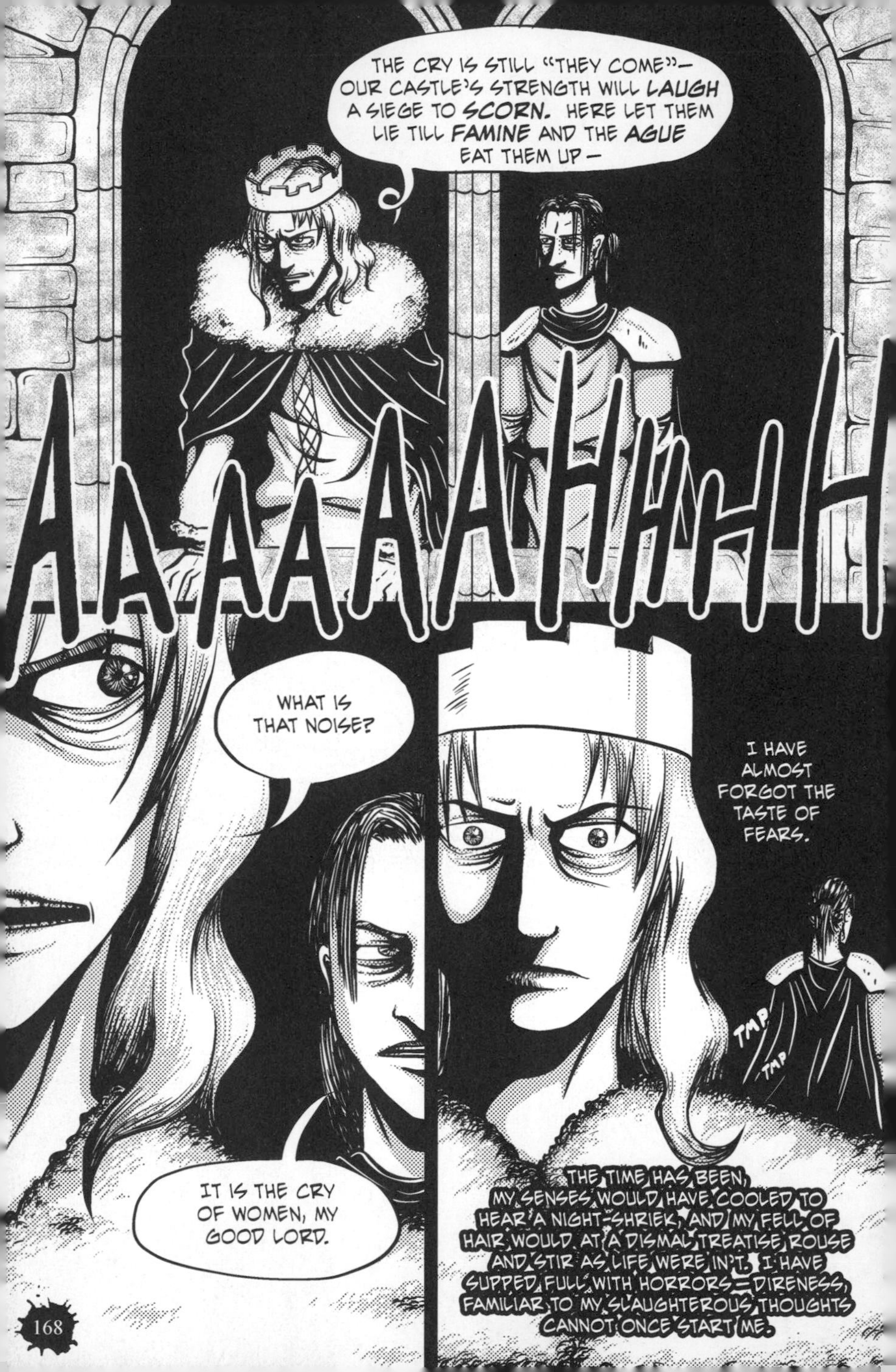
THE CRY IS STILL "THEY COME"— OUR CASTLE'S STRENGTH WILL LAUGH A SIEGE TO SCORN. HERE LET THEM LIE TILL FAMINE AND THE AGUE EAT THEM UP—
AAAAAAHHHHHH
WHAT IS THAT NOISE?
IT IS THE CRY OF WOMEN, MY GOOD LORD.
I HAVE ALMOST FORGOT THE TASTE OF FEARS.
TMP
TMP
THE TIME HAS BEEN, MY SENSES WOULD HAVE COOLED TO HEAR A NIGHT-SHRIEK, AND MY FELL OF HAIR WOULD AT A DISMAL TREATISE ROUSE AND STIR AS LIFE WERE IN'T. I HAVE SUPPED FULL WITH HORRORS—DIRENESS, FAMILIAR TO MY SLAUGHTEROUS THOUGHTS CANNOT ONCE START ME.

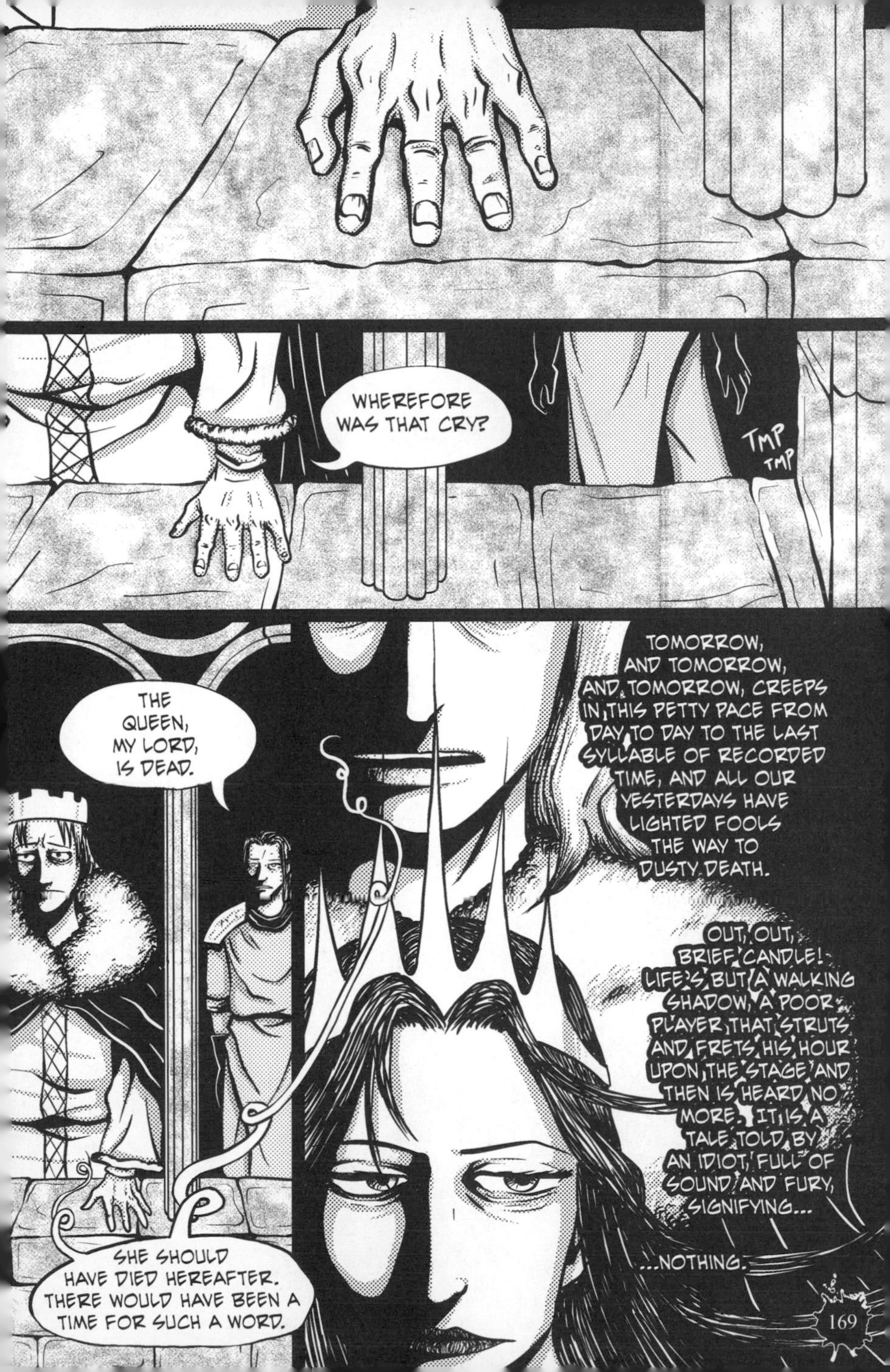
WHEREFORE WAS THAT CRY?
TMP TMP
THE QUEEN, MY LORD, IS DEAD.
SHE SHOULD HAVE DIED HEREAFTER. THERE WOULD HAVE BEEN A TIME FOR SUCH A WORD.
TOMORROW, AND TOMORROW, AND TOMORROW, CREEPS IN THIS PETTY PACE FROM DAY TO DAY TO THE LAST SYLLABLE OF RECORDED TIME, AND ALL OUR YESTERDAYS HAVE LIGHTED FOOLS THE WAY TO DUSTY DEATH.
OUT, OUT, BRIEF CANDLE! LIFE'S BUT A WALKING SHADOW, A POOR PLAYER THAT STRUTS AND FRETS HIS HOUR UPON THE STAGE AND THEN IS HEARD NO MORE. IT IS A TALE TOLD BY AN IDIOT, FULL OF SOUND AND FURY, SIGNIFYING...
...NOTHING.

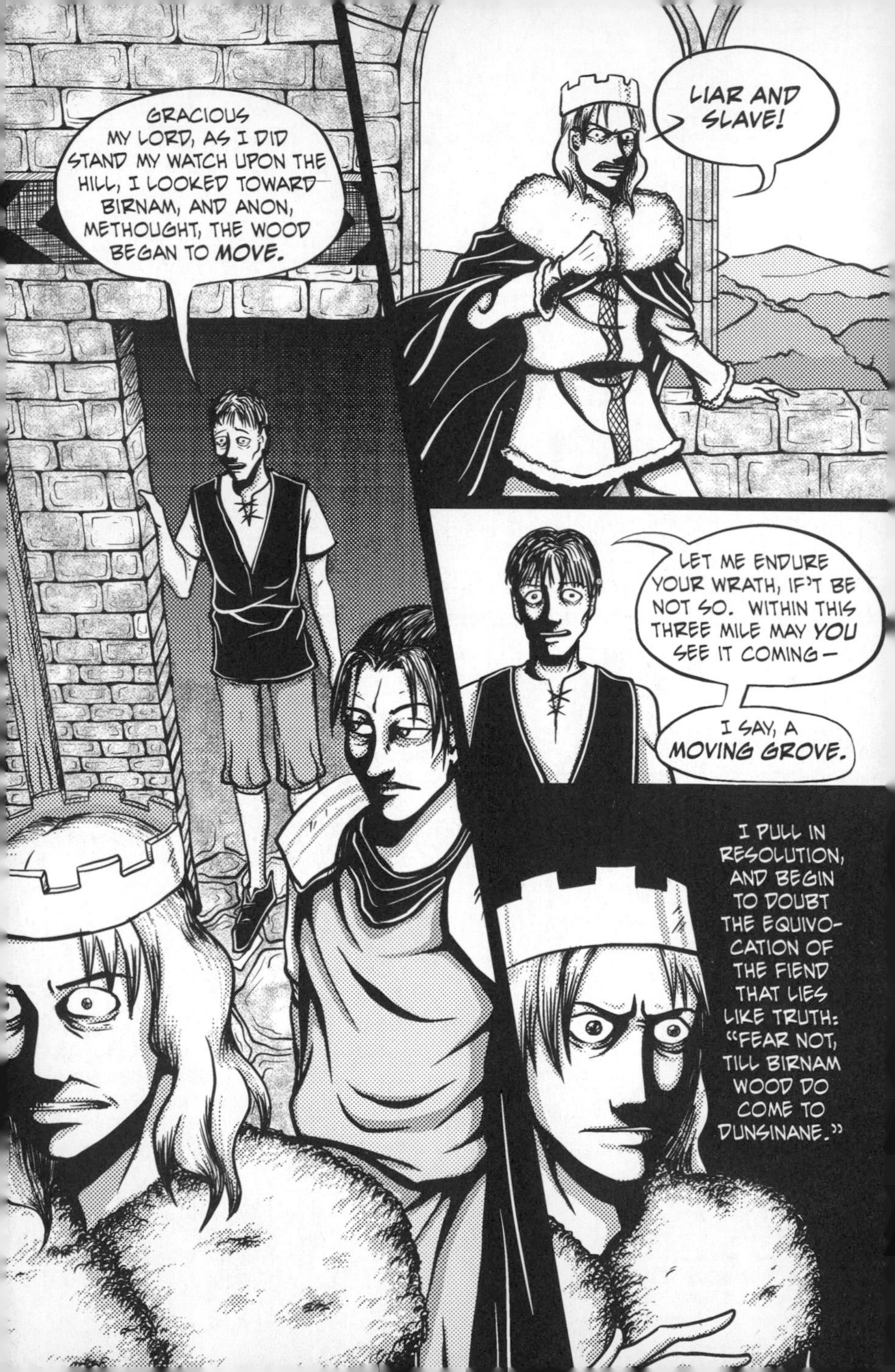
GRACIOUS MY LORD, AS I DID STAND MY WATCH UPON THE HILL, I LOOKED TOWARD BIRNAM, AND ANON, METHOUGHT, THE WOOD BEGAN TO MOVE.
LIAR AND SLAVE!
LET ME ENDURE YOUR WRATH, IF'T BE NOT SO. WITHIN THIS THREE MILE MAY YOU SEE IT COMING—
I SAY, A MOVING GROVE.
I PULL IN RESOLUTION, AND BEGIN TO DOUBT THE EQUIVOCATION OF THE FIEND THAT LIES LIKE TRUTH: "FEAR NOT, TILL BIRNAM WOOD DO COME TO DUNSINANE."

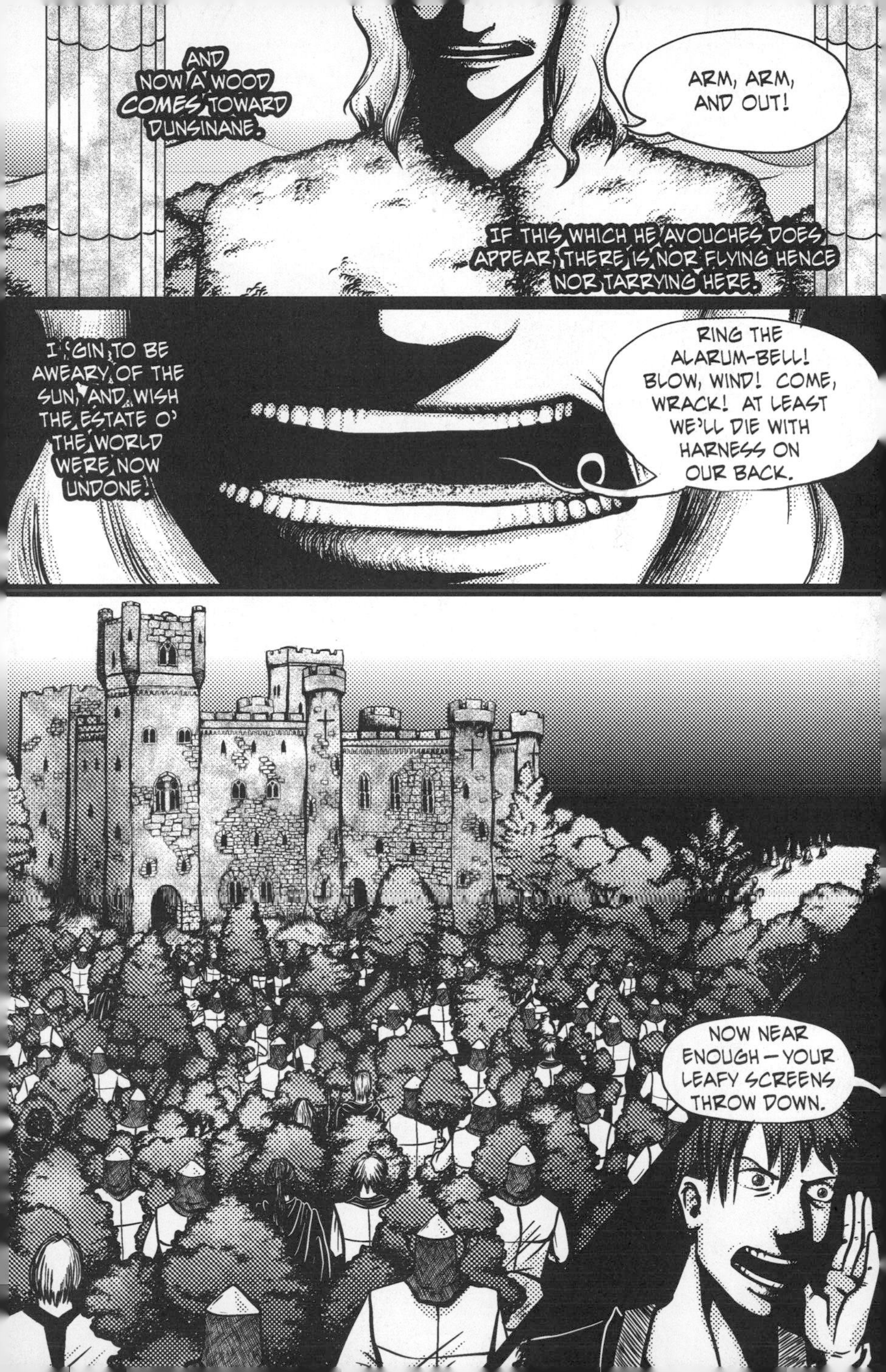
AND NOW A WOOD COMES TOWARD DUNSINANE.
ARM, ARM, AND OUT!
IF THIS WHICH HE AVOUCHES DOES APPEAR, THERE IS NOR FLYING HENCE NOR TARRYING HERE.
I 'GIN TO BE AWEARY OF THE SUN, AND WISH THE ESTATE O' THE WORLD WERE NOW UNDONE!
RING THE ALARUM-BELL! BLOW, WIND! COME, WRACK! AT LEAST WE'LL DIE WITH HARNESS ON OUR BACK.
NOW NEAR ENOUGH — YOUR LEAFY SCREENS THROW DOWN.

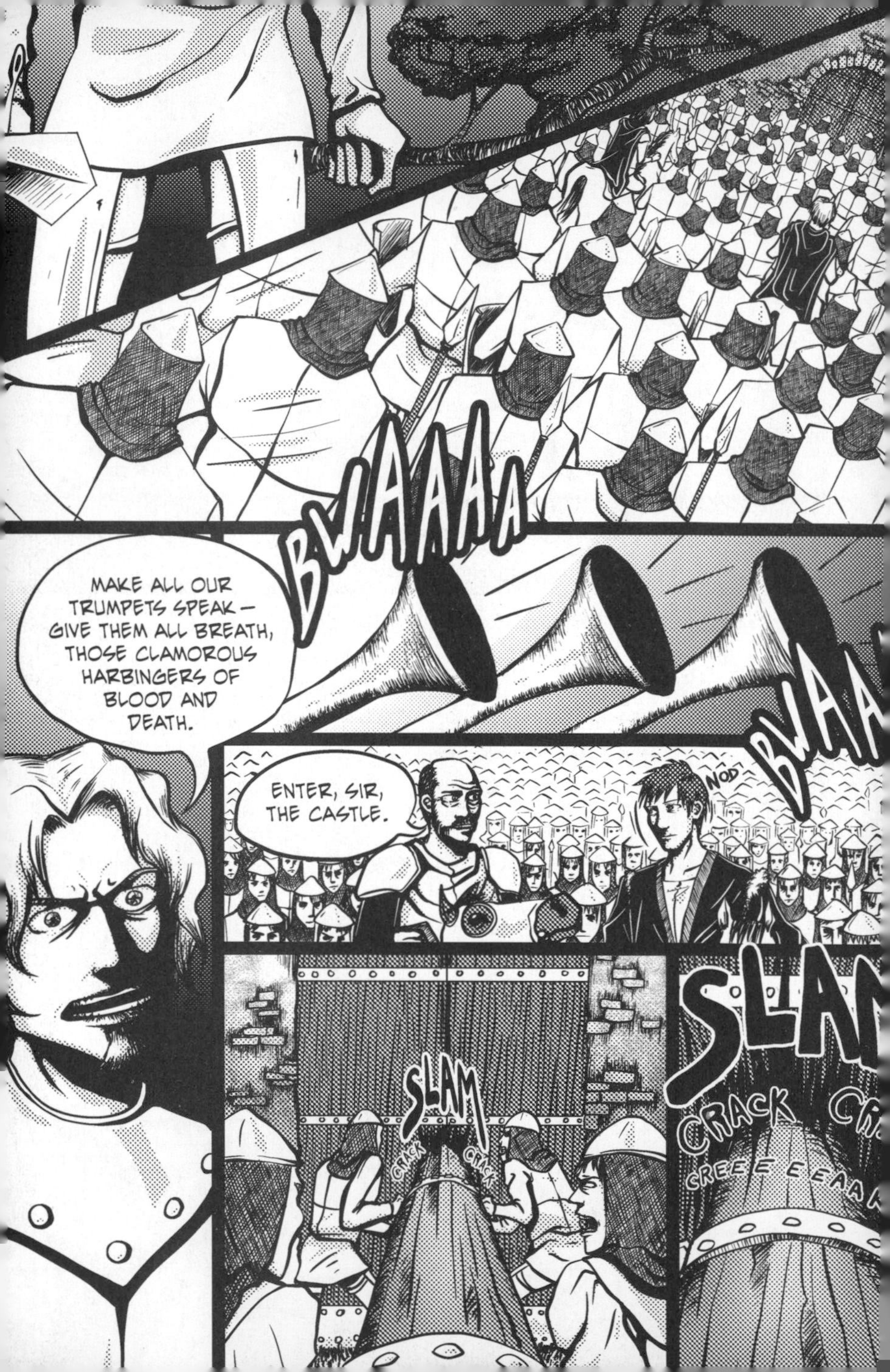
BWAAAAA
MAKE ALL OUR TRUMPETS SPEAK — GIVE THEM ALL BREATH, THOSE CLAMOROUS HARBINGERS OF BLOOD AND DEATH.
BWAA
ENTER, SIR, THE CASTLE.
NOD
BWAA
SLAM
CRACK
CRACK
SLAM
CRACK
CREEEEEAAA

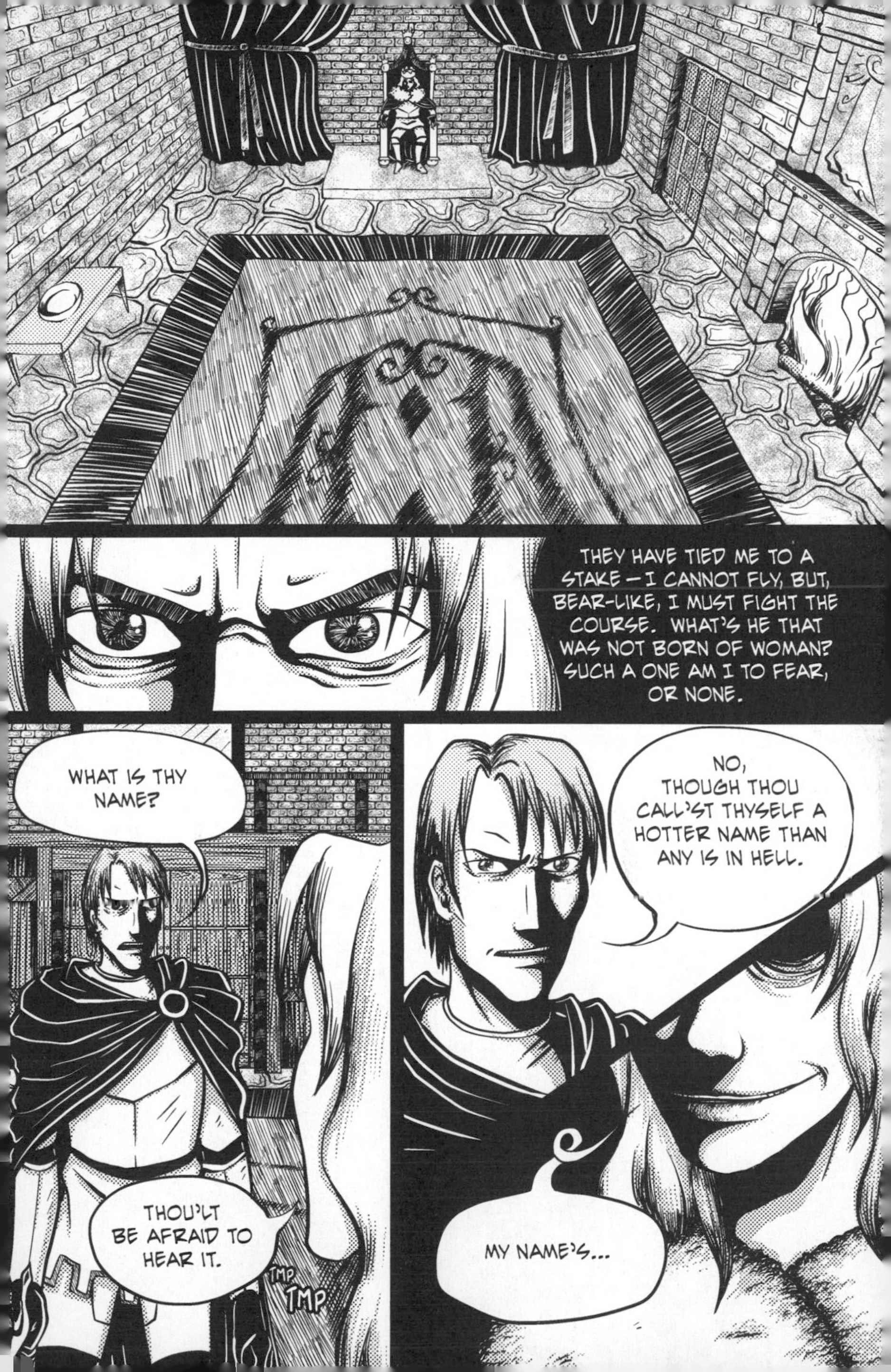
THEY HAVE TIED ME TO A STAKE — I CANNOT FLY, BUT, BEAR-LIKE, I MUST FIGHT THE COURSE. WHAT'S HE THAT WAS NOT BORN OF WOMAN? SUCH A ONE AM I TO FEAR, OR NONE.
WHAT IS THY NAME?
THOU'LT BE AFRAID TO HEAR IT.
TMP TMP
NO, THOUGH THOU CALL'ST THYSELF A HOTTER NAME THAN ANY IS IN HELL.
MY NAME'S...

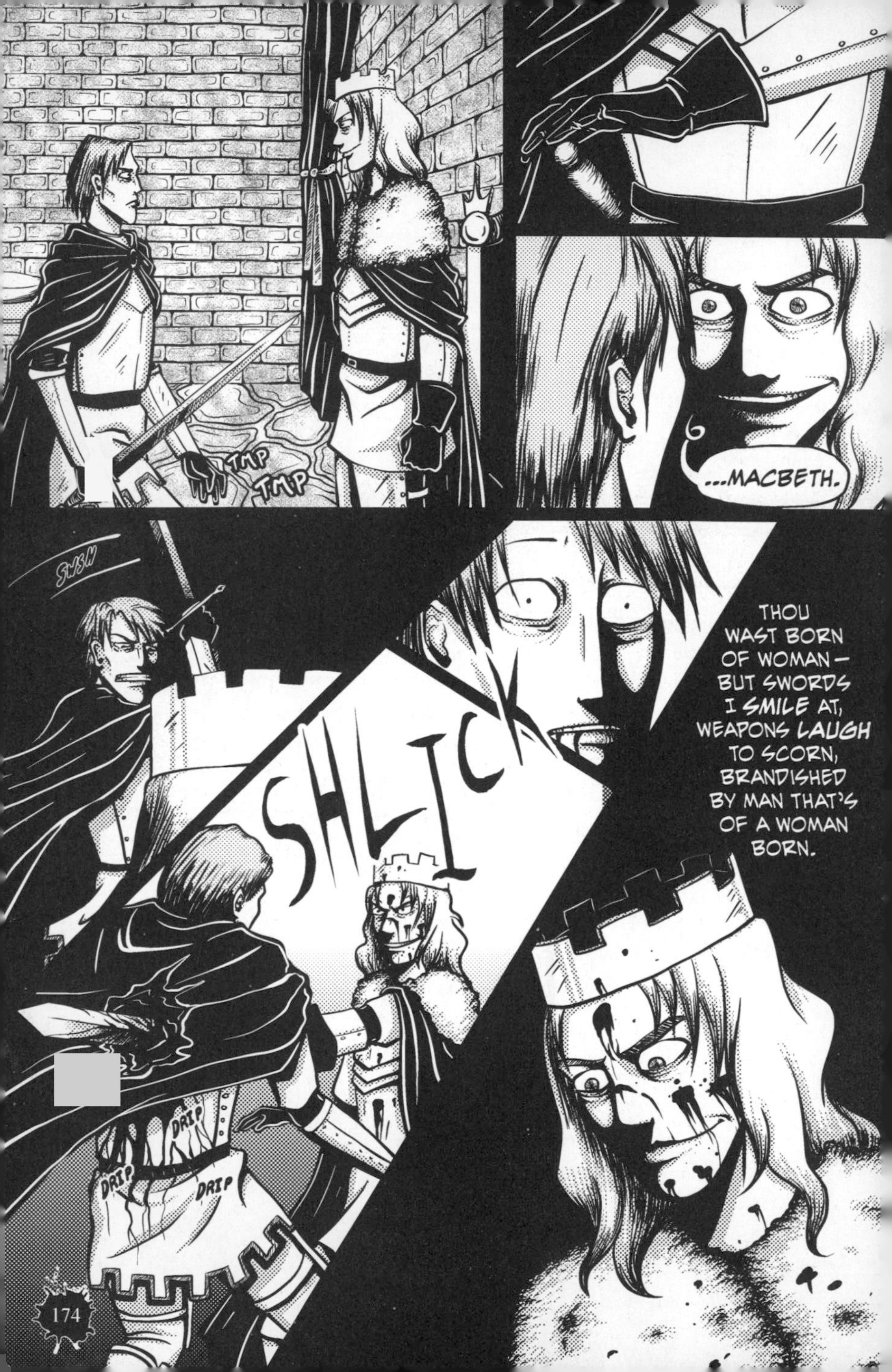
TMP
TMP
...MACBETH.
SWSH
SHLICK
THOU WAST BORN OF WOMAN— BUT SWORDS I SMILE AT, WEAPONS LAUGH TO SCORN, BRANDISHED BY MAN THAT'S OF A WOMAN BORN.
DRIP
DRIP
DRIP

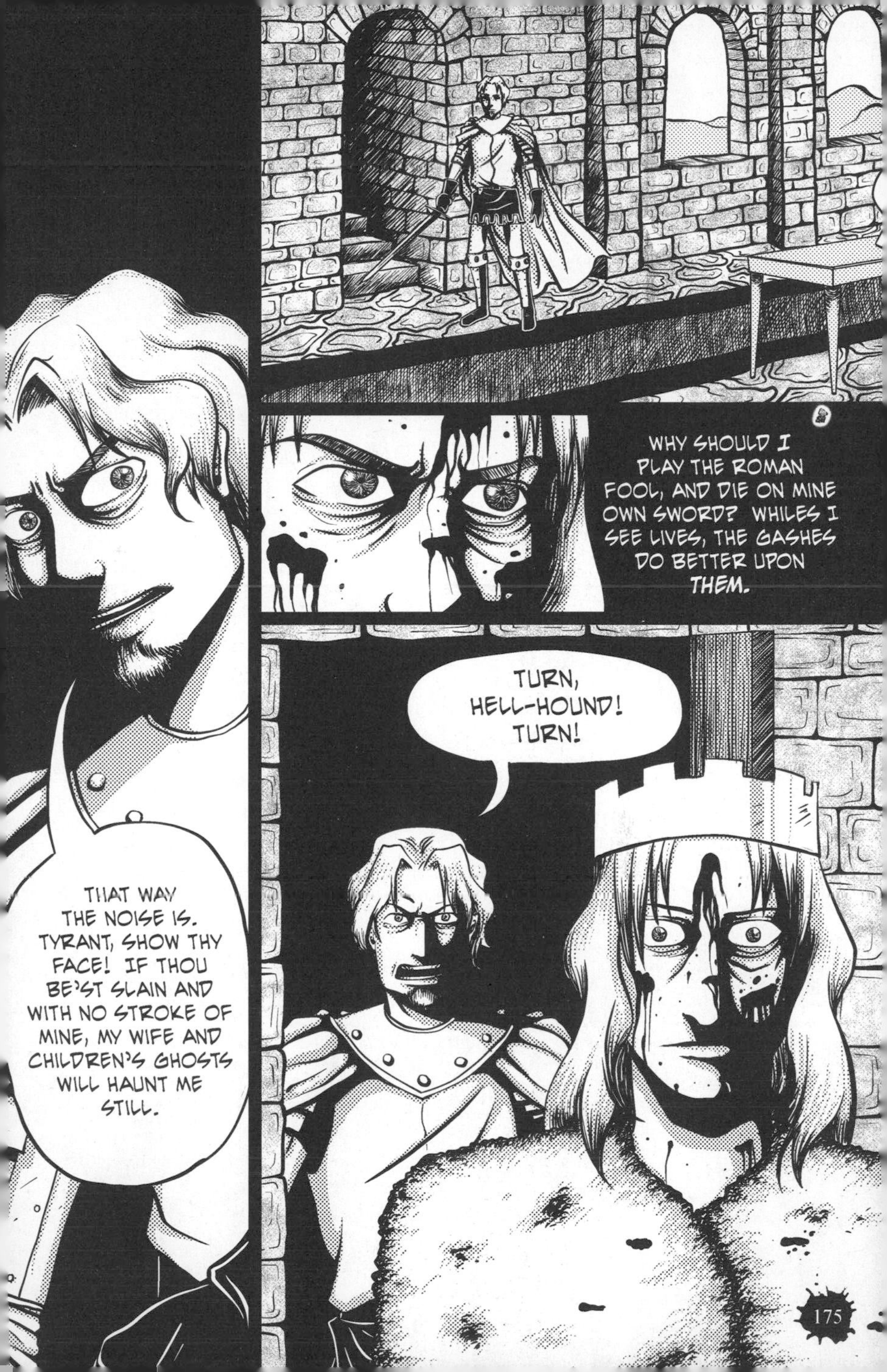
THAT WAY THE NOISE IS. TYRANT, SHOW THY FACE! IF THOU BE'ST SLAIN AND WITH NO STROKE OF MINE, MY WIFE AND CHILDREN'S GHOSTS WILL HAUNT ME STILL.
WHY SHOULD I PLAY THE ROMAN FOOL, AND DIE ON MINE OWN SWORD? WHILES I SEE LIVES, THE GASHES DO BETTER UPON THEM.
TURN, HELL-HOUND! TURN!

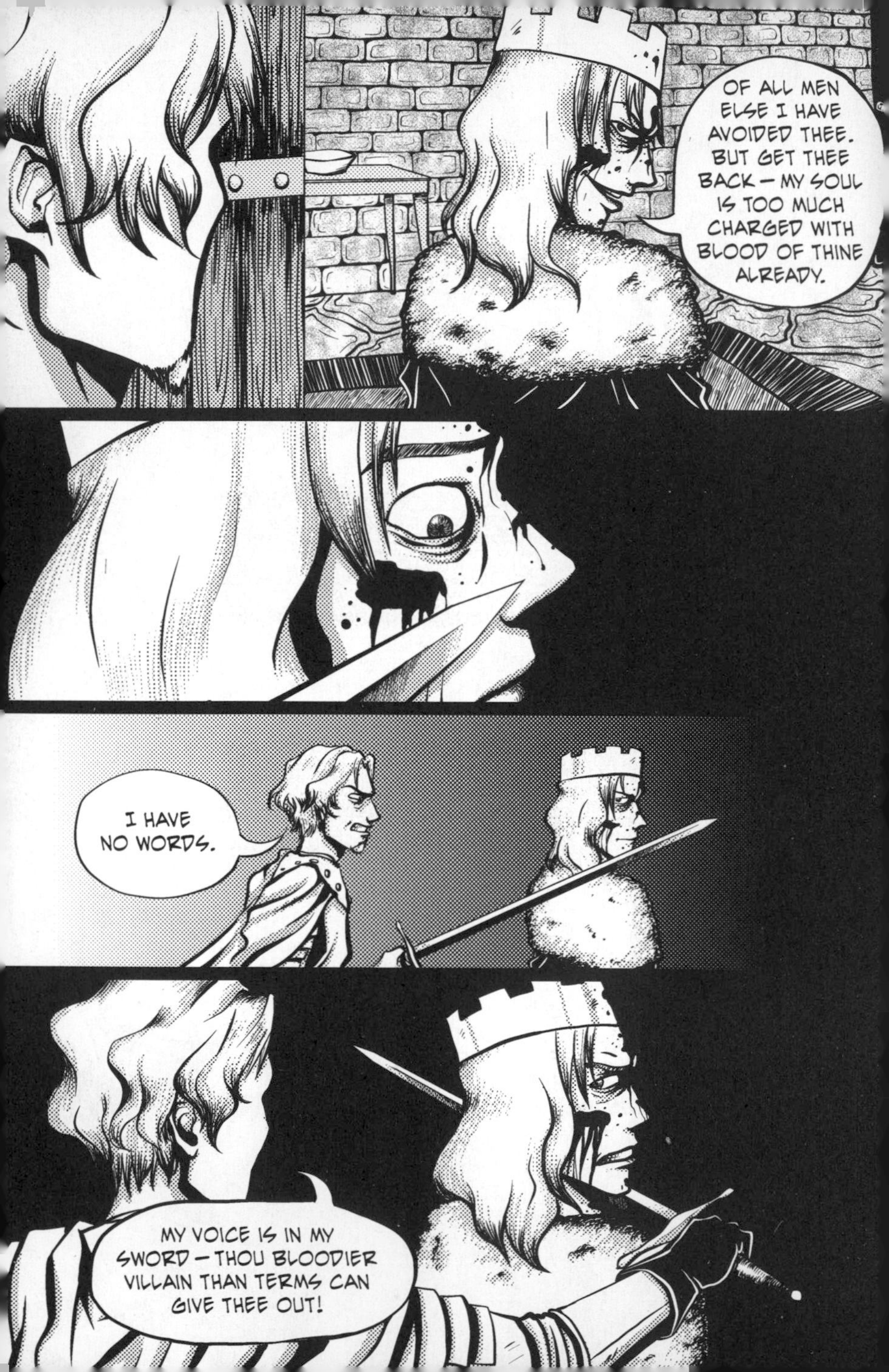
OF ALL MEN ELSE I HAVE AVOIDED THEE. BUT GET THEE BACK — MY SOUL IS TOO MUCH CHARGED WITH BLOOD OF THINE ALREADY.
I HAVE NO WORDS.
MY VOICE IS IN MY SWORD — THOU BLOODIER VILLAIN THAN TERMS CAN GIVE THEE OUT!

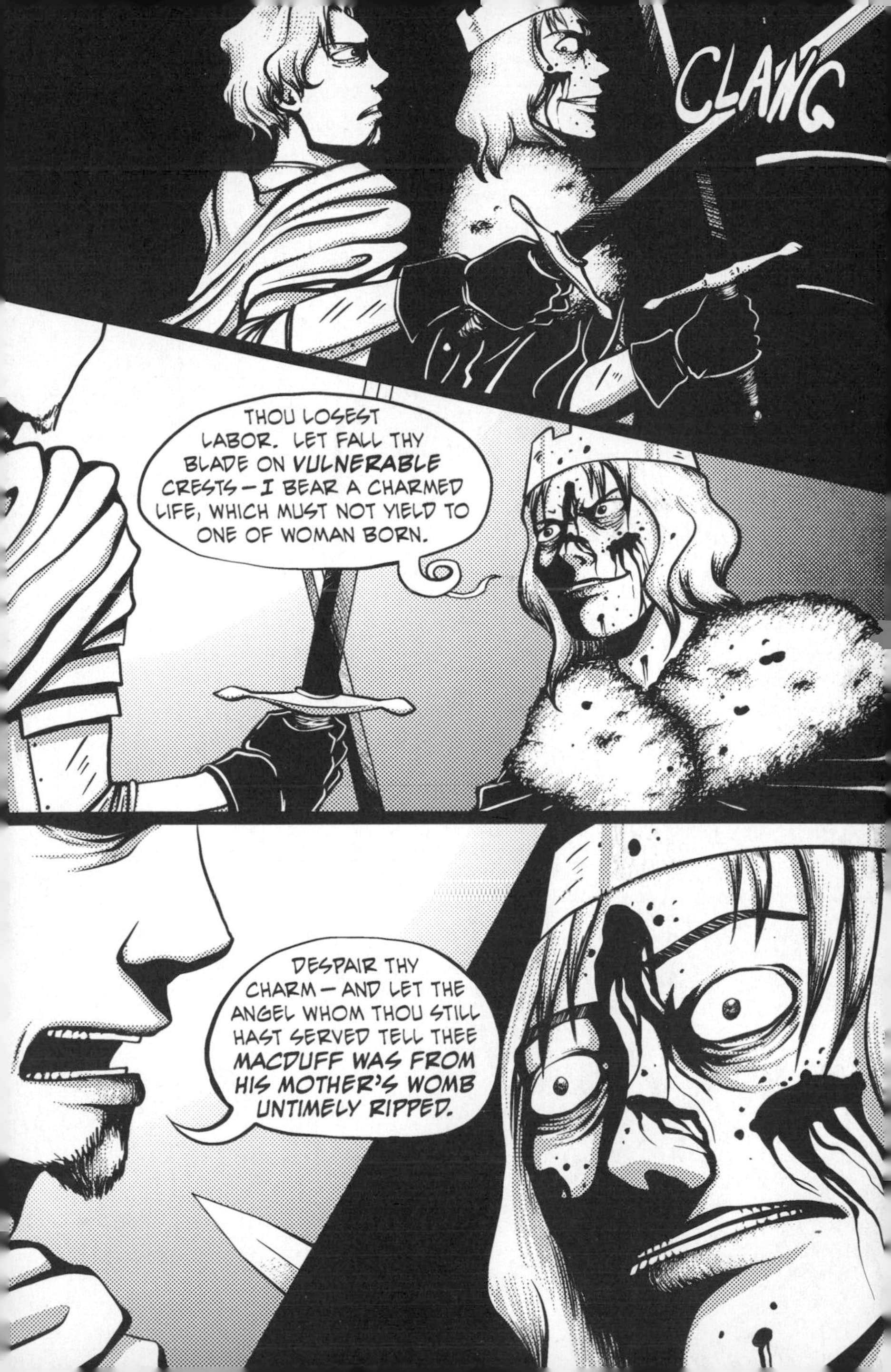
CLANG
THOU LOSEST LABOR. LET FALL THY BLADE ON VULNERABLE CRESTS—I BEAR A CHARMED LIFE, WHICH MUST NOT YIELD TO ONE OF WOMAN BORN.
DESPAIR THY CHARM—AND LET THE ANGEL WHOM THOU STILL HAST SERVED TELL THEE MACDUFF WAS FROM HIS MOTHER'S WOMB UNTIMELY RIPPED.

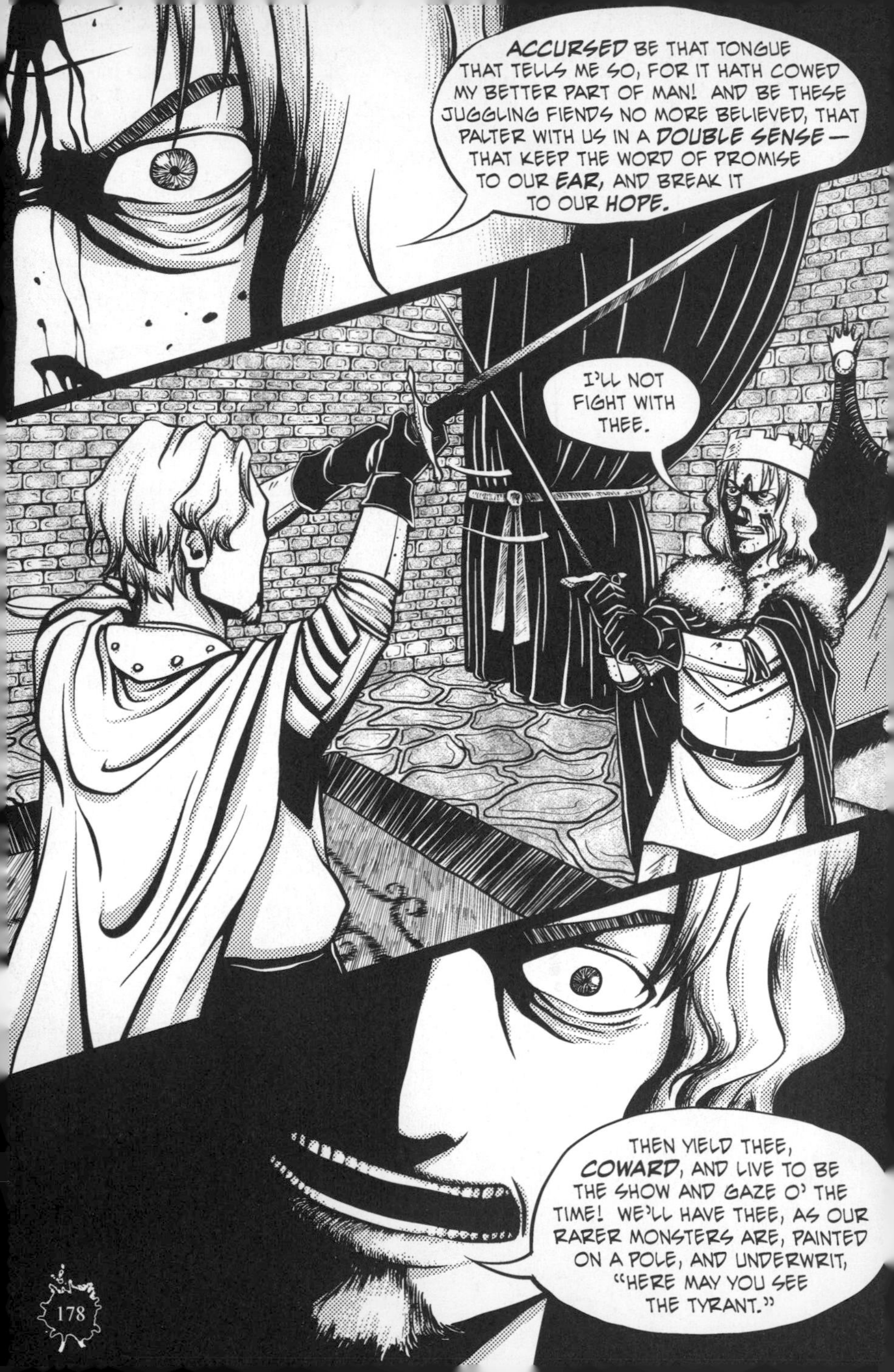
ACCURSED BE THAT TONGUE THAT TELLS ME SO, FOR IT HATH COWED MY BETTER PART OF MAN! AND BE THESE JUGGLING FIENDS NO MORE BELIEVED, THAT PALTER WITH US IN A DOUBLE SENSE— THAT KEEP THE WORD OF PROMISE TO OUR EAR, AND BREAK IT TO OUR HOPE.
I'LL NOT FIGHT WITH THEE.
THEN YIELD THEE, COWARD, AND LIVE TO BE THE SHOW AND GAZE O' THE TIME! WE'LL HAVE THEE, AS OUR RARER MONSTERS ARE, PAINTED ON A POLE, AND UNDERWRIT, "HERE MAY YOU SEE THE TYRANT."

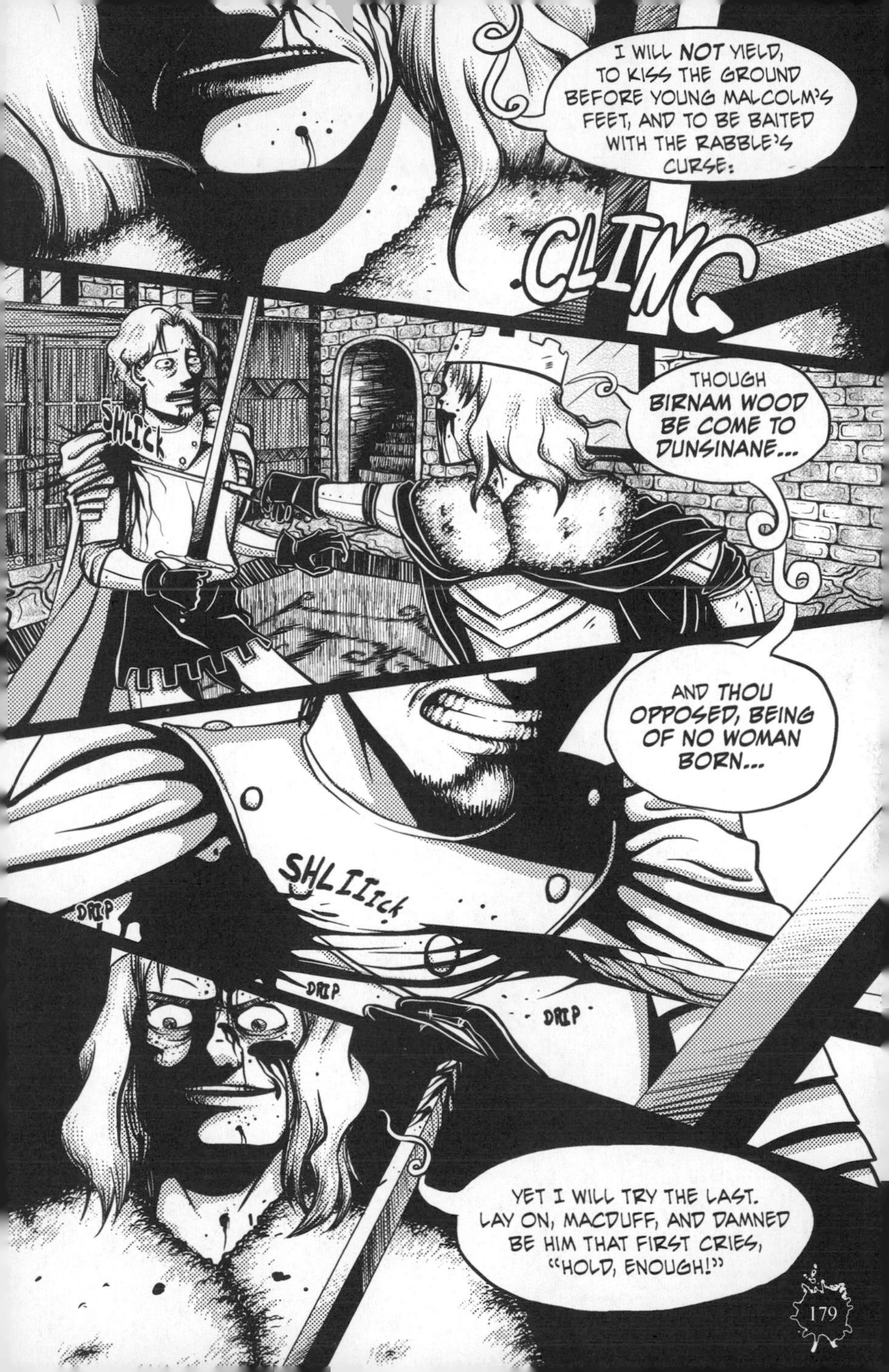
I WILL NOT YIELD, TO KISS THE GROUND BEFORE YOUNG MALCOLM'S FEET, AND TO BE BAITED WITH THE RABBLE'S CURSE:
CLING
SHLICK
THOUGH BIRNAM WOOD BE COME TO DUNSINANE...
AND THOU OPPOSED, BEING OF NO WOMAN BORN...
SHLIIIck
DRIP
DRIP
DRIP
YET I WILL TRY THE LAST. LAY ON, MACDUFF, AND DAMNED BE HIM THAT FIRST CRIES, "HOLD, ENOUGH!"

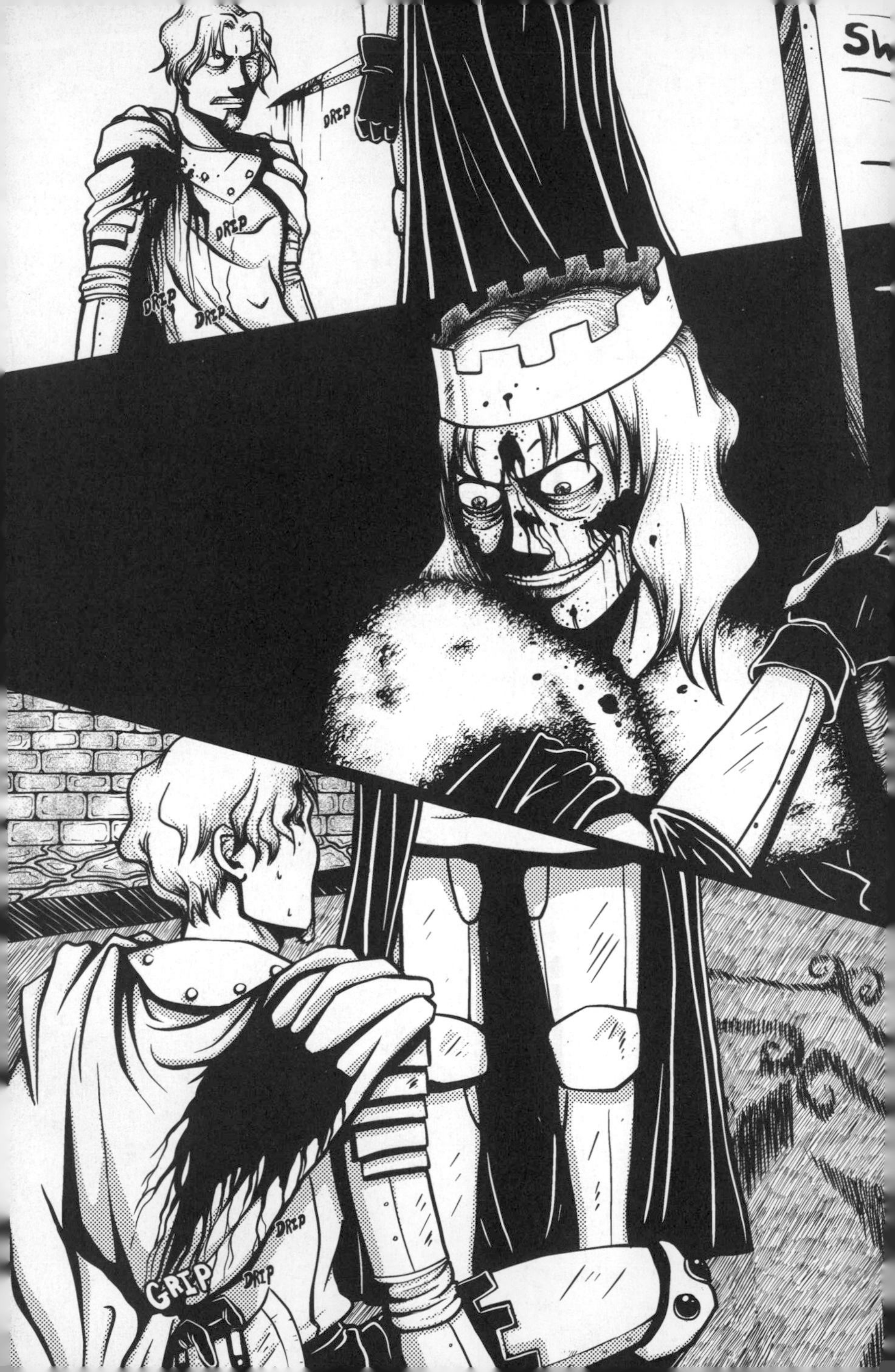
DRIP
DRIP
DRIP
DRIP
DRIP
GRIP
DRIP

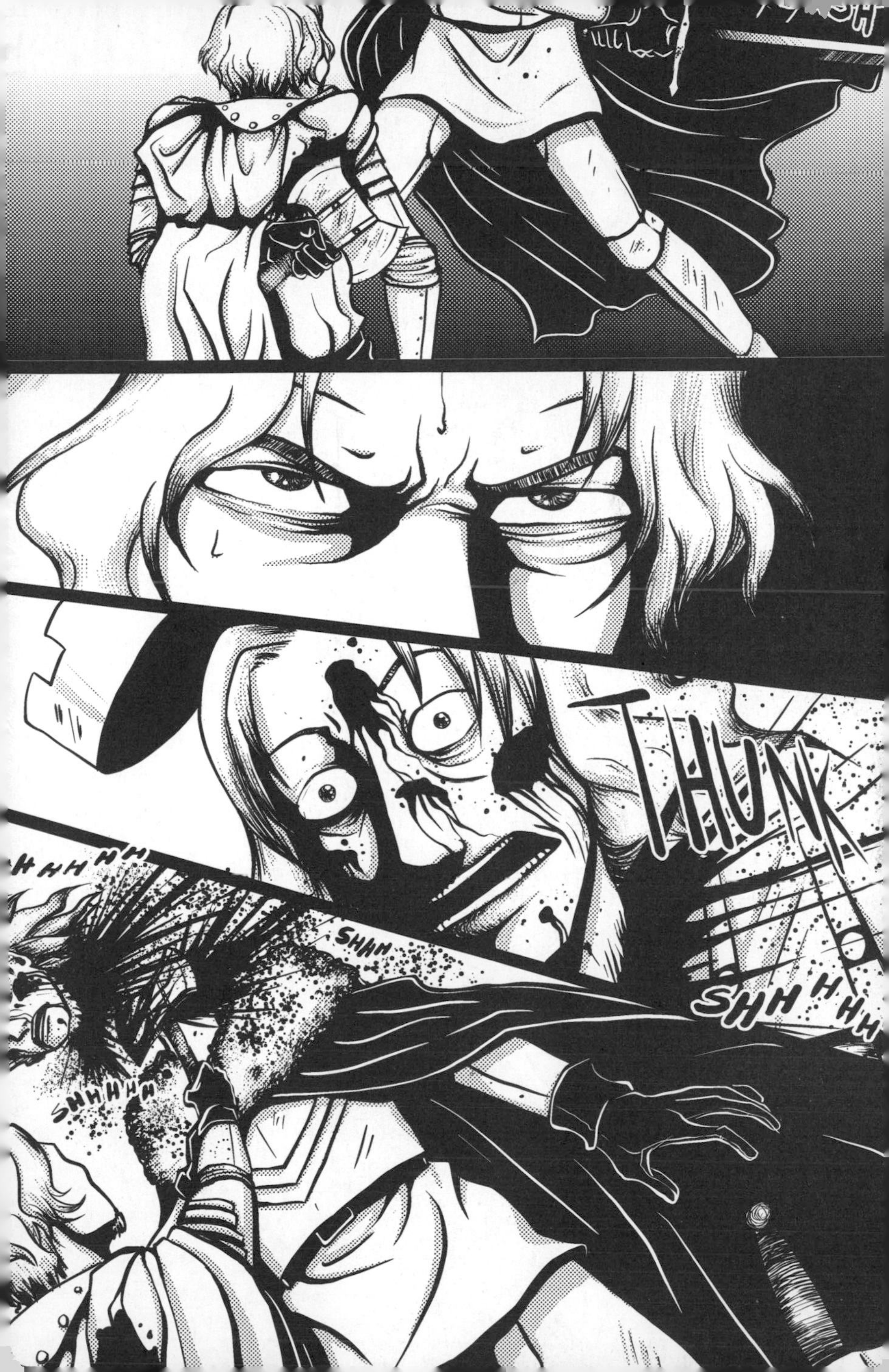
THUNK
SHHM
SHHHHHH
SHHHHH

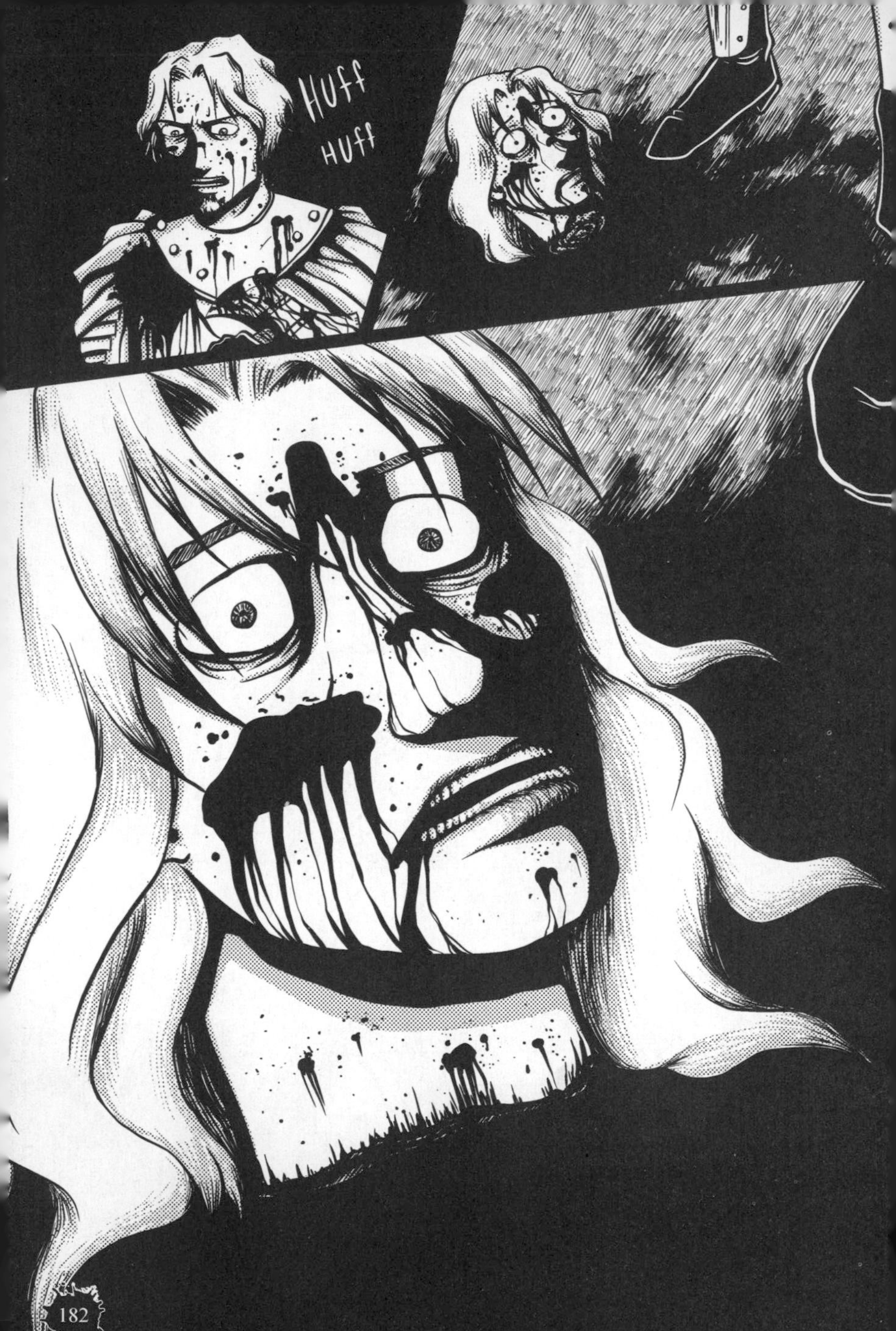
HUFF
HUFF

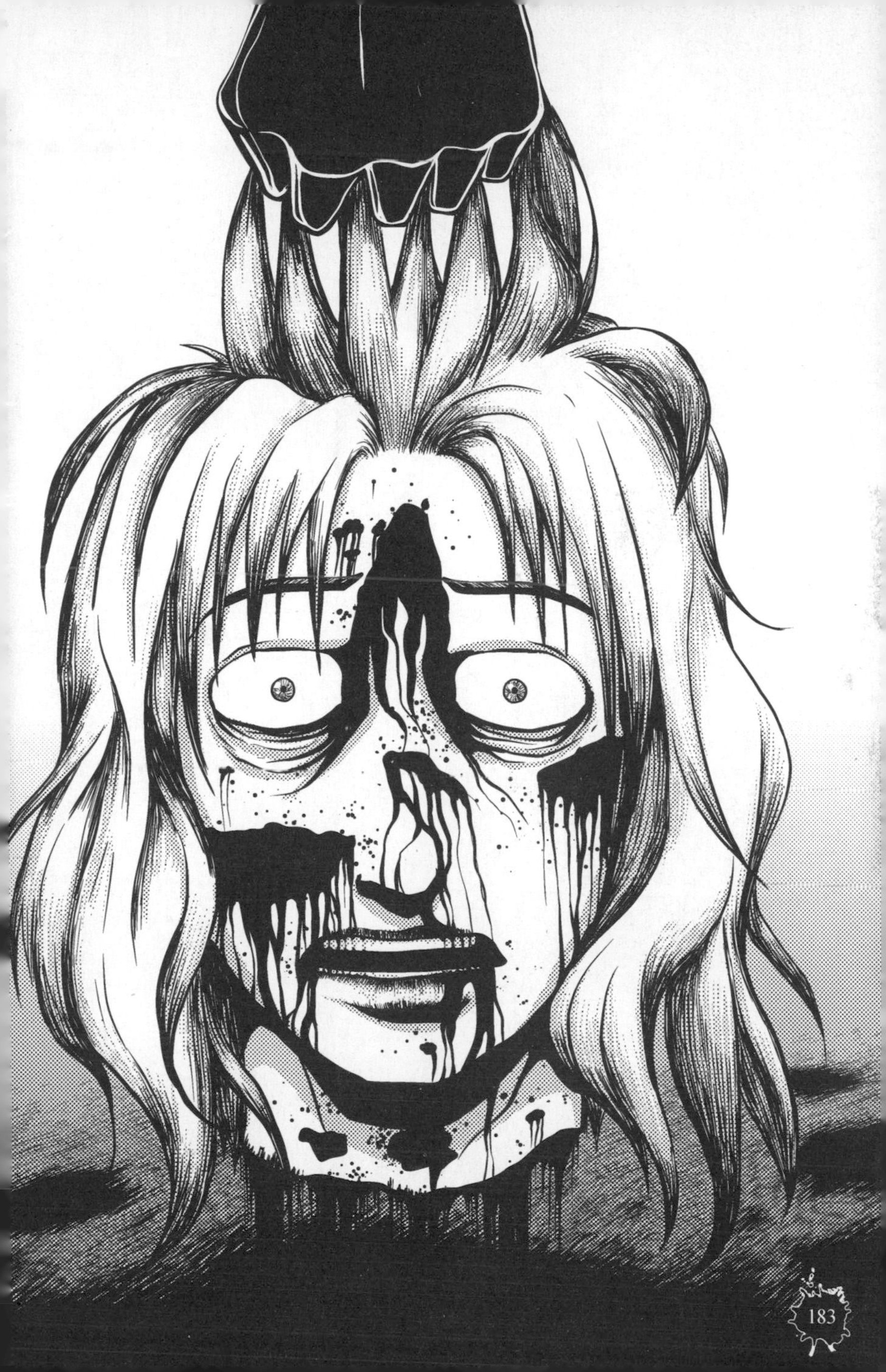

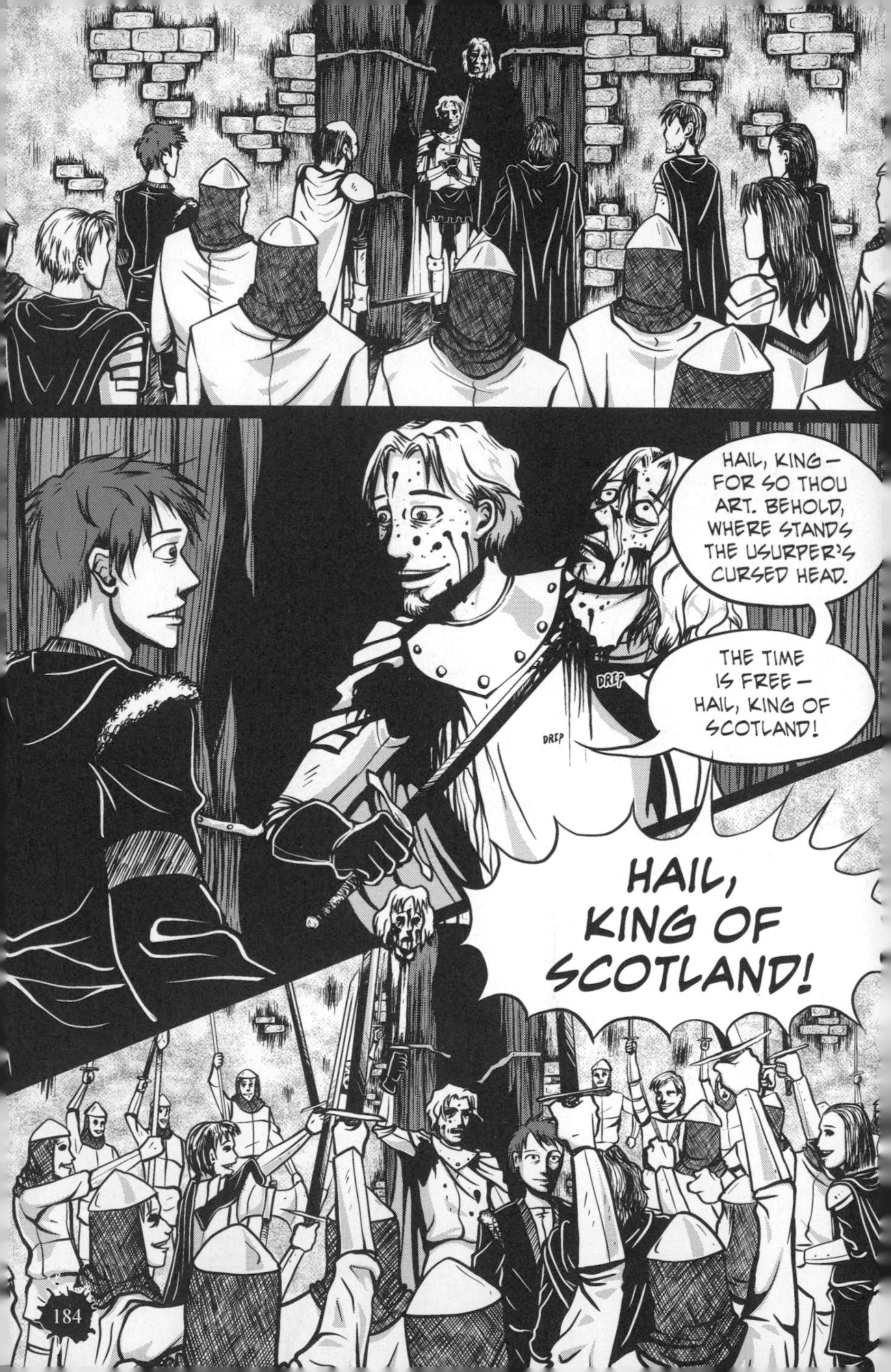
HAIL, KING— FOR SO THOU ART. BEHOLD, WHERE STANDS THE USURPER'S CURSED HEAD.
THE TIME IS FREE— HAIL, KING OF SCOTLAND!
DRIP
DRIP
HAIL, KING OF SCOTLAND!

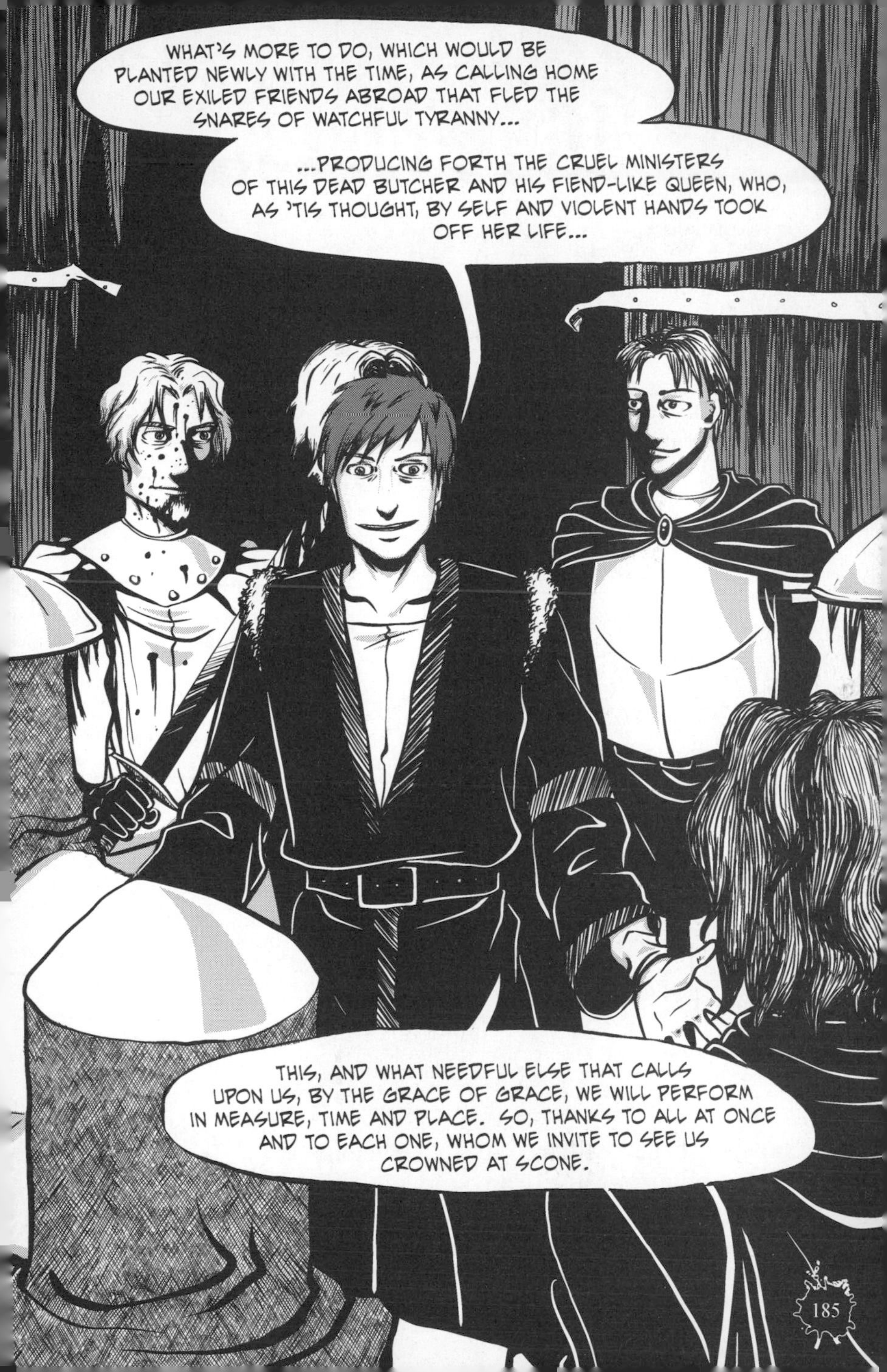
WHAT'S MORE TO DO, WHICH WOULD BE PLANTED NEWLY WITH THE TIME, AS CALLING HOME OUR EXILED FRIENDS ABROAD THAT FLED THE SNARES OF WATCHFUL TYRANNY...
...PRODUCING FORTH THE CRUEL MINISTERS OF THIS DEAD BUTCHER AND HIS FIEND-LIKE QUEEN, WHO, AS 'TIS THOUGHT, BY SELF AND VIOLENT HANDS TOOK OFF HER LIFE...
THIS, AND WHAT NEEDFUL ELSE THAT CALLS UPON US, BY THE GRACE OF GRACE, WE WILL PERFORM IN MEASURE, TIME AND PLACE. SO, THANKS TO ALL AT ONCE AND TO EACH ONE, WHOM WE INVITE TO SEE US CROWNED AT SCONE.